The Complete Fundraising Handbook

Sam Clarke
Michael Norton

3rd edition

DIRECTORY OF SOCIAL CHANGE

In association with the
Institute of Charity Fundraising Managers

Published by
The Directory of Social Change
24 Stephenson Way
London NW1 2DP
Tel: 0171 209 5151, fax: 0171 209 5049
e-mail: info@d-s-c.demon.co.uk
from whom further copies and a full publications list are available.

The Directory of Social Change is Registered Charity no. 800517

First published 1992
Second edition 1993
Third edition 1997

ISBN 1 900360 09 8

British Library Cataloguing in Publication Data
A catalogue record for this book is available from the British Library

Cover design by Kate Bass
Designed and typeset by Linda Parker
Printed and bound by Biddles, Guildford, Surrey

Directory of Social Change London Office:
Courses and Conferences tel: 0171 209 4949
Charityfair tel: 0171 209 1015
Research tel: 0171 209 4422
Finance and Administration tel: 0171 209 0902

Directory of Social Change Northern Office:
3rd Floor, Federation House, Hope Street, Liverpool L1 9BW
Courses and Conferences tel: 0151 708 0117
Research tel: 0151 708 0136

The authors also wish to acknowledge the following organisations for permission to reproduce their printed material:
British Airways; The Groucho Club Action Fund; Oxford Night Shelter; Ravenswood; LEPRA; Cancer Relief Macmillan Fund; RSPB; Jewish Care; Compton Hospice; Crisis; Actionaid and Greenpeace

Contents

Acknowledgements

To the International Fund Raising Group, for permission to use some of the material included in *The WorldWide Fundraiser's Handbook*, which is a version of this book specially produced for NGOs in developing countries who are starting to fundraise.

To the Institute of Charity Fundraising Managers, for their collaboration in producing the first edition of this book, for their continued association with the book and also for their permission to reprint their Codes of Practice in Appendix 6.

About the authors

Sam Clarke graduated from Oxford in engineering and economics and this was followed by a short spell with IBM. He joined Oxfam in 1974 and worked there until 1988 eventually becoming the Director of Central Fundraising. On leaving he took an MBA at Cranfield Business School, conceived and wrote the first edition of the *Complete Fundraising Handbook* and undertook consultancy work. He then became director of Oxford MIND. In 1992 he moved to head up World University Service. He is a trustee of the Refugee Council and is again working as a teacher and fundraising and management consultant. He is married with two children and lives in Oxford.

Michael Norton is the founder and was, until 1995, the Director of the Directory of Social Change, the UK's leading agency providing information, training and support to voluntary organisations. He has since founded a new charity, the Centre for Innovation in Voluntary Action, to develop new initiatives in the field of voluntary action. He is Executive Chair of Changemakers, a new initiative promoting voluntary action amongst young people in schools and youth organisations. He spends about one third of his time working on projects that relate to the development of the voluntary sector in India, where he is setting up a new charity called Books for Change, to produce and disseminate information to promote and support development. He has been a consultant to the Charities Aid Foundation helping them set up CAF in India to facilitate the flow of charitable donations into India, is author of *The Non-Profit Sector in India* published by CAF (1996), and is a founder trustee of the Asha Foundation, which raises money for projects in India. He has recently undertaken an evaluation for a consortium of UK development agencies on the development of an NGO management training programme in Africa. He is author of numerous books on fundraising and charitable status including *Tax Effective Giving*, *Writing Better Fundraising Applications*, *The WorldWide Fundraiser's Handbook*, and *Managing your Solvency*.

Foreword

This is a no-nonsense handbook for both new and experienced fundraisers. It is both a practical book and a very good read. I have no difficulty in recommending it to the reader.

If fundraisers want a patron saint, I can think of no better choice than the Good Samaritan who demonstrated all the qualities that are needed for success in their profession:

- compassion, when crossing the road to pick up a badly battered man lying in a pool of blood in a ditch;
- courage in getting off his horse on a particularly dangerous part of the road where the thieves might still be hiding;
- action and skill in knowing how to bind up the wounds with the use of a soothing oil;
- the funds to pay the Inn Keeper to look after the wounded man and a promise that, if it was not enough, he would provide.

This parable illustrates that fundraising is not primarily about money. Rather, it is about those human needs that cry out for help or for something to be done, the response to that need, and the desire to make things easier, to put things right, to make the world a better place.

So whenever you write or talk about your cause, start with the need and explain it clearly and simply in human terms, then describe how your organisation can do something to relieve that need. Never exaggerate what you are capable of doing or make false claims of success and do not forget that when you accept money from a donor, at the same time you are accepting a responsibility to ensure that the donor's generous gift is used wisely, effectively and with economy.

This means that you as a fundraiser must be constantly asking all your colleagues who are involved in the work of the organisation how the work is going, what successes you are achieving and how you can demonstrate that the organisation is being well run.

You will want to keep in touch with your donors, reporting back to them what you have been able to achieve with their money. Play your part as a truthful friend to your donor, telling of your successes and also your disappointments, and sharing your hopes and ambitions for the future.

People understand how difficult it is to bring about any real, lasting change for the better in human affairs, so you will find that an informed donor will support you through thick and thin – the first Director of Oxfam used to refer to this as 'the educated pound'.

Effective fundraising demands long hours, hard work, good communication skills and a proper understanding of the techniques that you will use to bring in the money, all supported by effective and well-managed administration.

At the same time it offers you a hidden agenda, as it is now called:

- a chance to be the agent of change for the betterment of the human condition, and to persuade others to help you in this;
- a chance to stand up effectively for human rights which are the key to human happiness, to justice and to the welfare of the human race;
- a unique chance to play a tiny part in a vision of a new society in which all of us may dwell in peace and harmony.

So take up this challenge, be successful and enjoy yourself!

Guy Stringer CBE FRSA
Former Director of Oxfam UK/I
Chairman Emeritus of the International Fund Raising Group

Introduction

This book provides a comprehensive overview of fundraising practice and techniques for those whose job it is to raise money – whether as a volunteer, as a paid fundraiser or as an external fundraising consultant. It is intended for people fundraising for non-profit organisations of all kinds. These include:

- **voluntary organisations and NGOs** (non-governmental organisations);
- **charities** – which are voluntary organisations established exclusively for charitable purposes, which conform with charity law, and are eligible for tax reliefs;
- **community organisations and self-help groups**, which operate at the local level;
- **campaigning and advocacy organisations**, which seek to promote change through research, information, campaigns and lobbying.

All share the need to obtain resources for their work, which they do from a variety of sources.

The book is published by the Directory of Social Change, the UK's leading provider of information and training on management, fundraising and communication skills for charities and voluntary organisations. It is published in association with the Institute of Charity Fundraising Managers (ICFM), the professional association which represents the interests of fundraisers and which promotes good practice in fundraising.

The aim is to show how fundraising works, explaining the processes of raising money and the skills needed to do this successfully. The book also covers the wide range of fundraising techniques which are now available to those seeking to raise money for charity, showing how each works and giving some basic practical information on how the technique can be used in practice, illustrated wherever possible with brief examples and case studies.

Raising money is never easy, particularly as the competition for available funds seems to increase every year. And fundraising cannot be taught in a book. It is best learnt through hands-on experience – trying and succeeding, which can give you the confidence to do even better next time; and trying and failing, when you can learn from any mistakes and improve your chances on the next approach.

What a book can do is:
- introduce you to a range of techniques, from which you can select those that are most appropriate;
- give you background information on how to proceed, and on points to consider;
- indicate sources of further information or advice.

The next step may be to talk to others with more experience, or to go on a training course (the Directory of Social Change and the Institute of Charity Fundraising Managers both run excellent fundraising training at affordable prices). Or simply get started.

There are some people for whom fundraising seems an insurmountable challenge and who never actually get started. Instead they spend their time trying to get all the information and advice they think they need. Getting going is a key stage in developing your fundraising competence. It enables you to find out what you can do, and to get experience and it gets easier and easier as you get more experience and gain more confidence.

If you believe passionately in the cause you are trying to raise money for, then you will want to convince people to support you and your work. Fundraising is not about getting people to give reluctantly, but about showing them how they can make a difference to something that is important – and then giving them the opportunity to do so. Read this book, get going, and we wish you every success in your efforts.

Sam Clarke and Michael Norton
1997

1. Background

1.1 Fundraising today

Fundraising is an extremely important component of your organisation's success. Some of the reasons for this are described below.

Survival

Every organisation needs money to survive – to meet project costs and develop programmes for the future; to pay the wages and salaries of its staff and all the office and organisational overheads that are needed for this; to keep buildings and vehicles in a good state of repair, and to pay for new equipment. The list of needs is endless. And the stark truth is that if the money is not raised, the organisation will not be able to do the work. And if the work is not done, then all those pressing needs will remain unmet.

The tool you will use to manage your fundraising is your annual budget. This will show the amount of money you plan to spend. It will also indicate the amount of money that has already been raised or has been promised, and what extra support needs to be raised during the year so that you can meet your outgoings.

You will monitor your progress in fundraising through keeping records of money received or promised, and by preparing and discussing management accounts at regular Management Committee meetings (which may be held monthly, or perhaps quarterly for smaller organisations). If the income isn't coming in as planned, then you will need to take some sort of action – put more effort into your fundraising, cut costs, defer planned projects, or agree to subsidise the deficit out of your reserves.

Expansion and development

If the organisation is to meet the challenges of the future, it may need to expand and develop its work – to improve its services; to extend its work into other regions and areas; to undertake research, campaigning and advocacy alongside its basic service delivery work; to experiment and to innovate. This all requires more money – money that will need to be raised.

You may want to prepare a business plan, or at least to prepare a 'sketch budget' for the next few years so as to plan for any major developments or expansion that you wish to undertake. In this way you can set about raising the necessary resources for this. Remember, fundraising always takes longer than you think. The more you plan ahead, the more successful you will be in getting the resources when you need them.

Reducing dependency

Many organisations are funded with one or perhaps several major donors providing most of the funds that they need. This can put the organisation into a state of dependency. If one of the grants is withdrawn, this could create a financial crisis and it may be difficult for the organisation to determine its own agenda when it is constantly having to adapt to the priorities of the donor organisation.

Broadening the fundraising base by bringing in other donors and by generating other sources of money can reduce this dependency. You have to decide whether your organisation is too dependent on any one source and, if this is the case, whether to negotiate some form of long-term funding partnership with your current donors or to develop alternative sources of income.

Building a constituency

Fundraising is not just about money; it is also about numbers of supporters. Each supporter is important to you. They can all be persuaded to give again and to give even more generously. They may be able to volunteer or to find friends who are willing to support you. They are an indication of the level of support that your organisation is attracting, and therefore can add strength to your lobbying and campaigning work.

You need to think about the sorts of constituencies that you would like to mobilise and who will be attracted to the sort of work you are doing. Is it businesses? Or middle class people? Or students and activists? Or women? Or retired people with time on their hands? Or doctors? Or lawyers? Or other special categories? You will need to think about how best to reach them and the sort of message they will respond to.

Creating a viable and sustainable organisation

Fundraising is not simply about generating the resources you need to survive from this year to next year, and planning for any expansion and development. It is also about helping create a viable and strong organisation which is able to sustain itself into the future.

There are many ways of doing this. One way is to build a substantial and active donor base – getting people to support you who feel involved and important to the organisation, and who will continue to give their support over a long period of time. Other ways include: organising successful fundraising events (which can create a regular and continuing source of income); creating capital within your organisation, such as an endowment or capital fund or buildings and equipment (especially when this reduces your need for running costs or can help you generate an income); and developing income generating schemes for the organisation itself.

Many organisations are addressing long-term needs – for example through community development which will not yield immediate results, or in looking after disabled or elderly people where there is a continuing commitment to provide care well into the future. It is important that you create an organisation that is financially strong in the long as well as the short term, rather than one that is plagued by annual deficits, or which is at or near bankruptcy, where the financial concerns are beginning to affect the morale of the whole organisation, and where the amount of fundraising work that needs to be done is affecting your ability to get on with the job. Most organisations should be able to find ways of strengthening their financial position and developing a sensible fundraising or income generation strategy for their future.

1.2 Prime challenges for today's fundraisers

Growing need

Britain along with many other countries is facing growing needs and a shortage of resources to meet its health, welfare and education programmes. Greater life expectancy, high levels of unemployment, changing family structures, higher standards expected or required, increasing costs of service delivery and high technology solutions, newer problems such as AIDS and drug related crime, and changing philosophies on the role of the state are all making it difficult for services to be provided for all those in need. This is creating greater burdens for the poor – and all the evidence shows that despite rising national wealth, the poor are growing poorer year by year, and a disproportionate number of our children are growing up in poverty.

There is also an expectation that voluntary organisations will intervene as a provider of last resort. The state seems to have withdrawn from this role, which is best illustrated by the Social Fund, a grant and loan fund run by the DSS for those in extreme need. When budgeted resources are used up (or when the individual is deemed too poor to pay back the Crisis loan), the applicant is advised to find a charity to help. Voluntary organisations are having to work within this situation of greater need and growing demands for their services.

It is not just a matter of raising more money to provide more services. The challenge for voluntary organisations is to develop solutions to people's needs rather than simply provide services that improve the quality of life. They need to create more imaginative and effective approaches to the problems that exist in society, so that they can respond to the growing levels of need without necessarily creating a continuing demand for funding that is just not there. This role as innovator is one of the strengths of the voluntary sector, as well as something that many funders welcome.

Competition

The fundraising world is extremely competitive. More organisations are thinking about fundraising and beginning to develop independent sources of income for themselves. This means that all the more obvious sources, such as grant-making trusts, the larger local companies and rich individuals, are receiving increasing numbers of requests for support – and they can't support all of them, however worthwhile the requests are.

New organisations, full of energy and enthusiasm, are continually being formed to meet many similar needs to those your organisation is addressing. Also, your existing competitors are each struggling to show that they are the best.

Your job is to try to show that your organisation is successful, effective, cost-effective and lively – in short that it is the best recipient of a donor's funds. Alternatively, you can think about developing new sources of money that nobody else is yet exploiting – the large trust that nobody seems to have heard of and which is not listed in any of the grant guides, a rich individual who has 'just made it', a new and exciting way of raising money (such as the Ravenswood Bike Rides) before everyone else has tried to imitate it.

Scrambling for funds

"There is intense competition for funds. Groups feel they must apply for whatever funds are available, although they know that their chance of success is low. There are so many initiatives from central and local government that it is difficult for voluntary organisations to respond without a full-time fundraising department. There is that sense of scrambling for funds whether or not they are appropriate for the organisations current needs. Small groups are told they should market themselves, when they are already fully occupied providing services in often impossible circumstances. Most voluntary groups cannot confidently see beyond the short term. It is very difficult for them to get funds for long-term development, and they continue to hang on in the hope that somebody – the Single Regeneration Budget, the Lottery, a future government – will rescue them."

Tim Cook, City Parochial Foundation

Developing long-term solutions to your fundraising

There is an increasing emphasis being given to the idea of financial sustainability. Many trusts and companies, for example, don't like the organisations they support to continue to be dependent on them for more than a few years. They want to be able to withdraw their support so as to be able to back new ideas and new projects. At the same time, an organisation can find that it has accessed all the ready sources of money, and that fundraising is becoming more and more difficult. At this stage, if you can develop mechanisms for bringing money into your organisation on a continuing basis, then this will provide you with the financial strength and confidence for a more successful future.

Different organisations deal with this problem in different ways. A committed membership paying subscriptions or covenanting donations; a major fundraising event which can be run annually; a network of local supporters groups, service agreements and other forms of funding partnerships with local authorities – these are all ways of developing continuing income and reducing the need to fundraise. Income generation is another way; but to develop this successfully requires new thinking, new approaches and new skills. There is, as yet, insufficient prominence given to this, and much of the emphasis of fundraising is still on the actual raising of money you need each year. But there is a body of experience building up as some organisations succeed. Hopefully this book will help to spread the word about the possibilities.

1.3 Who should read this book

The simple answer is that everyone who has any sort of fundraising responsibility needs to understand the fundraising process.

- **Board Members** (the generic term used for Trustees and Management Committee Members) will want to know what to expect of fundraisers, how to employ them, what qualities they should have and what support they will need to succeed. They will also want to know the options in income generating schemes.
- The organisation's **Director and other senior managers** will want to know when it is time to employ a specialist fundraiser or a fundraising consultant and how to manage them to achieve the best results. They will also want to know what is likely to be involved in starting an income generating scheme.
- **Fundraisers** will of course need to have a good background guide to the many techniques that are available, and an understanding of which are likely to be the most relevant to them.

- **Volunteers** who are raising money should have a copy to give them good ideas for improving their own contribution.
- **Consultants and advisers**, who will often be charging for their services, to ensure that they give the best fundraising advice to help their clients raise real money.
- **Trainers**, who might wish to use some of the material as handouts or checklists for those attending their courses.

This book has been written from as many points of view as possible, taking into account the interests of both large and small organisations, those with some experience of fundraising and those considering the possibility for the first time.

1.4 How this book is structured

The book is divided into seven sections:

- *Background*, which is this section, and which sets out why fundraising is important and the challenge for fundraisers;
- *First principles*, which describes some of the key principles of fundraising (to give a better understanding of the process) and some of the personal skills required in a fundraiser (so you will know your strengths and weaknesses for the job). It also shows how to write a fundraising proposal (which is a key skill you require to communicate what you want to do and what you need to do it);
- *Sources of funds*, which covers getting support from individuals, grants from trusts and foundations, company giving and business sponsorship, grants from government and other statutory sources and programmes, the National Lottery and the European Union, and a range of other possible sources for you to consider. This section will give you an understanding of how money is given away, and will help you identify opportunities for getting support for your own organisation;
- *Fundraising techniques*, which covers everything from house-to-house collections and direct mail to organising a fundraising event, getting a legacy, raising money through the radio, television and the Internet, and running a capital appeal. The full list of topics covered in this section is given on the contents page;
- *Fundraising strategy and resources*, which describes some of the factors to take into account and suggests ways of developing a fundraising strategy for your organisation, so you can decide where to put your fundraising efforts. Alongside having a strategy, it is equally important to have the resources available to implement your fundraising plans

successfully. Equipping a fundraising office, recruiting a fundraiser and using a consultant are all discussed. This section also covers testing, evaluation and control, to enable you to be more cost-effective in your fundraising;

- *Working with people*, discusses volunteers, celebrities and patrons, board members and donors, who can all be critical to your success;
- *Communication skills*, which aims to help you communicate the importance of the need and the cause, the effectiveness and impact of your work and the successes you have achieved to those with the resources to help you and to other stakeholders. This section covers producing effective literature for your organisation, using the telephone, marketing and market research, and effective public relations (which is an essential ingredient of successful fundraising).

The book ends with:
- a number of appendices, covering testing and evaluation, using computers, targeting systems, tax-effective giving (including model forms for you to use), and codes of practice on aspects of fundraising in schools produced by the Institute of Charity Fundraising Managers (ICFM);
- sources of information and advice, where we concentrate on just a few organisations and publications which we think will be helpful.

2. First Principles

This section covers some of the key aspects of fundraising. It will help identify the people, the attitudes and the approaches that you will need to get a successful fundraising programme under way.

2.1 Some key principles of fundraising

You have to ask

A piece of research commissioned by a major charity asked non-supporters what was their main reason for not giving. The answer was simple – the main reason for not giving was that they had never been asked.

Some fundraisers do not exploit the opportunities that exist to raise money. Others ask, but do not do so effectively. The whole purpose of fundraising is to raise money. It is often forgotten that the call to action, the punch-line asking people to give, is the essential piece of the message.

The good fundraiser must ask clearly for exactly what they want, having regard to the donor's ability and willingness to give when deciding what to ask for. They may also need to repeat the message to emphasise the point and they must make it as easy as possible for the donor to respond.

The personal approach

The general rule is that the more personal you can make your approach, the more effective you will be. So:

> asking in person at a face-to-face meeting is better than...

> giving a presentation at a meeting to a group of people, which is better than...

> telephoning someone to ask for support, which is better than...

> writing a personal letter to someone asking for support, which is better than...

> putting out a request on the Internet (at least the people who visit your site are interested in what you are doing), which you can consider alongside...

> sending a circular letter to lots of people.

Many fundraisers prefer to work by sending letters asking for support. This is not the most effective way of asking, and you may need to think carefully about how to make your approach. Two other approaches are worth considering:

- a **meeting** at your project where the prospective donor can see your work and meet some of the beneficiaries is often the most effective of all. If that can't be managed, you can try to illustrate your work with a short video, or with photographs, or by taking along some of the people you are working with to fundraising meetings;

- a **request** from someone who has given or from someone important (such as a business leader or expert in the field) can often be more effective than a request from a fundraiser or from the project director. Such requests are much harder to refuse. Part of the skill in fundraising is knowing the best person to do the asking.

Understanding the donor's viewpoint

In making a decision to give, a whole range of feelings and thoughts may be aroused in the donor. It is important for the fundraiser to understand this process.

The act of giving includes elements of faith, hope and charity: faith that the fundraiser truly represents the cause and will act as an efficient conduit for the donor's money; hope that the gift, however small, will make some difference, and charity which is an act of altruism, a gift without the expectation of any material return. It is also important for the fundraiser to understand that the donor might have some personal reason for wanting to give, and to build on that interest. People may want to support a cancer charity, for example, through fear that they might get the disease, or because a family member or close friend has recently died of it. They may feel strongly about an issue – such as the environment – and want to do something about it. In supporting your cause they are also supporting their cause, doing something that they feel needs doing and that they want to see done.

The return to the donor

People support charity without the expectation of any material return but they do want something for their money, even if it is intangible. For example:

- a feeling of having done something worthwhile, and perhaps that they have been able to make a difference to someone else's life;
- recognition from other people and from the public of their generosity – although some people prefer to give anonymously.

Fundraising is a people business

People do not give to organisations or to abstract concepts. They give to help people or to do something to create a better world. Your job as a fundraiser is to show how you are helping to achieve this. One way of doing this is through case studies – illustrating your work with actual examples of the people you have been able to help, showing how you have been able to change their lives, showing what you have done to create a better environment, and so on. In this way you can show donors how their money can make a difference.

Another is to focus your fundraising on particular aspects of your work: the income generation project you are planning to introduce in the village, that you hope will transform people's lives; the community publishing programme that is getting underway, where you are all full of enthusiasm and excitement about its potential. By focusing on specific projects rather than the overall work of the organisation, you make it easier to excite and enthuse your donors.

Fundraising is selling

Fundraising is a two-stage process. The first stage is showing people that there is an important need which you can do something useful about. If they agree that the need is important and that something should be done, and if they agree that your organisation is doing something significant to make a difference, and if you can show them how some extra support could be used to do even better – then asking for money becomes easy. Fundraising is more about selling an idea that the donor can make a difference than about asking for money. Once people have been sold the idea, then they will want to give. Fundraising is also more about 'selling' than 'telling'. It is about persuading people to give, and showing reasons why the work is important. Your success depends on your ability to get people to do something to help.

Credibility and PR

People prefer to give to organisations and causes that they have heard of. This means that the organisation's credibility and good public relations are extremely important. Press coverage of your work, trumpeting your successes in the newsletters you send to supporters, getting endorsements about the quality of your work from experts and prominent figures can all encourage people to realise the importance of what you are doing

Ways of asking for a specific amount

- Ask for a specific sum to cover a particular item of expenditure (for example, £500 to sponsor a park bench at a nature reserve).
- Give a shopping list of different items at different prices (for example, if you are equipping a hospice, you can list all the items you will need to purchase, put a price against each and ask a donor to contribute to one or more; the London Lighthouse did this when it was setting up). The price does not have to be just the direct cost of the item, but can include a reasonable overhead allocation as well.
- Show the cost per client, and ask the donor to support one or more units (for example, at a homework centre, show how much it costs for a child to attend for a week or a term, and ask a supporter to sponsor a child for a week, a term or a year).
- Give examples of gifts already received. This will give people a good idea of how much to give, depending on their level of generosity and whether they see themselves making a largish or a smaller gift.
- Break down the total into numbers of gifts of different sizes that you will need to achieve if you are to reach your target. This schedule of gifts is a technique much used in major capital appeals.

Examples of a shopping list

Intermediate Technology offer the following 'mini-projects' to potential donors:

- making improved beehives. £5,400 to fund tropical beekeeping updates, set up a business credit fund, supply woodworking tools and beekeeping equipment, and provide training;
- information dissemination. £4,800 to produce and circulate informative leaflets on solutions involving intermediate technology that can be put into practice;
- boat building centre in South India. When complete the centre will be able to complete between 38 and 40 extra fishing boats per year, of improved quality. The centre consists of 24 bays and is nearing completion. £339 to complete the construction work in each bay.

The Bromley-by-Bow Centre suggests the following to donors:

- £75 to replace some of the much used educational games in the Children's Toy Library;
- £180 to pay for the cost of 12 hours use of the kiln by the Supported Pottery Workshops for people with disabilities;
- £600 to enable the Kids' Club to hold outings, events and educational visits. They also contribute by raising small sums by their own fundraising initiatives;
- £5,000 to provide course materials for 20 Bengali women participating in the English Language Project (four ten-week terms, and three sessions per week);
- £1,000 or more for refurbishing the Centre will be acknowledged by a named plaque.

and have the confidence that you are doing a worthwhile and successful job – which makes it much easier for them to support you.

Donors don't know how much to give

One problem is that donors don't know how much they are expected to give. They may not want to give an enormous amount. On the other hand, they may not want to give too little, and so seem mean.

Saying thank you

Saying thank you is extremely important. It recognises and values the donor's generosity. It can also be an act of enlightened self-interest in getting donors to feel more warmly about your organisation, and perhaps to consider giving again at some time in the future.

Many organisations follow the policy of saying thank you to supporters only when they have actually received something. Those who say thank you on every appropriate pretext will see this investment repay itself handsomely in donor loyalty and may well be surprised at the level of repeat giving that can be stimulated by this process. But many donors complain that many of the organisations they support never even bother to say thank you!

Long-term involvement and commitment

What you really want are people who will give to you regularly and substantially. All the effort to find a donor and persuade them to give will really only bear fruit if they continue to give over many years and maybe increase their level of giving. If they are then prepared to ask their friends to help you or to put in long hours as a volunteer, then that's an added bonus.

To achieve this means getting them involved with the work of the organisation and committed to its success.

Accountability and reporting back

When you take money from somebody, you are responsible for seeing that:

- the money is spent on the purposes for which it was raised. Failure to do this is a breach of trust;
- the money is well spent and actually achieves something.

You may be obliged to report back to the donor as a condition of the grant, but you will want to do this anyway to show them that you have used their money effectively, and what difference you have been able to make as a result of having had their support. This is not only polite, it is good fundraising practice – an enthusiastic donor who has seen the money make a difference may consider becoming a more committed supporter.

If it turns out that the project has not worked, this can still be presented positively. Many voluntary organisations are in the business of innovation, and this inevitably involves risks and occasionally failure. But you will have tried, and you will have learned. The experience can lead you to develop new ideas and new ways of working, which you might then want to put into practice. If you have made a blunder of some sort (for example purchased an unroadworthy vehicle from a dealer that then went out of business), then admit what has happened and put it down to experience. Truthfulness is one of the key skills needed in a fundraiser, as we discuss below.

Saying thank you can pay

A former Director of a major aid charity made a point of telephoning donors who had given £500 or more at home in the evenings to thank them personally. "We're thrilled with your support. We're going to put it to good use immediately by using it to help establish a new health clinic for the Turkana. And we'll keep you in touch with progress." All this makes the donor feel that the charity is doing a good job and that their money is actually having some impact.

A fundraiser made a personal visit to thank a donor who had recently given £600. At the end of the visit, the donor made another donation of more than twice as much again.

Involvement and commitment

The difference between involvement and commitment is well illustrated by the Bacon and Eggs story. A hen and a pig were discussing the upcoming breakfast in which they were both to play a part. The pig said crossly to the hen, "It's all very well you being so cheerful. You're just involved. I'm committed!"

You want your donors to be committed. You can try to achieve this by:

- saying thank you immediately and telling them what you plan to do with their money
- regular reporting back showing them what you have achieved with their money
- sharing your ideas and hopes for the future
- encouraging them to visit you to see your organisation at work and getting them to meet some of the people that they have been helping
- offering opportunities for them to meet with the staff and volunteers who are actually doing the work, and with prominent personalities associated with the cause.

2.2 The skills required in a fundraiser

There are a number of important skills that you will need if you are to be successful. If you understand what skills are required, you can:

The starving baby syndrome

You are watching TV. There is a programme about a refugee camp in Rwanda. People have arrived there with nothing, absolutely nothing. They have walked days to get there and are near starvation. A picture flashes up of a starving baby, who seems to be crying out to you "Help me. Please help me. Please." How can you resist giving your support to the aid charity running the feeding programme at the refugee centre? Then you think about the cause you are working for. "How much easier it must be to raise money for starving babies", you think.

But your cause is important too. You have to make it seem as important to yourself and to others as saving starving children. Interestingly the fundraiser for the aid charity probably believes that it would be much easier to be raising money to save endangered animals from being poached, and the animal fundraiser would much prefer to be raising money for a cancer charity.

You have to believe whole-heartedly in what you are doing, and make your cause compelling to others. If you can do this, fundraising will become very much easier.

- assess your **strengths**, so that you concentrate on doing those things you are good at;
- learn what **skills** you need to acquire, and set about obtaining the necessary training or experience;
- find ways of compensating for your **weaknesses** by mobilising others to help you where appropriate.

Commitment to the cause

Commitment is one of the most important attributes that a fundraiser can bring to the job. If the cause does not seem important to you, then how can you convey to others the importance and urgency of doing something about it? You must really believe in the cause you are addressing and in the work that your organisation is doing. Your enthusiasm and commitment will encourage others to become equally committed through their giving.

The ability to ask

Many people feel uncomfortable with the notion of actually asking for money. Anyone who has this difficulty will not be a natural fundraiser – whether the task in hand is to write a four-page appeal letter, make a speech at a meeting of the Rotary Club, telephone a business to ask for an in-kind donation, organise a committee to run a fundraising event, or pay a personal visit to seek the support of a major donor. All this requires an ability to ask effectively for what you need.

Persuasiveness

People have choices as to what to do with their money. They have competing demands on what to spend it on. Your job is to persuade them that supporting your organisation is a really worthwhile investment of their hard-earned money. You need to make a really good case and to present it in a persuasive way. This requires good selling and communications skills. In particular you need to be able to marshal compelling arguments, to be able to write letters which excite interest, talk fluently and interestingly about the cause in public or in private, create a sense of excitement through your enthusiasm, and share your hopes and visions for the future.

Confidence and dealing with rejection

When you are asking for money, you need to radiate confidence. If you are apologetic or hesitant, people will not give to you.

One of the biggest problems is maintaining your confidence in the face of rejection. Since more people are likely to say 'no' than say 'yes' – that's a fact of fundraising life – it is very easy to get downhearted. Many approaches will be unsuccessful, simply because of the enormous competition for funds, or just through bad luck. After a couple of rejections, you really begin to believe that nobody wants to support you. You then start acting as if nobody wants to support you. You become apologetic and you talk as if you expect to be refused and maybe you even avoid asking – so as not to be rejected.

A good fundraiser has to be able to cope with rejection, starting each fresh approach as if it were the first, and to be prepared to learn from experience.

Persistence

Most fundraisers give up too soon. People often take 'no' to mean 'no' – rather than as a challenge to try to convert the 'no' into a 'yes'. If you give up immediately, then there's no chance at all. If you feel that they really should be interested in supporting you, then you will try to find a way of getting them to change their mind, or find some other thing that they might like to support. You have approached them in the first place because you need support and you feel that they might potentially be interested in giving it. Don't just give up at the first setback. You will find that persistence really does pay.

Truthfulness

The fundraiser has to be truthful at all times. The need to persuade people creates a pressure to tell only partial truths and to claim more for your work than is the case. The very complex socio-economic factors that create

"Some years ago I produced an environmental colouring book for children for a schools education programme. I thought that this might be sold to the public, so I decided to see whether bookshops might be interested in taking copies. I went first to my local bookshop. 'Not our sort of book', they said. 'No thank you.' I had a similar experience at the next three bookshops I visited. I really was beginning to feel that nobody wanted the book. But I decided to go to one more bookshop before giving up. It was just as well that I did. 'That's just the book we've been looking for. We'll take 70 copies for our Christmas table. What's the next title in the series, as we'd also be interested in that!' I felt elated." It is exactly the same with fundraising. Your next approach might be your big success! So keep trying.
(Michael Norton on his book *Colour in Your Environment*)

Persistence pays

I asked a group of fundraisers who were approaching charitable foundations to telephone them when they had received a letter of rejection to find out why they had been turned down, whether there was any possibility of their application being reconsidered, or what else they might apply for. What was interesting was how many eventually succeeded in getting a grant. If you are a donor receiving hundreds of applications, there is a tendency to say 'no' as an immediate response to any request. It is far harder to say 'no' to someone who feels that they have a good project which you really should be interested in and who has the courage to come back and try to enter into a discussion with you.

poverty today are a good example. If we are to raise funds by writing a short letter to a potential supporter, how can you hope to describe what lies behind the poverty? And can you give a proper explanation without straying into the politics of the situation, however unattractive or contentious that may be to the donor?

There is also a tendency to present the beneficiary as a victim. It makes it easier to elicit sympathy and support. This is true for people with physical disabilities as it is for families needing support or the homeless or those suffering from hunger or disease in the less-developed world. The beneficiary may see the fundraising material and even be represented on the Management Boards of organisations, and be offended at how the cause is being presented. The need to present a sensitive but truthful case, whilst making it powerful enough to persuade donors to give, can cause conflicts within the organisation. To resolve this demands sensitivity and understanding from the fundraiser.

Understanding your donors

"A fundraiser should never give up. Much depends on their approach and personality. To ask for financial or other support for people who are in need does not mean that you should look unhappy or ugly. Your good appearance, open smile, courage and challenge should light a beam in the heart of your donor. Your belief in the people you are helping should convince the donor. It is useful to remember that the donor is also a human being who lives in the same world as you, and is anxious to do their bit to improve the community. My modest experience in fundraising says that it is very important to create feedback with your donor. Generous people do not necessarily need to be praised up to the sky, but they will be delighted to know that their support has helped improved something or made a better world for somebody. We have become close friends with many of our donors and try to build long-term relationships with them."

Contributed by Ekaterina Kim, Contacts-I, a group with disabilities working for people with disabilities in Moscow

---

Social skills

A good fundraiser needs confidence, patience and tact. Confidence, because a confident appeal is harder to refuse. Patience, to deal with the particular concerns of donors (for example, when they ask to hear about the income ratios of the organisation for the third time). Tact and sincerity, to ask a supporter face to face for a legacy, or to suggest a variation in a Will. A good fundraiser should also really enjoy meeting and dealing with people.

Organisational skills

Fundraising often involves keeping in touch with thousands of supporters, all of whom imagine that they are special and that you have some personal relationship with them. Good organisation is essential. Fundraisers have to keep voluminous files of correspondence and information on donation history for each donor. All this must be organised so that no past event or piece of generosity is forgotten. A good memory for faces helps too.

Imagination and creativity

Fundraisers who come afresh to an organisation will find that imagination is an invaluable asset. The task may be to dream up new activities that will inspire existing supporters and to create events that the public is going to be enthused by, or to present your work in an exciting and imaginative way. Circumstances are continually changing and new opportunities emerging, so fundraisers need to identify new approaches and not simply rely on what has been done in the past.

Contacts and the ability to make contacts

The fundraiser who already has a number of existing contacts in an area or sector will be at an enormous advantage, but in no way is this a prerequisite. Having contacts does not necessarily mean that they will be the right people for the organisation. A good alternative is to have the confidence to ask anybody for what is needed, the ability to make helpful new contacts and the good sense to ask others to do the asking for you.

Opportunism

You need to grasp every opportunity that presents itself. For example, when a well-known supporter is awarded libel damages, should your letter asking for support not be in their in-tray next morning? Or if a leading company has just announced a major hike in profits or has been awarded a major construction contract in your area, then a cleverly constructed appeal for funds might just succeed.

The clearest examples of opportunistic fundraising are to be found in newspaper coverage. If, for example, there is a feature in the paper focusing on your cause, then the results of any advertising placed in the

---

How opportunism and persistence can pay

"Having nurtured the dream of an India-Israel Centre, I visited Israel in 1991, tramping the offices of umpteen cultural institutions, following up on every tenuous connection, meeting with Israeli government officials. Finally on my way back to the airport, I felt the kind of empty fatigue that comes with carrying a load of promises but nothing tangible. I knew we needed a respected and powerful patron, and many names came up, including that of Zubin Mehta, the Indian-born conductor and Music Director for Life. But it needed both familiarity and courage to access high places. That first time, in 1991, I'm not sure I had both. Suddenly, there was Zubin before me in the bustling airport. On impulse I went up and congratulated him, and said that he had done every Indian proud. He thanked me politely, then it was over. 'In that crowded place', I anguished with myself, 'I could have done more'. Two hours later, airborne, I noticed Zubin up front, reading glasses perched on his nose. I mustered the courage to send a polite note requesting to talk to him. From that and many subsequent meetings I realised that I was with a very special human being. Zubin's warmth and easy accessibility, his ability to get as excited as a child with an idea, astonished me. Here was something he had always wanted to do – to bring the people of the two countries he loved together culturally."
Salome Parekh, Hon Director and Trustee, the Shalom India-Israel Centre, Bombay

paper on the same day will be substantially greater (provided of course that the editorial coverage is supportive of what you are doing). So if you know you are going to get coverage, consider taking out an advertisement to ask for support – or better still, get the journalist to add this request at the end of the article, with a reply address where donations can be sent.

The annual calendar provides opportunities at different times of the year. For example in Christian communities, Christmas and the New Year provide extremely good fundraising opportunities. Other faiths have similar points in the year. There are also anniversaries, centenaries or events such as the Millennium, which can be used as a basis for major appeals.

2.3 Writing a fundraising proposal

Writing a proposal is probably one of the most important skills in the fundraiser's repertoire. For many smaller organisations, the difference between a good and a bad proposal will be the difference between success and failure. The fundraising proposal communicates the needs of the organisation to its potential supporters. And it is largely on the basis of the written proposal that many funders will decide whether or not to make a grant.

What follows should not be regarded as a blueprint which will guarantee success. What it aims to do is to identify the key points to enable you to produce a proposal which matches the requirements of a potential funder. The same basic approach applies when approaching any grant-making body, whether central government, a local authority, a trust or a company. Where differences do exist, these are identified in the text.

Planning your approach

In thinking about how to structure a proposal, you will need to consider who you plan to apply to: what their priorities and interests are; how you are going to make the approach; what procedure they have for selecting and assessing grant applications; what you need to say about yourself and what you propose to do, and when you will be submitting the application. There are several factors to consider at this stage.

- *Application forms.* You should find out whether the donor requires applications to be submitted in any standard format, or has an application form which has to be completed. There is nothing more frustrating than having completed a really good application only to find that it should have been submitted on an application form in a prescribed format, and everything needs to be rewritten accordingly.

- *Application dates*. Most donors work to a particular grants cycle. For local government this is an annual cycle, and applications have to be submitted in the early autumn for the grant year beginning in the following April; for many foundations grants are decided at quarterly meetings, and they may have a logjam of applications to consider at the next meeting so you would stand a better chance if the decision were delayed. This means that you can't just send off your application to get the money when you need it. You have to fit your fundraising into their grant-making timetable and this means planning ahead. If you need the money in three months time, this limits who you can approach.

- *How many donors you plan to approach*. If you are sending the proposal to a large number of donors, you should try to make it personal to each. The simplest way of doing this is by having a standard proposal accompanied by a personalised covering letter. This can include reference to any previous contact, how the project particularly fits within the donor's guidelines and current interests and (if relevant) whether and how the donor will benefit from the association (particularly important to companies).

- *The size of the donor*. Large funders, including major trusts and government funding programmes, will be interested in a great deal of detail. They will be receiving numerous applications from a wide range of organisations. They are looking not just for good ideas, but for evidence of need and professionalism in delivery. Smaller donor bodies, which include smaller trusts and most companies, simply do not have the time to read through a mountain of paper. They want everything shortened and simplified – a page or two at the most. If they need any more information, they can ask for it but you should try to include all the important points in a short letter.

- *The likelihood of success*. The larger the grant applied for and the greater the likelihood of success, the more it is worth putting time and effort into the application. Conversely, for smaller sums or where the chances are low, then you need to limit the time you put into the application if you are to be cost-effective. It is a general principle of fundraising that it is better to put more effort into fewer things than to scatter your efforts widely. So concentrating on a few applications which you think stand a greater chance of success, and following these written submissions up with phone calls, meetings and other activity, will be a better strategy. You can at the same time send a standard appeal to a selection of other donors in the hope that some may respond, although if it looks too much like a 'Dear Sir/Madam' circular your chances are pretty much zero.

Targeting your proposal

Who you send your proposal to will depend on a number of factors listed below.

- *Urgency*. If you need the money urgently, then your best chance may be to approach those who have already supported you. You have already convinced them of the worth of your work, and they may be willing to support you again.

- *Scale of need*. If you require large sums of money, you can either apply for a few large grants from the donors who are known to be interested in your sort of work (or who have already supported you) or from some government source, or you can mount a wider appeal seeking a range of donations from a larger number of donors. Remember that if you want a large donation, you will not get what you need if you approach a small grant-maker.

- *How many donors to approach.* Donors are often interested to know how many other people have been asked and whether others have already agreed to give. The general rule is that a careful selection should be made, based on an assessment of who is likely to be interested. If this is made clear in the proposal, those receiving it are more likely to take it seriously than a proposal mailed out widely. It also saves a great deal of time for both you and the grant bodies if you can cut down the number of applications you make.

- *Type of project*. New projects and new initiatives are more likely to be of interest to foundations and companies than simply contributing to the running costs of the organisation or providing a basic service. There is a skill to constructing a proposal which makes the work seem new and exciting, addressing matters of current concern in a fresh and innovative way. This is often simply a matter of presentation.

- *A personalised approach*. You should try to personalise the approach as much as you can, as this is likely to be far more successful than sending out a standard proposal or a form letter to a lot of people. Refer to previous contacts and any previous support. Match your proposal to their concerns as evidenced by their stated interests and policies or other grants they have made. Try to make them feel that you are writing to them personally. This is obviously much easier to do if you are writing individual letters to just a few donors.

Content of the proposal

You should decide whether you are seeking support for the core costs of the organisation or for a specific piece of expenditure or a particular project. Once you have done this, you should try to answer a series of questions, which are the questions that the donor will need to have answered before deciding to support you. Below are some examples of the sort of questions you will need to ask.

- What are the aims and objectives of this project?
- What is the problem or the need that is to be met?
- Are there any particular geographic or socio-economic factors which make it important to do something in the area where you plan to work?
- What working methods will be used to meet these aims?
- Why is the method you have selected the best or the most appropriate or the most cost-effective?
- What are the short and long-term operational plans?
- What are the expected outcomes and achievements of the project?
- Why should your organisation run this scheme?
- Why are you likely to be successful?
- If the work is innovative, what are you going to do to disseminate the experience gained from the project so that others can benefit?
- How are you going to monitor and evaluate the project?
- Do you have a clear budget for the work, and can you justify all the expenditure?
- What is going to happen when the funding runs out? Will the project continue on a sustainable basis; will you be able to identify and develop alternative sources of funding, or will the project come to a natural end?
- Will the project become self-sustaining in some way? Does the sum requested represent an investment which will continue to bring benefit into the future?
- What sources of funds have you already identified? And what has already been committed to the project?
- What other grants can be mobilised to add to the sum being requested from that particular donor?
- When do you need the money?
- Why is the need important and urgent and what are the consequences if nothing is done?
- Will you be able to harness the efforts and energies of volunteers, and how much value will this add to the work being done?
- Will you be mobilising the local community, and how are they involved?
- Will you be collaborating with other organisations and agencies, bringing in additional skills and resources?
- What are your plans beyond the project, to build on and develop from the work you plan to do during this next phase? (This should at least be considered, even if you have no firm plans at this stage.)

You need to answer all of the questions as factually and as honestly as possible. This should provide you with a structure for writing your

Checklist of things to include in your proposal

1. Have you got a strategy?

2. Have you planned ahead?

3. Have you selected a good project which will appeal to that particular donor?

4. Have you tailored your application to address the particular interests and priorities of each funder?

5. Have you done enough to establish your credibility?

6. Have you any personal contact and have you plans for using this to progress your application?

7. Have you prepared a realistic budget?

8. Have you been specific about what you need?

9. Have you a target for the amount you need to raise to get the project started?

10. Is your proposal clear, concise and factual?

11. Will people understand what you are saying? Have you assumed people know what you are talking about? Check for jargon, initials and acronyms, and other things that people may not understand.

proposal, and with many of the points you will want to include. You also need to demonstrate the importance of what you are planning to do and achieve, at the same time as describing your work and telling them about your plans.

When dealing with donors that have an application form, what they need to know will be evident from the questions they ask in the application form. Make sure that you answer all the questions as completely and as fully as you can.

When approaching companies, it is important to consider what you are able to offer them in return. For most companies this will be a key factor in their decision to donate funds, and for any sponsorship proposal it is crucial. Consider ways in which you can publicise the company's support (in your annual reports, newsletters, the local press, etc.); the interest of the company's own employees in becoming fundraisers or volunteers for your organisation; and the proximity of your organisation to any major plant or branch location of the company. Don't assume that the company will work out all the benefits themselves; you must point them out clearly and enthusiastically.

Deciding how much to ask for

You will have found out the sort of grant that the particular donor usually makes through your preliminary research. Very often this will be less than you need. In such cases, you will need to approach a number of funders, asking each to contribute part of the total. There are several approaches to this. You can approach, say, three different sources, and ask each to contribute one third of the total (or an appropriate proportion, depending on their size), or you can break the project down into separate components. Each of these might become the subject of an application to a particular donor, and in each application you will highlight the particular importance to the project of what you are asking that donor to support – as well as the value of the project as a whole.

Then there is the matter of strategy. Do you approach all your prospective donors at the same time? Or do you approach one of them first, hoping to gain their support, before approaching the others? This is something that only you can decide. If you have a funder with whom you have worked closely in the past and who is prepared to make a commitment to support the project, then the fact that you have been able to obtain that support might encourage others. On the other hand, if you have to wait to get a commitment from one funder before approaching others, then that can delay the funding process.

Whatever you decide, it is important to have a funding plan, and to explain to everyone you are approaching how you propose to raise all of the money you need.

Timing

It always takes much longer than you think to prepare a proposal. You should allow up to a month if you have not yet fully formulated your thoughts or if you need to consult others or gather more information. After you have prepared a first draft, it will need to be edited and checked before the final perfect copy is produced.

You must also consider the time requirements of the funders themselves. This may mean that some sources cannot respond within the timeframe you require. For example, applications for European Union funding may have to be submitted up to 18 months in advance. Government bodies have their own procedures and an annual budget cycle. Foundations may take up to six months, and smaller foundations may meet only once a year (although companies tend to respond more quickly). With the National Lottery Charities Board, you may have to wait until the theme of the grants round matches your work, and then there will be at least six months between the issuing of the application forms and the final decision.

There is the question of the length of time you want the money for and whether you require a single sum or continuing support for a number of years. It is frequently said that you get what you ask for; from this it follows that if you need three-year or five-year funding, you must remember to make this clear in your proposal, though that is no guarantee that you will get it.

There is also the question of what happens afterwards. If your project is to continue, how will it be funded after the initial grant period? If you are applying for money to purchase a piece of equipment or a building, how will the running costs be met? You may not have all the answers now, but you should at least be thinking about the problem.

Writing up the proposal

When writing up your proposal there are a range of factors to consider.
- *Length*. If you put in all your information, your application will be too long for most funders. For a major project, for example for a new

building, it may well be appropriate to produce a lengthy proposal, but you can also prepare an executive summary or a two-page covering letter which sets out the key points. For less complicated projects, try to keep the length to a minimum. This will make it much easier for the donor, who might be receiving a steady stream of proposals. A page to a page and a half for a company, or two to three pages for a trust will normally be sufficient for most proposals and you can append more detailed information if you feel that it will be of interest to the donor.

■ *The key points*. At the heart of your proposal, you will describe the needs you are trying to address, the aims of your project, and how you will achieve them. You should include as much detail as is necessary for a person who is not knowledgeable in your area. You should also give an indication as to how you expect to measure the success of the project.

■ *Your credibility*. If your organisation is new or the funder has had no previous contact with you, they may well want to ask who you are and why they should entrust their money to you. This can be overcome in a number of ways: providing CVs of the key organisers and others involved; listing the names of well-connected committee members or patrons; mentioning the support you have previously received from other major donors or a government body, will all help provide reassurance. If you have obtained press coverage, you can include the clippings. If you have had an evaluation done on your work, then that might provide ammunition. If you have received feedback from users, experts or others, then you can mention this or include a direct quote. If you have successfully developed other projects into on-going work, highlight this.

■*Recognition of the importance of the problem*. If the problem itself is not widely recognised, references to other respected reports or endorsements by prominent people will help.

■*The budget*. Your budget will always be carefully scrutinised by potential funders, and needs to be clear, complete and accurate. Most donors will not be interested in the small details of your stationery or postage bill. They will be interested in the major areas of expenditure and income. You should identify capital or other one-off costs, salaries, overheads and any other major operational costs. Similarly, income estimates will show the money you expect to generate from

---

Getting the budget right

There is a tendency to undercost proposals. If you do this, you will not raise the money you need to run your project effectively. So you should ensure that:

■ you include every item that you expect to have to pay for;

■ you put a realistic price on each item;

■ you take account of inflation. Different funders will have different systems for dealing with this, but you don't want to find that the price of something has shot up just when you need to purchase it;

■ you include administrative overheads associated with the project, where possible. The organisation as a whole functions to make the projects happen and the cost of running the organisation has to be paid for;

■ you include sums for dissemination and publicity.

Remember that a main reason why organisations get into financial crisis is that they undercost their applications!

the project itself or through fundraising. Beyond this, you may need to show the way in which the money you need in the medium term is going to be raised, say over a period of three years. This may require a summary income and expenditure statement and a capital expenditure statement, both spread over a three-year period. Additionally, you will need to supply your organisation's audited accounts for the latest year for which they are available.

■ *Information on the organisation and its status.* It is useful to include the formal and legal information about the organisation on the letterhead. This includes the registration details, names of trustees, board members and patrons, which can help create the impression that you are well established. Sometimes people include their bank account details – optimistically assuming a grant!

■ *Language and jargon.* Many applications are extremely badly written and boring to read. If you have the skill to do so, try to write the application in a lively upbeat way, concentrating on your strengths, the opportunities, the desirable outcomes and your hopes for the future. This is far better than the flat language that most reports are written in. The application is a selling document – selling the idea of supporting your project to a potential donor. Avoid long sentences, long paragraphs, meaningless words and jargon (which means something to you but nothing to the reader), and waffle. It is far better to have short words, short sentences, short paragraphs, bullet points and bold text to highlight key features, and headings and subheads to indicate the different parts of the application. The best advice is to get someone else to read what you have written before you send it off – and the best person is someone who knows little about your work, as that is the position of most of the people you will be sending your application to. They can challenge assumptions and ask for explanations where things seem unclear.

Dos and Don'ts for your proposal

DO
1. Address your appeal to the right person.
2. Tailor your appeal to the recipient.
3. Include a clear statement of your charity's functions and objectives.
4. State clearly the purpose for which the funds are needed and the amount required.
5. Break a large appeal down into manageable, realistic amounts for particular elements and items.
6. Include your latest sets of accounts.
7. Offer to go and see the prospective donor, and follow up the letter within a week.
8. Make full use of any contacts that can help your chances.
9. Keep it brief.
10. Be positive and upbeat about the exciting ideas you have.

DON'T
1. Make your appeal letter look mass-produced.
2. Include irrelevant information or large quantities of printed material.
4. Get angry at a refusal – funders cannot support every request, even those which meet their criteria.
5. Be put off by a refusal – try to find out why you were turned down, and try again next year or sooner.
6. Feel obliged to offer expensive hospitality to a prospective donor.
7. Leave too little time – it can often take months for your application to be processed and a decision made.
8. Drone on about what a difficult time your organisation has.

- *Facts and figures*. It is important to back up your claims – the extent of the need and the effectiveness of your methods – with facts and figures. Everything may be 'desperate', 'urgent', 'important', 'unique'; you need to prove this. Try to include a few selected facts and figures in your proposal (and you can also provide a wealth of detail in a background paper attached as an appendix to the application).
- *The human story*. If you can include case studies and examples of how people have been helped and what they have gone on to achieve as a result of your help, then this will demonstrate clearly that you are effective in helping people – which is what most donors are interested in supporting.
- *Presentation*. How you present your proposal is luckily not the most important aspect, but it can make a difference. Different standards and expectations apply to different donors. A sponsorship proposal directed at the marketing director of a major company will have to have a different feel to that being sent to a national foundation which is receiving dozens of others each day. Government agencies and international donors will have their own standards and preferred styles. Remember to tailor your style of communication to whoever it is you are talking to.

Getting in touch

Skilled fundraisers would not consider sending a proposal out of the blue to anyone but the smallest and the most remote foundation or company. To ensure a greater chance of success, applicants need to know as much as possible about those they are approaching. Equally, if the target already knows something about the applicant's work and reputation, then that will be an important advantage. For example, you will need to know:

- what **constraints** are imposed by the donor as a matter of policy (there is no point applying for something that they cannot or will not support);
- the typical **size** of a grant. Many funders make grants at two or three levels. Very large grants to major initiatives; medium-sized grants to a range of projects; and much smaller grants for local initiatives;
- what are the **donors interests** and what sort of things have been supported in the past ;
- **who to write to** (their name and job title), but also **who makes the decisions** and who they are advised by (so you can plan any lobbying);
- whether the donor expects any **recognition or benefit** in return for their support ;
- whether there are different **decision-making procedures** for different levels of grant. With some of the larger trusts a very large grant has to be decided by the full committee, but the Grants Director may be able

to agree to smaller grants between meetings;

- their **decision-making cycle** and the best time for applications to be submitted. This can vary from one grants meeting a year, to quarterly meetings; and some of the larger trusts and companies might be making decisions, particularly on smaller applications, even more frequently than this.

To find out about all of this you will need to:

- **research** the targets you plan to approach and keep this information on record;
- **telephone** the donor organisation to identify a contact person and the application procedure;
- suggest a **meeting**, if this seems appropriate, or think of other ways in which you can bring your work to the attention of the donor. This is particularly important for large applications;
- invite the donor to **visit** your project to see it in operation;
- find out as much as you can about the detailed decision-making process by asking the donor and by **talking** to others who have received support from that donor;
- **contact** any key advisers or trustees of the donor organisation to tell them about your proposal, if this is possible;
- **write** a draft proposal, personalised as much as possible to the needs of the donor organisation, seek comments on this from colleagues and then redraft;
- **produce** and send off the final application, together with appended information to fill in the detail as necessary.

You might want to ask the potential donor (tactfully) whether they could suggest other bodies for you apply to. Care needs to be taken here, as this may present an easy way for them to say no.

Some reasons for refusal

A large number of applications are rejected because they fall completely outside the funder's guidelines. The Commonwealth Foundation has a series of standard letters it sends out in reply to inappropriate applications, giving these reasons for refusal:

- the Foundation cannot support students at any level
- the Foundation cannot support non-Commonwealth citizens
- the activity is being held in a non-Commonwealth country
- the Foundation cannot help with general appeals
- the Foundation cannot normally support activities limited to one country
- the proposed activity is outside our terms of reference or priority areas of interest
- the Foundation cannot support research activities
- the application has arrived too late – the Foundation normally requires three months notice
- the Foundation cannot support activities of more than three months duration
- the Foundation does not provide capital grants.

Sending a completely inappropriate application is a waste of everyone's time. READ THE GUIDELINES BEFORE APPLYING!

3. Sources of Funds

This chapter sketches out the main sources of funding – individuals, charitable trusts and foundations, companies, government and statutory sources (including contracts), the National Lottery, European Union and other international sources, and a miscellany of other possible sources. It describes their characteristics, identifies the main opportunities for the fundraiser, gives practical advice and identifies the skills you will need to be successful.

3.1 Individual donors

There are a wide range of potential donors to your cause – each with different characteristics, each having a different motivation, each preferring a different way of giving, and each having a different pathway by which they can be reached and communicated with. It is important for the fundraiser to have a clear idea of who they plan to approach and how they propose to attract their support.

It is estimated that individuals give as much as £2,000 million a year to charity, with nearly half as much again coming through legacies and bequests.

Obviously, individual giving is a major source of funding for voluntary organisations, but the mechanisms for attracting it are far more diverse and complex than the grants process used for attracting support from trusts and government.

In this section, we examine how and why people give and in Chapter 4, we explore some of the techniques that you can use to get people to support you.

The range of potential donors includes:

- **individuals reached through institutions.** Institutions you might target include Rotary Clubs and other similar philanthropic groups of local business people, schools and colleges to reach young people, trade unions, companies and other employers through which you can reach employees;
- **the less well off as well as the rich**. It is often said that the poor are more generous, and response to telethons as well as anecdotal evidence of approaching the seriously rich seem to bear this out;
- **people of all ages**. People have different interests at different stages in their lives. When they are young, they may be more concerned with the environment, AIDS, drug-related issues or homelessness. When

they are elderly, it may be medical causes (such as cancer or arthritis or hospices) or animals which will attract them more;

- **those directly affected by a problem** to those who are only mildly interested. A parent of a disabled child will have a different level of interest in disability than a member of the public;
- **the general public** – everyone through to those with a particular perspective (such as lawyers or doctors or scientists or teachers);
- **the whole of the country** or just those living in a **particular city or region**;
- **family and friends** of existing supporters. Many people support charity simply because they are asked and if they are asked by someone they know well, it becomes quite hard to refuse.

The more clearly you can specify who is likely to be interested in your cause, the more successful you will be in reaching them. To find out about your organisation's potential for attracting support you could see who is already supporting you – perhaps by carrying out some simple market research. A survey could help you find out who they are (for example, whether they are male or female, old or young, living alone or in a family, busy or with time on their hands) and why they support you. Test different audiences to see what the response is. You may be surprised to find that a wider range of people want to support you and for different reasons from what you imagine.

The different ways of giving

There are not only different audiences, but there are also different methods of obtaining their support. A donor can support you by:

- giving a **one-off donation**;
- giving **committed support** on a regular basis (see section 4.7), through a membership scheme or a Deed of Covenant (see Appendix 3);
- making a **major gift** to an appeal or towards a project (see section 4.17);
- leaving a **legacy** to you when they die (see section 4.9);
- making a **gift in kind** – this can be anything from offering you office space to giving you items to sell at a charity auction;
- **purchasing a gift item** (such as Christmas cards or souvenir items) or promotional material (such as tee-shirts or posters) (see section 3.9);
- supporting a **charity fundraising event** (see section 4.2);
- participating in **lotteries**, raffles, sweepstakes and tombolas, by purchasing a ticket (see section 4.11);
- raising money from **family and friends**;
- giving time as a **volunteer**. Many organisations benefit very substantially from the time and effort put in by their volunteers – which can often be more important than the fundraising (see section 6.1).

Why people give

It is difficult to generalise about why people give because different causes generate different motivations. However, if you understand the main reasons for giving stated below, it will be easier to get people to support you.

- *Concern* is probably the single most important reason why people give. This will embrace the person who is worried about the environment, the parent who is horrified at the sexual harassment of children and the individual who sees the pitiful faces of starving refugee children on the television news and telephones in to make a donation. Giving provides someone with the opportunity to do something significant for a cause they believe in.

- *Duty* probably comes a strong second as a motive for giving. It is the idea that those of us who are rich or to whom life has been good should respond to their good fortune with some charitable act (giving their money or their time). Many religions promote the concept of charity and some even recommend that their members allocate a certain share of their income to charity.

- *Guilt* is another motivation, but unlike duty, if people give out of a sense of guilt, this is unlikely to lead to a long-term relationship. Guilt encourages the donor to give in the hope that the problem (and you) will go away.

- *Personal experience*. Those people who have themselves or whose families have been hit by cancer, heart disease or some other illness are likely to be especially motivated to give. Likewise, those who have children at school will want to support the school or anything that helps develop their child's education. All research indicates that personal interest is one of the most powerful motivations for giving.

- *Personal benefit*. Many people like the status or recognition that comes with giving when their generosity is publicised. They may like to be associated with any prominent people involved in the organisation – access to people and social ambition are important to some people, and giving to charity can be one way for them to achieve these personal objectives.

- *Being asked*. The main reason for most people NOT giving is that they are never asked. Research demonstrates this again and again.

- *Peer pressure* is also important, where people know that their friends and colleagues have given but they have not, or where friends and colleagues are asking them to give. It can be hard for one member of a group to refuse if all the others are giving.

- *Tax*, and in particular the ability to save tax on gifts made for charitable purposes. Tax is not usually the prime motivator for giving, but can be an important factor in encouraging people to give and to give more generously. (The tax concessions on donations to charity are discussed in detail in Appendix 3.)

It is important to be able to understand why people want to give, and more particularly why the particular person you are approaching might be interested in giving to you. This requires an understanding of human psychology, but also some good research before you approach particular individuals for support. This will then enable you to tailor your message and create an approach which makes it much harder for them to refuse.

It is equally important to understand why people might not be interested in giving. They may simply not be interested in your organisation and what it stands for, or they may have given substantially to something similar recently. Bad publicity can affect people's inclination to support you; people are often worried about high levels of administration costs or have the idea that little of what they give will actually reach the poor. The problem may be so big that it appears hard to make any impact or people may feel that it is the government's job to do something, and that the matter should not be left to private charity. And then there is the fact that some people are by nature generous, whilst others will always be looking for an excuse not to give.

Getting in touch

To be a successful fundraiser, you need to do five things:
1. Identify **likely supporters**
2. Create the **right message** to appeal to them
3. **Direct that message** to those people
4. Make it **easy** for them to give you the money
5. Support your promotional work with **good PR**.

The right people are those whose background and motivations indicate a likelihood that they will want to support your cause. Careful thinking, and possibly some research, will help identify such people and their characteristics.

The right message is the one that:
■ builds on the **motivation** of the potential donor;
■ starts from their **understanding** of the cause;
■ takes account of their **natural hesitations** or reasons they might have for not giving.

A good understanding of your cause and its appeal will help; but some simple market research can also be useful here.

Equally importantly, you will need to find the right method of reaching your target audience. In a sense you can only define a target audience if at the same time you can define a way of reaching it. For example, if senior business people are your target, then there are all sorts of channels you can use to reach them, including the business press, obtaining address lists of major businesses and writing to the names on this list, working through Rotary Clubs, Chambers of Commerce and other associations of businesspeople, using businesspeople to invite other businessmen to small receptions where you can give a presentation or ask them to ask their colleagues directly for support.

You will need to make it as easy as possible for the people who want to support you to pay you the money. This means ensuring that wherever possible every piece of literature you produce that aims to get people to support you has a reply coupon with a return address. This can also indicate how people might support you by giving several options. Try to get every feature article or news story, whether in print or on air, to include contact details. You can also consider using any of the following to make the response process simpler for the donor.

- A **freepost facility**. Often the lack of a stamp means that a letter goes unposted. Some organisations then suggest that using a stamp will save the charity money.
- A **dedicated telephone line** for donation enquiries, with a named person at the end. A fictitious name could be used for this, so that the name can be printed on promotional literature. This makes it more personal, and gives the donor a feeling that the organisation cares about customer relations. People staffing the line should be properly trained. You could also consider a freephone facility (an 0800- line) – although this does not really simplify the process.
- A **credit card donation facility**. This has now become commonplace for radio appeals.
- A **CharityCard donation facility** for Charities Aid Foundation clients, which include around 100,000 individual donors and around half the leading companies. Around 1,200 charities now welcome the use of the CharityCard and are listed in a small directory with their telephone numbers that is circulated by CAF to its clients.

Some tips for PR

- Keep a list of media people to send your promotional material to.
- Make friends with journalists, including journalists on local papers and radio, keeping them in touch with what you are doing.
- When you have a success, publicise it by sending out a press release. Follow this up with a phone call to encourage their interest.
- Use your beneficiaries to talk about your work, either through interviews or by quoting them in your press releases.
- Issue a press release with your annual report, and try to get publicity for it.
- When you win a substantial grant, or if you get support from a government body or from an important company, try to get publicity for this. You might be able to get the cheque hand-over photographed.
- Use 'stunts' to generate PR, especially those that illustrate the need or demonstrate the support that your cause is attracting. A stunt is an event specially designed to attract publicity – for example, going on hunger strike to draw attention to the plight of refugees in this country, or organising a prize for the 'worst work of art' to coincide with the Turner Prize to comment on the state of the arts.
- When you produce and publish research on the cause, try to get a feature written about it to coincide with publication, or make it newsworthy so that journalists will want to cover it, and issue a press release highlighting its news value.

Finally, people will be more likely to support you if they have already heard about your organisation, its work and the importance of the need you are addressing. This is where Public Relations comes in. It is often said that good PR is an essential ingredient of successful fundraising. So you need to spend some of your effort promoting your organisation and publicising its work (see section 7.6 for advice on getting publicity).

How British donors rate different causes

Helping children	3.7
Physical handicap	3.7
Sensory handicap (such as blindness or deafness)	3.6
The elderly	3.6
Mental illness and handicap	3.5
Hospitals and healthcare provision	3.5
Medical research	3.5
Youth problems and youth work	3.0
Housing and homelessness	2.8
Animal welfare and animal rights	2.8
Overseas emergency aid and disaster relief	2.7
Environmental concerns and conservation	2.6
Unemployment and training for employment	2.6
Education	2.6
Overseas development	2.3
Women's rights and women's organisations	2.2
Religious organisations	2.2
Sport	2.1
Museums and cultural institutions	2.0
The arts	1.9

This table is taken from the Charity Household Survey. It shows how people in Britain rate the various causes that they might be presented with. The greater the number, the higher the importance they give to that cause. In Britain, causes which relate to helping people – including children and people with impairments and disabilities – appear to rate the highest. Arts, education and the environment are much less popular causes. The culture and circumstances of other countries will be different, but in every country there will be causes which generate an extremely positive response and causes which are less attractive. The less attractive the cause, the more important it is to target your appeal at those more likely to support it.

Five good ideas when fundraising from individuals

1. In **approaching individuals**, always try to **identify clearly and precisely how much money is needed and how much you want them to give**. Show how their contribution can play an important part in what you plan to do. You should not suggest an unattainable figure, but you should make people feel proud to have done something significant to help you.

2. In **making the appeal**, try to **express the need in human terms**, giving graphic images of the problem and how your work actually helps individuals. Try to avoid giving abstract statistics describing the global importance of the problem unless you are trying to emphasise the point. It is said that:

One hungry person next door to you is equivalent to...

One hundred hungry people in a nearby town, who are equivalent to...

Ten million hungry people in some far off country.

The nearer you make people feel to the problem, the more successful you will be. If they feel that by helping you they are helping to solve a real person's problem, they will be much more likely to give than if asked to support a general cause.

3. **Ask for exactly what you want**. Prospective donors will not necessarily know the size or the nature of the contribution expected of them. One way of doing this is to suggest a range of donations, asking them to choose their own level of giving. Show what the different amounts can achieve – keeps one young person in a homework centre for a term, for example.

4. **Repeat the message** that you need their help, and that with their help you can do something. Repetition reinforces the message. It is good communication practice to:

Tell them what you are going to tell them.

Tell them.

Tell them what you have told them.

5. **Target your appeal** as carefully as you can, and make your message as personal and relevant to the prospective donor as possible. If you are approaching existing supporters, then refer to their generous support and what you have been able to achieve with it. If you are approaching doctors, tell them about your work from a medical perspective. If you are approaching local people, show the local benefits that will be achieved by your work. The more closely targeted the message, the more successful you will be.

Getting started

It is far easier to develop donations income from a base of existing supporters than it is to start from scratch. An existing donor is probably ten times more likely to support you than someone who has never given, but many organisations are in the position of having no existing donors. If that is the case for you, here are some things you could do.

1. **Produce a simple leaflet** that explains your work and shows that you are looking for money. This need not be anything more than a letter-sized sheet of paper (A4) printed in two colours and folded to make a four-page leaflet, and it should include photographs of the organisation at work. This should have a reply coupon with space for anyone interested to fill in their name and address so that you can enter them on your database. You could ask them to tick a number of boxes to show their interest in giving money, becoming a member, or volunteering their time.

2. **Get a feature written** about your organisation, and make sure that it includes an address to which anyone who is interested can write.

3. **Get coverage on local radio** – this is an accessible and often underrated publicity medium. Again, make sure that a response address is announced on air.

4. **Ask any existing supporters to suggest friends** whom you might contact, mentioning their name, or get them to ask. This supporter-get-a-supporter approach can work extremely well.

5. **Find an appropriate mailing list** which you could send a simple appeal to – for example, for a health charity, a leaflet and a short covering letter could be sent to doctors and health workers.

6. **Think about house-to-house collecting** or door-to-door canvassing for support. Remember that most people say that they don't give because they haven't been asked. House-to-house solicitation is an excellent way of asking, particularly for a local cause. Try to have some form of membership scheme so that you can enrol those who are interested. A personal approach will always work better than putting a written appeal through the letterbox, but obviously takes more time and effort. You need to strike a balance between ease and effectiveness.

7. **Consider running some sort of event** with a well-known speaker, and publicising this locally. You can then try to recruit those that attend.

8. **Take a stand or a stall at other people's events** (such as a local fair) or at a theatre or concert hall, which attract large numbers of people. You will need permission, and might be asked to make some sort of financial contribution.

9. **Organise a petition** if it is a cause which people are likely to feel strongly about.

10. Once you have recruited a donor, try to **keep them for life** (getting the most from your donors and supporters is covered in more detail in sections 4.7 and 4.8.; getting legacies is covered in section 4.9).

3.2 Trusts and foundations

Grant making trusts give away around £700 million each year for charitable purposes. They are an important target for most fundraisers. Each trust is different, so you need to research carefully first which trusts are worth approaching, what aspects of your work they are likely to be interested in, and the scale of their grant making.

Grant-making trusts, sometimes referred to as foundations, are independent grant-making bodies, deriving their income from investments or through some form of continued fundraising.

How a trust works

A trust has the following structure:

THE DONOR
who provides the money
▼
A CONSTITUTION or TRUST DEED
which sets out how the funds are to be managed and distributed
▼
THE TRUSTEES
who are responsible for seeing that the funds are properly invested and managed, and that grants are made according to the terms of the trust deed
▼
ADMINISTRATIVE STAFF
many of the larger trusts employ staff to manage the affairs of the trust, to deal with applicants and to assess applications (some use external assessors); the staff are accountable to the trustees, who retain the ultimate responsibility for seeing that the trust operates within the terms of its constitution
▼
THE APPLICANT
who applies for a grant from the trust (that is you!)

Trusts can be an extremely important source of support for any organisation, as they are set up with the express intention of giving their money away for charitable purposes and for community benefit. They are a must for most fundraising programmes – for well-established national and local charities, but also for new and smaller community-based projects.

One important role that some trusts play is supporting innovation – new ideas, new ways of doing things, new needs, new organisations. Many of today's successful organisations owe their existence to the support they received at the outset from progressive trusts who were prepared to shoulder whatever risk there may have been at that stage of the organisation's development.

How to be successful

Before approaching trusts, it is important to understand how they work, what sorts of things they like to support, and the type of support that they like to give. One feature of trust funding is the diversity of the sector. Trusts come in all shapes and sizes, founded for a variety of different reasons, with different social and political perspectives, and with different approaches to their grant-making. This means there will be many trusts which will not be interested in funding you but there may also be a few which could be extremely interested in your work and in giving you support.

Most trusts claim that they receive far more applications than they could possibly support, but that they do not receive enough good applications. Many are circular applications produced on a word processor, sent to a large number of trusts without being tailored to the trust's particular interests and priorities. These are generally rejected on sight. It is worth putting some effort into making sure that the application you send is as good as you can make it, that it is relevant to them and that it is for an appropriate amount.

Successful fundraising from trusts involves identifying those trusts that might be interested in supporting you, finding out as much as you can about them (and trying to get them interested in what you are doing even before you plan to approach them for money), finding some aspect of their work that they might be prepared to support, then persuading them to say yes. Easy!

The diversity of trusts as funders

- From very large institutions such as the Wellcome Trust, by far the largest trust in Britain, and the Tudor Trust, which funds across a wide range of charitable purposes, to tiny bodies with just a few hundred pounds a year to distribute.
- From those with an international remit such as the Aga Khan Foundation, which funds in Africa and South Asia, and Charity Projects, which works predominantly in Africa, or a national remit such as the Joseph Rowntree Foundation or the Gulbenkian Foundation, to those that operate regionally or locally.
- From those that support a wide range of activities to those that specialise in providing support for a particular type of work.

Understanding how trusts work

In this section we explore some of the key features of trusts, which you will need to consider when trying to identify trusts to approach.

1. Where trusts get their money from

Most trusts are established with a capital sum provided by a founder during his or her lifetime or on death through a will. This could be the shares in a company or the proceeds of the sale of a company, or perhaps even land. The founder could be a successful business person (such as Paul Hamlyn or David Sainsbury, who have both set up major foundations); but there are also many trusts that have been set up by individuals with much more modest sums.

Some trusts are set up by public subscription. The various royal Jubilee Trusts are examples, as is the Winston Churchill Memorial Trust, which was set up as a memorial after his death. The Church Urban Fund is another example, which sought money from Church of England congregations and businesses to realise some of the ambitions of the 'Faith in the City' report. Many of the livery companies, such as the Goldsmiths Company and the Clothworkers, have charitable trusts whose funds have accumulated from legacies and the philanthropy of their members.

Some trusts have no permanent funds, but rely on continuing fundraising activity to provide them with funds for distribution. The largest of these are the BBC's Children in Need charity and Charity Projects (Comic Relief), both of which raise money through television appeals. The Network Foundation, on the other hand, is a much smaller trust, which brings together a group of like-minded socially responsible individuals who pool their charitable giving to support projects which promote peace and a better world.

How a trust is founded has a significant impact on the style of its grantmaking in two ways. Firstly, the founder's wishes, sometimes set out in a letter attached to the founding trust deed, will guide the trustees in their grantmaking. Secondly, the founder and his or her family may still play a leading role in the affairs of the trust as trustees, and will want to support those concerns and projects which particularly interest them. This is perfectly legitimate. Trusts are not public bodies, but

> **Examples of major trusts established by successful business people**
> - **Esmee Fairbairn Charitable Trust** (Ian Fairbairn, M & G Group, unit trusts)
> - **The Gatsby Charitable Trust** (David Sainsbury, J Sainsbury, supermarkets)
> - **The Paul Hamlyn Foundation** (Paul Hamlyn, publishing)
> - **The Mackintosh Foundation** (Cameron Mackintosh, musical theatre)
> - **The Wates Foundation** (the Wates family, house builders)
> - **The Garfield Weston Foundation** (Garfield Weston, Associated British Foods)
> - **The Westminster Foundation** (Duke of Westminster, landowner)
> - **The Wolfson Foundation** (Sir Isaac Wolfson, retailing)

private bodies set up for public benefit. With the passage of time, the influence of the founder can diminish, as outside trustees are appointed. This is the case, for example, with the Joseph Rowntree and Nuffield Foundations.

2. The trust's objects and policies

The trust deed sets out the objects or purposes of the trust. This defines what can be supported and also what the trust cannot support. Sometimes the objects are very broad, for general charitable or educational purposes, for example. Sometimes they are much more specific. The trustees can also decide on a policy and priorities for their grantmaking (so long as this falls within the objects of the trust). Thus a trust set up for the advancement of education might decide to give all its money as bursaries to young people aged 16 to 18 in order to encourage them to stay on at school, or for primary schools to purchase new technology.

You need to check to see whether what you are doing falls within the trust's objects, but also that it falls within its current grant policy and priorities.

A trust may have been set up hundreds of years ago, and the trustees need to interpret the objects in the light of present social conditions and needs. In Victorian times, there were many trusts set up to 'relieve girls in moral danger'; this was to support sexually abused servant girls. Today society is quite different, but projects dealing with child sexual abuse or rape crisis counselling would be perfectly legitimate projects for such a trust to support. The Metropolitan Drinking Fountain and Cattle Trough Association used to provide drinking fountains and cattle troughs on the streets of London; today it provides drinking fountains in school playgrounds.

3. The beneficial area

Just as the trustees are restricted to giving support within the objects of the trust, so the beneficial area determines where the trust can give its support. A trust may be established with an international remit, allowing it to give overseas, or with a national remit – this might be England, Great Britain or the United Kingdom – and how this is termed will determine whether the trust can give in Scotland, Wales or Northern Ireland.

Many trusts have a purely local remit. For example, the City Parochial Foundation is restricted to making grants for the benefit of the people of London, and the Cripplegate Foundation can only benefit the people who live or work in two wards of South Islington.

4. Large and small trusts

The management of the larger trusts is highly professional and likely to

Read the guidelines before applying

Most of the larger trusts publish guidelines to what they will and will not fund. It is important to read these before applying to see whether what you are proposing fits within their policies and does not fall within their exclusions. For example, the **Bridge House Estates Trust Fund** was established by the Corporation of London to distribute money surplus to what is required for maintaining Blackfriars, Southwark, London and Tower Bridges.

The objects of the Trust are:
- provision of transport or access to it for elderly and disabled people in the Greater London area;
- other charitable purposes for the general benefit of the inhabitants of Greater London.

The policies of the Trust are to support the following activities in the Greater London area:
- transport and access to it for elderly and disabled people;
- environmental conservation;
- innovative projects which assist young people in deprived areas;
- schemes which assist elderly people to stay within the community;
- the provision of technical support to voluntary organisations.

The exclusions are:
- the Trust cannot fund: political parties or political lobbying; non-charitable activities; activities where there is a statutory duty to incur the expenditure. Nor can it make grants which do not benefit the inhabitants of Greater London;
- as a matter of policy, the Trust does not fund: individuals; other grant-making bodies; schools, universities and other educational establishments, except where the activity is an ancillary charitable activity; medical or academic research; churches or other religious bodies for construction, repair and maintenance of buildings or for religious purposes; preservation of buildings, except to provide access for disabled people; or applications where alternative funding is available;
- the Trust will not normally fund: organisations that receive a large proportion of their funding from central or local government sources, unless the application relates to a new initiative; umbrella organisations; or hospitals.

include a Clerk, Secretary or Director (the title varies), who is in executive charge of the grants programme with administrative support. Very large trusts sometimes have a team of specialist or regional grants officers. The Director will report to a Board of Trustees, who are ultimately responsible for policy and for seeing that the trust operates properly (within its constitution) and effectively. The Trustees will usually take or ratify the final decision on where the grants go, basing their decisions on the recommendations of their professional staff. The trust may also use local advisers or experts in the specialist areas who will be asked to assess larger grant applications.

Most of the larger trusts have well thought through policies for what they are interested in supporting. Grant applications will be assessed according to these policies.

Smaller trusts are often run by the family or the individual who set them up. They may be administered by a firm of lawyers or accountants who will prepare the accounts, and sometimes also provide an address for correspondence. These smaller trusts are unlikely to employ professional staff to assess grant applications – they simply do not have sufficient money to pay for this. Many simply support the charitable interests of the founder or family that established the trust. Some will not even consider applications received from charities they have no contact or connection with. Good contacts with their trustees or some form of personal or local connection is often important if you are to succeed in getting money from most of the smaller trusts.

5. How grant decisions are made

Most trusts are reactive, responding to the requests they receive for support, rather than going out to find projects they would like to support, so the first stage in the grant-making process is receiving a proposal from an applicant. What happens next depends on the size of the trust. Larger trusts will have a procedure for assessing applications, which could include:

- the trust director or a specialist grants officer **assessing the application** and making a recommendation;
- a **site visit** or a meeting with the applicant;
- engaging a **consultant** to investigate and report (which would only be done for very large applications).

A report will then be prepared for the trustees, which will recommend which of the applications should be supported, and this will go to a trustees meeting where the grant decision will be made. Some of the very large trusts allow their staff the discretion to decide smaller grants without reference to the trustees.

Some important considerations

1. Charitable status of the applicant

Trusts are governed by their founding constitution and, for almost all of them there is a requirement to support charitable work. There are a very few trusts which have been set up specifically to support non-charitable work, where charitable tax reliefs cannot be obtained on the income of the trust – the Barrow Cadbury Trust and the Joseph Rowntree Reform Trust, both of which are associated with larger charitable trusts, are the two most important; the Network Foundation also has a non-charitable arm.

This requirement to support charitable work does not necessarily mean that trusts have to give to organisations that are constituted and registered as charities, but the work they support must be for public benefit. Many trusts, however, have a policy of only giving to organisations that are registered with the Charity Commission or have an Inland Revenue charity reference number. Newly established organisations or those which have decided not to register as charities will not be able to obtain a grant directly from such trusts. It is possible to arrange that another charity receives the grant on behalf of the applicant in such circumstances. Some community trusts and local Councils of Voluntary Service are prepared to do this.

There are also trusts which have been set up to support individuals in need for educational purposes. The Buttle Trust, for example, is an important provider of welfare grants for individuals, and there are many local charities that provide this form of support (see *A Guide to Grants for Individuals in Need* and *The Educational Grants Directory*). Some trusts also provide bursaries to individuals – the Prince's Trust, which supports young people, and the Winston Churchill Memorial Trust, which provides bursaries for people to undertake study visits, are two good examples of this. Many of the trusts which make grants to charitable organisations specifically exclude making grants to individuals.

2. National or local projects

Many of the larger trusts have a national, or even an international, remit. They are interested in supporting national projects, important local projects, or projects of national significance – these could include pioneering local work, which has implications for the way things are done in other parts of the country.

Some national trusts will also be making purely local grants. Many will have a particular interest in supporting projects in the vicinity of where they are based. These local projects are more likely to be known to the trust, and it is easier to arrange a visit. Some will also have defined certain areas of the country where they are prepared to give their local support (on the basis that it is better to concentrate their resources on particular areas, and that it is difficult to assess applications from all parts of the country). For example, the Wates Foundation is keen to support projects in South London, the Joseph Rowntree Charitable Trust supports local projects in York, and 29th May Charity supports projects in the West Midlands, but not in Birmingham where the Cadbury Trusts are active. Some will want to focus on need, and any local project should try to make a convincing case that local needs are particularly pressing – comparative local data, possibly from census figures, can be used for this purpose.

Some trusts have been established specifically to make local grants. If yours is a local project, then it is important to establish what local trusts are active in your area.

One problem is the geographic distribution of trusts. Most trusts are based in the South East, and some areas and cities are less well served than others. For example, there are few trusts in Manchester or in Wales, but there are many important trusts and thriving trust networks in Scotland, Liverpool, Newcastle and Birmingham. If you come from an area with few trusts, then you will find it that much harder to get trust support for a local project. You could even make a good case based not just on need but on the dearth of available trust funding to meet that need.

3. One-off or continuing support

Most trusts either make one-off grants or give regular support for only a limited number of years (usually no more than three years, although some trusts are now prepared to consider five-year grants). Even if a one-off grant is obtained, it is possible that the same trust might be willing to support another aspect of your work next year. Some trusts, though, have a policy of not giving a second grant to an organisation until at least a year has elapsed since the first grant terminated.

Most trusts do not want to be committed to supporting a particular project indefinitely. This ties up their funds and prevents them from responding to new requests. They also don't want to feel that once their support has ended, there is little chance of replacement funding being found for the project to continue. Some have a maximum that they are prepared to give to any one organisation. For all of these reasons, it is important for the fundraiser to be clear about the long-term goals and funding strategy of the organisation. Where the proposal is for a building or to purchase a piece of equipment, the application should try to show how the facility will be used and how the running costs will be met. Where it is towards running costs, the application should try to show what will happen when the grant runs out. The phrase 'exit strategy' is increasingly being used to describe this.

4. Grants or loans

Most trusts simply make cash grants. Some foundations may be prepared to make interest-free or low-interest loans, but accepting a loan will require an ability to repay the loan at some future date, which can only happen if there is some return expected from the project. The Charities Aid Foundation has set up a social investment fund specifically to make loans to charities.

5. Trust preferences

Every foundation has a different approach to grant-making. Some prefer giving start up money, whilst others prefer to support the development of more established projects. Some preclude money for capital projects, while others will only provide support for these. Some prefer to support safer, more conservative work, whilst others are radical and pioneering. Some want to make a large number of small grants, whilst others prefer to concentrate on a few major projects. The least popular area of support is towards salaries and the overhead costs of the organisation (core funding, which is often what most organisations require); most foundations prefer to support specific projects and initiatives.

What support a trust is prepared to give can normally be ascertained from the trust itself (either by speaking to the director or by reading its literature – if it publishes anything). It is extremely important that you use all available intelligence to ensure that you send only appropriately targeted appeals to foundations, which match:

- their **policies and priorities**. There is no point sending an application to a foundation which has no interest in that sort of work;
- their **scale of grant-making**. There is no point approaching a tiny foundation for a large grant, or a major foundation for a small item of expenditure;
- their **ethos and approach**. You will have the greatest success with those foundations that share your outlook and values.

What trusts like to fund

On the whole, trusts like to fund projects which are particular aspects of an organisation's work that they can identify with and feel that they are having some impact on. They also like to back innovation, responding to new needs or meeting existing needs in new ways. Here are a number of project ideas that a local advice service might put forward to a trust.

- The training of volunteers to provide welfare rights advice.
- A nutrition advisory service using peer group advisers to provide advice to families with young children.
- A conference or research report on school bullying, which would get an issue of enormous concern further out into the open, with the opportunity to discuss some positive and practical approaches for dealing with the problem.
- Paying for a Desk Top Publishing system to produce and print leaflets on a wide range of topics for distribution throughout the community.

All these are likely to be much more attractive than simply applying for money towards the costs of running the organisation. The trick is to find things that you are already doing or want to do which are likely to appeal to a donor, and then to include in the budget a reasonable contribution towards the running costs of the organisation.

Getting started

1. First of all, find out what if **any links you have had with trusts previously**, and whether any have been successful. For those that have failed, try to establish reasons for your rejection. Those that have supported you once are often likely to want to support you again – especially if you have done a really good job with their money.

2. **Those that have turned you down** are also likely prospects for future support. You have already identified them as being potentially interested

in your work – but as yet, you have failed to convince them of the value of supporting you. Try to find something really interesting for them to support, and present a better case next time.

3. **Do your research** to identify and match possible funders with various aspects of your organisation and its work. The more you can match what you want to do with what they want to support the better. Go through the directories of grant-making trusts to identify trusts which might be interested in supporting you. Divide these in two ways: firstly, into those that seem most likely to give to you, those that might just be interested, and those that it's not worth contacting; and secondly into larger trusts which could make a reasonable sized grant, and smaller trusts where you could only expect to receive a small amount. Concentrate your efforts on approaching those that are most likely to support you. Find out whether the trusts on the list produce an annual report. If they do, then get hold of it. Thoroughly research your application from the available information.

4. It might be worth finding out when the **deadline for applications** is. Many trusts make grant decisions quarterly; but the smaller trusts may only do so annually, or may do so at any time on the decision of the founder, or may not respond at all to applications from people and organisations not known to them. Sometimes the trust will suggest that you delay your application until the next meeting, as there are just too many requests this time for your proposal to stand any chance of success.

5. Find out whether any of your trustees or volunteers or staff members have **good links or personal contacts** with any of the trusts you are planning to approach. Personal contact can be an important ingredient in your success – so if there is a point of contact, try to get a good word put in on your behalf or ask them to advise you on the approach to adopt and how to frame your application.

6. Remember that trusts are unlikely to give a very large grant to organisations they have never heard of. If you are looking for large sums, it may be more sensible to apply for something small now, and then when you have made a success of that, go back for something more substantial. Another strategy is to work in partnership with a larger, longer established and better known organisation. Their partnership with you will, in effect, vouch for your credibility.

Making contact

Getting in touch with trusts should be a several stage process. It might include the following:

Information about trusts

The Charities Aid Foundation and the Directory of Social Change both publish a range of grant directories on trust giving for fundraisers. The CAF directories cover more trusts, but the DSC grant guides go into greater detail, particularly for the larger trusts, where most of the money is.

Directory of Social Change publications:

- *Guide to the Major Trusts, Vol 1*: top 300 trusts (making grants annually of over £250,000), £18.95
- *Guide to the Major Trusts, Vol 2*: the next 700 trusts (making grants annually of over £50,000), £18.95
- *A Guide to Local Trusts*: four volumes covering local trusts in the North of England, the Midlands, the South of England, £16.95 each, and Greater London, £14.95
- The six trust guides listed above on CD Rom, £99.88, or with a copy of the *Guide to the Major Trusts* Vols 1 and 2 plus one local trust guide, £134.88 (prices inclusive of VAT)
- *The Scottish Trusts Guide*, £13.95
- *The Irish Funding Guide*, £10
- *UK Charitable Funding for the Republic of Ireland*, £9.95
- Specialist funding guides: *Arts Funding Guide*, £16.95; *Sports Funding Guide*, £15.95; *Pensioners and Carers*, £9.95; *Education Funding Guide*, £15.95; *Peace and International Relations*, £4.95; and the *Third World Directory*, £12.95.
- *Trust Monitor*, a journal to keep up to date, published 3 times a year, £25

from Directory of Social Change, 24 Stephenson Way, London NW1 2DP.

Charities Aid Foundation publications:

- *The Directory of Grant Making Trusts*, in two volumes, £69.95
- *The Directory of Grant Making Trusts: Grants Index* (lists recent grants by larger trusts), £14.95
- *The Directory of Grant Making Trusts: Trustees Index* (alphabetical listing of trustees), £14.95
- *Directory of Grant Making Trusts: Children and Youth*, £19.95
- *Directory of Grant Making Trusts: Environment, Animal Welfare and Heritage*, £19.95
- *Grantseeker: an Interactive CD Rom for Fundraisers* (runs on Windows 3.1 and Windows 95), £176.25 (inclusive of VAT)

from Charities Aid Foundation, Kings Hill, West Malling, Kent ME19 4TA

Other sources of information

- FunderFinder, 65 Raglan Road, Leeds LS2 9DZ. This is a database on disk to match your project proposals with funding opportunities. Your national association or your local Council of Voluntary Service may have a copy you can use.
- The Association of Charitable Foundations, 4 Bloomsbury Square, London WC1A 2RL. This is a network for trusts, which produces a newsletter, runs an annual conference for members, and organises special interest groups to keep members informed on particular areas of charitable work.

1. **General PR** to make people aware of your organisation and its work, so that when you approach trusts, they have already heard of you and understand the importance of what you are doing. Some ways of doing this include: sending out copies of your annual report or relevant publications well before you intend to raise money; getting coverage of your work and achievements in the press, and sending photocopies of any articles that are printed to people who you think might be interested; and being asked to participate in radio or TV discussions, or in specialist conferences.

2. **A phone call to establish contact**. This can determine whether there is a best time in the trust's year to apply, whether a trust is able to support your type of work, and the procedure for applying for a grant. You may also be able to get a clearer picture of the sort of work that the foundation is likely to want to support. An important thing to find out at this stage is whether an application form is required.

3. **A written application** setting out your request. Paper is the medium in which most foundations deal, and how your request will initially be judged. Make sure that you attach a copy of your latest accounts, and an annual report (if you have one) or some other description of your organisation and its work. (See Section 2.3 for advice on writing a fundraising application.)

4. Ask for an **appropriate amount**. You can find out from your research the typical levels of grant that a trust makes. Tailor your request accordingly. Some trusts make larger grants to larger national charities, and smaller grants to smaller or more local projects. You need to think carefully about the level of support they might be interested in giving.

5. Very often a trust will back the ideas and energy of a **key individual** in your organisation. If you have such individuals, make sure that their strengths are clearly being promoted in your proposal, include a CV, and try to get that individual to meet the trust.

6. For a **large proposal**, where you are unlikely to get the support you need from one single trust, you need to think carefully about what to ask for. One possibility is to invite trusts to consider matching their support to that of another trust, or to money raised from elsewhere. For example, if you are seeking support for a community venture, getting the local council to pay for the staff and premises and asking the trust to cover the project costs can be an attractive way for both to give their support. Or you might try to get four trusts each to contribute a quarter

of the project costs, where the total you require is beyond the reach of any one of them.

7. You might then **telephone** to see whether your application has arrived, and to ask whether any further information is required. At this stage it might be worth trying to get representatives of the trust, whether they be staff or trustees, to visit you. It will considerably enhance your chances if someone has visited the project. Make sure that everything is working well, that the premises look well kept and well used, and that they meet some of your clients and beneficiaries who can speak enthusiastically about your work and the help you have given them.

8. If you have **contact** with a particular trustee or with the Chair of the trustees, then you can try to discuss your proposal with them and enlist their support before the matter comes up for discussion.

9. Remember to **say thank you** if your application has been successful. Note all the conditions attached to the grant and the reporting requirements – and make sure that you comply with these.

10. **Keep in regular touch**, and let them know how the project is going, and tell them about anything that has been particularly successful. In this way, you will begin to build a relationship with them, which may lead to further support.

11. **Keep a record** of all the approaches you make, both your correspondence and a note of any phone conversations, and of the response you receive. This will be helpful when you approach them next time.

12. If you find you have raised **more money** than you need as a result of approaching several trusts, be truthful and go back to them with alternative suggestions. Offer to extend the project or improve it, rather than have to repay the money. They will almost always agree.

Community trusts

Community trusts work in a specific geographical area, to provide grants for local charitable activity. The idea is relatively new, and most community trusts are in an early stage of development. They operate in two main ways:

- they aim to **build an endowment** of capital raised from companies, trusts and rich individuals in their area, and through legacies. The

What trusts are looking for

1. Can you define the problem clearly?

2. What is the activity and process through which you believe you can make a difference? And does it work?

3. Can you show what difference will be made?

4. What period of time will you need before you can demonstrate an impact?

5. How do you see the problem and your approach to it fitting in with the trust's general orientation and priorities?

6. What skills will be needed for the project? Can you demonstrate that you have the required skills? Have you supplied details of your training and past experience, where this is relevant to the proposal?

7. How do you propose to secure the required skills, if you don't already have them?

8. What is it about the project which is innovative? And how far can the innovative aspects be replicated in other situations?

9. If the project isn't innovative, what is the particular reason you feel that the application justifies a grant?

10. How is it proposed to evaluate and disseminate any practical experience, outcomes and lessons learned from the project?

11. Does your organisation have a clear management structure (whether this is a traditional hierarchical structure or a co-operative structure)?

12. Does the application come from or clearly have the support of the senior people in the organisation – both the senior staff and the Management Board?

13. Have you supplied your latest annual accounts? And do they give a picture of a well run, effective organisation?

14. What are the major sources of income for your work at the moment, and will these continue into the future? If not, what are you planning to do to secure your organisation's future?

15. Is your budget realistic? A common problem in many applications is that applicants undercost their projects.

16. What proportion of the total you require is being requested from the trust?

17. Where do you propose to obtain the balance? Have you already made other applications? Have any been successful? Are any pending, and when will the outcome be known?

18. What will you do if you can't raise the whole of the budget you have proposed? Will you be able to work on less? Will you have to adjust your plans? Will you go ahead?

19. What will happen when the trust's grant runs out? Is there a strategy for obtaining continuing funding? Or will the project become self-sufficient or terminate at that point?

20. When do you need the funds? Most trusts have a decision process which takes several months to receive, evaluate and decide on the application. Many applicants apply far too late.

These 20 questions to ask yourself before approaching a trust for a significant grant have been adapted from a leaflet given to applicants by the Joseph Rowntree Charitable Trust. These are the sorts of things applicants may have to answer questions about in their written application and in any subsequent discussions with a grants assessor.

income from this is then used to make grants. Some also organise fundraising events to generate further income for their grant-making;

■ they work with other donors to **help them distribute their money more effectively**. Donors can direct their funds to a favoured cause or within a specified geographical area. Themed funds can address a particular issue, such as crime prevention, and can be supported with donations from several sources.

Community trusts are being promoted, supported and trained by the Association of Community Trusts and Foundations, 4 Bloomsbury Square, London WC1A 2RL. This is how they describe their mission:

"Community trusts and foundations are a new kind of charitable trust working in specific geographical area, which act as endowment builders, grant-makers and community leaders. Their broad purpose is to promote and support local charitable and community activity, through a programme of constructive grant-making. Individual donations pooled in an endowment, and wise governance by a board of trustees who know about the community, combine to make this possible. Those with a direct interest include donors, local voluntary and community organisations, and the wider local community.

"Community trusts and foundations also create partnerships through their work with local authorities and the corporate and voluntary sectors, and provide people with the information they need to make sound decisions about local charitable giving. Their work can generate new areas of action, and their independent status means that they are ideally placed to take a strategic approach to supporting local initiatives."

Community trusts are likely to grow in importance. They are worth approaching as a potential source of money for any local project – although many of them do not yet have large amounts of money to distribute. It impresses a national trust if you have already successfully raised money locally. They are also a possible source of advice on raising money from other local trusts.

3.3 Company giving, sponsorship and joint promotions

There is no particular obligation for companies to give their money to charity or to support projects in the local communities where they operate but they do give. The top 400 companies give £160 million in cash to charity each year plus a further £100 million in non-cash community contributions. Although the level of their support is far below what the general public, government or grant-making trusts contribute, they are an important target for both national and local fundraising.

The main reason for company giving is often said to be enlightened self-interest, rather than pure altruism or charity and they see their giving as 'community involvement' or 'community investment'. The following are some of the reasons why companies give.

> Companies give an estimated £200 million a year to charity. They also give support in kind, and some are becoming increasingly interested in encouraging their staff to volunteer.
>
> Alongside this, many companies get involved in sponsorships and joint promotions, where the payment to the charity is in return for some marketing or promotional benefit to the company.
>
> This section covers all aspects of company giving.

- To **create goodwill**: to be seen as good citizens in the local communities where they operate and as a caring company by society at large, but also to create goodwill amongst employees, who will get a better impression of the company from the good works that it is supporting. Pilkington, the glass manufacturer, for example is a major supporter of voluntary action and regeneration initiatives in St Helens, where it is based, and where it is still the major private sector employer.

- To be **associated with certain causes** that relate to their business. Mining and extraction companies often like to support environmental projects, pharmaceutical companies health projects, banks economic development projects, retailers and insurance companies projects working with young people and crime, and so on. This may be to enhance their image, but it could also be to find out more about matters that interest them from another perspective and build contacts with voluntary initiatives involved in the issue. Marks & Spencer and Prudential Assurance are both strong supporters of projects involving young people.

- Because **they are asked** and it is expected of them. They also don't want to be seen to be mean. If a major bank supports an important cultural project, then other large banks might also want to give their support, and to be seen to be generous in how much they give. There is a lot of peer group pressure amongst companies in a particular sector of business – banks, oil companies, pharmaceuticals, insurance companies, etc. They are concerned to see that the quantity and quality of their giving is appropriate to their status as a company.

- Because the **Chairman or other senior managers are interested in that cause** (and perhaps support it personally). There is also the Chairman's wife who can play an important part through her interests and influence – although this became less important as companies began to employ professional staff to manage their community involvement programmes.

- **Tax.** Giving to a charity or similar organisation can often be done tax free. This will be an added benefit for the company, but seldom the determining factor.

It is the shareholders' funds that are being given away. For privately owned companies or companies that are largely owned and controlled by a family, giving by the company is little different from personal giving. For public companies, the vast majority of shareholders are quite happy, even proud to see a limited amount of money given away in this way; but the company will always want to be able to justify the support it is giving by being able to show a good reason for it. And this is something that you can help them with when approaching a company – tell them not just why you want the money, but why it should be of interest to them and a good idea to support you. And also tell them what they will get out of it in return for their money – which is especially important if you are looking for 'sponsorship'.

Companies always appreciate thanks, recognition and good publicity for their support – whether they are giving a donation or supporting you through sponsorship. You can provide this by acknowledging their support in newsletters and in your annual report, and by trying to get press or media coverage for the activity they have supported, mentioning their support of course.

The Granada Challenge

In the North West, Granada and Business in the Community have been coordinating a challenge programme where five leading companies have each committed themselves to develop a community facility on a housing estate, contributing approximately £1.5 million to the project. Projects have included sports and play facilities, a youth centre and a pre-school centre. Sponsoring companies included Airbus, BNFL, Greenalls, Norweb and Manweb. Granada Television provided extensive TV coverage.

The Somerfield Community Charity

Money is raised through the sale of scratch cards at 450 of the company's participating stores. The target is to raise £3 million in the first year, and customers are asked to vote for their favourite local causes to receive grants from the Charity. For the company this demonstrates its commitment to the community, and builds both customer and community relations in the communities where the company operates. Far more is generated for charity through such a scheme than via traditional company giving. The 1996 annual accounts show the company earning £48.4 million in profit and giving £532,000 in donations (at just under 1.1% of profits this is more generous than many companies) to charities selected by staff, with local stores also being able to make donations in kind to local charities. This emphasis on staff involvement is new; two years previously, the company was giving away £154,000 to the British Red Cross, which was the company's selected 'charity of the year'.

The types of project that companies like to support

Companies support all sorts of projects but the following are the kinds of activity that they might be particularly interested in supporting:

- important **local projects** in the areas where they have a significant presence. Business in the Community capitalise on this by organising 'Seeing is Believing' events for business leaders, when they take them to visit local projects with a view to seeing problems at first hand and being shown that they can make a significant contribution to doing something;

- **prestigious arts and cultural events**. For example, the Midland Bank Proms at Covent Garden, or major exhibitions at the Tate Gallery or the Royal Academy;
- **sporting events and competitions**, especially those that attract keen public interest or mass participation. This would include events such as the London Marathon or the Cadbury 'Strollathon', as well as mainline sports sponsorship;
- **activities that relate to their product**. For example, NatWest has a schools programme promoting financial literacy, and banks in general target their giving at young people (who are potential customers), for example the Barclays New Futures programme encouraging young people's involvement in the community;
- **economic development projects** – because a flourishing economy will benefit business. Shell, for example, have supported Livewire, which is an award scheme for new enterprise, and the STEP programme, which provides undergraduates with work experience during the summer vacation;
- **environmental projects** – because these days everyone loves the environment. Shell, again, led the way through their Better Britain programme of support and awards for local environmental projects;
- **educational projects** – as education and training are building blocks for the future. This will assume added importance under a government whose three stated priorities are "Education – Education – Education"; and with the Business in the Community millennium programme of encouraging companies to help achieve national literacy targets;
- **initiatives which have the backing of very prominent people**. Who knows who is always important in getting support from companies, and the Prince's Trust is able to capitalise on this in their fundraising "finding that doors open for them without having to be pushed".

Looked at from the fundraiser's point of view, this can provide an interesting insight as to the sorts of company to approach, and how best to make that approach.

It is also important to know what companies are unlikely to want to support. Surveys suggest that most companies will not give to:

- **local appeals outside those areas where they have a business presence** – there is no reason for them to do this;
- purely **denominational appeals** for religious purposes, although this does not preclude support for social projects run by religious bodies;
- **circular appeals**, which are printed and sent to hundreds of companies and usually end up unread in the bin;
- **controversial causes** which might bring them bad publicity. They prefer to play safe, and they are seldom interested in supporting active campaigning bodies;
- **overseas appeals**, although some do support emergency and aid appeals on the basis that this is the sort of thing that the staff would like to see supported.

Special initiatives by companies in a particular industry

CRASH is the Construction Industry Charity for the Single Homeless. It aims to mobilise support from property companies, construction companies, builders supply companies and builders merchants, architects, surveyors and others with a stake in the construction industry to assist the single homeless.

- Support is mobilised in cash, including asking leading companies to become patrons.
- A CRASH Store is operated for furniture and equipment donated by supporters, including bedding from hotel companies.
- Materials and support in kind is gifted to building projects. As well as acting as a broker for these gifts in kind, a directory of 27 manufacturers and suppliers offering discounts or gifts in kind for CRASH projects is also produced.
- Empty buildings are located for possible use as winter shelters.
- Funds are raised through talks and presentations at conferences and events, such as at the Conference on Women in Property, the British Cement Association Lubetkin Lecture, the annual dinner of the National Housing and Town Planning Council and many others.

Single homeless projects should contact CRASH at The Barley Mow Business Centre, 10 Barley Mow Passage, London W4 4PH.

WaterAid is a charity set up by the water industry to focus charitable giving and technical expertise for water projects in the developing world. It mobilises support from the water companies, encourages employee volunteering and giving, sends appeals to water customers with their bills. The water industry contributes £1.11 million to WaterAid, and the customer appeal, which is sent to 19 million customers, generates £800,000, together representing 30% of the charity's annual income.

FashionActs is the fashion industry's initiative to raise money for HIV and AIDS. Over eight years it has raised and distributed more than £1 million via a calendar of fashion-related fundraising activities, including a designer jumble sale, an exhibition and sale of signed fashion photographs, a stand at the Clothes Show Live in Birmingham and a sponsored walk.

What companies give

There are a variety of ways in which companies can support charities:
- **cash donations** (usually a one off grant)
- **sponsorship** of an event or activity
- sponsorship of **promotional and educational materials** – the major banks, oil companies and drug companies are all active in this area
- sponsorship of **an award scheme** (such as the Whitbread Volunteer Action Awards, or the British Urban Regeneration Award, which is sponsored by English Partnerships)
- **joint promotions**, where the company contributes a donation to the charity in return for each product sold in order to encourage sales

- **making company facilities available**, including meeting rooms, printing or design facilities, help with mailings, and so on
- **support in kind**; giving company products or office equipment that is no longer required is often easier for a company
- **'secondment' of a member of staff** to work with the charity, where a member of the company's staff helps on an agreed basis whilst remaining employed (and paid) by the company
- **contributing a senior member of staff** to the charity's Management Board
- providing **expertise and advice**
- encouraging **employees to volunteer**
- organising a **fundraising campaign amongst employees**, including through payroll giving
- **advertising** in charity brochures and publications.

In recent years there have been a number of significant changes in the ways in which companies give. Companies are looking for ways of giving support that do not cost a great deal of money. The budgets for community involvement have not expanded in line with the growing demands for support being made on companies. In consequence, companies are always trying to find cost-effective ways of helping that are not a drain on their budget. Offering free use of facilities such as conference rooms, providing advice, donating product and equipment that is no longer required, encouraging staff to volunteer or collect and donate money will all cost less than making a cash donation.

Ten years ago it was still possible to mail the top 1,000 companies and get a good response. Today such an approach simply would not work. Every company receives far too many applications. Their response to this has been to focus on large and small donations. Many of the top companies have local donation programmes in areas where they have a major factory or business presence, where they give small grants. Some have matching funds schemes, where they match money collected or given by employees. Some have developed special grants programmes (like Shell Better Britain and NatWest's 14-30 fund). Some have a 'charity of

---

Major company programmes

Some of the largest companies now run large-scale programmes in partnership with a national charity. The following are two examples:

- **Prudential Youth Action Initiative**, with Crime Concern. The aim is to create safer cities by involving young people of Middle and Secondary School age in crime prevention activities through Youth Action Groups. The scheme publishes a directory of contacts and other publications, organises conferences and training workshops, provides partnership funding to develop local programmes and runs a national award scheme;
- **Barclays New Futures**, with Community Service Volunteers. This scheme offers £1 million a year in cash and professional support to help young people take positive action to benefit their communities. Schemes are assessed on the basis of student learning and personal development, student involvement, social relevance and sustainability. Cash awards of £3,000 (for an individual school) or £7,000 (for a group of schools) are made to 80 projects each year, plus educational resources, professional support and advice.

British Airways collects money from passengers

'Change for Good', an in-flight initiative run by British Airways for UNICEF, was launched in 1994 at the suggestion of staff and has raised £4 million to date. An envelope is circulated to passengers, so that their small unwanted foreign currency can be donated, and the message is reinforced with an appeal on the in-flight video. Staff also donate, and run local collections for the fund.

British Airways also encourages staff fundraising for four staff charities:

- an orphanage in Dhaka, where a former stewardess has taken a leading role, first as a volunteer and then overseeing its development;
- Dreamflight, where nearly 200 seriously ill children and their helpers are taken on a trip to Walt Disney World;
- Operation Happy Child, which provides holidays for underprivileged children;
- The Cargo Kidney Fund which purchases equipment for hospitals and supports aftercare for kidney patients.

Money is raised for these through a range of imaginative fundraising events, including parachute drops, kayak marathons, banquets, celebrity dinners, a charity supplement on a BA Holidays golf tournament.

British Airways passengers are asked to donate their foreign change to UNICEF using this envelope. So far over £3 million has been raised.

the year' for a major donation and as a focus for encouraging staff involvement. Many now have quite a narrow focus for their grant-making, whereas a decade ago they were making grants across the whole spectrum of charitable activity.

New themes have emerged as important areas for company support. Education and enterprise have been seen as important since the early 1980s, as these are thought of as investments in the future, and investment is a concept that companies understand. Crime prevention is a particular concern today, and a few companies have substantial budgets for this. It is as important to be aware of emergent themes, as it is to know what companies are currently interested in supporting.

There are two points to bear in mind:

- there are very many ways in which a company can help you. This is an important difference from other funding sources, as most other funders can only give you money. So think carefully about the best way in which the company might help you. You may find that they don't give very much at all in cash donations, and that it will be far easier (and less costly to them) for them to support you in some other way;
- there is an important difference between donation and sponsorship. With a donation, the company gets nothing back except some form of thanks and acknowledgement. With sponsorship, the company aims to get a return for the money it is spending. This return could be some form of publicity for the company, or it could be an opportunity to entertain customers and others (for example at a prestigious cultural event held in aid of charity).

The different types of companies that give

1. Foreign owned multinational companies

Many of the large multinational companies have global giving programmes. A trend in recent years has been for companies to extend their giving beyond their headquarters town and home country into the other territories where they have business interests, and also into countries where they are considering starting up (for example, American Express has been giving support to projects in Vietnam as a prelude to opening up for business in that country).

Some multinational companies have an international structure for managing their giving, with budgets set for each country and a common policy for the sorts of activity they are interested in supporting. This is the case, for example, with IBM. Others may give each country a small budget to spend on charitable projects of its choice. This has been the case with Microsoft up until now, where the bulk of its giving still remains within Seattle and Washington State – where the company is headquartered. With others, community involvement policy remains a purely local matter for company management in the country concerned.

Some multinational companies have tried to transfer projects and ideas form one country to another. American Express, for example, developed a travel and tourism project for schools in the South Bronx (New York), where the programme resulted in fewer school dropouts and higher grades. This has now been developed in Britain, where it was the first commercially sponsored educational course to get recognition as a GCSE subject. IBM developed a voluntary sector

Where multinationals give

If you look at the geographical breakdown of a multinational company's giving, you will find the following:

- most money is spent in the headquarters town or region
- most money is spent in the home country of the company. For example, ARCO, one of the leading oil companies spends most of its budget in the USA, but it has a strategy of trying to spread its giving more evenly in those countries where it does business
- the North gets more than the South. BP gives most in the UK and Germany, for example. This is despite the fact that money goes much further in the South, where due to currency exchange rates, everything is much cheaper.

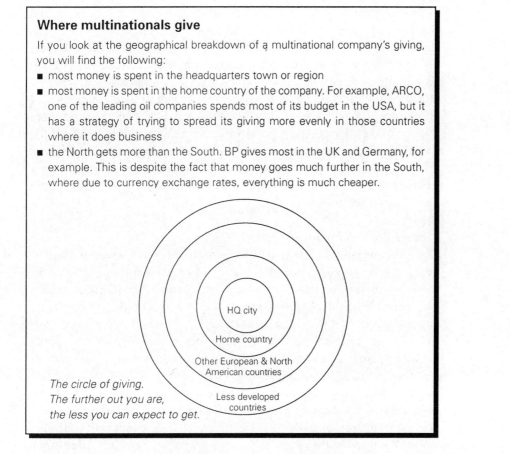

*The circle of giving.
The further out you are,
the less you can expect to get.*

management training programme in the UK, and IBM (UK) staff have been advising other IBM units on ways of developing similar programmes in their own country.

2. Leading national companies

The giving of leading companies is well documented in *The Major Companies Guide*, which covers around 500 companies and is published by the Directory of Social Change. This gives information on the scale and scope of the company giving programmes, with enough information to be able to identify those companies which might be interested in supporting you. About half the top companies are members of the 'Per Cent Club' organised by Business in the Community, which has set a target of 0.5% of pre-tax profit as a recommended level for community support (in cash and kind), with a higher target of 1% for those that want to do more. Some of the largest companies publish brochures which describe their community involvement programme or specific schemes that they sponsor.

The leading national companies will be supporting large national charities, many of which have whole departments to raise money from companies. Charities like Childline, Save the Children, Crime Concern, Turning Point and many others have been extremely successful in winning the support of companies. They may have their own sponsorship schemes and they will also be making smaller donations to local charities and sponsoring events in the area where they are headquartered or where they have a major business presence. National companies such as BT, make grants through regional offices. Retail stores, such as Marks & Spencer or B & Q, often use the store manager to provide advice on a local application, and give small budgets to be spent by each store at the manager's discretion.

3. Larger local companies

In any city or region there will be large companies who are important to the local economy. These companies will often feel a responsibility to do something to support voluntary action and community initiatives in those areas, and value the good publicity that this will provide. If yours is an important project, it should be part of your fundraising strategy to develop some form of relationship with the larger companies in your area. Boots in Nottingham, Allied Dunbar in Swindon, Pilkington in St Helens, ICI on Teesside are examples of this.

Then there are companies that have a regional remit. The water, electricity and independent television companies all have a specific geographical area within which they operate. Their community support will be confined within these regional boundaries. Brewers are another example. Some, like Vaux in the North East, still brew and distribute locally.

4. Smaller local companies

If you are mounting a general appeal, then you will want to approach smaller companies for their support. These present an important, often overlooked opportunity. Almost everyone is targeting the large companies, because good information is available on these for fundraisers and there is little available information on smaller local companies – which will range from manufacturing companies on trading estates to accountants and solicitors in the High Street. Many of these are privately owned, and the approach will often be through the Managing Director or Senior Partner.

The best sources of information on what companies exist in your area are:

■ the local **Chamber of Commerce**, where most of the more prominent local companies will be members;

- the *Kompass* **directory** of companies, which is regionally organised;
- the **Local Council**: the Rating Department might produce a list of major business ratepayers. The Economic Development section may have a list of major employers;
- the **local newspaper**, which will carry stories from time to time that mention local companies, and may provide information on new companies planning to set up in the area;
- **postcode directories**, where you can identify large users;
- **you** – by walking the streets and keeping your eyes open, you can often identify local companies that it could just be worth approaching.

Most of these companies will have no policy at all about what to give to and are likely only to give to projects which catch the fancy of the Managing Director or Senior Partner. Some may never have given anything before, and may not know about the tax treatment of charitable gifts so you may need to persuade them to give, and to show them how to give tax-effectively.

Some of these companies may prefer to give in kind – for example, a prize for a raffle or advertising in a souvenir brochure for a fundraising event. It might be easier to approach these companies for this sort of support in the first instance; and later on, once they have given something, to persuade them to make a cash donation.

Case Study - How GrandMet gives

GrandMet, which comprises the International Distillers and Vintners, Pillsbury and Burger King businesses, has been one of the pioneers in the field of corporate community involvement. It spent nearly £13 million in 1996 on community projects, which represented approximately 1.5% of worldwide pre-tax profits. Of this, 67% is spent in the USA, 26% in the UK and Europe, and 7% in the rest of the world. Cash donations represent 70% of the total spend, with the balance equally divided between product donations and social sponsorship. The main areas of support are empowerment, education and youth. A further £4 million is given for brand sponsorship and cause related marketing.

GrandMet's community relations policy states that it wants "to be seen to be contributing actively to the prosperity of the communities in which we operate (in addition to the economic contributions we make by doing business there), and playing a leadership role in helping others to help themselves". GrandMet strives to be innovative and at the forefront of issues, to act as a catalyst in forming partnerships between public, private and voluntary sector organisations, and to pursue community initiatives compatible with its competences, available resources and core businesses.

The GrandMet Foundation is the company's primary charitable funding and support vehicle. It focuses on four key areas: sustainable local economic regeneration to relieve poverty or reduce unemployment; education programmes in schools where there is the potential for employee involvement; charities with which GrandMet business have links, that are dedicated to helping people, particularly young people, achieve self-sufficiency; projects in local communities where the company operates, and transnational causes that reflect the global scale of the company's operations. In the UK, the main areas of support are:

- **matching funds** for employee involvement. The Trust matches charitable fundraising by employees pound for pound up to a maximum of £1,000 per employee per year, and also matches payroll giving by employees up to £250 per employee per year;
- working with **Cities in Schools** (CiS), a charity that supports young people excluded from school or at risk of exclusion through truancy to re-engage them in mainstream education and normal life. Through Burger King, GrandMet had been involved with CiS in the US. In 1990, GrandMet took the lead in establishing CiS in the UK, and by 1996, 75 projects had been set up in both urban and rural areas;
- **KAPOW** – Kids and the Power of Work. KAPOW educates primary school children about the world of work, using employee volunteers to deliver eight 'lessons', to help the young people understand the importance of what they learn in school and link this to success in adult life. Like Cities in Schools, this has been imported from the US and was piloted in one school in 1994 using volunteers from GrandMet's corporate HQ. By 1996, five UK schools had invited GrandMet companies to run KAPOW schemes;
- support for the **Foyer Federation for Youth**. In 1990, GrandMet formed a special homelessness unit to tackle the problem "that you can't get a job if you're homeless, but you can't get a home if you're jobless". In 1992, GrandMet teamed up with Shelter to launch the foyer concept in the UK, which had been developed in France, by setting up the Foyer Federation for Youth and supporting a demonstration project in South London. By 1996, 46 foyer residential centres were operating, with a further 40 in development, which had obtained the support of more than 150 companies;
- sponsorship of **Project Fullemploy**, which aims to stimulate economic activity amongst disadvantaged black and minority ethnic communities;
- support for **Business in the Community**, the **Prince of Wales Business Leaders Forum** and the **Prince's Youth Business Trust**;
- **Tomorrow's People**. In 1981, GrandMet decided to respond to the problem of youth unemployment, and set up the GrandMet Trust to

offer young unemployed people careers guidance, advice and skills training. Its work has been developed with £15 million of core funding from GrandMet, a further £15 million contributed by other companies, and government agency contracts of over £100 million. It is run as a non-profit business, and the Trust is being relaunched as Tomorrow's People, with the objective of becoming the recognised charity for the unemployed, addressing an issue of vital importance to business and aiming to involve small, medium-sized and regional companies that lack the resources to run programmes of their own.

Breakdown of GrandMet's total worldwide giving of £12,876,000
- **Charity: responding to appeals from the community**
  donations of cash to local and national appeals: £1,513,000
  social sponsorship, supporting causes or events with name recognition: £2,025,000
  employee volunteering, secondments and consultancy: value not quantified
  in-kind giving of product, equipment or use of premises: £554,000
  employee matched support and supporting causes to which employees are giving money or time: £816,000

- **Social investment: sustained involvement in issues important to the company**
  grants for programmes to achieve specific agreed goals: £4,350,000
  secondments and consultancy: £335,000
  in-kind contributions: £2,586,000
  in-house training: not quantified

- **Other items**
  sundry other support: £55,000
  managing the community support activities: £582,000

Who decides and who to write to

Practice varies from company to company. Larger companies will have a manager who is given the responsibility of dealing with and deciding on charitable appeals – although senior management through a Donations Committee may also have the final decision on what is supported. The largest companies may also employ specialist staff (rather like a foundation) to assess the applications that are received and make recommendations on what should be supported. Some large companies operate an independent foundation, where the foundation and its trustees will set policy and decide on applications. Sometimes community affairs staff are recruited from within the company – but some companies now recruit outside and look for voluntary sector experience.

With medium sized and smaller companies, it is nearly always the top person who decides.

You should write in the first instance to the person who has the responsibility for receiving and dealing with charitable appeals, and to make sure that you have the spelling and job title correct. You don't want to write to the wrong person, let alone someone who left the company ten years ago! You should also try to find out as much as you can about the company, and about its possible interest in supporting your project. If you have a top-level contact, then use it. It will always be helpful.

Getting started

As with raising money from trusts, research is important but in a way it is slightly less important for the following reasons:

- most of the larger companies have less well defined policies than trusts, although by looking at what they do support you can often determine a pattern to their giving;
- the chances of an application 'out of the blue' getting support are less. Companies are more conservative in their giving, and are less likely to support innovative projects (at least until they have got established) or anything that is risky or controversial.

Nonetheless research is important, not just into policies, but also into contacts – and not just your own personal contacts, but the contacts of any person you can get hold of to help you in your fundraising who has credibility in the business world. Here are some tips.

1. First find out what, if any, **previous contact** you have had with companies, and what previous fundraising approaches you have made, and with what success.
2. Through **research**, identify and match possible funders with various aspects of your work. In particular, try to find any local companies that are known for their generosity and might have an interest in supporting your cause.
3. Find out whether any of your Board Members or supporters (or even your volunteers) have any **personal contact** with any of the companies you plan to approach.
4. Think about enlisting a **senior business leader** to assist you with your fundraising. This can be someone to serve as Chair of a Development or Fundraising Committee, or just to contact a few colleagues and sign a few letters.

Ethical issues

Taking support from certain companies can be problematic if the business values or practice of the company conflict with what your organisation stands for. There are two approaches. Some organisations are prepared to accept money from anyone, on the basis that the money can be used to do good. Others define certain types of company that they are not prepared to accept support from. Tobacco, alcohol, gambling, armaments, extraction industries, polluters, companies operating in the developing world that underpay their workforce are all areas of business activity that can cause problems. This is of particular importance, where the work of the charity is directly connected with the issue, or where the relationship is high profile, as with a sponsorship, and promoting the partnership between the business and the charity is a major feature. Health and cancer charities would find it hard to accept money from a tobacco company, for example; peace and international relations organisations have similar problems with arms manufacturers; children's charities may not wish to be associated with those drinks manufacturers who are targeting their advertising at the young, and so on.

It is best for a charity to set out a sponsorship and donations policy that defines where it will and will not accept support, before approaching companies. This should be agreed by the Management Committee. There are two strategies for developing such a policy. The first is to define and agree a policy in consultation with staff, although sometimes the matter can be contentious and create divisions. In such cases it may be better to treat each on an *ad hoc* basis whilst moving towards some sort of consensus on policy.

Sometimes the issues are clear cut. It is relatively easy, for example, for a health charity to decide whether to accept money from a tobacco company, or a youth charity from a drinks company. The product relationship with the cause is clear, and all the charity has to do is agree a position on the issue. Some charities are happy to take money from anybody (perhaps feeling that there is no such thing as dirty money or that a grant is a first step to promoting greater social responsibility by the company). Others will want to adopt a more restrictive approach (either for ethical reasons or they may feel that it could affect the flow of donations from their traditional supporters). But what about Allied Dunbar, a financial services company with an unparalleled track record for its community involvement, but which happens to be a subsidiary of international tobacco giant, BAT Industries? Or Shell, with its link to the death of Ken Saro-Wiwa in Nigeria, or GEC which is a major armaments manufacturer, where the issue and the cause are not so closely linked?

There are two organisations that chart the ethical behaviour of companies, which can provide you with the information you need to formulate such a policy:

- New Consumer, 52 Elswick Road, Newcastle-upon-Tyne NE4 6JH, publishes *Changing Corporate Values* which explores the ethical performance of 128 leading companies;
- EIRIS, the Ethical Investment Research and Information Service, 504 Bondway Business Centre, 71 Bondway, London SW8 1SQ, which researches companies on the FT All-Share Index. Its main aim is to advise on socially responsible investment. A charge is made for its services.

Learning from experience – a case study by Michael Norton

Getting support from companies can be difficult at the best of times, simply due to the enormous demands being made for their charitable resources. Most approaches do not end in success. There is a tendency, however, for people to believe that everyone else is being successful, whilst they are failing. So it is important to understand the difficulties, but also to learn ways of improving your chances. Here are three examples which illustrate some of the different approaches that can be used.

1. Go for it!

Some years ago, I was running a fundraising course, and to illustrate how to get support in kind, I invited one of the participants to ring up the Managing Director of a company whilst we all observed the process. She was the fundraiser for a project which supported children with exceptional abilities, and she wanted an oboe for a child of limited means. We selected two companies that we knew to be in the music business – Chapple & Co, and Boosey & Hawkes. She rang Chapple's, and asked to speak to the Managing Director. She happened to strike lucky. Perhaps he was so busy, he needed a break. Perhaps the business was running so smoothly, that there was nothing to do. Perhaps he needed a bit of excitement during his day. "We need some advice", the fundraiser said.

Asking for advice is often better at the outset than asking for money. She described the work of the charity and the number of young people with musical abilities that needed help. He was interested, and invited her to lunch – that day. She went, and about two and a half hours later reappeared on the course, in a state of some excitement. No, they could not give her an oboe but he knew everyone in the music business, and could try to get free places at summer schools, provide sheet music at a discount, perhaps even become a trustee. This successful approach inspired many others on the course to do something similar, and with similar success.

2. A change of approach may be needed.
In the mid-1980s I was trying to establish the Urban Trust to provide grants to young people in inner cities for their social and economic development projects. We wanted to build up a grants fund. I did the rounds of Community Affairs Managers of leading companies, and after a few meetings I began to realise that the project was not of any real interest to them. There had been inner city riots, and several projects were competing for funds. Most of the larger companies had given to Fullemploy or the Prince's Youth Business Trust, and they couldn't see a reason to give to us – although our project had several interesting features which differentiated it from the others.

I decided that I needed someone to ask on my behalf who had more clout in the business world. Through a mutual contact I was introduced to the Chairman of a leading insurance company, who was also a promoter of the Per Cent Club. I explained my ideas and gave him a leaflet I had prepared. "Could you write to the top 100 companies", I suggested. "No", he said. "I will pick a small selection of companies I think will be really interested and people I know well, and send them your brochure with a handwritten letter saying that we're backing the project and asking them to do the same". He wrote to 12 companies. Seven agreed to support us with sums of between £5,000 and £10,000.

3. Slowly but surely.
More recently, I have been raising money for Changemakers, a national scheme which encourages community involvement amongst young people at school or in youth clubs. This project has been growing rapidly, and fits easily within the current concerns about good citizenship. We were full of hope that the project would appeal to companies. Although they were interested, our enthusiasm was not always matched by theirs.

We made a selection of around 20 companies from *The Major Companies Guide*, who we thought might be interested in supporting us, sent a letter with a simple brochure, and followed this up with a phone call asking to meet. About half the companies we approached agreed to meet us. The purpose of the meeting was to tell them about what we were doing and persuade them to support us, but also to discuss with them how they might provide help. One company was extremely keen to link their support to staff volunteering, and they were interested in making contact with schools in South East London. Two said that they would like to help us promote our scheme in the Local Education Authority Area where they were headquartered (discussions are still continuing on this). Three were happy to give us small sums towards producing promotional material for our launch to Head Teachers at the Secondary Heads Association annual conference. One gave us a large grant – we had applied at just the right time!

The main reasons for refusal were: that the company had recently supported something similar or had their own 'pet projects' with young people; that their budget had run out; that their grants programme was being reviewed and would have a different focus in the future.

A year on, we have drawn up a second list of major companies, including those we approached first time around, and will repeat the process. We also used a volunteer to write to a further 100 companies and follow this up with a telephone call. This produced three (very) small donations, but several other companies wrote back suggesting that we reapply later in the year. We have not yet been able to raise very large sums from companies – our main support at this early stage in our development has come from trusts – but we feel that if we persist, each year we will be able to do better.

Getting in touch

The personal approach is best, but often the most difficult to achieve. In smaller companies there is usually no staff member responsible for giving and therefore approaches have to be at Board level. As a first step you might telephone the company to see whether you can find out the following:

- **who is responsible** for dealing with charitable appeals;
- their **name**, correctly spelt, and **job title**, so that you get it right when you write to them or speak to them on the phone;
- what **information** they can send you about their company. The very large companies may have a brochure on their charitable support programme. They certainly will have a company annual report, which will tell you about their work. For private companies, you can try to find out as much as you can; and you can also look them up at Companies House if you need to;
- any **procedure or timetable** for submitting appeals;
- whether they might be interested in **coming to see your organisation** at work.

Visits are useful when discussing bigger donations with the larger companies, but are difficult to arrange for anything small. It is quite unusual to be able to persuade senior company executives to visit the projects that you are asking them to support. Business in the Community

Nine ideas for getting support from companies

1. **Put yourself in the position of the company**. Why should they want to give their shareholders' funds to you? Why should they choose your charity, rather than any of the other appeals they receive? Think about the benefits that they may get from supporting you and mention these in your appeal letter. If you are looking for sponsorship, then these benefits will be at the heart of your proposal.

2. **Suggest something specific** for the company to support, which you think will be of particular interest to that company; and in your letter tell them why they should be interested. It is often best to think of something quite small if you are approaching them for the first time.

3. **Use all the contacts you have** in the company to help get your appeal supported. Do you know the Chairman, the Managing Director or any other senior member of staff? Or their wives, who may be able to put in a good word for you? Or if you telephone, can you get into conversation with the Chairman's secretary or personal assistant such that he or she becomes interested and enthusiastic and will put in a good word for you. Do you have any volunteers who are helping you who also work for the company? They may be able to help you 'from the inside', and it will do you no harm if you mention their support for your organisation in your appeal letter.

4. **Think of all the different ways** in which the company could help. Cash might not be the best way for them to give their support. Might it be easier for them to offer staff time, perhaps giving you some expertise you lack? Or the use of a vehicle? Or access to company staff to circulate an appeal or to sell your Christmas cards to? It is likely that everyone else will be asking for cash. And the company may find it easier to give in kind; once they have given in kind and got to know you and your work, cash support may become easier to obtain next time.

5. Consider whether there is **a senior executive** of the company (the more senior the better) **who might become a trustee** of your charity or serve on a fundraising or development committee to bring new ideas, good organisation and a wealth of business contacts to your organisation that will be worth many times the value of a donation. Such an invitation, even if refused, may be seen as flattering. If this level of involvement is too much, a request for advice may succeed.

6. Does one of **your volunteers** – or someone else associated with your charity – have a paid job? If so, get them to make the initial approach within the company that employs them. They can ask who to apply to and sound that person out on your behalf. When you write, mention this contact. If the company turns your request down they risk alienating a valuable member of staff.

7. Don't assume that every company will give. Make parallel approaches to a number of different companies.

8. Consider who might be the **best person** to make the approach or sign the letter. It may not be you. Often it is another senior businessman who has already supported your organisation generously.

9. Every time you buy anything from a company, ask for a **discount**. This will save you money, but it is also a way of getting them to support you.

organises 'Seeing is Believing' days for senior businessmen and women. They find that when people visit projects and talk to project organisers and beneficiaries, they get really interested in the idea of giving their and their company's support. The interest and feeling of commitment that is engendered by this process raises the chances of getting support, and any support that you do get is likely to be more substantial and longer term.

Almost certainly your appeal to them will be in the form of a letter. Make this as personal as you can. Circular letters suffer the fate of most of the thousands of appeals a company receives each month. They are put in the bin. Letters should therefore be directed personally to a named individual. Make the letter short and to the point. A brief letter of a page is much more likely to be read (and responded to) than a longer letter, because companies receive so many appeals, their first instinct is to say no. They may not even read the letter. Many is the time when the sender of an invitation to an Open Day receives a standard letter of rejection – even though you have not asked for money – simply because the recipient has seen that the letter is from a charity!

Getting support in kind

Giving things rather than money is often easier for a company. Here are some of the things that companies might be able to give you.

1. **Product, materials and offcuts**. This can cost them little or nothing. An airline or cruise company offering free tickets may be just filling up empty places. Ends of lines can be a big earner for a thrift shop or a jumble sale, but be of little value to the company. Offcuts can be a staple for children's play programmes, and Scrap Projects have developed to 'broker' this for the community. A printing company could offer you free printing, if you paid for the paper – and you could try to get a paper merchant to donate the paper on this basis. Many organisations require office equipment (telephones, faxes, computers, photocopiers, etc.). Suppliers are inundated with requests, and mostly they are refused, but it is always worth asking (on the basis that if you don't, there's absolutely no chance of success). The following anecdote gives hope: "Some years ago we were launching a small project to provide employment to people with disabilities. We knew that one of the critical pieces of equipment we needed was a reliable photocopier. We decided to try to get a donation in kind, and settled on Rank Xerox as our first target. In order to get the attention of the Marketing Director who we reasoned would have access to reconditioned machines, we devised a carefully worded letter handwritten in blue ink. Within two weeks, we

were surprised and delighted to be awoken by an insistent knocking on our front door. It was the man from Rank Xerox. He had a machine to deliver now, he said firmly. Since our new office was not ready, we accepted delivery of a huge machine into our living room. And it was brand new!"

2. **Discounts**. A distributor may offer you something at a substantial discount – always ask for a discount as a charity on everything you purchase – and this can be considered a contribution towards the purchase cost of the item. Some of the major retail chains have a policy on charity discounts – some offering a standard rate, say 10% off, if requested, some giving no discount. It is always worth asking. Charity Projects, organisers of Comic Relief, go one step further and ask for everything to be donated (a 100% discount). If you go to lunch at their office, there will be sandwiches from the local Marks & Spencer; their post is put through the franking machine of a local company, and there is a rota for this.

3. **Facilities**, such as a meeting room for an important presentation, conference facilities for a seminar or annual meeting, the use of their DTP equipment to design a brochure, and so on. This will often cost them nothing, but be extremely valuable to you. It could also be the first step in developing a warm and profitable relationship with them.

4. **Technical expertise**. A surveyor or solicitor could donate professional time. A personnel officer could help you with employment law or to design an equal opportunities policy. Some companies now have schemes for involving staff in the community. Allied Dunbar, a leading financial services company, has the ALPHA scheme to provide professional help to local charities.

5. **Secondment of staff**. Some of the largest companies second staff to work with charities. These vary from long-term secondments of two years or more, through to short assignments of up to 100 hours during work time. They can be mid-career challenges or in the run up to retirement as an alternative to redundancy. Most long-term secondments are now to organisations such as Business in the Community, and there is little chance of any smaller charity getting the services of a business person on a long-term basis. Many companies work through Action: Employees in the Community (formerly the Action Resource Centre and now part of Business in the Community), and this could be a useful point of contact. Another possibility is a retiree, and REACH (the Retired Executives Action Clearing House) and RSVP (Community Service Volunteers' retired and senior volunteer programme), both offer a matching service, linking

Some practical tips on how to set about getting support in kind

1. Make a list of everything you need – this is called a 'wish list'. This can include services as well as products (such as the design for a leaflet you plan to produce).
2. Go through the list and try to identify companies that might have what you require. Personal knowledge is fine but you might also want to use business directories.
3. Make contact. Writing a letter does not work well. It is best if you can make personal or telephone contact. State your request, saying that it is for a charity and indicating how well used it will be and how important to your organisation's future.
4. If they refuse to donate it, they might be able to give you a hefty discount. This is worth getting and can be a fall back position in your discussions.
5. Be positive and enthusiastic. It can be very difficult for them to refuse if they know what you want and how important it is for you. It will always cost them far less to donate the item than it would cost you to purchase it.
6. Say thank you. Report back subsequently on the difference the donation has made. Send them your annual report. Try then to recruit them as a cash donor.

retired people to work as volunteers with charities on placements that match their skills and geographic availability.

6. **Board members**. With the publication of the NCVO report 'On Trust', attention was focused on the governance of charities, many of whom wanted to bring business skills on board. Some leading companies, such as W H Smith and Shell, encourage their employees to serve on trustee boards or management committees and this can provide a point of contact for subsequent financial support.

7. **Employee involvement**. Employees can get involved in all sorts of ways. They can undertake challenges for charity, and a national Challenge scheme has been developed to encourage this. They can be encouraged to volunteer, to collect money or to give money to charities, and some companies have matching schemes to match amounts raised or given or volunteer effort with a grant from the company. Some companies encourage their employees to link up with any charity they choose; others may select a charity of the year, and encourage everyone to support this.

Getting companies to advertise

Companies are often prepared to support you by taking an advertisement in a brochure or a publication – possibilities include your annual report and programmes produced for fundraising events. This is known as 'goodwill advertising' as it is paid for to create good will for the company rather than sell more of its products. Companies like it because they can treat the expenditure as a business expense rather than as a charitable donation, because they get publicity in return for their support, and because they are being asked to give a specific amount that they can afford. However, you do need to have thought through whether you actually want an advertisement or company logo to appear, say, in your annual report (getting advertising is covered in more detail in section 4.15).

Tax and company giving

A tax-effective gift by a company is one whose cost can be offset against the company's profits. The ways of giving tax-effectively are complicated and difficult to explain. You can expect a major company to know the rules, and to be making its donations tax-effectively but when you are approaching a smaller local company, you might want to explain how they can give tax effectively.

There are two important points to note. The first is that if a company is not making a taxable profit, then it does not matter how it gives. There is no tax to be saved. The second is that the rules only apply for gifts to charity. The ways of giving tax-effectively are:

- **Gift Aid**. This is available for donations of £250 or more. The company pays this amount, then signs a special form obtainable from the Inland Revenue. It has to pay over an additional amount in income tax to the Inland Revenue, which the charity then reclaims. The total paid by the company (the amount of the gift plus the income tax), is what is received by the charity, and what it actually costs the company; and this amount can be offset against the company's corporation tax liability. There are strict rules on the value of any benefits that can be given to the company in return for a Gift Aid payment, for example free tickets to a fundraising event (these should not exceed 2.5% of the amount of the donation);

- a **Deed of Covenant**. Where a company agrees to pay a regular donation to a charity for at least four years, it can then sign a Deed of Covenant – which it has to do before making the first payment. The procedure for reclaiming tax is as for a Gift Aid payment. Any covenanted donation should not create an appreciable benefit for the company. What constitutes an appreciable benefit is not as clearly defined as for a Gift Aid payment, but a reasonable acknowledgement of the company's gift is permitted;

How a Gift Aid payment works for a company

1. The company pays the charity £1,000.
2. The charity receives £1,000 direct from the company.
3. The charity sends the company a Gift Aid form, for the company to complete. Forms are obtainable from the Inland Revenue in Bootle.
4. The company pays the Inland Revenue the sum of £298.70. This is the Income Tax due on the Gift Aid payment. At 23% basic rate Income Tax, this is the amount of tax that has to be paid to create a net sum after tax of £1,000.
5. The company signs the Gift Aid form and returns it to the charity. This confirms that the Income Tax has been paid.
6. The charity claims the tax back from the Inland Revenue, using the same claims procedure as for covenant payments. In due course, it will receive a payment of £298.70 from the Inland Revenue.
7. The company claims £1,298.70 of charitable expenditure against its Corporation Tax liability. At a 33% rate of Corporation Tax, this results in a saving of £428.57.
8. The net cost to the company of making the donation is £870.13. The total received by the charity is £1,298.70. This benefits both parties. It costs the company less, and it provides an additional amount to the charity.

These calculations are based on a 23% basic rate of Income Tax, and a 33% rate of Corporation Tax. Income Tax rates are changed from time to time in the budget, and companies pay Corporation Tax at different rates depending on the amount of profits earned during the year. If a company is paying Corporation Tax, then whatever the rate of tax it is paying, a Gift Aid donation will never cost it more after tax than the amount it pays over directly to the charity.

- a **payment from a company trust**. Some companies have established their own charitable trust to make donations; for example the IBM (United Kingdom) Charitable Trust. The company transfers the whole of its charitable budget to the trust either by Gift Aid or by Deed of Covenant, and then makes payments from the trust to the beneficiaries. An alternative is for the company to use the services of the Charities Aid Foundation, which works in exactly the same way, with the company making payments tax-effectively to CAF and then instructing CAF to make payments to those charities it wishes to benefit; over half the top 100 companies use the services of CAF. Charities receiving donations this way do not have to go to the bother of reclaiming tax from the Inland Revenue. This will already have been done by the company trust or by CAF;
- a **business expense**. Any expenditure by a company which is wholly and exclusively for business purposes is deductible against corporation tax liability. This will cover most sponsorship and advertising payments to charity. This is the simplest way of obtaining tax relief;
- a **gift in kind**. The usual mechanism is that the company writes off the value of the item donated in its books before making the donation;
- **secondment of a member of staff**. There are specific provisions allowing the costs of a member of staff seconded to work for a charity, where that member of staff continues to be paid by the company. Provided that the secondment is of a temporary nature, then the cost is allowable.

Business sponsorship

Sponsorship needs to be carefully defined. It is not a jargon word simply meaning a gift from a company which is publicly acknowledged. It is an association between two parties with quite different interests who come together in order to support a particularly activity for two quite different motives.

The charity is looking to raise funds for its work and the sponsor hopes to improve its image, to promote and sell its products or to entertain its customers. The sponsor's contribution does not need to be money, though usually it is. It could also be a gift of goods (such as a car), or services (such as free transport), or professional expertise (such as promotion or marketing consultancy), or staff fundraising (to raise money for the charity), or the use of buildings (such as an exhibition centre), or free promotion (in a newspaper or broadcast), and so on.

An additional benefit of sponsorship is the way in which the link with the sponsor can be developed subsequently – depending on how the original sponsorship goes. If all goes well and they get to like you and admire your professionalism, then you might look for further sponsorships on a larger scale, and possibly also for getting a donation from the company charitable budget, being able to use company resources and facilities (such as a training centre or meeting room) free of charge, getting employees involved in the work of your charity or senior management to sit on your management Board. These are all things you might expect to flow from a successful sponsorship.

One of the future directions of corporate giving is through sponsorship – as companies want to get more back for their money than a simple acknowledgement. In recent years, sponsorship has extended from sport and the arts into environment, education and social projects. Many companies will give much more as sponsorship than they would as a donation, if they can see the benefits that they can gain for themselves. Developing links with the major national and local corporate sponsors – even if this effort comes to nothing – could be an investment in your future well worth making now.

Who sponsors?

Most sponsors are commercial businesses, including state-owned industries, but government departments, public authorities, utilities, hospitals, universities and other institutions sometimes undertake sponsorship when they can gain some benefit by doing so. There are four main opportunities for sponsorship:

- those businesses that are anxious to **promote themselves**, to create a better image of themselves, or to generate a public awareness in the local communities where they operate. This includes those companies with an 'image problem' – for example, mining and extraction companies associated with the destruction of the environment who want to project a cleaner image by being associated with a conservationist cause;

> **Why companies like sponsorship**
> - It helps them get their message across
> - It can enhance or change their image
> - It can reach a target audience very precisely
> - It can be very cost-effective advertising or product promotion
> - Further marketing opportunities may develop from the sponsorship
> - It generates good publicity for the sponsor, often of a kind that money can't buy
> - It generates an awareness of the company within the local community in which the company operates and from where it draws its workforce
> - Sponsors can entertain important clients at the events they sponsor.

- those businesses with a particular **product or service** that they wish to introduce or promote. This could include a new brand of toothpaste or beer, or a supermarket opening in the area. Public awareness is important if a product or service is to get accepted. It is therefore easy to see why companies might be open to proposals that give a particular product or service more exposure;
- those companies looking for **entertainment opportunities** to influence customers, suppliers, regulators, the media and other opinion formers. They may be interested in sponsoring a prestigious concert, theatrical

event, art exhibition, horse race or sporting event, which would provide them with an appropriate entertainment opportunity and the opportunity to meet and mingle with celebrities;

■ those companies that are **committed supporters** of your organisation. They may find something that they would like to sponsor, even if it is partly for philanthropic reasons.

> ## Sponsoring a fun run
>
> Community Links is a social action centre in Newham, East London, with an excellent track record of attracting sponsorship. Some years ago it organised a fun run. There were two main sponsors:
>
> ■ **Kia Ora**. The runners were joined by the cast of EastEnders, and there was a photograph of stars running in tee-shirts with the Kia Ora logo, which appeared in the company's house magazine. Raising the company's profile in this way can be important in building employee relations, and it was this as much as the good publicity which was the main benefit for the company.
>
> ■ **Barratt Housebuilders**. The run was routed through a new housing development that had just been completed. This created good local publicity which was used as part of the marketing of the housing. Support came from the marketing budget, and not from the charity budget.

What can be sponsored

There is an extremely wide range of things that can be sponsored. In fact anything that can offer some benefit to a sponsor. The most popular things to sponsor include:

■ **cultural and sporting events**

■ **mass participation** fundraising events, such as a marathon run

■ the **publication of a report or a book**, with an attendant launch

■ the **production of fundraising materials**, leaflets and posters, or the sponsorship of a complete fundraising campaign

■ **vehicles**, where the acknowledgement can be painted on the side

■ **equipment** such as cars or computers, produced by the company

■ **competitions**, awards and prizes

■ **scholarships**, bursaries, travel grants

■ **conferences and seminars**, especially to specialist audiences (such as doctors) where promotional material can be displayed.

The bulk of corporate sponsorship money goes to sports, with motor racing, golf, tennis, athletics, football and cricket all receiving huge amounts. These offer extensive media coverage, good opportunities for corporate entertainment and an association with a popular activity.

The arts is another big recipient of sponsorship – business support for the arts runs at around £70 million a year. Arts sponsorship has been promoted by the Association for Business Sponsorship of the Arts. The National Heritage Sponsorship Scheme provides government money to encourage first time sponsorship and companies to extend their sponsorship programmes.

Social sponsorship is much smaller by comparison, but is an area where there is a good potential for growth, as companies begin to realise that this 'market' is less crowded and that there are all sorts of imaginative ways in which companies can sponsor events and activities run by good cause charities.

Identifying possible sponsors

First you should decide what your proposed activity has to offer a sponsor. Is it a target audience? Access to public personalities? A prestigious event? Only when you have done this can you begin to define the companies who might be interested. They may be national companies looking for national publicity, or a major company located in your area or a purely local concern looking to develop local awareness. Remember that if you are looking for a substantial sum of money, only the larger companies will be interested.

You should draw up a list of potential sponsors that you plan to approach. You will need to do some research prior to submitting your proposal which will include finding out what the company has sponsored before, what sort of sums it might be interested in providing, and its current interests and concerns which might be met through sponsorship. For example a construction company that has just completed a residential estate will be interested in marketing it, or a new shopping centre may need a promotional event to coincide with its opening. All these are opportunities for sponsorship.

The next step is to prepare the written proposal, which will outline the project, and highlight all the benefits to be gained by the company sponsoring it. It will also have a price for the sponsorship which will reflect as much the benefits to the company as your own fundraising need.

You will need patience. Sponsorship can take a long time to negotiate, and it is best to plan well in advance. Start discussions at least a year, and possibly longer before the activity takes place.

Sponsorship involves a close working relationship between the company and the voluntary organisation which can create problems. It is one thing when a charity accepts or even solicits money from a company about whose activities it has some reservations; it is quite another when it actively seeks to promote the work of such a company, as it will be doing in a sponsorship relationship. For example, when Shell was a target of the anti-apartheid movement, its sponsorship officers used to discuss the implications of

Whitbread's sponsorship programme

"Whitbread's support for the arts reflects its commitment to encouraging innovative and diverse performances from groups which represent all areas of the cultural spectrum ... Whitbread hopes to stimulate groups throughout the UK to perform and bring their originality and talent to as many people as possible." Amongst the projects sponsored by Whitbread are:

- The Whitbread 'Book of the Year' Award
- Heineken Free Music Festival
- Boddington Arts Festival (in Manchester)
- Flowers Brass Band
- National Senior Citizen's Talent Contest
- Maidstone Prison Project (with the English Shakespeare Company)
- Portsmouth Blues and Pub Weekend
- 'Call that Singing' (in Glasgow)

Some of the sponsorships are linked to Whitbread brands; they cover the country, as does Whitbread's business; and they have an image of fun and participation, which is what the company wants to be associated with. Whitbread also sponsors the 'Volunteer of the Year' award, which recognises community involvement by all age ranges.

developing a close involvement with the company – as it was in neither side's interests to develop a relationship which could go wrong.

It is strongly recommended that you develop a sponsorship policy before you apply for any sponsorship – agreeing in advance which types of company you are happy to approach and which you are not.

The sponsorship package

Before you make your approach, you will need to decide whether the nature of the company, its products, its ethos and its performance conflicts with your own work and ethos, and whether you are happy to work closely with that company in a high-profile relationship. If the answer is yes, then you will need to decide:

- the exact **nature of the project** or activity, and how it is likely to work;
- the audiences that will be reached and the publicity that will be obtained. These should be quantified as far as possible (how many column centimetres of coverage and in which newspapers can be expected, how many and what sort of people will attend the event, how many posters will be displayed, etc.). Remember that the company will be primarily interested in reaching those people who are its target audience for the sponsorship;
- the **geographical coverage**. Is it a national or a purely local activity?;
- the **image** that will be projected through the event, and how this will fit in with what the sponsoring brand or company might be looking for;
- the specific **advertising opportunities** that will be available on poster hoardings, the sides of vans, in the event programme, on TV, in the press, and so on;
- some of the **other benefits** that the sponsorship might confer on the company. The effect it will have on staff, on business contacts, and on government and other authorities;
- the **cost** of the sponsorship – and the value of the sponsorship benefits, and how they compare with other ways of reaching the target audiences or achieving the same promotional objective.

All this should be produced in a professional (though not necessarily expensive) way, together with photographs and press coverage from previous sponsored events, and brief background material on your organisation and its work.

Where the money will come from

Which budget head the money comes from is important, as this will determine what sort of return is being looked for. The following are the main options.

- *Marketing.* The company may be undertaking all sorts of activity to market its products and brands – all within a limited budget. The marketing manager will be making choices based on the cost and expected return to the company from the money that is spent. If you are looking for sponsorship, then you have to demonstrate what return you can provide – in people reached, in media coverage, and so on.
- *Corporate image.* The very large companies undertake sponsorship out of a central budget to promote the name, image and logo of the company. With many companies this is handled alongside their charitable support, and sometimes even out of the same budget. Here the return to the company may be more intangible than with product or brand sponsorship but this is all part of the corporate image building process, which includes corporate advertising and PR as well. A good example of how this can pay off is when Shell was involved in an oil spill on the River Mersey. The judge fining the company said that the fine would have been far larger but for Shell's excellent record in sponsoring the arts and the environment.
- *Employee relations.* The human resources budget is often the biggest single budget that the company has; investing in better staff relations can be a cost effective way of enhancing staff loyalty, retaining and even recruiting staff. The whole community affairs programme of Allied Dunbar at its headquarters in Swindon (and with its self-employed sales force) can be seen as a way of creating a company to be proud of.

Making the approach

Having identified a potential company and developed your sponsorship proposal, there are a variety of ways in which you can approach the company.

It is best to make an appointment to visit the company to give a presentation of your work and discuss the sponsorship opportunities. Only then will you be in a position to find out what the company's needs are and how you might be able to meet them. You will need to make sure you are approaching the person who is able to make the decision. For product promotions, this will be the brand manager. For corporate PR, it may be a senior director.

If you are not able to arrange a meeting in the first instance, a phone call to the marketing department can elicit a wealth of information about who to send the proposal to, and what sort of sponsorships they are likely to consider. Send a summary proposal to see if it sparks any interest and follow this up with a phone call a few days later to try and arrange a meeting.

There may be an advertising agency or marketing consultant which will introduce sponsorship opportunities to sponsors. They will sometimes charge you a fee; more usually they will receive a commission from the sponsor. It depends who retains them, and in whose interests they are acting.

Contractual issues

Sponsorship involves your giving something in return for the money you are receiving, so it is advisable to agree terms through some form of contract, which can easily be done in the form of a letter. A number of important issues need to be included which should be settled when negotiating the sponsorship:

- **how long** will the arrangement run? Is it for one year, thus requiring you to find a new sponsor next year? Or can you get a commitment for three or more years? What happens at the end of this period – does the sponsor have a first refusal on the following year's event? Most successful sponsorship lasts for several years, and the benefit builds up over the sponsorship period, but companies don't like being tied to sponsoring something indefinitely – their sponsorship programme could begin to look stale;
- the **fee** to be paid, and when instalments are due;
- what **benefits** are to be delivered in return for the fee? These should be specified as clearly as possible, so that you know precisely what you are contracted to deliver;
- whether **VAT** is chargeable. This will depend on whether your organisation is registered for VAT and the extent of the benefits offered to the sponsor. If VAT is chargeable, this should be discussed at the outset, and the fee agreed should be exclusive of VAT. (Tax and sponsorship is covered in Appendix 3.)
- who is to pay the **costs**? This is something that is often forgotten. Who pays for the additional publicity that the sponsor requires? There needs to be a clear understanding of who is responsible for what, so that you can ensure that everything is covered and there are no misunderstandings later on.
- **who is responsible** for doing what? You will need to clarify who will do the public relations, who will handle the bookings, who will invite the guests, whose staff will receive the guests and so on;
- any **termination arrangements** in the event of the activity having to be cancelled;
- who is responsible for the **sponsorship** – on both sides;
- whether the sponsor is a 'commercial participator' under the terms of the **Charities Act**, when the requirements of the Charities Act will apply; this is discussed in the section on Joint Promotions (see below).

If everything is written down in the agreement, there are less likely to be problems later – and it will ensure that everything has been properly thought through at the outset.

Joint promotions

For larger charities, commercial promotions which involve the charity in helping market a commercial product (often known as joint promotions) can be another way of working with a company, which can bring in large amounts of money relatively painlessly and expose the name of the charity to millions of people for little or no cost. The method can also be adapted for use by local charities through local promotions.

This type of fundraising is an arrangement that benefits both the charity and the commercial partner. It is rather like sponsorship, but the relationships are reversed – you are linked to the company's products, rather than they to your cause. Commercial promotions can include on-pack and licensing promotional deals, competitions and awards, the use of phone lines, and self-liquidating offers. What they have in common is that they present an opportunity to raise money for your cause and to project your charity to new audiences but they require that you work with the company and on their terms to achieving this.

> **An example of a commercial promotion**
>
> SAVE THE WORLD WITH WORLD SAVERS
> "1989 has seen the launch of the Bank's biggest sponsorship to date – a guaranteed £3 million link with the World Wide Fund for Nature (WWF) over three years. Launched in January, the World Savers scheme offers accounts to children, paying a premium interest rate, which can be opened with a minimum of £5. A donation of £1 from the Bank's own funds will be given for each new World Saver account opened, and 0.5% of the total balances of all the World Saver accounts will be donated annually."
>
> This joint promotion has been designed to appeal to supporters of WWF and anyone who wants to do something for the environment. The bank reckons that if it can attract the savings of young people, they will continue to bank with the same bank for the rest of their lives, so they are offering an inducement to start an account, and a further inducement to keep money in the account. This is a classic example of the 'you buy this product and we give an extra £1 to charity' type of commercial promotion.

On-pack promotions

There are many variants of the on-pack promotion. They start with the need of a manufacturer to promote a product or service at a particular point in time – the promotion may be to the wholesaler, to the retailer or to the consumer. The basic mechanism is that with every purchase of the product through every label or coupon returned, the manufacturer agrees to give a specified sum of money to the charity, sometimes with an upper limit on the total that will be given as a result of the promotion.

Good practice requires that the amount to be donated is specified on the pack. Manufacturers like this sort of arrangement as they can predict quite accurately what it is going to cost to achieve sales at a given level. Fundraisers like it, since it presents their cause to literally millions of shoppers, and because they can usually expect to raise a substantial sum.

Diners supporting the homeless

The Groucho Club is a well known private restaurant in the heart of Soho in central London for people in publishing and the media. In 1995-96 it organised a promotion for the homeless, where diners were asked to contribute £1 on their bill.

The Groucho Club Action Fund for the Homeless

We have all seen an increase in the number of homeless people around Soho. In consequence, we have started a Grouch Club Fund for the Homelessto help people during the cold Christmas period. Having visited the Day Centres and Hostels in Soho, we realised one of the best ways of helping is to provide sleeping bags and warm clothing – there are enough soup kitchens – and we have arranged to buy these items direct from the manufacturers.

We are asking members to make a contribution of £1 on their lunch or dinner bill. The Groucho Club will then match pound for pound all contributions made by Members.

Thank you for helping us to help others.

They were able to collect £1,313 in the period to Christmas, which sum was matched by the Groucho Club, a further £941 came in after Christmas and a cheque was received from another restaurant 'Le Caprice' towards the appeal – a total of £4,567 was raised. A letter was sent out following the completion of the event: "To All Members: Thank you for supporting our £1 per meal homeless fund. I thought you might like to know the final destination of the monies raised. On the Friday before Christmas we gave CLASH 200 sleeping bags to give out on the street. London Connection, who feed and clothe young homeless received a cheque for £1,500 to enable them to remain open over the Christmas weekend. We hope you agree it was a worthwhile venture and we are hoping to do more this year."

Variations on this theme include the consortium promotion which brings a galaxy of well-known charities together in one promotion. Local and smaller scale promotions are also possible. A local Indian take-away restaurant in London donates all the proceeds of the sale of a lentil dish each Friday to selected charities supported by the owner. The Pizza Express restaurant chain has created a special pizza (Pizza Veneziana), where a specified sum is donated to an Italian conservation charity (the Venice in Peril Fund) for each pizza ordered.

Licensing

When a charity has become a well-known household name, consumer goods manufacturers can become interested in developing an association with the charity to enhance its sales. It uses the charity's good name to endorse its product. Out of this is born the licensing deal. The promotion is likely to involve a fixed number of uses of the charity logo or name over a given period in return for an often substantial fee. Precisely how it is used will be set out in the licensing agreement. The outcome is then not directly related to the level of public support, but is agreed at the outset as a fixed fee.

One particular form of licensing which has become an important income generator for many national charities is a special credit card for the charity's supporters. The charity agrees to promote the credit card to its membership list, and will receive a fee for each customer recruited plus a small percentage of the amount spent on the card. The University of Cambridge Visa Gold Card, which is a joint promotion launched in 1996 with the Beneficial Bank for alumni with an annual income of over £25,000, has no annual fee for the cardholder and a special introductory interest rate. The University appeal receives £5 for every new account opened and 25p for every £100 spent on the account. An earlier promotion of a Visa Classic Card launched in 1993 generated over £100,000 for the University. Not surprisingly, organisations like the National Trust, which have a large membership base of just the kind of customer that credit card operators are looking for, have had the greatest success with this venture. The Royal Bank of Scotland is the leading bank involved with this form of joint charity promotion.

Competitions

Another variant is the on-pack promotion that involves a competition. The competition is usually a prize draw, which is usually a game of chance rather than a game of skill (to encourage as many people as possible to enter) and may involve a tie-break question (for example, describe in 20 words why you like Brand X).

For the fundraiser, competitions offer several benefits. The promotion can be related in some way to the charity and its cause. If it's a charity working overseas, the prize could be a trip to that country. If a domestic cause, the competition questions could be designed to create a better understanding of your cause. Money will accrue to the charity, either through a contribution for each entry sent in, or from an agreed fee for the use of the charity's name.

Self-liquidating offers

The self-liquidating offer is the rather grand name for promoting one of your own products so that its costs are recovered from sales. You offer one of your products – say an attractive tee-shirt, with a design by a well-known designer – to a manufacturer to feature on the back of a pack. Consumers are invited to send in for this at the 'special offer price', which is set low enough to seem excellent value, but high enough to recover costs.

There are several advantages of such an arrangement. Depending on the pricing, you may end up making a profit on a large number of sales – something that charities do not often manage by marketing the same products themselves. Whether or not you do better than recover your costs, you can certainly expect to distribute a large number of items bearing your message. You should note the possibility of retaining the mailing list of purchasers as a suitable list for subsequent direct mail fundraising or trading. Finally, there will be an extremely large number of people who will see the promotion but not buy – which is additional publicity for the cause.

Getting started with promotions

Promotions of this kind are quite difficult to arrange. It is an area where professionalism will pay dividends, so you may want to talk about the possibility of your developing promotional links with companies with a marketing or advertising agency.

The first step is to decide whether you are the sort of charity which can expect a commercial link of this sort. Usually national household-name charities and those addressing popular causes, such as helping children, are more likely to benefit from this area of fundraising than the less well known charities and those addressing difficult causes, such as torture or slavery.

Then you need to decide whether to wait until companies or their promotional agencies contact you (they may not), or whether to take the initiative yourself and contact companies you think might be interested, or contact promotion agencies (not to be retained by you, but to be aware of the opportunities you are offering which they might include in their sales pitch when approaching companies in the future). In order to do this, you need to be absolutely clear about the nature of your cause and what your organisation can offer, and how a company can benefit from a link with you. The relationship is not one-way, so you also need to be clear about the extent to which you are prepared to associate your charity's good name with a particular industry, a particular company and a particular product.

Ideally, you need to research the industries, companies and products that are likely to make good partners for you. What are their marketing objectives? Who are their competitors? What might they gain through an association with you? With this information, it is worth trying to meet the marketing director to present the possibilities for working together and the advantages of an association.

It is preferable at this stage not to have too detailed a proposal in mind, so that you can react to what you find to be the company's own preferences and needs. You should take along examples of how other companies have benefited from an association with you – though this will not be possible if it is the first promotion you are arranging.

If you are approached by a promotional agency pitching for business, this does not mean that anything is certain. They may be working independently, hoping that a good idea that involves your charity can then be sold to a company. In nine out of ten situations, these ideas come to nothing, and you may find you have put in considerable effort without getting any payback.

Issues

Commercial promotions business bring charities face to face with a range of dilemmas – just as with sponsorship, but more so since the relationship is that much more public. The charity will be seen to be actively promoting the products of the company, so it is important that there are no ethical problems and that the product you are associated with is good value and good quality. As for sponsorships, you are strongly recommended to develop your own policy on what commercial associations you are prepared to enter into.

There is also the question of who is exploiting whom. How much you should expect to receive from a commercial promotion is also a difficult question. Your name is effectively being sold to the company to enhance theirs or their product's. It may be worth a great deal to them to be linked with you. Any negotiation should start from what you think the association is worth to them and whether it is worth your while to enter into the promotion at that price. Your need for money should not dim the value of your commercial worth.

Finally, there are important legal issues arising from the 1992 Charities Act. The Act defines a 'commercial participator' as 'any person who carries on for gain a business which is not a fundraising business but who in the course of that business engages in any promotional venture in the course of which it is represented that contributions are to be given to or applied for the benefit of a charity'. In other words, high street shops often promote products on the understanding that part of the sale price will go to charity (e.g. charity Christmas cards which are sold by a company but stating explicitly that for each pack sold some money will go to charity). This support for charity is seen as a major incentive for people to buy the product. The Act also covers advertising and sales campaigns or other joint promotions by companies with charities. This then requires:

- a written agreement in a prescribed form between the charity and the commercial participator. Model forms of contract can be obtained from the Institute of Charity Fundraising Managers;
- the public to be informed how the charity will benefit from its involvement, which shows what part of the proceeds or profits are to be given to the charity. This is a matter for professional advice.

Government, locally and nationally and through quasi-autonomous non-governmental agencies (QUANGOs), provides around £2-3,000 million a year to voluntary organisations through grants and contracts for services (this excludes the support given to housing associations through the Housing Corporation). It is therefore one of the major funders of the voluntary sector.

This section covers government grants (contracts are covered in the section 3.9 Income Generation).

The change of government in May 1997 is likely to lead to significant changes in the way in which government programmes are delivered, the functions of the Government Offices for the Regions and the relationship between central government and local authorities.

The Charity Commission also suggests that Trustees should consider the following points before allowing the charity's name to be associated with a particular business or product:

- the relationship is appropriate and will not damage the particular charity or the good name of the charity as a whole;
- the proposed fundraising venture is a more effective way of raising money than others that might be considered, and that the terms of the arrangement are generally advantageous to the charity;
- that the arrangement is set out in some detail and kept under review, such that the charity's name is not misused or improperly exploited, and that the charity has the right to prevent future use of its name if the arrangement proves unsatisfactory. It may be worth taking proper legal advice in drawing up the terms of the arrangement.

3.4 Government Grants

The money flowing from government to charities and the voluntary sector is huge, and it has been rising annually at about 8% in real terms in recent years. The total figure, estimated at £2-3,000 million, conceals many different components and trends. What has changed significantly in recent years is the relationship between the funder and the funded. Funding has become much more closely linked to a specific project or service provided in return for the money, with quantifiable benefits and outcomes. Many voluntary organisations, and this is especially true at local level, are being supported through some form of service-level agreement or a contract for delivering a service, which specifies what is expected in return for the money given.

Unlike voluntary sources, government, local government, the NHS and statutory agencies (the quangos) all have a particular remit, which sets out what they can and cannot spend their money on. This will limit and constrain their funding to the voluntary sector. There are three factors to consider.

- **What they can support?** They are only able to give for purposes that are linked to their particular mandate. For example, a health authority can only give to projects which relate to health, although there is some flexibility. A health authority could support a Citizen's Advice Bureau on the basis that there was a link between poor health and low income, and that, therefore, support for the CAB would assist in raising people's incomes leading to an improvement in health.

- **Where they can give?** Some agencies have a national remit and can only give to national organisations or to projects of national significance, some can give only in England (or Wales or Scotland or Northern Ireland), some can only give locally. Local government is organised differently in different parts of the country, with metropolitan councils, district and borough councils, and the new unitary authorities. Each has its own particular responsibilities, and you need to be sure that you are approaching the right body for the project you want supported.

- **When they can give?** All government works to an annual timetable, with their financial year running from 1st April to 31st March. Grants (but this is not the case for contracts) have to be approved within an annual budget, and there will be deadlines for submitting an application (mostly in the autumn of the previous year). This requires planning well ahead. There is also a second opportunity. If any budget seems likely to be underspent, and this applies at local as well as national government level, there is pressure to get the budget allocation spent by the end of the financial year. This means that in January or February, when the outcome for the year becomes clearer, sums and often quite large sums of money can become available at short notice for grants which have to be spent by 31st March (although there is some flexibility in how this is interpreted). Mostly this underspend funding goes to organisations that are already being supported, or possibly to projects which did not receive funding in the last grants round due to the shortage of available funds.

There is also the question of the boundaries between statutory provision and voluntary provision. Under charity law, it is a breach of trust for a charity to use its funds for something that the government has an obligation (a duty rather than a responsibility) to pay for. Equally, a statutory body will be looking to provide funding in one of two ways: to provide a service which it is responsible for, which it will be paying for; or to support a service which complements or supplements its existing provision. A third role for voluntary funding is to promote innovation – to support ideas and projects which may have significance for the way that statutory providers deal with the problem. There is a lot of interest, for example, at the moment in out-of-school clubs and homework centres. The government is providing funding for these in the hope that the idea can be tested as a means of engaging young people and improving school performance, such that they then become funded through mainstream education provision. In the following sections, we discuss the main areas of government giving.

Central Government

Although large sums of money are given by central government to voluntary organisations each year, it does not mean that it is easy for a new organisation to win support. Most of the money is continuing support for organisations that are already being supported. A wide range of government departments and agencies are involved in giving money to voluntary organisations. Some do it in a very planned and organised way, with application forms and deadlines. Others treat each application on its merits and deal with them on an *ad hoc* basis.

In general, there are three main reasons for a government department making a grant.

- Many government departments provide **core funding** to the more significant national organisations in their sphere of interest. For example, the Voluntary and Community Unit (VCU) of the Home Office is responsible for the promotion of volunteering, and supports national organisations such as the National Centre for Volunteering and Community Service Volunteers, as well as specialist agencies such as REACH and Action: Employees in the Community.
- It may be the department's policy to **use voluntary organisations to carry out its work**. An example of this is the Department for International Development and its grant making, where it has its major funding scheme specifically devised to give support to developing countries through NGOs. In these cases the charity may become little more than a contractor to government, for example in providing disaster relief.
- A department may wish to fund a voluntary project because it **innovates or researches** a new area that has national significance. An example of this might be the Department of Health's support for the development of a new centre for the study of schizophrenia.

In Scotland, Wales and Northern Ireland, most grant giving is handled by the Scottish, Welsh and Northern Ireland Offices respectively. For England the main departments making grants are Education and Employment, Health, Environment, Overseas Development, National Heritage and the Home Office. The Department of Trade and Industry funds Citizen's Advice Bureaux; the Lord Chancellor's Office funds law centres, and other departments have smaller grants programmes.

1. Voluntary and Community Unit of the Home Office

The VCU has responsibility for co-ordinating government activity in the voluntary sector and in overseeing charities. It has a number of very specific objectives in relation to voluntary organisations. These are:

- to increase the effectiveness of the UK voluntary sector by encouraging efficient and effective practice, and by supporting and developing organisations which provide resources and support to the sector generally;
- to encourage, support and promote volunteering;
- to encourage involvement in all aspects of voluntary activity in the work or running of charities, and in support of the services provided by government;
- to support and sustain initiatives promoting community development;
- to encourage the involvement of individuals, trusts and companies in supporting the sector.

Besides supporting a number of national voluntary organisations (including the Women's Royal Voluntary Service, the National Council for Voluntary Organisations, the Community Development Foundation, Community Service Volunteers and the National Centre for Volunteering), the Department also makes grants of up to £50,000 under three main headings as follows:

- increasing the effectiveness of the sector
- promoting volunteering
- promoting community development.

You can be a national charity or a specific project which has lessons for the whole sector. The Voluntary and Community Unit can be contacted care of 50 Queen Anne's Gate, London SW1H 9AT (0171-273 3000).

Grants by Government Department 1993-94	
	£,000
Agriculture, Food and Fisheries	243
Defence	18,919
Education and Employment	56,003
Environment	2,582,870
Foreign Office	3,594
Health	52,984.
Home Office	64,418
Lord Chancellor's	1,125
National Heritage	21,051
Northern Ireland Office	71,206
Overseas Development Administration	158,500
Scottish Office	356,786
Social Security	13,110
Trade and Industry	14,435
Transport	442
Welsh Office	147,284

(Taken from *Dimensions of the Voluntary Sector*, 1996. The Department of the Environment total includes grants to housing associations, which total approximately £2.5 billion)

2. Home Office

In addition to the Voluntary and Community Unit (which returned to the Home Office from the Department of National Heritage in 1997 – see above for separate description), the Home Office also makes grants in a number of areas of interest to the voluntary sector, including:

- refugees and asylum seekers
- immigrants
- victim Support
- drugs and Crime Prevention
- the Safer Cities Programmes.

The Home Office can be contacted at 50 Queen Anne's Gate, London SW1H 9AT (0171-273 3000).

3. Department for International Development(DfID)

The DfID (up until 1997, this was called the Overseas Development Administration) has a stated policy of working through NGOs. The DfID maintains desk officers for most of the regions of the world who are in a position to advise on policy in their region. They also have a refugee office, disaster office and food aid office as well as a volunteer scheme, all of which are there, in part, to liaise with charities operating in developing countries. The biggest pool of money that the DfID administers is its Joint Funding Scheme. This is a competitive scheme which receives project proposals from UK based international organisations and funds a wide variety of development projects. Grants given are in the region of £30 million each year, and are funded on a matching basis (the applicant has to raise at least 50% of the project's costs from other sources). The DfID deals additionally with the funding of the British Council and other scholarship schemes to introduce people overseas to things British.

The DfID can be contacted at 94 Victoria Street, London SW1E 5JL (0171-917 2000).

4. Department of Health

The Department funds a wide range of voluntary bodies under its Section 64 provisions. Mostly they are looking at new ways of delivering health services. They will give:

- core grants to national organisations
- funding for national or nationally significant projects which test new ideas
- occasional local project grants where more than one local health authority may be involved
- capital grants for priority projects of great significance.

The Department can be contacted at Richmond House, 79 Whitehall, London SW1A 2NS (0171-210 3000).

5. Department for Education and Employment

Since the merger of the Education and Employment departments, they have become one of the major funders of the voluntary sector. Major programmes include:

- grants for national youth work for 13-19 year olds
- grants for local projects
- grants for adult education organisations
- educational research
- supported (sheltered) employment
- support for training through TECs and ESF funding.

The Department can be contacted at Sanctuary Buildings, Great Smith Street, London SW1P 3BT (0171-925 5000).

6. Department of the Environment

There are a number of different schemes run by the department including the following (some of which are now being absorbed into the Single Regeneration Budget – see below):

- special grants programme for urban regeneration
- home improvement agencies
- homelessness grants
- tenant participation grants
- housing management grants
- Environmental Action Fund
- grants to Groundwork Foundation and trusts
- litter prevention grants
- energy efficiency grants.

The Department can be contacted at 2 Marsham Street, London SW1P 3EB (0171-276 3000).

7. The Department of Culture, Media and Sport

The responsibilities of this new department (earlier the Department of National Heritage) include:

- television and broadcasting
- the Arts, museums, libraries and national heritage (where grants are made through agencies such as the Arts Council of England)
- sport (where grants are made through the Sports Councils)
- the National Lottery.

Further information can be obtained from Department of Culture, Media & Sport, 2-4 Cockspur Street, London SW1 5DH (0171-270 6000).

8. Department of Social Security

DSS grants are limited to the following:

- Voluntary Organisations dealing with mobility for disabled people

(grants to Motability and the British Limbless Ex-Servicemen's Association)

■ via the Resettlement Agency, grants to assist outside organisations providing accommodation where no resettlement unit exists, or as an overflow for an existing unit. Contact the Resettlement Agency, 286 Euston Road, London NW1 3DN.

9. Department of Trade and Industry

The DTI funds three voluntary organisations only: the National Association of Citizens' Advice Bureaux, Citizens Advice Scotland, and the Royal Society for the Prevention of Accidents.

10. Scottish, Welsh and Northern Ireland Offices

The Scottish, Welsh and Northern Ireland Offices serve as the lead government departments in these areas for a number of the main functions of government. These include agriculture, environment, education and employment, health and home affairs. All the main functions covered by the appropriate Departments in England will be their responsibility in Scotland, Wales and Northern Ireland, and there will be a certain amount of coordination between them and their English counterparts. You can contact them at:

The Scottish Office, New St Andrew's House, St James' Centre, Edinburgh EH1 3SX (0131-556 8400).

The Welsh Office, Crown Building, Cathays Park, Cardiff CF1 3NQ (01222-825111).

The Northern Ireland Office, Stormont Castle, Belfast BT4 2AZ (01232-763 011).

QUANGOs and government agencies

Much of the work of government is no longer carried on directly by a government department. In the past two decades a range of agencies have been created, as the responsible bodies for delivering government programmes, and for disbursing funds to voluntary organisations for work that falls within their remit. These agencies are responsible to the relevant Secretary of State and accountable to Parliament. Their Boards, who are charged with the responsibility for the work of the agency, are comprised of appointees (although there are moves to select Board Members through open competition). In this respect, they tend to be less accountable than a government department itself. Although they are operationally separate from government itself, there is pressure on them to respect the fact that they are spending government money, and often pressure from the responsible Minister on what they fund.

Grants from the larger Quangos

	£,000
Arts Council for England	225,600
Scottish Arts Council	176
Northern Ireland Education and Library Boards	288
Youth Council for Northern Ireland	1,421
Youth Exchange Centre	1,634
Commonwealth Youth Exchange Council	164
Countryside Commission	4,178
Countryside Council for Wales	1,400
English Nature	804
Scottish Natural Heritage	7,800
Historic Buildings and Monuments Commission	40,542
Road Safety Council for Northern Ireland	100
Rural Action for the Environment	680
Commission for Racial Equality	5,213
Equal Opportunities Commission	35
Northern Ireland Community Relations Council	761
Rural Development Commission	2,900
Rural Development Council for Northern Ireland	205
Urban Development Corporations	11,036
Highlands and Islands Enterprise	1,075
Welsh Development Agency	398
Northern Ireland Tourist Board	1,043
Wales Tourist Board	287
Westminster Foundation for Democracy	1,679
Housing Corporation	2,510,000
Scottish Homes	273,302
Housing for Wales	122,082
Northern Ireland Housing Executive	49,293
Sports Council	20,219
Sports Council for Northern Ireland	728
Scottish Sports Council	1,898
Sports Council for Wales	1,645
Health Education Authority	1,250

Other Quangos making grants include: the Arts Council of Wales, the Forestry Authority, the Natural Environment Research Council, the British Library, Belfast Action Teams, the Equal Opportunities Commission for Northern Ireland, the Economic and Social Research Council, English Partnerships, Scottish Enterprise, the British Tourist Authority. This list excludes grants made by Health Authorities and Hospital Trusts.

(1993/94 figures from *Dimensions of the Voluntary Sector* 1996)

Probably the largest group of these Quangos are the Health Authorities and Hospital Trusts. Although their Boards are appointed and not elected, because of their local remit and knowledge, their funding for voluntary organisations is organised in a similar way to local authorities, and the two should be considered together.

Owing to the wide variety of Quangos and the schemes that they administer, it is difficult to give general advice on how to approach them. The following tips may be useful.

1. Ask for details of **grants schemes**. There may well be a printed brochure or an annual report which sets out the aims and objectives, and the purposes for which grants are made.

2. Get hold of **application forms**.

3. Note the **timetable and deadlines** for applications, any conditions for receiving grants, and the range of grants available.

4. Contact a member of staff to give **advice and support**. The larger bodies will all have specialist staff dealing with grants to voluntary organisations.

5. Consider what you can do to **demonstrate your credibility** as an organisation and to show that you will be spending the money cost-effectively. These are both important considerations in disbursing government funding.

6. Don't see them as mere cheque-writing machines who are there simply to fund what you want to do. Show how you **share their policy concerns** and would like to work with them to develop strategies for meeting the needs and problems which you have jointly identified.

Single Regeneration Budget

In 1994, the Single Regeneration Budget (known as SRB) was created, bringing together funding from 20 separate government funding lines. This was done progressively, and will see a number of well known funding schemes disappear altogether as they are absorbed into the SRB. The idea was to co-ordinate government funding so that it would be spent more effectively through focusing different programmes to deal with the problems of regeneration. Government Offices for the Regions were set up to administer the SRB, and this should be seen as the start of a continuing process of decentralisation of government spending.

The SRB encompasses the City Challenge and other employment-related funding schemes. Employment is its first priority. Housing, ethnic minorities, environment, crime prevention and community development are all on the list too. The idea of the programme is to encourage partnerships, and bids are encouraged on this basis. The SRB represents a major opportunity for many local voluntary organisations concerned with community regeneration, but also creates problems in finding an appropriate way into the scheme.

A voluntary organisation can become the lead partner, developing its idea for a bid, and then bringing in other partners from the voluntary, public and private sectors as appropriate. Constructing a bid can be a major task. The scale of the funding is big and the required application paperwork takes a long time. You will need to negotiate with the range of partners you assemble for the bid. Alternatively, a voluntary organisation might be associated with a bid led by another agency or organisation. Here the problem is to ensure that your organisation is not being included as a partner in the bid for cosmetic purposes (to show the involvement of community organisations) but with no real role in delivering the programme and no real funding either. This becomes a matter for negotiation. You may not want to be left out of a bid, but at least you should ensure that your contribution to the bid is significant and adds value to the programme through the skills, resources and community mobilisation that you bring. You will also need to ensure that you are not expected to deliver impossible outputs, and that you are rewarded properly for your contribution.

Since the whole aim is to make funding more accountable locally, the main promoters of SRB bids have been local authorities, TECs and other local agencies promoting economic regeneration. None of these are necessarily easy for a small voluntary organisation to work with but there are now examples of bids developed by voluntary organisations receiving funding.

Decisions are made by the Government Offices for the Regions, which are increasingly co-ordinating regional strategy and government spending on training and regeneration. There is a wide range of experience ranging from the helpful to the impenetrable among the different regional offices.

Local authority expenditure on voluntary sector (1994-95)	
	£000
Housing	33,285
Education	187,208
Social Services	624,257
Recreation/Arts	97,214
Economic development	26,236
Environment	14,429
Policy, other	171,037

(figures from *Dimensions of the Voluntary Sector*, Charities Aid Foundation, 1996)

Local Government

Local government giving has come under a great deal of financial pressure in recent years but it is still an important source of funds for local voluntary organisations. What is different now is that it is much more volatile. Whereas in the past there was some certainty that a grant might continue, today there is the ever-present fear that it might be cut back significantly or cut off completely.

There are a number of different local authority types (Metropolitan, County, District, London Borough, and Unitary Authorities), and the system is yet again in the throes of change. This means new shapes and structures for grant-seekers to understand, new people to meet and new funding opportunities. Many counties are now moving towards becoming unitary authorities (a single tier of local government that is responsible for the whole range of local service delivery), and they are taking this opportunity to change the way they have traditionally done business. In other places, the old three-tier pattern of parish council (which may have very limited grant-making potential), district council and county council remain. In metropolitan areas, the local authorities have already operated effectively as unitary councils for a number of years.

The different levels of local authority will each be responsible for providing a specific range of services and it is only within these areas of responsibility that they will consider making a grant. However, irrespective of what level of council your work relates to, they are obliged to support things which are for the benefit of their local community. If your work does not provide any local benefit, then you will not be funded. If your work covers a wider area of benefit, then you will have to demonstrate the local need and the benefit that you are providing locally. There is no reason to expect say Liverpool to support a national scheme, for example, unless they are supporting just the part that affects the people of Liverpool.

What local authorities support

Local government has responsibility for a wide range of activities which may be of interest to voluntary organisations. These include:

- recreation
- housing
- health
- environment
- equal opportunities
- poverty and community development
- advice and guidance
- old people
- young people
- education
- art and museums
- recreation and leisure.

Local authority funding for voluntary organisations varies wildly from one council to the next. Some conduct much of their business through voluntary organisations and other independent providers, rather than trying to provide services directly themselves. Some welcome the voluntary sector as contributing a great deal at relatively low cost to community life. Some see voluntary organisations as yet another hungry mouth to be fed from their limited resources.

The exact departmental organisation, the name of the department and what each department is responsible for will vary from council to council. Some councils have a central grants department which undertakes all voluntary sector liaison and acts as the channel for distributing grants. With others, the grants are made by the responsible departments. Whatever the procedure for grants, there will be separate channels for contracts, where arrangements will be made through departmental officers whose job is to purchase specific services within budgets that they are responsible for.

It is hard to be categorical about which level of council does what. There are examples of education charities successfully obtaining support from District Councils (education is usually handled by County Councils) and of children's charities not getting support from County Councils (although this is their statutory responsibility). Most councils though will produce guidelines for charities which indicate the services they run, and the aims and priorities of their various committees.

Type of support available

Councils can provide a number of different types of support to a voluntary organisation, including:

- a **grant**, which is usually for one year at a time. This may be a smallish sum for a particular project or core funding representing the major slice of funding for the organisation;
- a **funding agreement**, which sets out what is expected from the voluntary organisation in return for the money and can run over a number of years. This is more tightly defined than for a grant, and concentrates more on outputs and outcomes against which the expenditure can be evaluated, rather than simply requiring the recipient to account for how the money was spent. It can also run over a longer period of time, thereby giving the recipient some stability within which to plan and develop the programme of work. Some local authorities now support their more important voluntary sector clients in this way – for example, a CAB to provide advice, Age Concern to run a day centre for the elderly or the Council for Voluntary Service to provide voluntary sector liaison;
- a **contract** for providing a specified service, which is usually a service which the council itself wishes to provide. It becomes the 'purchaser', and the contractee, which may be a commercial organisation, a non-profit agency or a voluntary organisation, becomes the 'provider'.

(Contracts, which are sometimes also called service agreements are discussed in section 3.9);

- **publicity** for events. Many councils have the means to publicise specific events – especially those which they are providing support for. They have mailing lists, they publish newsletters which are sent out to the whole area, and they have access to many notice board sites, such as in public libraries, which can be made available to local organisations;
- **staff time**, either by providing someone on secondment or delegated duty, or simply by assisting on a particular project. This is one way in which they can offer really useful support. For example, if an organisation is already getting support from a Social Services department, then it is very much in their interests to ensure that finances and staffing issues are in good order by making available relevant advice and expertise. Key staff can be asked to help with specific problems and, in the development phase of new projects, they are often prepared to spend significant time in helping to plan the way ahead;
- **access to and use of council owned premises and facilities**. Some councils have access to significant numbers of properties which are owned by them yet are standing empty. The success of some projects will depend very much on access to some sort of a base from which to provide a service. From the local authority's point of view, it is often better to have a building occupied for community benefit, even if there is no rental stream rather than to risk vandalism, however District Auditors, who oversee local authority finance, are now advising that even favoured voluntary organisations should be required to pay market rents for premises. This problem is overcome by councils then giving the rent back by way of a grant. This will involve some careful negotiation with a council to ensure that you don't end up with something you cannot afford to be responsible for. And there is an opportunity for you to get a grant that will cover more than just the rent;
- **rate relief**. There is mandatory rate relief of 80% for any charity occupying premises for its charitable purposes. This is subsidised by central government. The local authority may also offer discretionary relief of the remaining 20%, which it has to bear the cost of. You should make sure that you are receiving mandatory relief – it has to be applied for during the rating year (by 31st March in respect of rates payable during the year to that date), and cannot be granted retrospectively for previous years. For the discretionary relief, you need to apply for this in the same way as for a grant;
- access to **training**. Some local authorities provide training for voluntary organisations; some subsidise the cost of training;
- **partnership arrangements**. Very significant is the help that the council

can give in setting up partnership arrangements which may involve your organisation. The SRB, a local authority led National Lottery bid and European Social Fund may all require some sort of partnership arrangement. Much of this work is done through economic development departments in councils and they are used to working with voluntary organisations.

Lobbying councils

Unlike most of the other funding bodies mentioned in this book, councils are democratic organisations. This means that they are very open to pressure being put on them to try to influence their decision making. Most council officers expect the local councillors to be interested in what gets supported, and very often the decisions that are made are overtly political. This means that if you wish to be sure of getting your money, you need to play the game. You need to be aware of the political complexion of your council: many are now hung which makes lobbying more complex. You need to do what you can to make your application difficult to refuse. Here are some ideas to help you do this.

- **Meet the local councillor** for your ward, and get them interested in your idea. Their support is critical for any very local project, whether or not they are a representative of the party running the council.
- **Prepare your case** carefully with details about local needs and what happens in neighbouring areas. Be as factual as possible. The more information you can gather on the extent of need and the current pattern of provision, the better. If you can show, for example, that according to latest census data or local authority research there are particularly important unmet needs in your area, then this is a good basis for your application to be taken forward.
- Take any opportunities to **meet councillors on the committee** that may be considering your application. The Committee Chair is a particularly important person to get on your side. You can also try the party route, and get the Leader of the Council interested in your plans. Many decisions are taken in party caucuses.
- Invite these people to **visit your project** and share your excitement about it.
- If yours is a major issue for the people of the area, ask to **address the whole council meeting**. You may be invited to address the full meeting for just one minute – but this is still very worthwhile.
- Make sure that you have **taken on board any concerns** of the officers dealing with your application or responsible for your area of work, so that you will have their support.
- Get as much **local publicity** for what you are doing as you can. This will demonstrate that you can also mobilise publicity when they dare

Getting in touch with your local council

1. Identify the relevant local authorities which cover your geographical area and your area of work – there may be more than one responsible authority.

2. Phone their main switchboard to identify whether there is anyone delegated to act as the main voluntary organisations contact.

3. If there is such a person, contact them by phone or visit them in person to find out what their committee and decision structures are, and what are their main funding lines. If funding is handled through an individual council department, then you need to find out which departments have the responsibility for what you are proposing. Find out who is the responsible person and who you will need to contact – this could be an officer, a senior director, your local ward councillor, the committee chair or the council leader. In larger authorities, you may find it easier to contact your local councillor. They will be interested in what you are planning and will be able to put you in touch with the right people. Visit them, if possible.

4. Approach your Council of Voluntary Service or its equivalent to find out what is the best way to approach the council. They are there to give this sort of advice.

5. Consult the Council Minutes of the previous year's grants meeting, to see what sorts of projects have been funded with what amounts. This will give you guidance on what they are likely to fund. It will also warn you if a major initiative in your particularly area that is very similar to what you are proposing has been funded.

6. Research the need as well as you can. Also find out whether the Council has a stated policy of supporting what you are proposing. Census data is useful. There may also be policy documents or manifestos from the last election. The local Reference Library is a good starting point.

turn you down, as well as provide good publicity for them if they decide to support you. A prime concern of every councillor is to get re-elected, and the possibility of good publicity can facilitate this (or at least they see it that way).

- **Attend the meeting where the decision is to be made** in person, if you are allowed to, so that you may answer any questions that arise.
- **Contact all the committee members** before the meeting and offer to answer any queries they may have in advance. By doing this, even if they have nothing to ask you, the call will make them more aware of your application.

London Boroughs Grants Unit

For organisations based in Greater London whose work extends beyond a single London Borough, the LBGU is of special interest. This is the organisation which has taken on residual responsibilities from the old Greater London Council to make grants to London-wide organisations and those operating over a number of London Boroughs. It is a highly professional grant-making organisation which is modelled rather on a local authority department. Each Borough puts up a councillor to sit on the board and it takes its lead from them. They do not consider it their role to support projects whose area is within one borough, nor is it their intention to support national organisations. However, they do support national organisations where much of the work is in London. The contact address for the LBGU is 5th Floor, Regal House, London Road, Twickenham TW1 3QS.

Getting Started

When considering government funding it is important to know the likely sources of funding suitable for your project or organisation, and to get as much information as you can on how they operate. There are two good starting points:

- for central government and QUANGO funding, consult the *Central Government Grants Guide* published by the Directory of Social Change in which are listed all the central government departments, their agencies and the funds that are linked to them;
- for local government funding, contact your local Council of Voluntary Service, or its equivalent. Most, but not all, areas have such an organisation as a central information point for voluntary action.

When doing your research, the key thing is to find out what they want to fund. Too many organisations assume that because it is government money the authorities are simply there to underwrite your core costs. If this was ever true, it is certainly not now. You may even consider arranging a meeting simply to hear about what they are trying to do rather than you telling them what you want money for. You can then frame your application around their concerns, not your own ideas (as these may be of absolutely no interest to them).

Having researched the likely sources, the next step is to draw up a short list of potential funders you might contact. Your initial contact should be on the phone to establish whether they are the right people to approach for funding, who is the person responsible for dealing with applicants, what printed information is available, and any deadlines that you will be expected to meet. With this information, you might then decide to write to them with an outline of you proposal, requesting a meeting to discuss the idea further; this is always likely to be better than sending in a completed proposal without any prior consultation. They will be receiving a wide range of applications, they will know the current priorities and interests, and they can give you invaluable advice. More importantly, if they are involved in the process of constructing the application, they are much more likely to want to recommend it.

It can take a long time for central or local government funding to come to fruition – even several years. It requires persistence. If you feel that your work deserves government funding, then that is a good starting point. You have to develop a fundable proposal and gather around you enough support to make them say yes. Once you have received funding, it is important to be fully accountable for the money you are spending, to evaluate your work to show the level of benefit you are creating, and to maintain good relationships with the funder. Although there is never a commitment to continue funding over a long period of time, practice shows that those who get government support continue to get such support provided they deliver and manage the relationship properly (and put time and effort into doing this).

> The National Lottery has come from nowhere to be the largest single source of funds for voluntary organisations, and for arts, sports and heritage projects.
>
> It distributes some £1,500 million a year through its five Distribution Boards. It is of such size and importance that many organisations are now gearing a substantial part of their fundraising effort towards getting support from the Lottery.

3.5 The National Lottery

In late 1994, the National Lottery was launched with a degree of opposition from the voluntary sector. There were several different objections:

- that the Lottery would compete with charity fundraising, both by being an additional call on people's disposable income and because people would confuse the purchase of a lottery ticket where a part of the proceeds were to be channelled to good cause with the direct support of a good cause;
- that the lottery would compete with existing charity lotteries. This method of fundraising is marginal for most charities, but for a few such as Tenovus, the Welsh cancer charity, it was a major component of its fundraising;
- that it would benefit certain causes at the expense of others. There was particular concern and hard lobbying by the medical research charities for a slice of the income;
- that the lottery was raising money through gambling, and encouraging people to gamble. Certain religious denominations were not prepared to receive money from such sources, and this ruled them out of the potentially huge source of support;
- that the lottery would impoverish already poor people, and create greater needs than any benefits it provided to charities;
- that the lottery would benefit 'rich' causes rather than 'poor' causes, and be regressive in its impact.

Some of the fears were unfounded, and some have been taken on board in determining the policies for distributing lottery funds. Now after more than two years, the National Lottery has become a fact of life. There have been many 'winners', with large numbers of voluntary organisations succeeding in gaining substantial grants. Of the nearly £5 billion of lottery ticket and scratch card sales, £1.3 billion was channelled to good causes in 1996 through the eleven lottery Distribution Boards. This has represented a new and very substantial flow of funds to voluntary organisations, and has been especially important for the smaller ones. The impact on established fundraising methods and on the total donated to charity by individuals is still much disputed, with research offering differing stories.

More important, the lottery has completely transformed the way in which organisations think of funding. Many organisations now look to the National Lottery as a major potential source of funding, and even as an answer to all their funding problems. Although many applications succeed, many more fail (for the Charities Board, the failure rate is around

80%), but the average level of grant is way above what one might expect from a trust or a company. The gaining of a lottery grant has become something of a lottery itself, but many organisations are treating the lottery extremely seriously, and spend significant time and effort planning their next bid. Some are even adapting how they operate in order to meet the assessment criteria more closely (for example, organisations which have some non-white or disabled trustees stand a greater chance of getting a Charities Board grant than those that don't).

How the National Lottery operates

The National Lottery is operated on a seven-year licence (which runs from 1995) by Camelot plc. They were awarded the licence on their ability to run the lottery successfully, to generate large sums for good causes and to keep operating costs to a minimum. They now run a twice weekly lottery game (on Wednesdays and Saturdays,) and sell scratch cards for instant prizes. The costs of running the lottery and selling the tickets (including any operating profit) are kept to 10% of the total take. After the prize money, the tax due to the Treasury and these operating expenses, 28% of the total take is passed to the National Lottery Distribution Fund for distribution to good causes.

The Distribution Fund then passes this money on in five equal parts to the Distribution Boards for the five 'good causes', each of which gets 5.6% of the proceeds of the lottery. The boards are:

- The **National Lottery Charities Board**
- The **Arts Councils** in England, Scotland, Wales and Northern Ireland
- The **Sports Councils** in the same four countries
- The **National Heritage Lottery Fund**
- The **Millennium Commission**. The continuation of this as a beneficiary is to be reviewed after the millennium.

A sixth distribution mechanism is being developed through the 'People's Lottery' proposals of the new Labour Government. **The New Opportunities Fund** will draw its resources by cutting back on the funding available to all distribution boards apart from the Millenium Commission, and will fund healthy-living centres, after-school clubs and computer

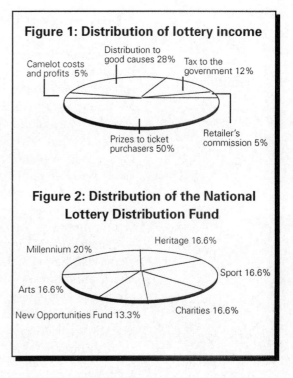

Figure 1: Distribution of lottery income

- Camelot costs and profits 5%
- Distribution to good causes 28%
- Tax to the government 12%
- Prizes to ticket purchasers 50%
- Retailer's commission 5%

Figure 2: Distribution of the National Lottery Distribution Fund

- Millennium 20%
- Heritage 16.6%
- Sport 16.6%
- Arts 16.6%
- Charities 16.6%
- New Opportunities Fund 13.3%

Camelot's costs and profits 5%

technology for teaching. The redistribution of money to allow for this 'sixth' good cause, and the consequently reduced income for the original five, began to be implemented by agreement in autumn 1997. The revised proportions are shown in figure 2 on p. 113.

The National Lottery is the responsibility of the Department of Culture, Media and Sport. The Boards are QUANGOs run by an appointed Board and distribute public money. Although nominally independent, their distribution policies and even specific grants are subject to influence from the Secretary of State. Their policies, and the operation of the lottery itself, are under close public and media scrutiny, and there has been criticism and debate, for example on the purchase of the Churchill papers by the National Heritage fund and the purpose of the Millennium Exhibition, being supported by the Millennium Commission.

Camelot, the National Lottery operator, does not have any influence on the distribution of the funds, although it does have its own community giving programme (which operates in exactly the same way as for other prominent companies). One pressure on Camelot is the level of profit it earns. There is considerable public interest in this, particularly as Richard Branson's failed bid had promised to pay over any profit it earned into the distribution fund.

The National Lottery Charities Board

The Board which most voluntary organisations think of first is the National Lottery Charities Board (NLCB). The Board's stated aims are to 'help meet the needs of those at most disadvantage in society, and to improve the quality of life in the community'. Unlike the other Distribution Boards, it has not required any matched funding to be provided from other sources, it is prepared to give grants to cover salaries and running costs, and grants can be for a period of up to three years. Unlike any of the other Boards, it has had poverty at the heart of its grant-making. At the time of writing there their scheme is only operating in Wales, Scotland and the north east and south west of England.

The way the Board has operated so far has been to identify a theme for each grant round (there are two a year at the time of writing) and to invite applications within these themes. The themes have been quite wide in their scope, and for most organisations there is likely to be a theme coming up into which they could reasonably fit a proposal. Examples of themes during 1996-97 are: health, disability and care; new

---

Grants made by the National Lottery Charities Board

In the first two grant rounds:
- the largest grant awarded was £682,000
- the average grant was £68,000
- over half the grants were for less than £40,000
- two thirds of the funding was given for two and three-year projects.

And in the first round:
- one in five eligible applications received a grant (2,460 grants were made out of 13,000 eligible applications).

opportunities and choices; and improving people's living environment. An additional theme was launched at the beginning of 1997 relating to the development of the infrastructure for supporting voluntary action, and this theme will continue in future rounds.

Additionally an International Grants programme for work overseas in developing countries and Eastern Europe was launched at the end of 1996 (the first allocation was £25 million), and this will run annually.

However, as from 1998, the Board has said that for its main areas of work it will be moving from themes to a system of receiving applications on a continuous basis.

Assessment of applications

Applications have to be made on a standard form, and the assessment of the application goes through a number of stages, including:

- completion of application form to **meet all the requirements** (which includes submitting annual accounts and a copy of the organisation's constitution, providing a business plan for large projects, three signatures which have to include a trustee and a third party referee, besides answering all the questions). Inadequately completed applications are rejected at this stage;
- **assessment** by a National Lottery Charities Board assessor;
- **consideration by the appropriate panel** (UK-wide, England-wide, or one of the nine regions of England, Scotland, Northern Ireland, Wales).

> **Key requirements for grants**
> - Relevance to the theme of the current programme
> - Benefit to the community
> - Capital and/or revenue projects
> - Funding for 1,2 or 3 years
> - Financial and technical viability of the project
> - Effective management of the organisation and project
> - Meeting a need (not duplicating existing services or replacing statutory provision)
> - Involvement of users or beneficiaries

The application forms run to around 24 pages, but nonetheless are a model of their type, with considerable effort going into making them easy to understand and complete. The application form comes with a detailed guide to their completion (a separate guide is published for each grant round), which sets out the criteria against which the application will be assessed, gives advice on completing the application form and makes it very clear what is required.

Assessment usually involves either a face-to-face meeting with the assessor, or discussion over the phone for smaller applications. This can be quite an intensive session, and it is important that the right people are present to ensure that a correct presentation of the organisation and the proposal is given. Assessors have mostly been experienced freelancers with voluntary sector experience, but more is now being undertaken in-house. Your application is scored numerically against a set of criteria,

Types of grant

There are a number of restrictions relating to the size and types of grants you can get. You can apply for:

- one, two or three-year funding
- some or all of the project's costs
- revenue costs (including core costs, as long as they are not being paid for by anyone else)
- capital costs
- matching funds for European Union funds.

You cannot normally apply for:

- endowments
- loans or loan payments
- retrospective funding
- making up deficits
- promoting particular religious beliefs
- sports, art or heritage projects (as these are the responsibility of other Lottery boards)

No grants will be awarded which replace (or may replace) lost statutory funding, nor where the money will subsidise statutory provision, nor where it will make up a deficit on a service otherwise funded by the state.

which are published for each round. This is quite a rigid process, with little scope for rating something highly because it seems imaginative or a good thing.

It is as important to have a project which genuinely meets all the criteria as it is to complete the application form skilfully. To help you in preparing applications, the Directory of Social Change run a course on increasing your chances. For example, applicants need to know that there may be extra points for having disabled or non-white trustees; and that user involvement in management and decision making is rated highly. Some of these you can do something about prior to making your application, others will influence how you design your project, but being aware of the assessment criteria will ensure that you present a good case well and do not slip down the score sheet for the wrong reasons.

Grants are available not just to charities, but also to a wide range of organisations that have benevolent objectives – although the vast majority of grants awarded by the NLCB have been to charities. Recipients can include associations, societies, cooperatives or companies acting in a benevolent way. Grants will not be made to any educational institutions (schools, FE colleges, universities, etc.), local councils, NHS trusts or appeals on their behalf. The reason for this is that the Board may not use public funds to support statutory services, but the ruling ignores the very valuable work that can be done by statutory bodies that builds on their statutory responsibilities. Applications may not be made directly by professional fund-raisers, though they can assist in the preparation of applications.

One application from an organisation can be made to each of the five grant-making committees (England, Wales, Scotland, Northern Ireland and the UK) in each grant round, and an organisation can only be in receipt of a maximum of one grant at a time from any of the five committees (i.e. you can have up to five grants from the Charities Board at once, one from each of the five committees) – this restriction does not cover grants awarded in the first grant round, or grants from the international programme, or for organisations submitting an application or holding a grant as part of a consortium. This has led to some organisations setting up a new organisation to apply for a NLCB grant, which will be activated if the grant succeeds, or left dormant if the application fails. This may be an appropriate strategy for a community group already in receipt of a project grant and now seeking to set up a community centre, as much as for an organisation in receipt of a grant for its national work in England and now seeking support for a regional initiative.

Grants mostly range between £5,000 and £250,000, but are typically £30,000 to £80,000. The minimum grant amount is £500, and some larger grants are made. The maximum awarded in the first two grant rounds was £682,000. Any project with a budget in excess of £200,000, whether

---

Dealing with an assessment – 10 tips from a National Lottery Charities Board assessor

1. Remember that not all assessors have experience of your kind of work. Do not assume too much knowledge of what you are trying to do and how you do it.

2. Have all your documentation to hand. If an assessor rings and you do not feel prepared with the necessary information, ask for another more convenient time when you will be organised. Ask what information they will be looking for so that you can everything to hand. An assessment phone call usually takes about an hour (some have taken up to three hours). It will save you time and stress, and make the assessor's job easier, if you are organised and prepared.

3. Remember that assessors are human. There's no need to go overboard but make sure they feel welcome. Cocktails and canapés are too much, but coffee and biscuits will probably be welcome.

4. If you are having an assessment visit, make sure that the person conducting the tour and answering the questions knows the details of the application.

5. Be open and honest. Don't be over the top or try to cover the cracks. If your organisation is perfect, why do you need the money anyway?

6. See the assessment as a discussion not an interrogation.

7. Use friendly, jargon-free language. Be straightforward in your answers.

8. If your proposal is for a mini-bus or a building or a salary, you may need to supply copies of your supporting documentation to the assessor if they don't have them.

9. Keep a record of what you have been asked for. This will help you after the assessment to make sure you have fulfilled your side of things. At key points in the conversation, ask the assessor to reflect back his or her understanding of what has been said. This will avoid misunderstandings.

10. At the end of the assessment, do not be afraid to ask questions about anything you are unsure of. It should be a two-way process, and this is your chance to get some first-hand knowledge of when you can expect to hear, what happens next, or anything else that is needed.

or not the amount being applied for from the NLCB is below or above this figure, will receive extra scrutiny.

Unlike the other Distribution Boards, matched funding for a NLCB grant is not a requirement. However, the Board is quite prepared to match funding that is coming from another source – for example, from the European Social Fund.

Typical management criteria for assessing projects

- Is the organisation **financially sound** and **well managed**? For example, does it produce annual accounts which show a reasonable surplus? Does it pay its bills on time? Does it have a reasonable amount of money in the bank? Does the management committee meet regularly and review what is going on? Does the organisation have a good track record in delivering the kinds of services it is applying for?
- Is the project **properly planned and organised**, and staffed appropriately? Is there a project plan? Does it seem sensible? Has it got measurable targets? Are they realistic? Are the management structures clear?
- Is the **budget accurate** and does it offer value for money? Are all costs covered, including overheads? Do they seem appropriate for the work that is being done? Can you show that this is money being very well spent?
- Will the project be **monitored and evaluated** in a meaningful way? Are there clear targets for the project? Will there be regular progress reviews? What will happen if targets are not met?
- What will happen when the Charities Board money runs out? Will the project simply stop? If you want it to **continue**, how is it going to be funded (not by the Charities Board, although there is some discussion now as to whether continuation funding might be offered to projects that have been supported once the original NLCB funding has run out)?
- Is the organisation committed to **equal opportunities**? A statement on a piece of paper is not enough. You have to show that you are genuinely representative of your community at management committee level, among the project leaders, volunteers and users. If you are not, what are you doing about it? (The argument that "I don't think we have those kinds of people here" does not carry much weight.) How many people with disabilities are involved in your activities? What access do we offer to people with special needs?

Charities Board – grants awarded between April 1996 and April 1997
(excluding Small Grants Scheme)

Size of grant (£)	No. of grants	% of total grants
0–5,000	424	10
5,001–20,000	769	18.2
20,001–50,000	921	21.6
50,001–250,000	1986	46.9
250,001–1,000,000	138	3.3
Total number of grants		4238
Total value of grants		£318,625,135

In this period the Charities Board also awarded 380 small grants with a total value of £826,206

- How does the project **encourage the people who benefit to be involved** in the planning and running of the project? You need to show that you have actively consulted potential users or beneficiaries in the planning of the project and how they will be part of the management, monitoring and evaluation of what is happening (e.g. by setting up a project steering committee which will include users).
- Does the organisation have the necessary **financial and management experience** to cope with the added workload and responsibility associated with a grant?
- Have you **researched the work of other voluntary groups** in your locality, and are certain that your project will not duplicate existing services?

Small Grants

Alongside the procedures discussed above, there is also a small grants programme which has been launched in Wales and is being extended to other parts of the UK. This runs continuously, and is not linked to the changing themes of the main grants programme. The small grants programme makes grants in the range of £500 to £5,000, and is open to organisations with an annual income of less than £10,000 (although if your income is less than £10,000 a year, you don't have to apply just to the small grants programme – you can also apply to the main programme). At the moment, the facts show that it is rather easier to succeed in getting a small grant than in getting support from the main programme. If you meet the criteria, there is a high chance of success. The application procedure is similar to the main programme, but with a simplified application form and a lower level of assessment. However, the same rules apply; if you get money from the main programme in Wales, you cannot get a small grant from the Wales board. You could get money from the Wales Board and a small grant from England if you had separate projects, one benefiting people in Wales and one for people in England.

Getting started

The first thing to do is to contact the NLCB to find out about future grants rounds. If you decide that a particular grants round is appropriate to your work, then contact the NLCB at the address below to receive guidelines for the particular grants round.

Read through the guidelines, paying particular attention to the criteria against which the applications will be assessed. If you still feel that your project fits within the priorities of the grants round, then make a decision to proceed, noting the timetable for receiving applications and all the information and signatures that will be required.

Carefully formulate the project that you wish to submit for consideration, and complete the application form answering all the questions as fully and as factually as you can. On key questions, such as the level of need, the degree of benefit, the extent of user involvement, your equal opportunities approach, the detailed breakdown of the budget, make detailed notes giving information in more detail than is required for the application form. This can then be referred to during the assessment process when particular questions are asked.

Send off the application form in the envelope provided, retaining a copy for yourself. This has to be sent by post, and cannot be delivered in person. It must arrive by the due date. Applications received late cannot be considered, whether or not the delay was your fault. Then wait to be contacted for the assessment process. You will hear whether your application has been submitted properly and can go forward for assessment. Once the assessment has taken place, you just have to sit and wait for the letter informing you as to whether the application has succeeded or failed.

The address to contact for general information is NLCB, 7th Floor, St Vincent House, 30 Orange Street, London WC2H 7HH. The telephone number for application packs is 0345-919191, and the enquiry line is 0171-747 5299. Packs are available in English and Welsh, in printed and audio form. The guide to each particular round is also available in Braille and large print, in a variety of minority languages, and in a special edition for people with learning difficulties.

Key requirements for Sports Council lottery grant

- It must be for a recognised sport only (from the Sports Council list).
- The project must have long-term financial viability.
- It must be a quality project.
- The proposal should have breadth of appeal and command public support.
- The proposed facility should be accessible.
- The proposed development should be relevant to the organisation's strategy and other plans.

Sports grants

In 1995, its first year of operation, one in three of applications to the Sports Council of England was successful, and 749 grants were made valued at £120 million, with a further £25 million being distributed in Scotland, Wales and Northern Ireland. All grants are required to be match funded. The Council provides a maximum of 65% of the project budget in most cases, but sometimes as little as 10%. The minimum grant is £5,000. Applications must be for capital rather than running costs.

The types of application that are likely to succeed cover a quite wide spectrum of activity. They can be on behalf of any recognised sport, which includes 112 different activities. The main focus for the board remains on the provision of facilities that are for the benefit of the wider community, which means for the recreational aspects of that sport rather than for the development of professional sport or the provision of spectator facilities.

In its first year 95% of the money was spent on this, but the situation is now changing. Revenue funding schemes are now being developed to increase excellence in various sports (following the disappointing performance of the British team at the 1996 Olympics). In England, the Priority Areas Scheme, which covers named areas containing over 25% of the population, encourages applications by requiring lower levels of matched funding.

There are a number of organisations interested in bringing sport to people with disabilities or to others, such as the unemployed or ethnic minorities who may have wider social needs. This idea of sports for social development is likely to become of increasing interest in distributing sports lottery money, as part of a strategy to distribute an increasing slice of the lottery cake to the poor. Applications for such projects might well fit within the criteria of the Charities Board as well as the Sports Council. However, the NLCB has indicated that it expects to see applications for sports-related projects going to the Sports Council rather than to itself.

Each of the four sports distribution boards (for England, Wales, Scotland and Northern Ireland) imposes somewhat different conditions. However, all projects require some sort of matched or partnership funding. For a local activity this almost inevitably means having the support of the local council, which may or may not have capital funds available to provide the counterpart funding.

Only capital projects will be considered, although the definition of what is capital is quite wide. This will include the building of new facilities or the upgrading of existing ones. The acquisition of rights or land are acceptable as is the purchase of equipment.

To apply, first get an application form from the relevant Sports Council. Applications are accepted at any time from almost any body. (See Useful Addresses for details of individual bodies.)

Arts grants

Arts grants, in a similar way to the sports grants, are handled by the four national Arts Councils (for England, Scotland, Wales and Northern Ireland). All grants have to be match funded from other sources, and most of the money is for capital, albeit defined in a broad way. There is considerable concern that the large amounts of capital grants will create pressure on trusts and companies for matching funding, and that the system favours those projects in local authorities rich enough to be able to provide matched funding. There is also a growing concern that there will not be sufficient income to run the capital projects once they are built. At the time the lottery was launched, there was a commitment by government that the arts funding available through the Arts Councils as grant-in-aid from government would not be affected by the arrival of lottery funds. However, since the lottery started, government funding for the arts has declined in real terms. Recently, access to the arts, bursary schemes to support young artists and a scheme to bail out arts organisations that have got into debt by paying off past debts and funding the plan to get the organisation back on to a sound financial footing, are being developed as additional themes.

Most of the grant money awarded in 1995 and 1996, the first years of operation, was for large-scale projects based disproportionately in London. It is not expected that this represents a preference so much as a bias in applications, and that as these large claimants get their long-planned capital developments funded, so the balance of the distribution of arts money may begin to shift. There is considerable public and media concern about the arts money going predominantly to fund the leisure activities of the rich, which will provide additional pressure for change.

The key requirements are that projects should:
- be for **capital programmes** (for revenue programmes, see Arts 4 Everyone below). Capital expenditure includes buildings work (new developments and refurbishment); the purchase of equipment or instruments or vehicles; the commissioning of works or art. All forms of art are included – from circus to video;
- offer the widest possible **public benefit** (including maximum access for disabled people);
- have **long-term financial viability**;
- involve **high quality in design and construction**;
- demonstrate a **high quality of planned artistic activity** and contribution by artists;
- be of **relevance** to other plans for the arts;
- meet a **demand** which is not currently met;
- demonstrate **proper planning** for education and marketing activity.

Almost any type of organisation may apply for a grant – there are a very few exclusions. The lower limit ranges from £2,000 to £5,000, depending on which Arts Council is being applied to. There is no upper limit. The largest grant awarded so far is the £78.5 million for the Royal Opera House redevelopment in Covent Garden.

Matched or partnership funding is required for all the boards and will vary depending upon the size of the grant. For small applications in England, for example, 10% is required while for larger ones 25% is the minimum.

Arts 4 Everyone

This is a revenue scheme in England which aims to reach new audiences and to involve new groups in the arts. The two parts of the scheme are

Arts 4 Everyone and Arts 4 Everyone Express and both look to encourage more young people to become involved in the arts. This scheme is particularly good for groups which may not have any experience of raising money for arts activities.

Arts 4 Everyone Express suits small projects looking for grants from £500 to £5,000. Applicants will not necessarily be arts groups, but may be voluntary organisations setting up a small arts project, perhaps for the first time. (Large, established arts organisations will be eligible under the larger Arts 4 Everyone scheme which gives grants from £5,000 to £500,000). Up to 20% of an A4E Express grant can be spent on overheads and administration, and a further 25% on equipment which is part of the project.

There is a matched funding requirement of at least 10% of the total cost of the project. At least 5% must be cash, and the rest can be in kind such as buildings, volunteer work or materials.

You cannot get an Express grant if you have received £5,000 for arts projects from any public source in the last three years, or if you have a fixed term, regularly funded or franchise status with the Arts Council, Arts Board or a local authority. The emphasis is on getting new organisations and new people involved in the arts.

Your project will qualify if it meets at least one of the following:
- encouraging and developing **participation** in arts activity – helping people take part in the arts through voluntary and non-professional organisations;
- getting more young people **actively involved** in arts and cultural activities – the intention is to support and develop the talents and skills of those under the age of 30;
- supporting **new work** and helping it develop its audience – the funds are intended to stimulate new work which is then promoted and presented in a way that builds an audience for it;
- building people's **creative potential** through training or professional development – including work experience, training, study or international exchange;
- **encouraging new audiences** to experience high-quality arts activity.
  (This applies more to A4E projects than for those under the A4E Express) The Scottish Dimensions and Advancement programmes are similar but by no means identical. Ring the Scottish Arts Council Lottery Unit on 0131-243 2443/4.

To apply for a grant from one of the Arts Councils you should first obtain an application pack which gives full details of the process. Addresses for regional Arts Councils are given at the end of this book in the Useful Addresses section.

Millennium grants

The purpose of the Millennium Fund is to help celebrate the passing of the old millennium and, presumably, the arrival of the new one. It will cease to exist on 31st December 2000. So far it has funded a small number of very large projects of national importance together with a number of smaller local projects, many of which have been in the area of the environment. However, by the time of publication of this book, its main grants programme will have come to an end. From 1st January 1997, the Commission will concentrate on three main objectives:

- **The Millennium Festival** to take place around the country in the year 2000, and an associated programme of national events from 1998 onwards
- **The Millennium Exhibition** to be held at Greenwich in the same year
- **The Millennium Awards Scheme**, the first round of which was decided at the end of 1996.

The Millennium Awards Scheme will be distributing around £10 million annually, and will survive the new millennium. It is intended to benefit individuals who have ideas for particular projects which will be of benefit to their communities. The first 13 awards schemes have been announced and others will follow. Each award scheme is organised by a different organisation on behalf of the Millennium Commission. There is not the scope here to cover the details of each scheme. To illustrate the diversity of the different award schemes, the first 6 schemes were:

- **Help the Aged Millennium Awards** (St James's Walk, London EC1R 0BE), who are making 1,250 awards for people over 60 to create new networks.
- **Raleigh International Millennium Awards** (27 Parsons Green Lane, London SW6 4HZ), who are making 360 awards for a 10-week overseas project.
- **The Royal Society/British Association for the Advancement of Science Millennium Awards** (BAAS, 23 Savile Row, London W1X 2NB), who are making 500 awards to people to bring science alive.
- **Earthwatch Millennium Fellowships** (57 Woodstock Road, Oxford OX2 6HJ), who are making 550 awards to teachers to make field trips.
- **The Farmington Institute Millennium Awards** (Harris Manchester College, Mansfield Road, Oxford OX1 3TD), who are offering 75 grants to primary school teachers working in religious education.
- **Techniquest Pantechnicon Millennium Awards** (Smart Street, Cardiff CF1 6BW), who are making 30 awards to science popularisers in Wales.

The Millennium Commission, Portland House, Stag Place, London SW1E 5EZ (0171-880 2001).

Heritage grants

The Heritage Lottery Fund is designed to support a wide range of activities within the purview of museums and galleries, libraries, manuscripts and archives, the national heritage and transport and maritime heritage. Uses of the fund include:

- the buying of **property**, and the repairing or the restoring of older properties
- acquiring **land**
- acquiring **objects** or collections
- improving the public **understanding** or access to buildings.

Only capital grants are made, although the first award, which was for a National Trust purchase in Scotland, included an endowment element to generate a continuing income for the maintenance of the property. The minimum grant is £10,000. Partnership or matched funding is required and is expected to be in excess of 25%.

As with some of the other Distribution Boards, the Heritage Lottery Fund has come under close scrutiny regarding the extent of the benefit it is providing to poorer people. One area in which the fund has specifically encouraged submissions is for urban parks. Guidelines have been sent to local authorities to stimulate proposals in this area.

Almost any organisation can now apply for a grant. A charity in occupation of a historic building might be eligible for a grant towards its restoration or refurbishment, for example. Contact the Fund to receive one of their application packs. Criteria for projects are that they:

- be for **capital expenditure** only
- provide **tangible benefits** to an existing heritage asset
- be **significant** at a local, regional or national level
- be for **public benefit**
- **improve access**
- have long-term **viability**.

The Heritage Lottery Fund, 7, Holbein Place, London SW1W 8NR (0171 591 6000).

Issues regarding the Lottery

1. *Gambling.* The most obvious issue that will concern many organisations considering seeking grants from the lottery will be the question of receiving money derived from gambling. Some religious based organisations are not prepared to accept money from such sources, and thereby exclude themselves from this enormous source of funding.

2. *Impact on the poor.* Many charities are there to relieve poverty, but what if the lottery itself is leading to increased poverty as a result of

increasing the spending pressure on the poor? National lotteries have been described as "the most effective way of redistributing money from the poor to the rich". Although the National Lottery involves over 80% of the adult population and attracts people broadly equally across classes, there is evidence that the poor are spending a greater proportion of their income on lottery tickets.

Alongside this there is the question of gambling addiction – people being attracted to buying several tickets for each draw, the extension to two draws per week, and the purchase of scratchcards which have proved enticing to some because of the instant prizes that can be won. The National Lottery is clearly extremely popular, but whether it is leading to an increase in poverty and adverse consequences for the most vulnerable sections of the community is an issue that each organisation must debate and decide for itself.

3. *Matched funding*, euphemistically called 'partnership funding', can be a headache for many. This is especially true for the arts and heritage funds, where large capital appeals have been launched by many successful applicants (including the Tate Gallery, Sadler's Wells and the Royal Opera House). This has increased the competition for voluntary funding, particularly for big gifts, trust funding and business funding for the arts. It has been suggested that there simply is not sufficient charitable funding in the economy to meet all of the matching requirements, and that some of the successful applicants may in the end fail through their inability to meet matched funding requirements.

Although there has been some relaxation in the matched funding targets as the lottery has progressed, and there is likely to be continuing change and a move away from providing capital funding only, the matching requirements are still an issue and a problem for both intending and successful applicants. The best advice that can be given is to raise your lottery funding early in your fund-raising timetable to give yourself sufficient time to meet any matched funding requirements, and be creative in how you account for gifts in kind or volunteer support that you receive.

4. *Capital versus revenue funding*. This will prove a problem for many projects. Until the arrival of the lottery, there was a dearth of public funds for capital projects, particularly for the arts, in sport and for heritage projects. The lottery has made funds available for capital developments beyond the wildest hopes of most fundraisers, and has enabled many projects to be taken forward which were stuck for lack of funding, but this will create a further demand for the costs of operating the additional capital facilities. Some boards are slowly moving towards revenue funding, and as the backlog of capital projects gets funded, there is likely

to be more movement on this score. As with the question of matched funding, this has not been an issue for the National Lottery Charities Board, which has always provided grants for revenue purposes and been prepared to fund up to 100% of the project.

5. *Impact on government funding*. Although the funds for good causes generated through the National Lottery are technically public funding, a commitment was given when the Lottery was agreed that the funds from the lottery would not substitute for government funding. It should be noted that in the arts, sports and heritage, the advent of lottery funding has coincided with a huge squeeze on public expenditure and a decline in traditional government funding for these purposes.

6. *Impact on fundraising*. When the lottery started, the NCVO began a research project to examine the impact on fundraising by charities. Further evidence of any impact would come from the Charities Aid Foundation's annual survey of charity income, published as *The Dimensions of the Voluntary Sector*. The evidence is not conclusive, nor could any decline in voluntary fundraising income be attributed directly to the advent of the Lottery. Some charities have suffered a decline; others have not, but the general fear that the public would confuse a lottery ticket purchase with a donation to charity has not been realised. There is always the challenge for fundraisers to respond to changing circumstances and trends, and the amount of income that could be raised through successful asking far exceeds any reduction caused by spending on lottery tickets.

The development of the National Lottery is being carefully monitored by Luke FitzHerbert with funding from the Joseph Rowntree Foundation. This includes logging every grant and assessing the geographic distribution of funding in relation to social need. This together with a myriad of facts and useful information on the lottery is published as *The National Lottery Year Book*, by the Directory of Social Change, 24 Stephenson Way, London NW1 2DP.

3.6 The European Union

The European Union provides a very large amount of money for social and economic development in member states, some of which is available to voluntary organisations. The amount received by the UK through the European Social Fund alone is estimated at £1.6 billion, which goes to local government, TECs, regional regeneration initiatives as well as to voluntary organisations. The annual reports of the top 500 charities show them receiving some £70 million annually from Europe – the actual total may well exceed this sum quite substantially.

Before deciding to look to Europe as a potential source of funding, it is important to recognise that getting money from Europe is a long, slow and painstaking process, which can easily end in frustration – though the rewards if you are successful can be great. There is increasing competition for the funds, and the programmes, priorities and guidelines are constantly changing – so it is important to keep up to date and to make contact as early as possible.

There are three main types of funding that are available from the European Union through the European Commission.

- *Budget line funding*. This involves an existing allocation of funds, and is open for organisations to put up proposals. There are a large number of budget lines, which we list later in this section, many of which may be of interest to voluntary organisations. These budgets are controlled by officials in Brussels operating within one of the Directorates of the European Commission. A full list of current budget lines and who to contact is printed here along with which directorate to contact. To an extent these can be influenced by MEPs in Strasbourg. Almost all applications have to have a significant transnational dimension – UK-only projects are unlikely to succeed.
- *Structural Funds*. These include the European Social Fund and the European Regional Development Fund and some lesser funds. These funds are controlled by member governments and need to be matched by funding within the UK. The European Social Fund (ESF) is of particular interest to voluntary organisations.
- *Contract and research funding*. This is for specific work which the European Commission wishes to commission, either on behalf of itself or another government. This is usually put out to tender. It can support research across a range of issues likely to be of interest to NGOs in the areas of health, environment, socio-economic affairs, energy, transport and medicine. There are also opportunities to host European Commission conferences and events.

The following is a list of European budget line funds

Budget	Line	Million Ecus	Contact	Brief description of budget line
A	3020	3	SG	Grants for advancing idea of Europe and to training European networks
A	3021	8	SG	Town twinning schemes in EU

Budget	Line	Million Ecus	Contact	Brief description of budget line
A	3040	1	SG	Support for internal non government youth organisations
A	3041	0	DGI	Support for international NGOs working for establishment of international criminal jurisdiction
A	3054	0	SG	Preservation of Nazi concentration camp sites as historic monuments
B2	1410	641	DGXVI	Interreg II: border development, cross-border cooperation and selected energy networks
B2	1420	70	DGV	NOW: new opportunities for women
B2	1421	132	DGV	Horizon: training orientation and jobs
B2	1423	58	DGV	Youthstart: job market
B2	1424	343	DGV	Adapt: adaptation of the workforce to industrial change
B2	1433	198	DGXVI	RETEX: diversification of zones heavily dependent on textiles and clothing
B2	1430	154	DGXVI	Rechar II: economic conversion of coal mining areas
B2	1431	183	DGXVI	Resider I: economic conversion of steel areas
B2	1432	189	DGXVI	Konver: conversion of defence industries
B2	145	144	DGXVI	Urban: city development: development of new small economic activities
B2	600	6	DGXVI	Promotion of inter-regional cooperatives

Budget	Line	Million Ecus	Contact	Brief description of budget line
B2	514	6	DGVI	Training and information for farming
B2	144	105	DGXVI	Regis II: ultra-peripheral regions
B2	605		DGXVI	Measures concerned with regional disparities for long-term unemployed
B2	146	313	DGXVI	Leader II: rural development
B2	147	243	DGXVI	Adaptation of small and medium enterprises to internal market
B2	602	2	DGXVI	Regional measures and studies
B3	1001	173	DGXXII	Socrates: education including Erasmus and Comenius
B3	1010	24	DGXXII	Youth for Europe III
B3	1021	152	DGXXII	Leonardo: training
B3	1000	4	DGXXII	General education measures and youth policy
B3	1020	3	DGXXII	General measures for vocational training and guidance
B3	1006	4	DGXXII	Promotion and safeguarding of less widespread language and culture
B3	1007	3	DGXXII	Co-operation with 3rd countries in education and vocational training
B3	1008	5	DGXXII	European Year of Lifelong Learning
B3	1025	12	DGXXII	European Centre for Development of Vocational Training
B3	304	3	DGX	Jean Monnet: European integration in universities
B3	2000	10	DGX	Raphael: community action programme in the field of cultural heritage

Budget	Line	Million Ecus	Contact	Brief description of budget line
B3	2011	2	DGX	European dimension in the audio-visual industry
B3	2001	8	DGX	Kaleidoscope 2000: artistic and cultural activities with a European dimension
B3	300	41	DGX	General information and communication work concerning the EU
B3	301	8	DGX	Information and documentation outlets
B3	302	8	DGX	Information programmes for non-member states
B3	2002	3	DGX	Ariane: support in field of books and culture
B3	305	4	DGX	Sport in Europe
B3	2003	6	DGX	Other cultural measures in Europe and co-operation with 3rd countries
B3	2010	60	DGX	Media II: measures to provide the development of the audio-visual industry
B3	306	50	DGXIII	PRINCE: information programme for EU citizens
B3	4000	7	DGV	Industrial relations and social dialogue
B3	4002	8	DGV	Meetings of workers organisations in the Community
B3	4012	9	DGV	Measures to achieve equality between men and women
B3	4010	11	DGV	Labour market, research, cooperation and monitoring
B3	4011	17	DGV	EURES: European employment services
B3	4103	9	DGV	Measures to combat poverty and social exclusion
B3	4113	1	DGV	Measures to assist refugees
B3	4102	13	DGV	Helios II: integration of disabled persons

Budget	Line	Million Ecus	Contact	Brief description of budget line
B3	4100	3	DGV	Measures and studies to assist families
B3	4104	7	DGV	Measures to assist the elderly
B3	4110	12	DGV	Free movement of workers, migrant workers and immigrants from outside EU
B3	4111	2	DGV	Social security and coordination of social security legislation
B3	4114	5	DGV	Measures to combat racism and xenophobia
B3	420	12	*	European Foundation for Living and Working Conditions
B3	4300	13	DGV	Public health, health promotion, information health education and training
B3	4301	12	DGV	Combating cancer
B3	4302	7	DGV	Health aspects of drug abuse
B3	441	6	DGV	European Monitoring Centre for Drugs and Drug Addiction
B3	4303	9	DGV	Combating AIDS and other transmissible diseases
B3	440	2	DGV	Combating drug abuse
B3	4313	2	DGV	SAFE: preparatory action for safety at work in Europe
B3	4310	5	DGV	Health protection, hygiene and safety at work
B4	304	16	DGXI	Fifth Action Programme on the Environment
B4	307	3	DGXI	Nuclear safety and radiation safety
B4	306	8	DGXI	Awareness and subsidies
B4	3200	45	DGXI	Life II: nature protection

Budget	Line	Million Ecus	Contact	Brief description of budget line
B4	3201	45	DGXI	Life II: environmental protection
B4	3300		DGXI	Cooperation on a civil protection and eco-emergencies
B4	3400		DGXI	Emergency aid to disaster victims in the Community
B5	100	4	DGXXIV	Representation measures and consumer redress
B5	102	4	DGXXIV	Consumer information and comparative tests
B5	105	5	DGXXIV	Quality, safety and monitoring of products and services
B5	800		SG	Cooperation in fields of justice and home affairs
B5	722	11	DGXIII	Information society
B5	321	3	DGXXIII	Operations relating to cooperatives
B5	300	41	DGIII	Strategy programme on internal market
B5	323	5	DGII	Growth and the environment
B5	325		DGXXIII	Conservation measures to assist tourism
B6	7111	110	DGXIII	Telematic applications of community interest
B6	7112	94	DGXIII	Advanced communication technologies and services
B6	7113	499	DGIII	Information technologies
B6	7131	119	DGXII	Environment and climate
B6	7141	230	DGXII	Biotechnology
B6	7142	126	DGXII	Biomedicine and health
B6	7143	181	DGXII	Agriculture and fisheries, food technologies, rural development

Budget	Line	Million Ecus	Contact	Brief description of budget line
B6	7151	171	DGXII	Technology for cleaner and more effective energy production and use
B6	7161	84	DGVII	Transport
B6	7171	18	DGXII	Targeted socio-economic research
B6	7211	145	DGXII	Cooperation with 3rd world countries and international organisations
B6	7411	268	DGXII	Training and mobility of research
B6	792	32	DGXII	Scientific and technological support to policies on competition issues
B7	2000	530	DGVIII	Food aid
B7	210	150	ECHO	Aid for developing countries hit by disasters or crises
B7	214	102	ECHO	Humanitarian aid to central and eastern European countries
B7	215	45	ECHO	Humanitarian aid to independent states of former USSR
B7	217	15	ECHO	Emergency aid for refugees and displaced persons in developing countries
B7	219	7	ECHO	Operational support and disaster preparedness
B7	410	403	DGI	MEDA: reforms to structures in non-EU Mediterranean countries
B7	320	150	DGVIII	Programme for reconstruction and development in South Africa
B7	321	20	DGVIII	Rehabilitation in South Africa
B7	420	52	DGI	Support for Middle-East peace process

Budget	Line	Million Ecus	Contact	Brief description of budget line
B7	212	60	DGI	Self-sufficiency for refugees and displaced persons
B7	501	16	DGI	European Training Foundation
B7	6212	5	DGVIII	Mother and child health care
B7	631	3	DGI	Population policies and programmes in developing countries
B7	520	498	SG	Technical cooperation with independent states of USSR
B7	542	35	DGI	Special aid to refugees in the former Yugoslavia
B7	545	35	DGI	Europe for Sarajevo
B7	6000	174	DGVIII	NGO schemes carried out in developing countries
B7	541	27	DGI	Reconstruction of the republics of former Yugoslavia
B7	6004	2	DGI	NGOs operating in Vietnam
B7	6005	1	DGI	NGOs operating in Cambodia
B7	6006	1	DGI	NGOs operating in Cuba
B7	6007	3	DGI	Aid and rehabilitation for Kurdish communities in Northern Iraq
B7	6008	2	SG	NGOs operating on behalf of Tibetan refugees
B7	610	2	DGVIII	Training and awareness raising of development issues
B7	615	10	DGVIII	EU action regarding anti-personnel mines
B7	6200	15V	DGIII	Environment in developing countries
B7	6201	50	DGI	Tropical rainforest
B7	6210	10	DGI	North-South cooperation in campaign against drug abuse

Budget	Line	Million Ecus	Contact	Brief description of budget line
B7	6211	15	DGVIII	Health programmes and fight against HIV/AIDS in developing countries
B7	632	3	DGI	Migration observatory and measures to deal with immigration
B7	6330	4	DGVIII	Small credit schemes for women in developing countries
B7	6410	75	DGVIII	Rehabilitation in developing countries
B7	6430	6	DGVIII	Decentralised cooperation in developing countries
B7	6440	2	ECHO	Aid for the people of Western Sahara
B7	500	1	DGI	PHARE: economic restructuring for countries of central and east Europe
B7	7000	11	DGI	PHARE democracy programme
B7	7001	5	DGI	Democratisation and peace process in republics of former Yugoslavia
B7	701	11	DGI	Democracy in independent states of USSR
B7	702	19	DGVIII	Human rights and democracy in developing countries
B7	703	14	DGI	Democratisation process in Latin America
B7	7040	7	DGI	Grants to NGOs for the protection of human rights
B7	705	9	DGI	MEDA democracy programme
B7	707	6	DGI	Rehabilitation centres and direct assistance to victims of human rights violations

This indicates the diversity of the interests of the EU in providing funding. Look for those budget lines which relate to your work; then contact the relevant Directorate for further information. Budgets are given in millions of ECUs. (Adapted from A *Guide to EU Funding for NGOs*, ECAS, 1996.)

Accessing the Budget lines

Budget lines are all handled by the various Directorates of the European Commission, or their Technical Assistance Units, which are based in Brussels. The lines are those that have been approved by the European Parliament as part of the budget process. In order to get access to these funds, there are a number of straightforward processes.

1. **Make an initial contact**. Contact the relevant Directorate or Technical Assistance Unit and ask to be put in touch with the individual who controls the budget. Telephone systems are good and English is universally spoken. The system appears to work in a rather more open manner than British Government departments. For many budget lines there will be written criteria or conditions.

2. **Discuss your project** with officials. Officials are well used to being seen in their offices and happy to discuss ideas, indeed many welcome it. You will inevitably then be required to send in a formal application and this is where the system can break down. The time it takes for a decision may well exceed one year (by which time your need may well have altered). This is something that officials are only too well aware of and will give you the latest lead times on.

3. **Lobby**. There may be value in lobbying MEPs – if you can find one interested in your project. They do not have any control over the budget, but officials are often influenced by their interest.

4. Get **agreement** from the appropriate Directorate to support your project. Once you have their agreement, you will be asked to sign a contract with the Commission with a number of conditions. Possibly the most onerous of these are the reporting

Directorate responsibilities of the European Commission

DGI	External relations
DGII	Economic and financial affairs
DGIII	Internal market and industrial affairs
DGIV	Competition
DGV	Employment and social affairs
DGVI	Agriculture
DGVII	Transport
DGVIII	Development
DGIX	Personnel
DGX	Information and communication
DGXI	Environment and nuclear safety
DGXII	Science and research
DGXIII	Telecommunication and IT
DGXIV	Fisheries
DGXV	Financial institutions and law
DGXVI	Regional policies
DGXVII	Energy
DGXVIII	Credit and investments
DGXIX	Budgets
DGXX	Financial Control
DGXXI	Customs and VAT
DGXXII	Enterprise, commerce and tourism

For full details of contact names and direct phone numbers, call the European Commission on 00-32-2-299 1111 or contact their office in London on 0171-973 1992.

requirements, which are especially complicated as they need to be done in your currency and in also in ECUs (to be renamed Euros after Monetary Union). Advice should always be sought about the problems of fluctuating exchange rates which can leave you with either less or more money to spend than you had planned on.

5. Have **trans-nationality**. Almost all the budget line funds require a trans-national aspect to the work they support. However, if you don't already have trans-national contacts, don't worry. Ask the officials to help you identify possible partners.

Accessing structural funds, including the European Social Fund

The structural funds are some of the largest of EU financial allocations but differ from the budget line funds in that the programme for the UK is wholly administered within the UK. Along with the European Regional Development Fund, which is only relevant to certain regions of the UK, the European Social Fund (ESF) is the main structural fund and has a number of different objectives (see box overleaf). Its main focus is on the labour market, supporting projects to help people back into work either through direct provision or by giving guidance. To make access to ESF easier, the Department for Education and Employment, which is responsible for the fund in the UK, has provided a number of routes which may be used by voluntary organisations. These are through intermediary organisations, called sector managers, whose task is to administer all applications within a particular field. Their responsibility includes publicising the programme, the distribution of guidelines and application forms and providing training on making applications. The whole system seems to be in a process of continual change which affects how it is run. For 1997, at least the main routes are:

- **Ecotec**, for programmes including Horizon, Now and Integra. Contact them at Priestley House, 28-34 Albert Street, Birmingham, B4 7UD
- **NCVO** for other voluntary sector projects. Contact them at Regent's Wharf, 8 All Saint's Street, London N1 9RL

Structural Fund Objectives

Objective	Purpose
Objective 1	Development in regions lagging behind. This includes the Highlands and Islands of Scotland, Northern Ireland and Merseyside.
Objective 2	Regions seriously affected by industrial decline including many parts of UK (e.g. the Midlands, the North of England, Scotland and Wales).
Objective 3	Combating long term unemployment, integration of youth unemployed and those affected by social exclusion (for all of the UK).
Objective 4	Facilitation of workers' adaptation and upgrade of professional qualification (for all of the UK).
Objective 5a	Adaptation of structures of agriculture and fisheries (for all of the UK).
Objective 5b	Development and structural adjustment of rural areas (many individual areas).
Objective 6	Economic adjustment of sparsely populated regions (in Finland and Sweden).

- **ICOM** for co-operatives. Contact them at 20 Central Road, Leeds LS1 6DE
- **local authorities**, for community projects
- **universities** and **colleges**
- **Training and Enterprise Councils** (TECs).

You are able to choose which route you take. Each has somewhat different guidelines and is suited to a particular type of organisation. The system is changing to a route that has become familiar to applicants to the Single Regeneration Budget (see section 3.4), where the Regional Office of Government will co-ordinate applications in the region. Details of how this procedure will work were not available at the time of writing.

It is important to note that you may well be able to access ESF through local authorities, Training and Enterprise Councils and universities by entering into a partnership with them. Many local authorities have officials or special departments set up to access European funding, and they are prepared to help small local voluntary organisations get their work funded through ESF money.

ESF grants are highly competitive and a rigorous points system is used in assessing applications. This means that you have to structure your application very carefully. Some successful projects play the score system effectively, appealing against scores that they feel will not enable them to succeed. Regional committees have been used to help identify and prioritise among the many competing projects.

Tips on making applications to Europe

- **Don't expect clarity**. Procedures vary from one office to another and even published guidelines change from time to time. Careful research is well worth the time and effort involved.
- **Talk about ideas not money**. Officials are there to develop their programme areas, not yours. You should be prepared to understand the wider picture, discuss your ideas and adapt them to meet their interests as well as yours for those budget lines and programmes where there are no clearly set out guidelines.
- **Don't be in a hurry**. Expect to be talking to officials early in one year to be getting money in the next year. Sometimes it can take far longer than this. Response times in some departments are very long. In other words, plan ahead.
- **Think partnership**. This is becoming increasingly important for projects. It takes more time, but adds strength to your application.
- **Check out which Directorate is the most likely to be interested** in your proposal, and approach them direct. Find out the name of the official, and speak to them directly. Try to go to Brussels to meet them. European officials are far more accessible than government officials in the UK.
- **Consider using an expert** to help you make your initial approach: there are now a good number of people based in Brussels and elsewhere who specialise in this sort of work. There are also a number of liaison groups who can advise you, such as the Euro-Citizen-Action-Service (ECAS).
- **Don't underestimate the red tape**. Ensure that you commence nothing before you have a signed contract. Be careful to charge only that expenditure which has been agreed. Be clear where your co-funding will come from. Finally, make sure everything is fully documented.

How to find out about EU funding

There are a number of useful publications that are available that provide detailed information. These are given in the Further Reading section at the end of this book.

How to get started with Europe

The following are the main steps you will need to take:

1. Find out as much **information** as you can on the many programmes and budget lines that connect with your work. There are considerable opportunities other than the ESF, and it is often those that find out first and make their approaches before others do that are successful. Useful starting points are suggested above. But you can also ask people in other organisations where they have tried, and try to learn from their experience.

2. Establish whether what you have in mind fits in with the **conditions** of that particular programme. This can be done by phoning the named contact person and by asking for any written conditions. In addition, ask for the application deadlines and for information on how soon a decision on any proposal submitted to them might be made.

3. At this stage, you may decide either to send in a **firm application** or, if appropriate, to submit a **brief outline** of what you are proposing. Firm proposals are most suitable where you are approaching a large funding programme with tight requirements. Where this is not the case, it may be better to submit an outline in order that you can discuss what you are planning with the relevant officials. It may be useful to meet officials in Brussels or the UK. This can be arranged simply and at relatively low cost (the opening of the Channel Tunnel has made contact with Brussels even easier). It will give you a chance to explain your ideas, and find out their priorities and any special requirements.

Issues on European funding

1. *Matched funding*. Most grants are given on the basis that matched funding will be found by the applicant organisation. Fundraising for this can sometimes be an insuperable barrier, and it is always important to assess the feasibility of raising the matching funds before making any decision to apply. Match requirements vary from 0% to 55% of the total project costs according to the particular budget line. Very often you will be able to use some existing funding that you are already receiving, perhaps from membership income or other undesignated funds or from funding received for a specific project where you are enlarging the scope and the budget of the project in your application to Europe. Wherever you get the funds, you will have to convince the Commission that the matched funding you have promised to raise actually exists, and there is a risk that you might have to return funds if the matched funding requirements are not fully met.

2. *A European dimension to the work.* Increasingly the idea of subsidiarity has meant that European funds have to be used for a project that is Europe-wide or covers several member states – apart from the Structural Funds, where the European funding is made available specifically for local and regional development projects within one member state. Any European involvement in a project which does not have a wider benefit would be seen as an intrusion into the member state's affairs. With some funding programmes there is a specific requirement for projects to cover more than just one member state, whilst in other cases, having this wider geographical remit will improve the chances of the project being funded. What this means in practice is two things:

■ you may be required to submit your proposal in conjunction with one or more partners from other European member states;
■ it is likely that your project itself will be more successful if it contains within it elements that strengthen links across Europe. This could involve the dissemination of your results on a Europe-wide basis; research involving the collection of information or comparison of practice across Europe; pilot projects addressing an important issue in more than one country; or exchanges between a number of member states.

The implication of all this is that you should build relationships with like-minded organisations across Europe even before you consider submitting a proposal. Go to conferences, use the e-mail, and develop contacts by joining any relevant Euro networks and liaison groups. This is not always as daunting as it sounds, as many organisations are in a similar situation to you, and will welcome the opportunity for contact and partnership.

3. *Delays in making decisions and providing funds.* The competition for funds and the relatively poor resourcing of the Commission itself often mean that applications take a long time to be processed. This causes difficulties for dynamic projects where, by the time that a decision is reached, you may find that your ideas have moved on and that you need to make changes to your application. Worse than this is the problem, particularly for the ESF, that grants may only be approved after the project has started – often three months or more into it. For a new project this may mean that you are not able to start exactly when you want – although you still have to spend your allocation within the European financial year (which runs from 1st January to 31st December) for which the grant has been awarded. For a continuing project it may mean that you have to finance the programme yourself and risk a negative decision. This situation is being remedied to some extent by some ESF programmes moving towards providing three-year funding.

3.7 International sources and funding for international work

International foundations

Most of the larger international foundations are based in the US, but there are many in Europe and a few in Japan which give internationally. The main sources of information on international foundations are:

- the **literature produced by the foundations** themselves, although only the largest publish reports or guidelines for applicants, and these may not always be in a language that you understand;
- a number of published **grant directories** produced by information and documentation centres.

Raising money from an international foundation is difficult. You are a long way away, and they may not even have heard of you – even though you are a reputable and successful organisation in your own country. Their view of the world and their priorities may be completely different from your own (there are a large number of US foundations, for example, promoting 'democracy' defined in different ways according to their political stance). Moreover they will prefer to give in their own country to organisations they know, even if there is an international purpose to the grant. Nevertheless, there are opportunities if:

- you are undertaking work in which they are particularly **interested**, where you can demonstrate your track record, expertise and international credibility;
- there is an **international dimension** to your work. The Medical Foundation for the Victims of Torture, the Oxford Centre for Refugee Studies and other organisations dealing with refugees, for example, are addressing an international problem of wide concern, and such organisations could expect to generate some of their funds from international sources. Equally rainforest preservation has attracted support from around the world;
- the project is **bilateral or trilateral**, comparing approaches and practice in different countries;

Five don'ts in dealing with overseas foundations

- Don't assume that because they are rich and philanthropic they will want to support you. They have plenty of other calls upon their resources.
- Don't write a begging letter out of the blue. You will either get no reply at all, or a certain rejection.
- Don't ask for money for your existing work. Try to find a project which has some international aspect or dimension and which they should be genuinely interested in.
- Don't leave it to the last moment. You will need plenty of time to make contact, discuss your ideas with them, even meet, before submitting a full proposal.
- Don't assume that they have heard of you and your work. You will have to build your credibility with them. Getting world renowned experts to endorse your work can help. Good literature clearly explaining the problem and how you work will help. Meet people at international conferences, and follow up on these contacts. If you travel abroad, set aside some time to develop contacts with larger foundations in that country. Telephone or fax them in advance and ask to visit, or even telephone them on your arrival to try to arrange an appointment.

■ the project is a **joint venture** between you and an organisation supporting similar issues in the home country of the foundation. They will have heard of your partner organisation, who can then act as a conduit for the money, a source of technical and other aid, and even a guarantor of the project's success, as they will be ultimately accountable for the grant. This is certainly a sensible strategy if you are serious about getting support from a US foundation, as most grants given by

---

Information on international foundations

United States

The Foundation Center publishes a wide range of grant directories, including an *International Funding Directory*. You can turn up at their offices (or at any of the documentation centres they run) and access information on particular foundations, including grants lists from previous years and current policies and priorities. CAF America, an affiliate of the Charities Aid Foundation in the UK, publishes *The Guide to Funding for International and Foreign Programs*. This prepares grant-seekers for an informed grant search with up-to-date information on over 600 foundations and corporate giving programmes. *US Foundation Support in Europe*, published by the Directory of Social Change, details US foundations with significant grant programmes in Europe.

The Foundation Center: 79 Fifth Avenue, New York NY 10003-3076, USA. CAF America, 90 Park Avenue, Suite 1600, New York NY 10016, USA.

Europe

The European Foundation Centre in Brussels keeps information on European foundations and can provide informal advice. The EFC publishes two directories which are distributed in the UK by the Charities Aid Foundation: *European Foundation Centre Profiles*, £40, which gives information on 112 foundations, and *Cultural Funding in Europe*, £35, which gives information on funders interested in the arts and culture.

The European Foundation Centre: 51 Rue de la Concorde, B-1050 Brussels, Belgium. The directories are available from the Charities Aid Foundation, Kings Hill, West Malling, Kent ME19 4TA.

Other countries

Other countries, such as Australia, Canada, Japan and South Africa have 'foundation centres' which act as focal points and publish information on foundations operating in their country. For further information on foundations in these countries, contact the following: **Australian Association for Philanthropy**, 4th Floor, 20 Queen Street, Melbourne 3000, Australia; **Canadian Centre for Philanthropy**, 1329 Bay Street, Toronto M5R 2C4; the **Foundation Library Centre of Japan**, Elements Shinjuku Building 3F, 2-1-14 Shinjuku, Shinjuku-ku, Tokyo, Japan; and for South Africa, there is *The Donor Community in South Africa: a Directory* which is published by the **Institute for International Education**, 809 UN Plaza, New York NY 10017-3580, USA.

US foundations for international purposes go to US-based organisations;

- you plan to approach US foundations on a systematic basis and feel that there is a real potential of attracting money from this source, you might then consider the possibility of setting up an **affiliate organisation** in the US as a vehicle for raising the money. By recruiting a US board of trustees and having a US correspondence address, you will make your cause that much more acceptable to US donors. You will also have a vehicle for tax effective giving by both trusts and individuals which complies with US Internal Revenue Service requirements.

Commonwealth Foundations

Some money is available to support projects that link together Commonwealth countries. There is no published grants guide to sources of Commonwealth grants, but you may be able to get advice from the Commonwealth Secretariat, Marlborough House, Pall Mall, London SW1Y 5HX.

There are a number of foundations which support travel, exchanges and community service in the Commonwealth. These are given in the Useful Addresses section at the end of this book.

Money for work abroad
UK trusts

Few UK trusts have significant overseas programmes. You will need to go through the directories of trusts to identify those that do. The following are some of the large UK foundations that support work in other countries:

- The **Aga Khan Foundation (UK)**: supports innovative, cost-effective and replicable projects in child development and education, family health and nutrition, rural development, skills training and professional exchanges in low income countries of Asia and East Africa. The Aga Khan Foundation has its own projects in developing countries, with branches in many countries in East Africa and South Asia, and also undertakes fundraising for these;
- **The Charity Know How Fund**: this is a fund created by around 20 leading UK trusts with funds matched from the Foreign Office, and is administered by the Charities Aid Foundation at their London office. The Fund provides small grants for the development of voluntary organisations in Eastern Europe and the former Soviet Union. Through East-West Link, it also encourages the sharing of technical expertise between UK voluntary organisations and partner organisations in the region;

- **Charity Projects**: this major trust supports projects in Africa which empower indigenous peoples through rights and building participatory institutions, small-scale trading initiatives which promote fair trading, education, training, literacy, improved communication and networking within Africa and projects addressing the needs of those suffering the effects of long-term disruption (e.g. war, AIDS and drought). It is the largest UK non-governmental fund for work in Africa, raising money through the Comic Relief telethon;

> ### Information on UK funding for work overseas
>
> - *The Third World Directory*: covers UK sources of funds for work in developing countries.
> - *Peace and International Relations*: covers UK, US and international sources for work relating to peace and security, which includes the strengthening of civil society in Eastern and Central Europe.
>
> Both books are published by the Directory of Social Change

- **The Gatsby Charitable Foundation**: supports projects mainly in the Cameroon and East Africa which assist farmers, artisans and small business;
- **The Paul Hamlyn Foundation**: their overseas policy is under review; up until now the bulk of the support to the developing world has gone to the Indian Sub-Continent to support dissemination of the 'Jaipur Foot' an artificial limb and other disability aids;
- **The National Lottery Charities Board**: their international programme launched in Spring 1997 provides £25 million for projects overseas, and is open to applications from UK based voluntary organisations. There were six themes in the first round of applications: community economic development; improving environmental management; empowering communities; advocacy work; promoting and protecting human rights; and enhancing the understanding of development. A seventh category available for projects in Eastern and Central Europe is capacity building amongst NGOs in these countries. The Board expects to run this programme annually;
- **The Joseph Rowntree Charitable Trust**: this trust has a particular interest in rights and justice, and promotes corporate responsibility, racial justice and disarmament issues in Southern Africa;
- **The Westminster Foundation for Democracy**: this was established by the British government with all-party support, with the aim of strengthening democracy overseas, and concentrates mainly on Central and South-Eastern Europe, the former Soviet Union and anglophone Africa.

Government funding for development

There are two main sources of government money for UK-based organisations for their work in developing countries:

- **The Joint Funding Scheme** of the **Department for International Development**. This can be contacted at Abercrombie House, Eaglesham Road, East Kilbride G75 8EA. The ODA itself is based at 94 Victoria Street, London SW1E 5GL
- **The Co-Financing Scheme of the European Commission**, which can be contacted at Unit VII/B/2, Directorate General for Development, Commission of the European Communities, Building G-1 Astrid 1/18, Rue de la Loi 200, B-1049 Brussels.

Both require matching funds to be raised or provided by the applicant organisation. They each have different guidelines, and an information pack should be obtained before applying.

Most of the wealthy nations of the North have government funding programmes that support development. These and non-governmental funding sources are listed in the following directory: *The Oxfam Handbook Resources Directory*, £7.95 from Oxfam, 274 Banbury Road, Oxford OX2 7DZ.

3.8 Membership and other bodies

Many people at work or play participate in some sort of group, and some of these groups play a significant role in supporting both local and national charities. Such groups may have money, influence and the human resources to support your organisation, and can make an important contribution to the success of your fundraising. There are many different organisations which can potentially fulfil this role. We are not able to list here all the possibilities, but we consider four main types:

- **Trade Unions** and **professional associations**
- **membership bodies**
- **local groups**
- **churches** and other religious bodies.

Unless there are clear links between what you are doing and the interests and concerns of these bodies, this area of fund-raising is not one with the greatest potential for generating funds. The amounts actually raised are likely to be relatively small, as compared with the other sources discussed in this chapter, and there are no clear statistics for the total giving from this source as a whole. Although there are thousands of small trade unions and other groups, the potential for raising money is relatively small and identification of donors can be difficult except at a local level.

Trade Unions have a particular basis for their giving. It is invariably an extension of their political stance and will be expressed by some campaign or sectional interest. For example, many unions contributed to the fight against apartheid by making donations to the voluntary organisations concerned with combating apartheid, in pursuance of resolutions passed on the subject at their annual conference. The structure of giving can be through the TUC itself, through the Union's headquarters, through local branches, or from the membership at large. Giving can be in the form of gifts in kind, advertising in brochures or journals, appeals to or collections from the membership, or a small cash grant. A possible place to get started is by using personal contact at a local union branch.

Professional associations are another potentially useful target. The Law Society (for solicitors), the Institute of Chartered Accountants, the Royal Institute of Chartered Surveyors, the Royal Institute of British Architects, the Institute of Practitioners in Advertising, the Institute of Personnel Management are just a few of the bodies you might consider. Some even have social responsibility programmes to encourage their members or member firms to get involved in community projects.

Membership bodies such as the Women's Institutes in rural areas and Townswomen's Guilds in urban areas, Young Farmers, Round Tables and Rotarians (and other similar bodies for men or women), Masonic Lodges (if you have an active supporter who is a freemason) can provide assistance of some use. Usually they don't make large grants themselves, but they can encourage their membership to support a particular appeal.

Each organisation has its own special characteristics, and time taken in getting to know these will pay off. If you are not successful in attracting the attention or interest of the national headquarters then you may well be able to get the support of your local branches or get invited to speak at a function. If you do get invited to speak, make sure that you bring along plenty of literature about your organisation and the sort of help you are looking for, which can be circulated to those present. This could be supplemented by having an article in a newsletter or being given access to write to the membership afterwards. A few organisations have been able to develop significant support from these sources, perhaps using enthusiastic volunteers who are willing to be used as speakers.

The Scouts, Cubs, Girl Guides, Brownies, sports clubs and dance schools can all help. You may be running a sponsored walk or a fun run, or a fete or a fair, and require personpower to staff the event. Such organisations can be a useful source of people, perhaps in return for a small grant to their own funds. The Junior League is an association of American wives committed to voluntary service, who may agree to provide similar support.

A wide range of church and religious bodies give to charity. Many local congregations decide to allocate an annual collection to a particular cause – and it certainly does not need to be religious in nature, and can be in addition to traditional collections, such as for Christian Aid Week. Groups within congregations often meet to explore particular themes and this will lead them, for example, to become interested in homelessness or poverty. At a diocesan and national level, the Churches have boards of social responsibility or their equivalent whose role is to mobilise support for social action. The Church Urban Fund, which is organised at a diocesan level, harnesses the support of Church of England members. Other religions and denominations too have extensive networks that can be supportive.

Support you can expect

Depending upon the organisation you are approaching, and whether its remit is local or national, you might look for a range of different types of support and assistance. These include:

- a **cash donation**, from a national body and from many local ones too
- a gift of **equipment** for a local project
- mobilising the involvement of **volunteers** for your project or for a fundraising event
- mobilising **support** from their members or organising a collection for you
- the **running of a fund-raising event** to support your work, for example by a Rotary Club
- an **invitation to speak** at meetings or to appeal to members
- an **endorsement** for your work.

A very useful first step is to get an invitation to address one of their meetings. They may hold meetings regularly, and always be on the look out for an interesting speaker. From this initial opportunity a number of offers of help may then develop. If a chance to speak comes up, do not turn it down. Some local groups are well attuned to the needs of local voluntary groups and may be willing to actively support your cause. This might involve appealing for your charity in pulpits, raising volunteers for a street collection, or running a fund-raising event.

Getting started

1. **Consider what support you are looking for.** Is it money? Is it people's time as volunteers? Is it access to a network of individuals with influence or contacts? Is it the availability of facilities you wish to make use of? Or is it an endorsement of your work?

2. **Review your own records** for the evidence of past support from the organisations you plan to approach, and from other similar organisations and networks.

3. **Check with your own committees and supporters** to see if they are members of organisations who might be willing to help. This can provide a first point of contact.

4. **Draw up a short list** of possible organisations who you believe have the resources or interest to support you.

5. **Make contact** at the appropriate level (locally or nationally) to try to establish what might be of interest to them.

6. Follow up this contact with a **specific proposal** but make this something that they could reasonably do for you.

3.9 Income generation and contracts

Income generation means developing or participating in some form of commercial enterprise, with the intention of making a profit. This could include:

- **charging the users** of a service for providing that service
- providing a service under some form of contract with another body such as a local authority
- **selling items made by the beneficiaries** of the organisations
- **selling items to members, visitors and supporters**
- earning money through **selling publications**, running conferences, providing training, undertaking research or selling consultancy within the organisation's area of expertise and competence
- entering into some **commercial activity** completely unrelated to the work of the organisation simply to make money.

Some reasons for income generation

- It can provide an additional independent source of income for the charity's work
- It forces a more commercial approach to the management of the organisation, such that the cost and value of each product is known
- It creates a more lively entrepreneurial approach
- There is positive feedback – the more successful you are, the greater the income return
- It fits within current culture and attitudes.

Some arguments against income generation

- It is far easier to ask if donors are around and with income generation, it's only the profit (after all costs) that is available to support the charitable work
- It makes the organisation too commercial, distorts priorities and distracts from the real agenda
- Too often it LOSES rather than makes money
- Many organisations do not have the skills, the management capacity or the organisational structure to undertake income generation activity successfully.

The profit from this commercial activity is then used to support the main work of the organisation. Put like that it sounds a simple and logical thing to do – and, in the right hands, and under the right management, it can be so – but the experience of many organisations suggests that successful income generation is more difficult than it seems, and that a lot of thought and preparation needs to be put into such an idea before it is put into practice.

If it was that simple to make money (for yourself – or for your organisation) then a lot more people would be doing so. It is quite possible for your organisation to become involved in an enterprise which not only makes no profit, but which becomes a drain on its resources and siphons off management and staff time which would otherwise be spent on the work of the organisation. This leads us to perhaps the most important warning for anyone thinking of developing a commercial activity: the enterprise is only a means of earning money for an end – which is to support the mission or main purpose of the organisation. If the enterprise becomes too demanding in time and resources, and if the income it generates is relatively small or non-existent, then stop.

The reasons for getting involved in income generation activity are in many ways the same as the reasons for fundraising:

- a question of **survival** (in an era when the competition for charitable funds is becoming greater, especially for smaller organisations)
- to generate **funds** for expansion and development
- to **reduce dependency** on outside support and on major grant sources
- to **build a constituency** of support in your local community
- to help **create a viable and sustainable organisation**.

In this section we will look at the different ways of generating income, and the risks and opportunities involved in each.

Making a charge for services

This involves asking the beneficiaries to contribute something towards the cost of the services that they are receiving (possibly where these were previously being provided free of charge). There is no problem under charity law with a charity charging for its mainstream services. This form of trading is often called 'primary purpose trading'.

A lot depends on the nature of the clientele of the charity. Many theatres and opera houses, for example, are constituted as charities, and people expect to pay for attending a performance. The income generated from ticket sales depends on the nature of the institution, but in general will vary from around 35% upwards of the total budget – the remainder coming from grants and sponsorship, and from the profits from the bar or restaurant, programme sales and other income generation activity.

Similarly, the major public schools are all charities, and they charge fees to their students.

The main argument against charging is that it can exclude those who are unable to pay (creating a charity for the rich). Trustees should consider carefully the implications of charging a fee on what the charity does and who uses its services, but the fact that the organisation is charging has a number of benefits:

- it forces the organisation to calculate the **cost** of providing the service. Oscar Wilde once said that: "a cynic is somebody who knows the price of everything and the value of nothing". One could turn this around and say that most charities know the value of everything but the cost of nothing. This is an unsatisfactory basis for running any activity;
- once the price is known, then the organisation can decide a **subsidy policy**. It is not a matter of the service either being provided free or at full cost. Decisions can be made on the level of subsidy and who it is directed towards. This could lead to a differential pricing policy (special rates for local residents, or concessions for UB40s and over 65s or for children and students), and can be an extremely effective marketing tool;
- it allows a **marketing budget** to be set aside for promoting the service. If income is going to arise from sales of the service, it creates a more powerful argument for setting money aside to promote it to potential customers;
- it creates a different relationship with the funder. The funder is assisting people who are prepared to pay for something, and not enabling a service to be doled out free of charge;
- it creates a different and possibly more equal **relationship** between the service provider and the service user;
- there is a demonstrable **commitment** from the service user, and an indication that what is being provided is what is needed and wanted.

This may be all very well for opera goers at Glyndebourne or Covent Garden, but many charities claim to be working with poor people – if not always the very poorest, at least with people with very little disposable income. It has been customary in the past to offer such services free, in the belief that poor people could not pay for them. Experience in the developing world, where grants are harder to obtain, has shown that even the very poorest may be prepared to pay something. A health scheme for tribal people living in the forests of South India is partly financed by a mutual insurance scheme where families pay monthly contributions; a village library scheme which is bringing books to people covers over half its costs from subscriptions from users.

Charities might ask themselves whether such techniques could be used in the UK, and especially where the alternative is that the service be withdrawn for lack of funding. Another consideration is the immediate and future benefit to the service user. If there is a demonstrable benefit, either in cost saving or income generation for the beneficiary, then it might be seen as reasonable to charge a fee – for example for the administration costs of a credit union. If there is a conscious decision to provide the service free, at least the matter of charging is discussed and the economics are worked out.

Contracts for services

The contract culture has been one of the major changes that has confronted the voluntary sector in recent years. Particularly in the provision of care in the community, but also extending into many other aspects of health, welfare, education and leisure activity, statutory authorities now work in partnership with independent providers to deliver a service. The authority becomes the 'purchaser', providing the funds and setting the guidelines for how the service is to be run and who is to benefit. The 'provider' may be a charity, a non-profit agency set up specially to deliver the service, or a commercial enterprise running the service and hoping to make a profit.

The provision of residential care for the elderly is now done, for example, by the local council itself, but also through a range of for-profit and not-for-profit providers. A suitable provider is selected by the purchaser, which is done either by negotiation or through some sort of tendering or bidding process. In awarding a contract, price is an important consideration, but issues of quality and the ability of the provider to run the service successfully will also be taken into account. Once a provider has been selected, a contract is then issued (this is sometimes called a service agreement), which defines the service to be provided and the payments to be received.

The contract culture provides many opportunities for voluntary organisations to access funding for their work, but it requires skills that are different from traditional fundraising to operate successfully. The payment is a payment for a service, which may have penalties for non-performance, and is not a grant. When entering into a contract, a provider undertakes to deliver a specified service with performance requirements which will be based on both quantity and quality. A meals-on-wheels service, for example, would be contracted to deliver so many lunches, but the quality of the lunch might also be defined by nutritional value and temperature.

When negotiating or submitting a bid for a contract, a charity should note the following:
- the arrangement is quite different from a funding relationship. It is a payment for a service, not a grant. The price is fixed at the outset, there can be penalties for non-delivery, and some element of risk is involved.

The terms of the contract are set by the provider, which is the other way around from a funding application where the applicant sets out what they want to do and seeks funding for that. You are working to their agenda and their priorities. It is a world of purchasers and providers, rather than funders and applicants. However, it is not always quite as clear cut as this. Some service-level agreements or funding agreements between funders and voluntary organisations, whilst not having the rigour of a contract, specify much more clearly what the organisation is expected to do with the money provided than would be the case with a grant (see below);

- in some cases the fact that you are a charity is irrelevant. The purchaser is buying the best available service at the best price. You won't get anywhere by simply saying "give it to us because the charity benefits";

- the way the bid is costed is extremely important. A charity could submit a bid at cost, at a profit, or even at below cost, hoping to raise the balance through fundraising. In most circumstances it is sensible to include an element of profit and even contributions towards management costs of the organisations, depreciation of equipment, research and development, the costs of bidding for contracts and other hidden costs. In some cases, there may be specific guidance in the bidding documents as to what costs are eligible; for example depreciation of equipment is sometimes not allowed;

> ### Guidance on contracts
>
> The Directory of Social Change with the National Council of Voluntary Organisations has published three handbooks and two resource packs to assist people with contracts:
>
> Handbooks
> - *From Grants to Contracts*, £8.95
> - *Getting Ready for Contracts*, £8.95
> - *Costing for Contracts*, £8.95
>
> Resource packs
> - *Finance for Contracts*, £35
> - *Managing Contracts*, £35

- the contract work may be a diversion from the real mission of the charity, and be undertaken solely because the money is there. This was a real worry in the days of the Manpower Service Commission's job creation schemes, and is something that trustees should review today in the context of the contract culture;

- because finding running costs is a problem for many charities, they are seeing contract work as a solution. They are often put in competition with one another to obtain contract work. For example, the three main advice work groupings (the Citizen's Advice Bureaux, the Law Centres and Independent Advice Centre services) were asked to bid to run the advice services in Lambeth. In such circumstances, there is a pressure to lower your bid in order to get the work, with the hope that any shortfall can be fundraised. This puts charities in an extremely difficult situation. It is not a proper use of charity funds to subsidise public sector services, and underfunding can soon lead to financial crisis. It is natural to do what you can to get the contract – and the larger charities with reserves or a well-resourced fundraising department will always have an unfair edge.

There are other examples of charities being bullied by purchasers. One charity was asked to provide a complete statement of costs that had been incurred in running a contract. Despite the fact that the purchaser had been extremely happy with the service delivered, when they wanted to renew the contract, the price offered was reduced to the cost price. Desperate to get the work, the charity agreed to this. This sort of situation should not be allowed to occur, as organisations will find it hard to survive in the long-term, if they are continually being paid cost price only. Commercial providers would not tolerate this sort of behaviour.

Exploiting skills and expertise

Many voluntary organisations have specialist skills and expertise which derive from their working methods and experience, and it is possible to market these at a profit to others. This can be an important part of the dissemination process, encouraging better working practice, and enabling other similar projects to be developed, or it can be done simply as a means of income generation. Home Start Consultancy, for example, is a resource centre for local Home Start projects, providing them with training and support – for a fee – and the Child Poverty Action Group provide training on welfare matters and publish the *National Welfare Rights Handbook*. Both these organisations are exploiting their expertise whilst directly pursuing their mission.

The following opportunities exist for exploiting expertise:
- organising training courses and workshops
- organising conferences
- selling publications
- offering consultancy.

The following should be taken into consideration when deciding how to proceed:
- is there a **market** for what is being offered? And if so, will it pay an economic price? As with other forms of income generation, it is extremely important to know the costs involved. If you can provide something that people really need or want, that is a good starting point;
- does the organisation have the **marketing skills** and the **administrative capacity** to make a success of the venture or would it be better to link up with another organisation to assist;
- is there a **marketing budget** to ensure that people know about what is on offer and that they have a means of responding? Too many

organisations produce a publication, for example, and only then think about what to do with it. If they had thought about marketing at an earlier stage, they might have created a budget to pay for this;

■ is what you are planning one off? Or can it be **repeated** in the future?

Selling products made by beneficiaries

There are all sorts of situations where an organisation has something to sell as a result of its work with its beneficiaries:

■ products made in **sheltered workshops** for persons with disabilities or impairments

■ products made in **rural development projects** in the developing world

■ **training programmes**, that develop skills with the long term unemployed or people with special needs.

■ the **sale of produce** from a city farm or community garden.

The goods being produced and sold can be the main purpose of the enterprise, or simply a spin-off benefit. But it is important to ensure that they are of marketable quality, and that there is a market which can be reached – whether through a retail outlet, by mail order to supporters or by wholesaling the merchandise to a retailer.

Selling gift items to supporters

Some of the larger charities raise money through catalogue trading, where new goods are offered to supporters and to the general public by mail order, or as in the case of Traidcraft (which sells products from southern rural development projects to northern customers) through local agents. Successful charities may earn as little as a 10% profit from trading in this way, since the cost of the merchandise, the marketing of it and the management of the operation have to be taken into account. It is often the associated donations that purchasers add to the purchase price that brings any profit at all. The following are some key points.

■ *The merchandise*. When selling goods in this way, high standards are needed. The goods are described in print and have to live up to their description when received by the purchaser. If they don't, there will be disappointment, and it will reflect badly on your charity. The goods should also in some way aim to reflect the values of the organisation – either in the use of materials (recycled paper, for example) or through the design. The items in the catalogue should be conceived as a range, rather than be a collection of unrelated products, and the range must appeal to the target market. The goods must be available in sufficient quantity to meet likely demand, or a serious loss of confidence will arise, and the cost must be low enough in relation to the selling price to give the possibility of a profit.

Promotional items that can be sold to raise money with the charity's name, logo and message

- Greetings cards
- Calendars
- Diaries
- Address books
- Pens and pencils
- Tee-shirts
- Wallets
- Mugs
- Posters

■ *Promotion*. Merchandise can be sold successfully through charity shops, but there are tax implications unless the shop is selling mainly donated goods or items produced by the beneficiaries of the charity. The more common way of promoting and selling gift items is through a catalogue. Unlike a charity shop where customers can walk in off the street, a catalogue needs vigorous promotion. The mechanism normally used is direct mail, the aim being eventually to build up a list of regular purchasers which will create an assured market for the merchandise. Although some sales will be made through word of mouth and personal contact, most will be made as a result of sending the catalogue to previous purchasers, to your supporters and to other likely mailing lists.

■ *Control and administration*. The management of catalogue trading involves a major buying operation, with all the control and cash flow worries that are associated with that. Then there are the warehousing and order processing systems required which for catalogues of any size can be a major logistic operation. There are the questions of proper pricing, cost control and good management of what is a business activity, very different from the normal work of the charity and perhaps requiring quite different skills. Finally, there is the question of how to finance such a fluctuating business, where the purchases may need to be paid for well in advance of the revenue actually being received.

On a more modest level, many smaller charities produce and sell some of the following in an attempt to raise money:

- **Christmas cards** and **gifts** to their supporters
- **souvenir items** to visitors (at heritage sites, museums, arts centres, etc.)
- **publicity** material, such as tee-shirts and lapel badges.

Done well, all these can generate useful income for the charity. In addition, the items can carry a logo, a slogan or a message, thereby publicising the cause. But you need to be clear at the outset whether you are producing and selling the items to raise money or for publicity purposes. Sometimes a charity gets into this sort of trading because they believe that their supporters want them to, or they see other charities doing it and feel that they ought to. They can end up selling quite small quantities of Christmas cards, for example, and be making a loss and involving themselves in a lot of worry and management time. This becomes a waste of effort, which could better be used more effectively to ask people for money.

This form of trading at whatever level it is carried out does not directly further the work of the charity. To that extent it is a marginal activity, and its success should be judged by the amount of money generated in return for the effort, capital, risk and management time put in. It is also an activity which cannot always be carried out directly by the charity itself, and a separately managed and funded trading company may need to be set up (this is discussed below).

Charity shops turning donated gifts into cash

One common area of trading for a charity is running a charity shop, selling donated items such as second hand clothes, in order to turn the donated goods into cash.

Most charity shops are simply a retail outlet, selling merchandise to generate a profit for the charity. Some aspire to do more than this by being an information point, promoting the cause and the work of the charity, and perhaps recruiting new supporters. Whatever the purpose, running a shop requires a considerable management effort. The following are some of the key factors in doing it successfully.

- *Location*. Finding the right location is essential. The shop must be sited in a place that can attract passing trade, must be near enough for the voluntary helpers who will staff it, and you have to balance these needs with the rent.

- *Staffing*. Most charity shops depend extensively on volunteers for their staffing. The usual pattern is to employ one professional manager for a shop of any size, who will co-ordinate a team of 20-40 volunteers. Some shops have a separate volunteers committee which takes responsibility for running the shop. Training, recruitment, supervision and management of this whole group of people is a key determinant of success.

- *The merchandise*. Charity shops tend to sell three types of merchandise: goods donated to the charity by well-wishers in order to raise money (such as second hand clothing, household items and jewellery); goods produced by the beneficiaries of the charity (for example in workshops for the handicapped and rural development projects); and goods produced by the charity (such as greetings cards). The quality of the merchandise is an important factor, and this is particularly true where the shop is selling donated goods which should be cleaned, repaired or checked, sorted and priced before they are sold.

For further information, read *The Charity Shops Handbook* published by the Charities Advisory Trust, who also coordinate the Charity Shops Group, a forum for those charities (large and small) who are running charity shops. Further details from the Charities Advisory Trust, Radius Works, Back Lane, London NW3 1HL.

Letting space in a building

Some charities are fortunate enough to own premises which they can let out to generate an income. There are several ways of doing this:

- a strictly **commercial letting**, where the tenant pays the landlord a rental which (after the costs of running the building) is used to support the work of the charity. Technically this is investment income, but both the tenancy and the building have to be managed properly;
- letting out the **premises** to further the work of the charity. The charity itself may create independent projects which will operate from the building, and which will have their own budget and be able to contribute a share of the rent. Alternatively it may find other organisations which are running services that it wishes to be associated with as part of its work, for which it can offer space in the building. Here the motives are twofold: to ensure that the project or service contributes towards the rent, and to further the work of the charity;
- hiring out **conference and seminar rooms** to other charities and commercial users. This can be part of the charitable work of the organisation (for example, a local Council of Voluntary Service providing facilities to support local voluntary organisations), or it can be a commercial activity;
- running a **commercial service** on the premises, such as a print shop or a community cafe, either on a commercial basis or somehow linked with the charitable work of the organisation.

It may be possible for a charity to consider acquiring or renting premises which are larger than it needs for its own work, as a mechanism for generating income for its work (in one or other of the above ways). If you have the capital to invest, this can be an interesting strategy for creating sustainability. If you are leasing the building, there will be an element of risk, in that you are committed to paying the rent on the larger building. Two things are important if a success is to be made of the venture:

- That the additional costs can be more than met from the income generated.
- That the building is managed properly and be kept in good repair.

Running a service as a business

A well known national charity runs a specialist medical facility for children with multiple disabilities. The facility is acknowledged as a centre of excellence. It found its income was falling due to a shortfall in places being taken up by local authorities – as a result of spending cuts. The immediate response to this was that money would have to be raised to make up the deficit. But it is not a particularly good idea to go to funders only when your service delivery targets are not being met. A marketing approach to the problem might involve thinking of yourself as an airline, and trying three new approaches to win back the business you have lost:

- 'commercial espionage': find out as much as you can about the purchasing habits of your customers, to see what other services are on offer, how they compare for quality and what price they are being offered at. This information can be researched cleanly and honestly;
- a 'frequent flier club': to lock in your major customers through discounts linked to scale of purchase and forward commitment. In this way you may be able to assure a large part of your annual income;
- a 'bucket shop': to sell off any vacancies at the last minute at a discount, in order to ensure that you are operating at or near capacity. This can be important when it comes to raising money, as well as being a sensible use of resources.

This approach is something that many theatres adopt in their marketing. It can equally be used by social welfare providers.

For further information on this, Community Matters produce a book on *Managing your Community Building*, £13.95, which is obtainable from the Directory of Social Change.

Problems and issues

1. The need for an entrepreneurial approach

For so long the reliance on grants has discouraged an entrepreneurial approach amongst many voluntary organisations (except for the honing of skills in how to approach donors and package proposals for them). A very definite change in approach and attitude is needed if you are going to make a success of income generation.

Voluntary organisations have usually been run by budgeting their expenditure against available funding – the concept of a revenue budget with targets for income to be generated is often foreign. The idea of using marketing and selling techniques to generate an income (rather than fundraising) and of investment (spending money now to produce a return later on) will need new skills and new approaches. This is well illustrated by the following example.

It can be a hard for many organisations who are convinced of the value of moving towards a greater financial self-reliance to actually implement such a strategy. The decision to do this involves more than simply seeking alternative sources of funds. Developing a new approach to the funding of the organisation can be very difficult, and it is easy to slip back into running to donors when you are short of money. A decision to travel this road has to be a serious one, arrived at after serious consideration of all the options, and with a clear understanding of the organisational changes that will be required. It is often a good idea to undertake a serious strategic planning exercise first.

2. Kinds of people and skills needed

Very few voluntary sector people have the necessary entrepreneurial approach for successful income generation. It is possible that you will need to extend your recruitment to people from the private sector, rather than recruit traditionally from voluntary sector sources. Not all business people are interested in profits and personal income alone. There are many who are interested in working for a good cause, who share the values and goals of the voluntary sector for a better society, and who may have the skills you need to succeed.

3. Losing the vision

Voluntary organisations are driven by a shared vision of a better society.

The work that they do, for the most part, reinforces that vision. The health outreach, the credit scheme, the welfare programme, for example, bring project workers into contact with their client group – the needy – and reinforces their motivation to continue doing the work. When the main purpose becomes making money (albeit that the money is being made in the course of the work of the organisation), a new set of attitudes starts creeping in – a more commercial approach to the work – and many organisations become concerned that they will lose their internal cohesion which comes from the shared vision.

Because of this, some organisations prefer to separate out the income generation from the rest of the work of the organisation, and they do this even where there is no legal requirement to set up a separate trading operation. They recognise that a different kind of staff will need to be hired, and that reward systems may be different, with salary structure, incentives and benefits likely to evolve differently.

Charity law

Provided your income generation activity involves the pursuit of your charitable objectives (this is sometimes known as primary purpose trading), or the sale of products made by beneficiaries or the sale of donated goods, there are no problems. However if it involves activities outside these three categories, then there may be charity law problems and tax problems. This will only be significant where:

- the **trading activity is substantial and involves the use of the charity's assets**. It is not a proper function of a charity to get substantially involved in a non-charitable activity (trading), or to apply its assets for this purpose;
- a **profit** is being made, which would be taxable if made directly by the charity itself. Very often after allocating all relevant overheads, a charity will find that it is not making any real profit from the activity. Where a substantial profit is being earned, then an associated but separate trading company may be needed to avoid paying tax;
- the **charity's resources are being put at risk**. Where the trading activity is substantial, then this could involve a degree of risk. A loss might be made rather than a profit, and there are many cases, including some large well-known national charities, who have run up large losses on their trading which have had to be made good out of charitable funds.

In such circumstances, a separate trading company might be needed as the vehicle for undertaking the trading. This is tax effective, as the profits can be covenanted or Gift Aided to the parent charity. This is an extremely technical area, and good professional advice is required on the best structure for carrying out the trading. For more detailed information, read

Sources of loan funding

Most voluntary projects will not qualify for a commercial loan from a bank, or the bank will require a personal guarantee from the trustees or other persons. There are a number of loan schemes that have been developed especially for voluntary projects:

- **The Triodos Bank**, a Dutch social bank which merged in 1995 with Mercury Provident which had been operating in the UK in 1974, lends to charities, community projects, environmental initiatives and social businesses. It provides mortgage, secured loan or overdraft finance. It also arranges lending schemes where the bank mobilises supporters who are prepared to make 'socially responsible' loans to the project at low interest. It has launched an Earth Saver Account with Friends of the Earth to direct savings into renewable energy and conservation projects in the UK. It has an associated Triodos Foundation to provide grants alongside the loans that the Triodos Bank makes. Contact Triodos at 11 The Promenade, Bristol BS8 3NN.

- **The Local Investment Fund** (LIF) is a £3 million charitable loan fund established jointly by the Department of the Environment and the private sector (the major supporter is the NatWest Bank, who piloted an earlier scheme in the North East), managed by Lancashire Enterprises plc and ICOF, and administered by Business in the Community. Loans are made to community-based enterprises which can demonstrate economic viability, and this is interpreted flexibly. Money is lent at commercial rates, and generally within the range of £25,000 to £250,000. Access to specialist advice is offered as an 'after-sales service'. Contact LIF at Business in the Community, 44 Baker Street, London W1M 1DH.

- **Investors in Society** has been established by the Charities Aid Foundation (CAF) to provide "low cost, sustainable finance for charities, to bridge the all-too-frequent gap caused when urgent needs cannot be met by traditional sources of funding". The scheme is funded by interest-free loans and donations, and CAF is encouraging its individual and corporate clients to support the scheme. Contact Charities Aid Foundation, Kings Hill, West Malling, Kent ME19 4TA.

- **ICOF** (Industrial Common Ownership Finance) was established to provide investment finance for common ownership schemes. It manages a number of revolving loan schemes, often on behalf of local authorities. Some are specific to cities such as Manchester, London and Cardiff, and others cover larger areas such as the West Midlands and South Wales. For those areas not covered by specific loan funds, it makes loans through the ICO Fund. A recent initiative has been to establish ICOF Community Capital to make loans for community and social projects in the 'social economy', particularly to agencies providing social and welfare services in the 'contract culture'. This is quite a small fund at the moment, and its success will depend on ICOF's ability to attract investors for this fund. Contact ICOF, 12-14 Gold Street, Northampton NN1 1RS.

- **Your own supporters** can be invited to make an interest-free loan to you. They will not be charged tax on the notional interest forgone so long as the letter of loan is worded correctly. For any substantial loan, professional advice on the terms of the loan should be sought, to protect the interests of the lender. A loan can be subsequently converted into a gift, but if it is to qualify for Gift Aid tax relief (for amounts over £250), the loan has to be repaid to the charity and the sum given as a gift in two separate transactions.

Charity Trading and the Law, published by the Directory of Social Change, which is a practical guide to the legal, fiscal and charitable status implications of undertaking trading.

Sources of capital

The most important step in getting started in income generation is making the decision to do so. Trying to generate your own income for your organisation is likely to be very different from your usual methods of fundraising from donors – either domestic or foreign. But once this decision has been made, where can you find the money which will help you make the money?

1. From borrowing, renting or use

Do not always think in terms of owning capital in order to generate income. It is equally possible to lease or rent property and equipment. It is also possible to borrow the money you need. There are a number of 'socially responsible banking services' that specialise in borrowing and lending out money to good cause organisations at below commercial levels of interest and without the onerous guarantees or security that commercial lenders may require. The pioneer in this field was Mercury Provident, now operating as Triodos. Two interesting developments here are the social banking service being offered by the Charities Aid Foundation, which has ambitions to develop substantially in this area, and the loan fund operated by Business in the Community to support regeneration initiatives. (See opposite).

2. Savings

If you are thinking of acquiring money in order to make money, then consider how you can build up your own capital fund from a variety of sources to create a sufficient sum to invest in the enterprise. Such a capital fund might be built up by budgeting for a surplus each year in order to create a reserve fund. It might also be possible to allocate a small percentage of the charity's income across the board to a development fund (this should not be hidden from funders, but could be justified as a R & D cost). This needs to be done tax effectively, and good professional advice is essential.

3. Grants

The thinking of funders has become astonishingly conditioned to the idea of 'projects' (i.e. time-limited agreements whereby money is given to an organisation to enable that organisation to deliver certain specified goods and/or services to certain specified people). Most donors proclaim their belief in the virtues and value of the voluntary sector, and the importance of promoting and supporting civil society but very few of them have followed the logic through to the extent that they are prepared to invest in a sustainable voluntary sector, rather than just covering the costs of discrete time-limited projects delivered by a specific voluntary organisation.

The donor's usual expectation is that, once the funding for a particular project is finished, the organisation will find funding from somewhere else for another project. Very few have thought about how to promote the organisation's financial self-reliance and ensure its long term viability. Organisations need to start educating their donors about the value of capital grants to provide the investment needed to set themselves up with a source of sustainable income.

4. Fundraising Techniques

4.1 Fundraising through local groups

Whether you are an established national organisation or a small group just starting out, raising money locally through events and collections can be an important source of income. However, organising a fundraising event or collecting money locally requires time and effort.

There are two main approaches: using staff to do the organising, or getting a group of volunteers to take responsibility for raising the money. Much depends on the scale of the fundraising. Using paid staff will cost more, and should only be considered where large sums of money are being raised. Using a group of volunteers can make a lot of sense, particularly if you can find people with the right abilities and enthusiasm who are prepared to do the fundraising work for you.

Groups of volunteers can be given responsibility for running a particular event, or for raising money in a specified area. You can establish local fundraising groups in different towns and cities, or in different areas of the same city. They will work largely independently, but you will need to provide proper management and some back up in the form of literature, ideas and advice. Another benefit in working with volunteer groups is that the more groups you establish, the more money you will raise.

Setting up a local fundraising group requires effort and patience. It can take a long time to get the group established and raising money successfully, but the investment can be worth it. The volunteers you recruit, if properly supported, may stay involved with your organisation for many years.

> **Getting started**
>
> To establish local fundraising groups, you need to:
> - find people who are willing to put in the time to raise money for you, and in particular
> - find someone to lead the group (as the Chair)
> - establish the group with a constitution, which defines how it will work and its relationship with the organisation it is raising money for
> - help the group identify appropriate (and ideally repeatable) fundraising activities
> - supervise and support the group in its fundraising work.

Getting a local fundraising group going

The following story illustrates how you might set about forming a local fundraising group. The key is to follow up on every idea or contact, and to ask persuasively.

My brief was to form a fundraising group in a large city. Where should I start?

My usual way of working is to check my address book and contact my friends for their suggestions. I knew one person in the area who was worth approaching; a priest I had known for thirty years. I felt sure that he would set me off in the right direction. I made an appointment to see him.

The meeting gave me a detailed insight into the social needs of the town, and was a fascinating morning, but I left realising that anyone the priest knew who was at a loose end would have already been snapped up for the much needed social work of the parish.

I wrote to a Member of Parliament I had met some 25 years ago, to a business man from my home city who is on various local boards in the town and to other luminaries. All wrote back most helpfully, but only one suggested any specific people to visit. I followed this up and it led me to a wives' group which I don't think wanted me to recruit their people as they met for purely social reasons. However, through this contact I did meet one person who said that she would be free to help in a couple of years. Too long to wait, alas!

In driving around the well-heeled suburbs, I felt that there must be someone in there longing to help the cause. But who? And when would I find them?

Then I was invited to speak at a Rotary luncheon. My hopes were high. Unfortunately the meal was so delicious and the company so convivial that my allocated time to speak about our charity was severely cut, and the one-to-one cultivation didn't happen (no-one 'offers' on these occasions!).

My big break came in a totally unexpected way. I was arranging for a group of people from another town to visit a city child-care project. I said that I would send them a map to show the location of the project. "Don't worry", was the reply, "I was brought up in the city". This was my cue to act. "Do you know anyone who lives here who is at a loose end and could help me form a fundraising group?", I inquired. I obtained the name of a relative and another name.

I set off with new enthusiasm having ascertained that the first person would probably be in on a certain morning. I knocked on the door, and although the lady had been rung by her relative to explain who I was and that I would be making contact, I received a strict telling off for calling unannounced. I apologised and, grasping my diary, suggested that we might find half an hour for a chat another time. "Half an hour!" was the horrified reply, "Where have you come from?" I explained, and said it was about 45 kilometres away. It must have sounded like the other side of the world, as I was invited into the kitchen for coffee. Immediately we got on like a house on fire. We might have known each other all our lives. How easily I could have fled at the first tirade! Names and suggestions flowed and an agreement that she was willing to be part of the new group in spite of her numerous other commitments.

The visit to the next person was also quite alarming. I was invited into the house. "I was wondering if you know anyone who would be free to join a fundraising group?", I asked. "Are you asking me, or asking me if I know anyone?" I kept my cool and said, "I was really asking you if you knew anyone, but if you are able to help as well that would be wonderful!". Not only was she willing to help, but she thought deeply, and made suggestions of others who might be interested. She contacted them. She telephoned me. I visited most of the people she suggested. Others I just spoke to on the telephone. All agreed to help.

The most exciting introduction was to a person who had that very month given up her job (although still young and very active!). She was an obvious candidate to take the chair. Soon we had twelve people and were able to have our first meeting over lunch, kindly arranged by one of the group. This is always a highly charged occasion. Are people going to get on well together? Is anyone going to offer to be Secretary (and be responsible for the dreary organisational work)? I had already arranged that three of the people take on the posts of Chair, Treasurer and Secretary after some undercover work beforehand. The democratic procedures can follow once the group is established – at future AGMs.

The first fundraising function was fixed for a few months later, and all members worked well together and enjoyed themselves. My initial idea was to hold two functions a year, and also to sell Christmas cards and perhaps to distribute some collecting boxes. The first two events organised within the first 13 months raised £1,200 and £1,400. We were on our way.

Recruitment is the key to success. You may need to find people to serve on committees and fundraising groups or you may be looking for one key person to chair a committee or take the responsibility for a particular area of fundraising. You will want to identify the skills and resources that they will need for the job (time available, use of their homes, their contacts, ideas, initiative, enthusiasm, and so on). You should allow yourself plenty of time for this. You can also ask the people you contact to suggest other people (their friends and other people who they think will be able to do a good job).

As the group begins to organise fundraising events (and starts to be successful), you will find that there will be more interest in what you are doing and more people will be come forward to volunteer their time. At any stage in the process, good publicity in the local press or on local radio can bring further support. If you are setting up a local branch of a national organisation, a good starting point are the names of existing supporters who live in the area the area. They will be already interested in the cause, so when you approach them you may find them keen to help.

Constituting the local group

You need the people, and you need something for them to do but you will also need a constitution, which defines how this group of people will operate and clarifies their relationship with the central organisation (that is with you). If you are setting up lots of local groups, then you will probably want to draw up a model constitution.

Recruiting for a County Committee

The steps you need to take:

- Recruit a researcher
- Train the researcher
- Identify key individuals
- Meet key individuals
- Seek contacts from key individuals
- Organise inaugural meeting

Notes:

Joining a committee is an opportunity to make a contribution to the welfare of the community in an interesting and enjoyable way, which leads to personal satisfaction.

It is an opportunity to acquire a personal profile and influence in an acceptable way, to meet other business contacts and to be seen as the supporter of a (national) charity.

People of the calibre of those invited to join a county committee have very limited free time, but are in a position to select and actively support fundraising events that fit into their lifestyles.

Funds raised through the efforts of the county committee will be spent in the county on projects based in places where it might be difficult to raise money locally.

There is satisfaction to be gained from becoming part of a (national) charity with the occasional opportunity to meet and talk with the decision makers in the organisation.

This exercise can take up to twelve months and is from the **Help the Aged** strategy of forming local committees.

You will need to decide whether the local committee is simply a sub-committee or branch of the main organisation, with no separate legal identity of its own, or whether it is a separate organisation in its own right, constituted independently as a charity, but with the object of supporting the main charitable organisation.

A separate legal structure will be more expensive to operate, but it will give full responsibility and control to the local group – who will be completely accountable for what is raised and how the money is spent. The most appropriate structure depends on a lot of things, including the length of time the committee has been in operation, the amount of money it raises, and the number of local groups around the country who are raising money for you.

You will want to ensure that the group operates in the interests of the parent charity and does nothing to bring it into disrepute. One way of doing this is through some sort of licence agreement, which authorises the use of the organisation's name and logo provided that certain standards are met and values adhered to. The Charities Act provisions on unauthorised fundraising (see Appendix 4) is another.

Local fundraising activities

There are an enormous range of fundraising activities that local support groups can undertake. Here we list a few that work well to give you some ideas:

- coffee mornings and other 'socials'.
- bridge tournaments and other games (whist, chess, etc.)
- sponsored walks, jogs, cycle rides, fun runs and anything else that can be sponsored
- heritage walks or cultural evenings for tourists
- craft fairs and sales of work
- fashion shows
- film premieres
- concerts and other cultural events
- dinner dances and balls
- discos for young people
- picnics and outings for families, if possible at interesting locations
- auctions of donated goods and 'promises auctions' (where a promise to do something useful or interesting is auctioned)
- raffles, lotteries and sweepstakes
- competitions with an entry fee to participants
- sports events and tournaments
- New Year's Eve parties, and events on other festive occasions
- getting supporters and businesses to advertise in calendars and diaries, brochures and annual reports
- sales of greetings cards
- public and house-to-house collections.

(Organising fundraising events is covered in Sections 4.2 and 4.3, organising public and house-to-house collections in Section 4.4, lotteries and raffles in Section 4.11, and getting companies to advertise in Section 4.15.)

Supporting and managing the local group

The point of having a local group to do the fundraising is that the bulk of fundraising work is farmed out to a group of volunteers, leaving you free to concentrate on other tasks. It often is not cost-effective for a paid

---

Constitution of a Local Committee

The following are some of the headings for the constitution of a local fundraising committee. These responsibilities are not to be taken lightly.

- The committee and the charity
- Support to be provided by the charity
- Responsibilities of committee members
- Name
- Location
- Bank account
- Objects of the committee
- Structure including: patronage, election of officers, responsibility of officers
- Meetings and operation: quorum for meetings, frequency of meetings, voting, resignations, termination of memberships, annual general meetings
- Remuneration of members
- Alteration of constitution

member of staff to spend time organising craft fairs or dinner dances or coffee mornings. However, you need to make sure that the group you have established to do this actually does the work, does it well, works consistently with the values and aims of the charity it is raising money for, and does not call unreasonably upon staff time.

You will need to support and manage the group to get the most out of it.

- Provide the group with some form of **induction**, so that they understand the importance of the work being done by the organisation, see the staff at work and meet and talk to staff and beneficiaries. If they can see the work at first hand, it will help fire them with enthusiasm, so that they know what they are raising the money for and can convince those they are asking of its importance.
- Help steer the group towards those **fundraising methods** which are most likely to work. Your experience will help, and you can also research what the local fundraising groups of other organisations are doing.
- Give the group a **budget** (they will need to spend some money to raise money) and fundraising targets to achieve. Don't expect too much too soon. It is best for them to start slowly, and to allow more time than they think will be necessary. If you are too optimistic at the outset, there will be a sense of failure when the targets are not achieved.
- Continue to show your personal **interest** in what they are doing and, at every opportunity, acknowledge your appreciation of their hard work.
- Monitor their **progress** and be available to advise them if they have difficulties.
- Provide them with appropriate **literature** about the organisation that explains its work clearly and powerfully.

The characteristics of a good fundraising leader

1. The leader must be an efficient and capable **organiser**.
2. Leaders must be able to **plan** an event in every detail.
3. Leaders must be able to **communicate** with their helpers. They should enjoy working with people and should be able to **lead** without causing offence.
4. A leader must be able to **motivate** others and inspire them with enthusiasm and zeal.
5. Leaders must be good judges of people. They must get to know the committee and helpers well and be able to **recognise and use the talents and abilities of individual members of the group**. They must also be able to understand each person's strengths and weaknesses in order to be able to **direct** and **guide** them in a way that they can accept and enjoy.

Source: *Complete Guide to Fundraising*, Sterrett.

4.2 Organising a fundraising event

All sorts of events can be organised to raise money, but whether you want to organise a concert in your home town, arrange a charity cricket match or celebrate your organisation's centenary in Hyde Park, you have to think not just about the fundraising potential but also about the possible risk of losing money from the event. You need to have the organisational skills. For every event that attracts thousands of new supporters and gives everyone a good time, there is another that collapses, is rained off, or whose sponsorship founders at the last moment. While there is money to be made from a well run event, many absorb a great deal of energy and deliver only small returns.

Objectives of the event

An event may be of almost any size and complexity, but what all events have in common is that you will be asking your supporters or the general public or a selected audience to participate, and you will be giving them something to enjoy in return for their money. This last point is important. You should not just aim to generate as much money as you can from those who attend. You should also try to give them a good time – so that they will contribute enthusiastically and be happy to participate next time.

You must be absolutely clear at the outset about the purpose of the event. Is it for PR, to get your name known? Is it to raise money directly? Is it simply an opportunity to entertain volunteers and supporters? Or is it to give an enthusiastic bunch of supporters something to do? Don't say that it's for all of these reasons; you will end up achieving none. Set a clear, primary objective for the event. This will help mould the exact form of the event and set targets for what you get out of it.

Whatever your event, there are five principal groups of people involved. Get these working in harmony and you are well on your way to success. These are the sponsors, the media, the performers, the audience and the charity.

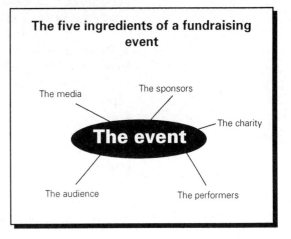

The five ingredients of a fundraising event

The media · The sponsors · **The event** · The charity · The audience · The performers

1. The sponsors

Sponsors, who may be underwriting much of the costs, have a good deal to gain too. They will be interested in reaching your audience (to promote their product or company) and in being seen by the general public and by their employees to be supporting something worthwhile. If you make the most of the next ingredient (the media), then your sponsors will regard the event even more enthusiastically. However, you have to ensure the event meets their business objectives (i.e. it gives access to their target audience, key opinion formers, celebrities or whoever).

2. The media

The media are in business to report events such as yours, especially if there is a star performer or a news story of particular interest. Whether the event is genuinely newsworthy depends on the nature of the event itself and or how creative you are in generating media interest. They may be interested in being given exclusive coverage of the story in return for a publishing major feature or picture coverage, or they may be interested in becoming a 'media sponsor', offering you not money, but free advertising and press coverage to promote the event in advance, and thus attract an audience. There is no doubt that star names and celebrities attract the media more than anything. You may get some coverage by talking about the good work you do or the fun of the event; a celebrity will guarantee massive coverage.

3. The performers

The performers are those people upon whose skills and appeal the event is centred: the band that is booked to play at a ball; the auctioneer undertaking a sale for you; or the football teams and celebrity players who will be playing in a charity match. They are critical to its success but they also have something to gain from participating in the event. It could be a fee (although you should always try to get a reduced fee or a free performance), or good publicity and an association with a good cause – which is good for their image.

4. The audience

Some 10% of the public attend charity events. Some go simply because they want to participate in the event, but many consider it a way of supporting a charity. People do not go to a charity auction feeling the same way they do about going to a commercial auction. They are much more likely to be generous with their bids. People do not go to a charity concert without expecting to be asked to give to a plate collection or to listen to an address by a luminary of that organisation. Their enjoyment of the occasion will in part be determined by the quality of the performance (get that wrong and you risk your reputation), and in part by the degree to which it is benefiting the charity.

5. The charity

The final ingredient is you and your organisation. Your involvement gives the event a focus – the real reason for its happening is to raise money to support your good work. The audience may come because they are your supporters, or because they are interested in your cause. The performers will not come to just any event, because they may have many other commitments but an event for your organisation could be something that strikes a sympathetic chord with them. The sponsors will decide to back the event because of your reputation and the audience that you can deliver for them. Your contacts with royalty, celebrities and other important people can be a further inducement.

Deciding what to organise

One starting point is to examine your market. Who is likely to attend the event? What are the interests of these people? Can you persuade them to bring their friends? Are they old or young, active and energetic, or particularly interested in your cause? What are you and your helpers interested in – and what contacts do you have? (access to performers, for example).

An alternative starting point might be to think in terms of some of the major types of event and see whether any seems appropriate. A short list might include:

- sporting events
- musical and cultural events
- balls, dinners, auctions and other entertainment events
- exhibitions, festivals and fairs
- events involving schools and young people
- mass participation events, with the participants collecting sponsorship money.

Most events are run on a one-off basis – although you will always want to re-run the event next year if it is successful, thereby creating a regular source of income for your charity. The initial event usually takes the most time to organise but having invested all this time, it is a shame if next year you have to start again from scratch. Therefore, try to develop repeatable events. Some events take place over a period of time – for example a knockout football competition or a film festival. More complicated (and more risky) events should perhaps be left to when you have more experience.

Depending upon the nature of your plans, you may need some sort of licence (to run the event, to collect money in a public place, or to run a bar). Check the legal requirements with the local administrative authority before you start any detailed planning.

Management

The ability to run the event well is crucial. It will almost certainly take much longer and involve more effort than you think, but skimping on the organisation will lead to an event which fails to meet your objectives. There are three main approaches to running an event. Each has its drawbacks and their advantages.

1. **Do it yourself**. Doing it yourself (or getting a member of your staff to do it) will help you learn how it should be done and provide you with the experience to do it better next time. However, if you haven't run an event before then you may be jeopardising the chances of success with your own inexperience. This can be countered by taking advice from more experienced people.

Perhaps the single most important problem of doing it yourself is the opportunity cost that organising it will involve. What else could you be doing with your time? How much money could you be raising if you were not stuck with doing the organising? Almost any event will require constant attention to detail, and checking and double checking at every stage. If you are in the middle of a busy fundraising programme, then organising something that requires so much of your time may not be feasible.

2. **Engage a professional** to organise the event for you. Very often the event will be run through some sporting or theatrical body, whose job it is to organise this sort of activity. It could make sense to engage them to do all the organising. You could try to persuade them to do it free as their charitable contribution. If not, there are professional event organisers in the musical, sporting and entertainment fields. For a fee they can be engaged to take over all the day-to-day administration from you. Alternatively a suitable public relations company could be used. If you are dealing with a commercial event organiser on the basis that a certain proportion of the ticket price or the proceeds goes to them, they will be a 'professional fundraiser' under the terms of the Charities Act, and certain requirements will need to be met to comply with the Act.

3. **Establish a committee of volunteers** to take responsibility for running the event. The key appointment will be the Chair (it could be you). This need not be someone who knows how to run an event, but someone who has the leadership qualities and the good management sense to link the commercial needs of the event to the requirements of the charity. You will probably then need to select a multi-disciplinary team that embodies all the skills necessary to make the thing work: from people with the sporting or musical background to deal with the programme, to the accountant who will tell you whether VAT is chargeable on the ticket sales and what the legal requirements are. You need to give yourself plenty of time to find the right people.

There are several important aspects of successfully managing the event.

- *An accurate budget*. It is essential to control costs, if you are to run the event profitably. Your budget will also give you an indication of the size of audience you will need to attract and what price to charge for tickets. At an early stage you will need to make an assessment of all the likely costs and the potential sources of income – and just to be safe you should include something for contingencies. On the income side it is worth making a high and low estimate to illustrate what may happen in different circumstances. This will highlight the risk involved.

- *Plenty of time*. Although it is possible to organise an event in a short space of time, the longer you leave yourself the better. The best is an annual cycle, with the planning of the next year's event starting just after the completion of this year's. Booking a venue or obtaining the services of star performers may take a lot longer and be an important factor in how far ahead you need to plan.

- *Legally binding contracts*. You will also need the arrangements with performers, the venue and any sub-contractors, expressed through some formal written agreement. This sets out precisely what has been agreed and is signed by both parties to confirm the agreement. This avoids disagreement later on. It is especially important that you agree how any money is to be split (both expenditure and income); who has the rights to the recording of the event; who is responsible for what costs, and what the obligations are in the event of cancellation. Where considerable sums are involved, the agreement should be drawn up by a lawyer.

- *Good administration and record keeping*. For your first event, you have to start from scratch but next time it will be much easier, since you will be building on experience. Keep records of everything, so you will know what to do next time – for example whether insurance is needed, where to go for it and how much to pay. Immediately after the event, have a de-briefing – find out what went really well, what went wrong or could be improved, what suggestions there are for doing better or raising more money next time, and all this can be used to ensure that the event is even more of a success the next time you run it.

Reducing the risk

An accurate budget is essential if you are to run a profitable event. At an early stage you will need to make an assessment of all the likely costs and the potential sources of income. You should include a good amount for contingencies. On the income side it is worth making a high and a low estimate to illustrate what may happen in different circumstances. This will set targets for you as well as highlight the risk involved. An additional idea is to set yourselves a financial strategy. You might decide, for example, not to pay for services but instead get everything donated or sponsored. As a general rule, costs tend to be higher than anticipated and income lower, so be realistic.

The best way of reducing risk is to have a well thought out event, and good planning, organisation and marketing, but things have a habit of not going to plan, so you need to think about your exposure to risk and how to reduce it. There are several ways of doing this.

- *Financial sponsorship*. Get all the costs of the event covered by a sponsor, so that there is nothing to lose, and everything to gain. An additional advantage is that you can tell everyone coming that all proceeds will go to the cause (since all the costs have already been covered). This can be a tremendous encouragement for ticket sales.

- *Commitments and guarantees*. One way of running a charity ball is to have a committee of say 20 people, each of whom agrees to get 12 people to come to the ball. They take responsibility for selling the 12 tickets, or for paying for them themselves in the event of being unable to find others to contribute. This means that you have a guaranteed attendance of 240 people – enough to fill the venue or make sure that the event is a success.

- *Cost cutting*. You might try to get as much as you can lent for the occasion, donated or sponsored, so that you do not have to pay for it. Venue costs, performers costs, and the cost of prizes can all be substantial, and if they are too high can jeopardise the success of the event. Not having to pay or paying less is a simple way both to get more out of the event and to reduce risk at the same time.

- *Insurance*. It may be possible to insure against public liability, theft or damage (in case something goes wrong), and for an outdoor event if weather is a problem, even against the possibility of bad weather.

Promotion

Effective promotion will turn an event from being a modest success into one that is really profitable. Consider who is likely to want to come to the event – this is your target market – and then decide how best to reach them

For an important event, try to get the backing of one of the main TV or radio stations. Local radio can be a powerful force for local events. Many radio stations send mobile recording studios to events; others may send a reporter to cover the event live. This sort of link can create its own promotional momentum. The station will have an interest in giving frequent plugs during the run up to the event, mentioning the date and how to get tickets. Another possibility is to offer free tickets as prizes to be given away by the radio station. You could devise a competition, or the station or newspaper might do this to suit its listeners or readers.

Advertising is another medium you can use. Posters and handbills displayed or distributed locally, advertising in the local press and being included in listings magazines should all be considered.

One way of encouraging publicity is to feature celebrities who may be attending the event or performing in it. For sporting and musical events, the performers will be one of the main attractions. Alternatively, you can invite a celebrity to act as compere, to open the event, to present the awards or announce raffle winners at the event. Having famous names adds credibility to the event, and encourages people to come along; it also encourages people to be there during a whole day of activity. The presence of royal patrons or visitors can also add a great deal, although it will create considerable security and protocol headaches.

Selling tickets can be extremely hard work, and it is through having a full house that the event will appear successful. Give yourselves the best chance by having:

- a really **attractive event**
- plenty of **ticket sellers** who will take responsibility for selling all the tickets
- a readily identifiable and reachable **target audience**
- an **arrangement with local outlets** or ticket agencies.

You also need a strategy for getting people to come if ticket sales are slow, but not so disappointing as to have to cancel the event. Once you are sure the event is going to run, it is important for everyone that the event is well attended. At that stage it is more important to see that people are there than that all the tickets are sold. This means that you should be prepared to give tickets away free to groups who might be interested in coming – through schools and student unions for young people's events, through hospitals and other institutions for other events, or via a media promotion.

This small flyer was distributed to those who had expressed interested in this event. The result was that £20,000 was raised and lessons have been learned for next year

Sponsorship

Events are ideal vehicles for sponsorship, for the sponsor because they offer a range of facilities and benefits that can be attractive, and for you because sponsorship can help reduce your risk and defray the costs.

Sponsors will need to know a good deal about the event and its expected audience – how many people will come, who will they be and how they will be exposed to any advertising messages. This applies particularly large scale events and where you expect substantial media coverage.

You should have a clear idea of how much money you are expecting from the sponsor and what you can give in return. You might be offering special hospitality facilities, opportunities to meet royal patrons, opportunities to place the sponsor's message in a prominent place, or the chance to publicise the sponsorship through the advertising or public relations undertaken for the event.

One of the key items that can carry the sponsor's message, and those of other advertisers too, is the brochure. Almost any event needs a brochure or a programme of some sort. This should contain details of the programme but it can also carry advertising, which can generate considerable income. Each copy can either be given away free (to create maximum circulation) or be sold on the day to generate further income (brochure advertising is covered in section 4.15).

Developing extra income

For many events, such as a dinner dance or a ball, the ticket price will cover the cost of organising the event and not much more. If you want to generate money for your work, then you will have to devise ways of getting those who are attending the event to give or spend at the event. It is by generating this extra money that your event becomes a real success. There are all sorts of ways of doing this. Here are a few ideas:

- getting local businesses to take **advertising** in the programme. This is called 'goodwill advertising', and is sold on the basis that they are helping a good cause and being associated with a successful event;
- having an **auction**, where interesting items are auctioned during the course of the evening. A holiday donated by a travel company is often the 'star item'. Alternatively, the items can be prizes in a raffle or prize draw;
- having a **tombola** or a **raffle**, where small gifts donated by local shops and by supporters are the prizes. Each prize is numbered, and each ticket purchased has a number which corresponds with a prize or does not win. To be a success there should be lots of prizes and a good chance of winning something;
- offering a **prize** for the table that contributes the most;
- having **pledge forms** for each person to fill in, and making an appeal during the evening, or collecting money from those present in a bucket. To make sure that people respond generously, you should say what the money is for and perhaps suggest a level of donation. You might get the performers to say something during the evening;
- **advertising the appeal** in the event programme. Not everyone there will be an existing supporter or know about what you are doing and why the work is important.

Spin-off for future fundraising

A great advantage of a successful event is that you can build up a clientele for future occasions. By keeping the names and addresses of those who have attended, you can invite them to participate next time you run the event.

You will also want to capture the interest of the people who attend the event so that they learn about your cause and understand the importance of your work. You can also add the participants' names to your mailing list and make sure that they receive any appeal literature you are sending out. You might even make them an honorary member for three months to get them used to the idea of being a supporter. You could think about organising an open day where they could come and see your work, meet your staff and talk to your beneficiaries.

Organising a particular type of event can help you reach new audiences. For example, if you want to appeal to the middle-class cultural elite, you might consider running a concert or art exhibition; if you are interested in the educational establishment, you might think about an exhibition of children's paintings; or if you want to appeal to the business elite or top politicians, an event involving leading TV or cinema or sporting stars might be worth considering.

However, you need to be careful. People attend or take part in charity events for many different reasons. Commitment to the cause may be one of them but the attractiveness of the event can be just as powerful. It may well be that a substantial number of those attending do not and will not care about your charity; they simply wanted a good time – which you must give them. Therefore, sending them expensive appeal literature over a long period of time may simply be a waste of money. It is much better to ask them what they want to receive from you – if anything – and give them that. The response rates to this kind of strategy are usually as high, if not higher, than the blanket approach, but at lower cost to you.

Fundraising events and tax

When income to a charity is given freely there is no tax payable on it. However, many events involve the sale of tickets to the public. This is considered trading rather than fundraising and may be liable to tax. This is a complicated area involving both VAT and income tax. There is a tax concession (ESCC4) for those organising occasional events which allows the income from such events to be treated as a donation and be free of tax. For further information, see the Inland Revenue publication *Trading by Charities*.

For VAT, there is also a concession. Normally the sale of a ticket to an event would be treated as a taxable supply and be subject to VAT if the seller is registered for VAT (or obliged to register because the ticket sales take total taxable income above the VAT registration threshold). However, if the ticket price is split into two components, a reasonable price for attending the event and a donation, and if the wording is such that the donation element is optional, then only the attendance price would be treated as taxable income for VAT purposes. It is worth taking professional advice or consulting your local VAT office if you are in any doubt.

4.3 Sponsored walks, fun runs and other mass participation events

A sponsored event is very different to getting business sponsorship. In a sponsored event, which might be a walk or a swim or a cycle ride, the participants get their family, friends and colleagues to sponsor them by contributing a certain amount for each kilometre or each lap they complete. These events can generate substantial amounts of money for your organisation.

Remember though that people are supporting their friends who are participating in the event (and perhaps doing something interesting or unusual) because they are asked. The participants may become involved in the event because it is a fun thing to do or a challenge or simply because they support your charity and want to contribute to its success.

Sponsored events are one of the most commonly used ways of raising money for charity. You can sponsor just about anything! Ideas that have been used include:

- giving up smoking (number of days without a cigarette up to a specified limit)
- slimming (amount of weight lost during a set time)
- knitting (centimetres knitted during an afternoon)
- litter pick (amount of litter cleared from a river bank)
- marathon runs (kilometres raced plus a bonus for completing the course)
- penalty shoot outs (goals scored if you are the penalty taker, or goals saved if the goalkeeper).

In deciding the event, find something that will be sufficiently popular to attract lots of participants (the more participants you attract, the more money you will raise), as well as something that is trouble-free to organise. Also you want something that you can repeat, building on your experience and success to achieve greater returns the next time you run it. A sponsored event can be used to get across an important message about your cause (an environmental charity could organise a sponsored clean up, Alcoholics Anonymous a sponsored give-up-drinking, for example).

You need to take into account what will attract your target audience, and whether you can reach them. Younger people may be interested in disco marathons, but will not be interested in a sponsored knit. For older people, it would be the other way round. If your target audience is young families, can you think of something that will involve them all during the weekend? Family strolls, fun runs and swimming are all popular – your imagination is the limit to what is possible.

You can expect four types of person to join in:

- **those who have participated before** and who know it will be a lot of fun (so it is important to keep a record of who has participated in previous years);
- **supporters** and **sympathisers** of your cause. Mail your members and donors; they may be interested in doing something to help raise money;
- **those who simply enjoy the particular activity** you have chosen (cycling, walking, marathon running, etc.) but who may not know about your work – although their participation gives you the opportunity to interest them in it;
- **those involved in your organisation**: your Management Board (it is a good opportunity to get them doing something; your staff (their involvement in a sponsored event can improve morale and teamwork); and your beneficiaries. (See box for example.)

> ### Ravenswood Charity Bike Rides
>
> In 1996 Ravenswood, a charity working with 1,600 children and adults with learning disabilities, organised a series of sponsored events with the aim of raising £1 million.
>
> For the less ambitious a five mile walk through Windsor Great Park was organised on a Sunday in July. For those who liked the idea of the young doing their bit, a junior mountain bike ride was arranged. This had a £10 entry and a target sponsorship of £50 per participant. For the more ambitious adults, two further one-week bike rides were organised. Each had a strong link to Jewish interests, and were more than just a physical challenge. The first was from the pyramids to Eilat; the second from the Dead Sea to Eilat. The organisation was done in conjunction with a tour operator. The price for each entrant was £375 to cover travel and other costs and a minimum sponsorship of £2,000 was required for each adult participant.
>
> These bike rides have been held for several years, and the income has been steadily building up. Ambitious sponsorship targets are set, which is appropriate to the market that Ravenswood is aiming at and reflects the appeal of the event, and assistance and encouragement are given in helping participants meet their sponsorship targets.
>
> Ravenswood tries to involve participants in its work, through open days and reunions at the Ravenswood village, and by encouraging volunteering and further support from ride participants.

Organising a mass participation event

Organisation takes place in three stages:

1. Before the event

Before the event, you will need to:

- decide the event and agree the **route** or the **venue**
- get any **permission** or **insurance** necessary

- plan the **promotion**
- prepare the **sponsorship** forms and explanatory materials about the work of your organisation
- provide **advice** and **support** to participants to help them collect pledges
- **organise** volunteers and stewards to help on the day
- **mark** out the route
- prepare a **certificate of completion** for participants to take away after the event.

Preparation of the sponsorship forms requires thought. The form must describe exactly what is being done, but should also say why the money is needed. It should list the names and addresses of the sponsors (the participant will need the address to collect the sponsorship that has been pledged afterwards; you will want the addresses so that you can mail your appeal literature and try to get further support afterwards) and a phone number to contact the sponsor if they fail to produce the money they have promised; and finally the amount pledged. You want to encourage sponsors to commit themselves to a generous amount of sponsorship. They need to know how many miles (or whatever) they are likely to be paying for. Is there a maximum number of miles for example? Remember that you are likely to get more if your sponsorship is per kilometre than per mile, per minute rather than per hour, and so on. Most sponsors do not know what level of sponsorship is expected, and are guided by what others have written before so encourage participants to approach their more generous supporters first. Alternatively you might indicate some preferred amounts. Some people may prefer to give a fixed sum. The form should allow for this too.

Since the ultimate success of the event depends on the amount raised, it is important to have lots of participants raising lots of money. Once you have got the participants, you can encourage them to raise more money by:

- setting a **minimum sponsorship requirement** which they guarantee to pay;
- giving them a **target**, both in terms of the number of sponsors they should aim to get and how much to ask for;
- having an **entrance fee** for participating in the event.

You will be surprised by the range of sums people raise. This depends as much on the effort put in by the participant (this can be encouraged by you) as on their financial circumstances.

2. On the day

On the day, you need to make sure that everything runs smoothly, that there are sufficient helpers, and that they are properly briefed. You also need to ensure that participants are welcomed (especially any celebrities who are participating), that newspaper and radio reporters are welcomed and briefed about anything unusual (including anyone participating in fancy dress, any stunts, anything unusual about what the money will be used for), that there is information at the start of the event to advise performers and the public what the route is, where the refreshment and toilet facilities are, and for events that involve physical exertion, where medical help can be obtained. You will need to have sufficient helpers to staff the various check-in procedures, to mark the route and to certify completion.

3. After the event

After the event, the key activities are to:

- collect the money
- thank those who helped
- record the names and addresses of those who took part.

Collecting the money can be surprisingly difficult. This must primarily be the responsibility of the participants who took part and who were sponsored for doing so. Keep a register of all participants. Stress the importance of collecting the money and give a deadline date. Follow up in person if you can or by phone, or if all this fails, by letter. Offer prizes for the largest amount actually raised by an individual or a team – which can also provide an incentive for people to collect their sponsorship money.

Finally you should de-brief. This is important as it will enable you to identify your successes, but also the weak points and problems, so that you can improve next year.

Sponsored event checklist

1. Make sure you plan well ahead
2. Choose the right activity
3. Set a date and find a suitable venue
4. Get any permissions you need, for example to use a public place
5. Produce sponsorship forms
6. Involve other organisations, as they can be a good source of participants
7. Organise local publicity and get media sponsorship
8. Get local business sponsorship to cover costs and pay for any prizes being offered
9. Prepare for the day: ensure you have all the stewards, equipment and information that you need for the event
10. Tidy up afterwards
11. Thank all the participants
12. Chase up all uncollected pledges
13. Add the names on your sponsorship forms to your mailing list. You will then be able to send them an appeal letter in due course suggesting that they continue supporting your work.

4.4 Collections

Organising a local collection can be a successful way of raising money. It requires a good deal of planning, a well briefed and enthusiastic team of volunteers and a certain amount of equipment. The main advantage of a local collection is that it reminds the many local volunteers about your cause, as well as getting your name across to those who see you in action. Collections can take several forms:

- **house-to-house collections**, where you knock on doors and ask for support, or leave an envelope and information about your work, and call back next day;
- **street collections** and collections in public places. Typically here a collector will have a collecting box, and may give some token in return for the donation (such as a sticker);
- **collecting boxes placed on shop counters**, in pubs and in restaurants for people to leave their small change;
- **static collecting devices** placed outside shops;
- **collecting boxes in supporters' homes**, where they can leave their small change or ask their friends to contribute.

The great strength of local collection schemes is that over time they can reach very large sections of the public. Not only does this have advantages in fundraising terms (you will be asking lots of people), it can also have a great educational or publicity impact. Imagine the impact of a national AIDS campaign that contacted every household, not just to raise money but also to provide information. You could provide information on the disease, gain publicity for the organisation concerned and of course raise funds. Equally important is the converse, where sloppy volunteer work which is replicated across the land will quickly bring an organisation into disrepute.

Organising a house-to-house collection

House-to-house collections are very popular with both national and local charities, and are a good way of asking everyone in a specified area to give their support. The collectors need to be well briefed, as they are the link between your organisation and the public, and may be asked all sorts of questions about the work of the organisation and how it spends its money, which they will need to answer.

The first step is to obtain a permit from your District or Unitary Council (or in London, from the London Borough). In your application for a permit, you will need to specify the date or time scale of the collection, the localities in which you intend to collect and the manner in which the collection will be conducted. A licence may be refused on several grounds including the possibility that:

- it will cause inconvenience to the public;
- it is on the same day or the day immediately before or after another collection;
- the expense is too high or too little will be generated for the cause;

- the promoter has not acted properly in past collections.

The detailed requirements for conducting a collection are set out in the regulations attached to the 1992 Charities Act. These cover such things as who can collect money and how the collection has to be run. You only need a licence for a collection in a public place (which is a place to which members of the public have access) or when you are collecting in more than one location. A collection restricted to a private house, school office, public house or hospital does not require a licence. However, even if you are not collecting cash (i.e. you are going from house to house asking for jumble, paper etc.), you still need a licence.

If you are organising a national collection (throughout the whole or a substantial part of England and Wales) then you can obtain an order from the Charity Commission authorising the collection. For details of the rules on collections in Scotland and Northern Ireland, consult the Scottish Council for Voluntary Organisations and the Northern Ireland Council for Voluntary Action.

A successful house-to house collection requires:

- carefully recruited volunteers
- well chosen streets in which to collect
- good advance planning
- delivery of collecting materials in good time
- reliable collection of envelopes
- careful recording of donors.

A good example of a house to house envelope giving an example of what money can do and, on the back, inviting you to send for information

Before applying for a permit, you should plan how you will run the collection. Local knowledge should help you decide which sorts of houses are likely to be responsive. For larger collections you may want to collect throughout the area.

Those who have spent many hours carrying out house-to-house collections are convinced that going to the largest (and richest) areas is not always the most effective strategy. Long drives slow you down and results are often poor in the richest areas. The best results appear to come from those leafy suburbs where mortgages have been paid off, where education levels are high, and yet where the householder will open the door to you.

An important factor is the group of volunteers that you have. Typically you may want one volunteer to take responsibility for one street, ideally their own street or one nearby. Volunteers can be recruited on a networking basis or, as is increasingly the practice now, by telephoning them (although this is not universally popular or accepted). It is important to provide some initial training and induction. For example, they can be given a general briefing about the charity and its work and the purpose of the appeal, and be told when to call, how to introduce themselves, what to say, what difficult questions to expect, and so on. You may be able to do this by arranging a training session, or by briefing people personally, or by preparing a pack containing all the necessary information.

Their main function will be to deliver an envelope on which there is some message, possibly with an accompanying brochure or letter from the charity. After a short interval of days, the collector should return to collect the envelopes. At this point they will encounter responses ranging from hostility to apathy to enthusiasm. There will be those who decline to help you and those who choose to be abusive. Most people will be polite. Some people will offer a range of reasons or excuses in justification of why they will not give. In most cases these are people who find it hard to be seen not to give without a clear reason; if you stay to demolish their argument you will find another argument springing up hydra like in its place. In the meantime, you may be missing other supporters elsewhere in the street.

Some people will be genuinely interested in what you are doing. This is an ideal opportunity to recruit a new member or a volunteer, to give more information, or to sign them up for a covenant.

Record keeping is very important. For those who simply return their envelope, make a note of their address. You have identified a new donor, and you will therefore want to keep in touch. They may well respond to postal appeals later on, become a member or enter into a Deed of Covenant. Those who appear interested in the cause could be visited again, put on a volunteer register or asked to contribute more regularly. In any event, this information should be passed back to you, the fundraiser.

The returned envelopes should be handed in at one central point, and the envelopes opened under the supervision of two people, with the amounts from each address logged in a register. This is good practice, and an attempt to avoid fraud. A local bank manager or clerk may agree to help with this. You should also try to keep track of how much money is coming from each area, for future reference.

Checklist for organising a collection

1. Check the **date**. Avoid holiday periods or times of the year when there are other collections going on.
2. Seek any **authorisation** that you will require: from the police or local authority, and from the landlord if appropriate.
3. Identify the **areas** and **locations** for collecting and think about the best time of day to call.
4. Recruit your **team** of volunteers; the more you have, the more you will collect. Get those who have agreed to suggest their friends.
5. Prepare any **materials** you will need, including collecting boxes or envelopes, leaflets about the work of the organisation and details of any membership scheme, and stickers.
6. Brief the **volunteers** about the work of the charity, and provide some basic training in effective asking.
7. Organise how the **money** will be received and accounted for. Bank all proceeds immediately upon receipt.
8. **Thank volunteers**, telling them how much they raised and how important this will be to your work.
9. **Thank all the donors**, by sending them a letter (with a further appeal). Follow up on those who have been noted as being particularly interested.
10. **Debrief** with your volunteers. Find out what went well, and what not so well. Suggest ways of doing better next time. Keep a record of which locations or neighbourhoods did best.

There is always the possibility of fraud being perpetrated on your charity by someone carrying out an unauthorised collection in your name. If you receive any reports of unauthorised collecting, you should investigate these as fast as you can, as any bad publicity will damage your organisation and the voluntary sector as a whole. Under the 1992 Charities Act you now have the power to prevent unauthorised collections by seeking an injunction from the courts (see appendix 4).

Organising a street collection

Running a street collection is in some ways more difficult than a house-to-house collection. The differences lie in the fact that volunteers find it a less agreeable way of spending their time; yet the collecting has to be concentrated into just one day and you, the organiser, have to provide enough collectors to cover the whole of the area.

As with a house-to-house collection, you need a permit and should apply to your local council for this. Do this well in advance, as others may have laid prior claim to important collection dates and sites. If you have an annual flag day or collection week, you will need to apply each year.

There are two requirements for a successful collection.
1. You need plenty of **volunteers** to carry out the collection. Draw up a rota for each collection point, using people for not more than an hour or two. They can then link this with visits to shops and pubs in the area.
2. The choice of **location** is important to ensure that collectors have access to the maximum numbers of people. The high street or shopping centres are usually best, though collecting at well populated events, such as outside a football stadium, can also work well. The ideal site is one where you are visible to passers by as they stroll up the street. This gives the potential donor time to think about giving. If you are stationed immediately outside a busy entrance to a shop, people have to make a split second decision to give. If you make it difficult, this gives them one more reason not to give.

To make the most of your location you need to train collectors to be a little assertive. Although collectors are not allowed to solicit on the streets, they should not shrink back from passers-by. The collector who is prepared to vigorously rattle the tin, who is prepared to look people in the eye, and who is prepared to station themselves in the middle of the thoroughfare will do very much better. Street collection requires a very positive attitude.

Having the right equipment is important. You will need a sealed collection device that is convenient to carry, convenient for the public to put money into, and easy to get the money out of again after the collection. The main choice is whether to go for a more expensive plastic collecting box that can be reused, or whether to use a cheaper disposable box. This will depend on your future plans. A number of commercial suppliers now provide a range of fundraising devices which can be personalised with your charity's name and logo.

Your collectors should wear a sash or other strongly visible item with your charity's name on it. Again you need to be a able to signal at a distance what you are collecting for. It is not good enough to hope that passers by can see the label on your tin. You may wish to offer sticky lapel badges indicating that someone has given. It certainly helps spread the idea in a busy centre and particularly encourages parents with young children to give. It is also important to have a number of general leaflets about your organisation for those who are genuinely interested.

What you need for a successful street collection

- A good date and location for the collection
- Lots of enthusiastic volunteers
- Good organisation
- The right equipment: stickers or flags to offer people, and collecting boxes suitably labelled to advertise your organisation
- Printed information about your appeal to brief the volunteers, and to hand out to interested passers by
- Good local publicity
- A proper system for receiving and banking all the cash that has been collected.

Static collection devices

Static collection devices are the large, often brightly coloured, free-standing collecting boxes placed near the exit or just outside shops in the high street, pubs, cinema foyers, superstores, service stations and other suitable premises. They can provide a regular source of income for any charity, but considerable care needs to be taken to ensure that the money reaches the charity.

Suitable locations are anywhere where people are paying for things and the device is visible. It must be on private property, although the street outside a shop may well be within the boundary of the premises. There are two types of device.

- Those that appeal to **children**, which need to be visually inviting or have some sort of moving part that is operated by inserting money. For example, the RNLI box which launches a lifeboat.
- Those targeted at **adults**, which need to be functional and have a design or a label, which clearly expresses the cause or need.

Finding locations for static devices can be delegated to a persuasive volunteer. The challenge is to arrange for the money to come back reliably. One approach is to make the box the responsibility of the proprietors of the establishment, for example in a pub. In this case, it is the responsibility of the landlord or landlady to send in a cheque when the box is full. This would be inappropriate in places such as shops, where the turnover of staff is high. In such places, volunteers should arrange to make regular collections or keep in touch by telephone.

If boxes are not looked after regularly they can be vandalised or stolen. Larger devices should be chained so that they cannot be removed by over enthusiastic supporters! It is always worth checking up regularly to see how they are being displayed, and taking the opportunity to chat to the shopkeeper and enthuse them about your cause.

Many shops have one or more smaller collecting boxes on their counter for customers to put their change in. As with the larger collecting devices, these need to be properly maintained and managed. The box needs to be durable. If it is falling apart, it gives out a message that the charity does not look after its money properly. It needs emptying regularly, as it can fill up quickly with 1p and 2p coins.

It is also helpful to write clear thank you letters showing how much has been raised and what has been done with it. This can be displayed to encourage further giving.

Mass collection schemes

A local collection scheme which has been tremendously successful in the past, but whose results have declined in recent years, is the 'cascade' or 'penny-a-day' collection. This is based on the chain letter principle. A collector is recruited to collect regularly from ten people in their locality; the collector remits the money to a coordinator who has recruited ten collectors, and then passes the proceeds back to the charity. Recruiting coordinators, collectors and donors can be done by an enthusiastic team of volunteers, and the coordinators and collectors can be asked to help recruit donors. In return for a contribution of maybe 50 p each month, donors are sent a newsletter and other promotional material.

Another possibility, for those organisations with large memberships of committed and enthusiastic people, is to ask supporters to place a collecting box in their home. This can be used to deposit their small change, or encourage friends and visitors to contribute (perhaps when they make a telephone call). As with a cascade collection, a system is required for retrieving the money that has been collected.

> **Further information**
>
> ■ Codes of practice on the conduct of house-to-house collections and use of static collection devices are given in Appendix 5. These have been developed by the Institute of Charity Fundraising Managers as an attempt to promote good practice.
>
> ■ A useful source of suppliers of the equipment you will need is the ICFM year book. A long established supplier of collecting devices is Angal, who can be contacted at 68 First Avenue, Mortlake, London SW14 8SR.

4.5 Postal Appeals

The post provides one of the most flexible and powerful tools in fundraising. A postal appeal or direct mail programme can provide both regular and quick income. The key is to build up and maintain an active and enthusiastic list of supporters, which will require time, effort and money. So postal appeals will not be an immediate source of income for those organisations that do not yet have an active supporter base.

The essential feature of this medium is the ability to direct a personalised message of the length that you choose to a target audience at a time of your choosing. It requires the use of:

- a list of **addresses** to send the letters to;
- a **'communication package'** – usually a brochure with a covering letter and some mechanism for replying;
- a system for dealing with the **response**.

The main areas in which direct mail can be of value to the fund-raiser are:

- **'cold' mailings** to people with whom you have had no previous contact
- **'reciprocal' mailings** where you swap your member list with that of another organisation and use their list to recruit new members for your organisation
- **'warm' mailings** to your existing members and supporters.

Response rates on warm mailings are the highest, and can vary from as low as 7% to as much as 30% or even higher. Reciprocal mailings to other people's supporters also work relatively well – these people are known supporters of charity and responders to direct mail appeals. Response rates on cold lists also vary enormously, from virtually nothing to as much as 3%, depending on the cause and the list. The average seems to be around 0.5% to 1.5%. However, once people have given, they become part of your warm list.

The power of the medium comes not only from the ability to target your message precisely, but also from the ability to send the same message to very large numbers of people, which provides an economy of scale. The whole idea is to make the medium as personal as possible

---

The three elements of a mailing

- **The audience**. There can be an enormous variation in the response rate you achieve. Sending the letter to people who are more likely to respond will reduce the costs of acquiring a new donor considerably.

- **The message**. Likewise what you tell them and what you ask for is extremely important. A powerful message that will move them to give will be the most effective. The creative approach, that is the way you angle the story you are telling them, and the 'offer', what you are asking them to do, are the two important components of the message.

- **The timing**. Some times of the year may be better than others. The period leading up to Christmas works best, as it is a time when people feel predisposed to give. If there is a good reason for the appeal, for example as a response to a natural disaster, then the immediacy of the need and demonstrating that you are responding efficiently and effectively means that you should get your appeal out as quickly as you can.

– the ideal is to be able to write a letter by hand to a friend or make it appear as if you are. As the numbers on your list get larger, then the opportunities for making it personal get smaller. The difficulty, for example, of producing a hand-written greeting on 5,000 letters or even 500, becomes very great, and it is much easier to print "Dear friend" for every one. This depersonalisation will inevitably have an impact on your returns.

You also have the possibility of sending slightly different messages to different groups of people. This is called segmentation. You will certainly want to say something different to your existing donors to those you are trying to recruit who have not yet given. You may want to subdivide further, treating larger donors differently from smaller donors, those who have supported you consistently over a number of years differently from recent recruits, and so on.

Ten ways to personalise your mailing

A personal letter works far better than a circular letter. If you are writing to thousands of people, you will have to send a circular letter but you can personalise it to make it appear to the recipient that it is written specially to them.

1. Handwrite the donor's name in the salutation at the start of the letter (Dear...) and handwrite the signature at the end of the letter. With large mailings this can be done by a volunteer. Or use a word processor to incorporate the donor's name in the salutation ("Dear Mrs Smith" rather than "Dear Supporter") and where appropriate also in the body of the letter.
2. Personalisation is not just a matter of name and address. It is also any personal detail which might be incorporated into the body of the letter – such as the amount of the last gift and the purpose for which it was given. Such details can often be incorporated using a word processor.
3. Type or handwrite the address on the envelope.
4. Use an ordinary postage stamp rather than put it through a franking machine.
5. Make handwritten notes or underline parts of the text of the letter even if this is then going to be printed!
6. Have a handwritten postscript at the end of the letter which reinforces the message. Again this can be printed.
7. Ensure that the response form has the donor's name on it.
8. Use a reply envelope with the sender's name handwritten or printed on it, as well as the organisation and reply address, on it (so that the reply letter is addressed to someone and not to an anonymous organisation).
9. Stamp the reply letter. Although this will double the postage bill, it should generate much better returns. Keep track of the response to ensure that it is worth doing this.
10. Even think of handwriting the whole of the appeal letter – which can be short, with the work of the organisation and the purpose of the appeal being explained in an accompanying leaflet.

Components of a mailing

The components of a mailing vary widely. A well used model consists of five parts:

- an **outer envelope**: with a window to carry a name and address on the reply device. This can be overprinted with some teaser copy to encourage recipients at least to open the letter;
- a **letter**: this should be regarded as the main communication, and which should be written as interestingly and personally as possible;
- a coupon or some **reply device**: summarises what the appeal is, gives examples of expected donation levels and carries any codes and donor identity so that you can keep track of the response;
- a **reply envelope**: this can be extremely helpful in securing a gift. Use Freepost if you can. Making it simple for the donor to reply will increase the response considerably;
- a **brochure** or leaflet: this helps provide illustrations of the need highlighted in the letter. This is not always necessary but can be helpful in building a clearer picture for the donor.

One advantage of this form of appeal is that you can include as much information as you feel you need. There are several schools of thought about how long a letter ought to be; however there is little doubt that even the skimpiest mailing package can include a great deal more information than an expensive newspaper advertisement. Beware, though, of producing mailing packages that are too full of words. There is a great danger that they will go unread. Use pictures to tell the story, case studies and quotes to illustrate that you can make a difference, and all sorts of graphic devices to break up the text.

Getting the message right

Like any other printed communication, getting the message right is at least half the battle (the other half being sending it to the right people at the right time). For a mailing however there are a number of important components.

- *The proposition*. Each mailing should have a central proposition. It might, for example, be "£21.60 can help a child in distress" or "urgent action is needed to save the rainforests of Brazil". This central idea should be the visual and verbal theme throughout the mailing pack.

Improving your appeal response

Here are six ways in which you could increase your response rates or average donation values. Before committing yourself to any of these you should attempt to test the idea first.

1. Wherever possible, **personalise** your communication.
2. Mail a **different** appeal to your large and regular supporters which refers to their past giving, recognises its value to the organisation and asks for a generous response to this new request.
3. Read through your letter and **rewrite** it to improve its impact.
4. Introduce **case studies** of how people are being helped.
5. Try including **pictures** of your work.
6. Ask for **specific amounts** to achieve particular things: "50 Rupees will buy a new syringe", for example, and mention this in both the letter and in the response device.
7. Put a **stamp** on return envelopes. No one likes to see a stamp wasted, and the only way to avoid this is to reply to the appeal! This would not be the case with a pre-paid or freepost reply envelope.

- *Making the request*. The creative feel of the mailing must be subservient to the essential purpose of the letter – which is to get someone to help you. It is often assumed that the recipient will know what you want. A good letter will repeat the request for help up to six or seven times. Then there can be no mistaking what you are really wanting from the reader.

- *The length of the message*. There is no rule about this. The important thing is to say what you want and to say it effectively. So you need to focus on quality rather than length.

Warm mailings

Sending letters to your own donors can be the most profitable way of raising money. Although not everyone can expect to raise £1 million by mailing 80,000 people, it has been done! The principle is to get the audience, the message and the timing right.

This warm mailing was personalised and included a small crayon which could be returned for a child's use. It also contained a donation form and a reply envelope.

The relatively high response that you can get from warm mailings to previous donors is the main reason for maintaining a mailing list. When you include the longer-term support from covenanted donations and membership subscriptions, you might be able to raise as much as £10 for each £1 of fundraising costs.

There are a number of factors to consider when writing to existing supporters. They are one of the groups on which your organisation depends for its success. You are, therefore, communicating with one of

---

A sample Mailing Plan for a Year

A - *appeal sent out* **R** - *annual report sent out*

	Feb	Apr	Jun	Aug	Oct	Dec
Covenantors			R			A
Standing orders			R	A	A	A
Recent major donors	A	A	R	A	A	A
Recent donors	A	A	A	A	A	A
Old donors			A			A
Enquirers			A			A

An example of how a small charity might structure its mailing programme, taking into account the need to appeal more often to good but uncommitted donors, to report back to major donors with an annual report, and to appeal rather less frequently to enquirers or lapsed donors. Each of the segments in the plan will demand a different package even if appeals are going out at the same time.

your most important audiences. Get the approach and message right, and you will succeed in raising lots of money; get it wrong, and you risk killing this 'golden goose'.

There are varying views about how often you should write to your donors. Some people feel that twice a year is an invasion of privacy, while some organisations keep in touch at least once a month (when all the different mailings are included). Trustees often take a very conservative view of this, which can effectively block the sensible development of your direct mail income. Testing is sometimes the only way for you to prove the point that more frequent mailings will be productive. The best advice is that if you find it cost-effective to mail more frequently, then do so; if not, then don't. Another possibility is to ask your donors how often they would like to receive information from you, and if your list of donors is large enough, you can then divide this into different groups who wish to be mailed at different frequencies.

However frequently you plan to mail, you need to develop a mailing strategy and have a good idea of the mailings that are to follow when you are planning the next one.

Most organisations will be using direct mail to seek money directly. There are a number of variations on this that can work well, helping vary the approach and making any high frequency mailing programme less repetitive. For example:

- inviting existing donors to enter into a **covenant**. This can be extremely effective since you are asking for a reasonable sum to be paid over a number of years, even though the response rates will be much smaller than for a single donation;
- asking donors to organise an **event** or participate in a **local collection**. This can help get new initiatives going locally. The majority of Oxfam shops started with an appeal for volunteers in the locality;
- suggesting to existing donors that they leave a **legacy** to your organisation. This does not produce cash now, although you can give an extra option of making a donation as well or instead.

There are great attractions to using mail as a medium for communicating with your supporters. Most important is your ability to target particular groups of supporters. Depending on the size and sophistication of your mailing list, you will be able to subdivide it into different segments, separating out your covenantors from people living in Wales and from those who have given large gifts, for example. This gives you the power to address a

---

Reducing your mailing costs

Mailings of 4,000 letters and more which are sorted into postcode sequence by the customer may qualify for discounts under Royal Mail's *Mailsort Scheme*. There are three options:

Mailsort 1 – aim to deliver next working day

Mailsort 2 – aim to deliver within 3 working days

Mailsort 3 – aim to deliver within 7 working days

For further details contact the Royal Mail Sales Centre on 0345-950950 (local rate call).

different message to each group. Indeed, there is a great danger in ignoring the information that you have. If, for example, you appeal to everybody on your donor list for a donation, you might well expect criticism from your existing covenantors who are already giving regularly. Surely you knew this, they will say. The best way of dealing with the particular circumstances of each donor is to have a general message and produce a series of variations – which may only require a change to one paragraph of the letter – to suit each segment.

Cold mailings

It's all very well to dream about the returns you could get if only you had 10,000 existing, active supporters on a computerised mailing list. Somehow these people have to be identified and won over to your cause fast. One of the main ways of doing this is through the use of cold mailings. 'Cold' because the person in receipt of your letter has not demonstrated any warmth to your cause before.

The practice is to create a mailing list from directories or to rent lists from someone who specialises in this; to put these lists together with any other promising lists you can obtain, and then to mail an appeal package as before. The difference between warm and cold mailings lies in the cost and the message. Because the people you are contacting are not your existing supporters, you can expect a poorer response from them. Thus to get the same amount of money you may need to mail to ten times as many cold names at ten times the cost. Then there is also the cost of renting the list. This often forces fundraisers to look for a cheap way of circulating the large numbers necessary to get a response of any size.

Most of the recipients of a cold mailing will not know much about you, so you will need a slightly different appeal. The degree of understanding of the issue will be that much lower; this may demand a rather more basic description of your work, and they will need some reassurance about its value and importance. This might take the form of providing endorsements from well known people; you might present the answers to frequently asked questions, like the amount spent on administration, or you might highlight your achievements and successes.

Not all of the people on the list will be new. Some may be duplicates of people who are already your supporters. If you can't find a way of removing these duplicates, this can create sticky situations when you find you have sent what is perceived as an inappropriate message to your own Chair or other key supporters.

Since it costs around 50p to send each letter, a 1% response rate would require an average donation of £50 just to cover the costs. Cold mailings rarely pay for themselves. Why do it then? Simply to get new supporters

Issues in Cold Mailings

1. Whether to buy other people's lists. Many members of the public regard selling mailing lists as an invasion of their privacy and do not like to receive unsolicited mail. These people will contact you from time to time and complain in the most vocal way. Be prepared with your response.

2. It can appear a waste of money. If only 3% of people respond, then 97% will be throwing all that paper away – which is why it is sometimes referred to as 'junk mail'. It is those who reply, not those who don't, who make direct mail an effective fundraising method, but you do have to watch the response rates and mail out costs to ensure that you are being effective. Even if you are, those that are not responding will think you are wasting both your money and the world's resources. Using recycled paper can give the right signals, despite its greater cost; suggesting the letter is handed on to a friend may also help.

3. It is expensive. You must ensure that you have the capacity to invest in this form of fundraising which requires a large expenditure commitment, a significant degree of risk and a payback period of several years. If you can't do it properly, then don't do it.

to add to your donor list. If you don't do this, the list will decline as supporters die, move or lose interest. You need to recruit new supporters just to stay where you are, and you want to increase your supporter base. You have to balance the cost of acquisition against the likely support you will receive from those who respond. If half the donors continue to support you at an average of £30 per year for five years, this puts the original acquisition cost into a better perspective. Some may even go on to leave a legacy.

When starting from scratch, a direct mail programme can be extremely expensive in the first years. Depending on the sort of response rates you get, you may find that the programme does not begin to generate any surplus for three or four years. However, at that point, the income should gradually build up, given good management of the programme. Local charities may have a significant edge here. It may be easier to find suitable local lists, the local connection can generate additional interest in the work, and cheaper methods of distribution than the post become possible. The question for a small organisation is how to develop this medium cost-effectively without having to invest in expensive professional advice and design work.

Reciprocal mailings

One answer to the low response rates to cold mailings is to undertake reciprocal mailings. The idea is that your best potential donors are those people who have recently given to you (warm mailings); but the next best are those who are giving to similar organisations. These people are likely to be socially concerned and are known to respond to direct mail appeals. They may also be happy to support two similar causes. So that if you mail your supporters with an appeal from a similar charity and they mail your supporters, you will both gain. And that's how it usually turns out in practice. Typically, response rates can range from 2.5% to 10%.

The best results will be obtained by choosing to swap lists with organisations that are closest to your own, even though they may be your competitors. Before you do make sure that your organisation backs you in doing this. Most organisations will want to devise a simple policy to safeguard the interests of themselves and their donors. A code of practice on reciprocal mailings is printed in Appendix 5 at the end of the book.

Finding the right lists

Your success in cold mailing will depend very substantially on the list you are mailing. Some lists will work extremely well for you, whilst others will achieve much worse results. There are several places to look:

- **publicly available information**, such as electoral registers and telephone directories. The electoral register (if published) can give you names and addresses in particular areas, and you can then select those areas which you feel are more likely to give – because of the affluence of the neighbourhood. The telephone directory at least gives you access to everyone who is able to afford a telephone. Not everyone is predisposed to respond to a request sent by post, and these lists compiled from public information do not always work that well;

- **lists compiled from directories**. Typically these could include lists of leading business people or the largest companies, which should be treated with care, as you may find that such people are the target of many appeals. There may be directories available which provide you with just the right list of names to send your appeal to;

- **lists that you obtain from other sources**. These may be lists of people who have purchased something by post, lists of account holders at a bank or with a credit card company, lists of subscribers to a magazine or information service, lists of graduates from a university.

The market for lists is served by list brokers who keep details of what is available and charge for the use of the list. The choice of lists is usually left to hunch or past experience. If you are doing a large-scale mailing, you will want to test them on a small quantity of the names first to see whether the people who subscribe to a magazine or buy a particular product through the mail want to support your charity to a sufficient extent to justify mailing them.

Other ways to identify good lists in advance, are to find out whether the list is already mail order responsive, whether there are a high percentage of people on your own list of donors who are also on this list and whether they seem to be the same sort of people as your typical donor.

Issues in reciprocal mailings

1. The first issue relates to the ethics of the idea itself. For most, the objection is to letting names of supporters out of your hands. The recommended way of doing this ensures that you keep firm control of your own supporters' names. However, you will have to argue it out with your trustees (who will usually take a cautious view).

2. If you do decide to do it, do you come clean with supporters and tell them what you are doing or do you keep it quiet? The Data Protection Act dictates that you must register yourself if you plan to do this. But you might wish to insist that any mailing from a reciprocal organisation to your supporters carries a slip or message to the effect that they are being mailed as a supporter of yours.

Evaluating mailing lists

Eleven questions to ask before you buy a mailing list:

1. Are the people your supporters or someone else's? If so, could you get them to endorse your appeal?
2. Are they mail order responsive? If this is a list of mail order buyers or postal donors they will be more used to responding in the post.
3. Is this a compiled list or a list of someone's customers/supporters? Compiled lists do not respond as well.
4. Are the people on the list similar to your own donors; by age, gender and attitude?
5. How up-to-date is the list and when was it last updated? Don't buy names of people who are no longer there.
6. Is there a name and a home address for each person?
7. Are these people buyers/donors or just enquirers?
8. Have these people bought or given recently? Can you take only the recent ones?
9. Is there any information on frequency of activity? The more frequent the better.
10. When was this list last mailed? The more recently the better.
11. What was the amount of money on average that was given/paid? Are these people likely to be able to give what you need?

Getting the right mailing lists is essential when you are trying to find new supporters. The difference between getting a good mailing list and a poor one may be as much as five times. Taken from Drayton Bird's **Commonsense Direct Marketing**.

Before you purchase or rent a new list, you should check a few things. Has this list been used recently? How old is it? Has it been updated recently? You do not want to be sending letters to out of date addresses or people who have died. Another thing to check is whether the list has been run against the Direct Mail Preference Service list recently, in order to remove all those people who have asked not to receive direct mail letters.

Your own list

The most valuable resource you have is your own list of donors or supporters. Guard it carefully and manage it properly. You need to keep it up to date by adding all new donor contacts as soon as you 'capture' their name. You need to change donor details as soon as you are advised of, for example, a change of address or a death. You need to check for duplicates occasionally.

You need to remove all inactive supporters. Just because someone has not responded for a year or two does not mean that they won't respond in the future – but they are less likely to. Periodically you should review the names of people who are no longer active donors. One way is to segment this part of your list in the mailing, and examine the results. You would expect the response to be low, but is it so low that it is no longer worth mailing these names? Or should they be mailed just once a year? Where the yield is below that of a cold mailing you should consider dropping or archiving them. Maybe you could try ringing some of your list to see why they haven't been giving (see 4.6 Telephone solicitation) before you remove them.

If your list is held on a computer, have you obtained a licence under the Data protection Act? Have you got a security copy of your file held somewhere else for safety's sake? You should produce regular back up copies of your files. If you lose the data, you may never be able to re-create it without a massive investment of time and money.

Management

The management of your mailings and the maintenance of your donor list is of great importance. The first thing to look at is the way you intend to communicate with your supporters. This should be planned a year or 18 months ahead. You should segment the list into different groups depending on when they became a supporter, how much and how they gave, and other relevant characteristics. Since each group will be receiving rather different messages from you, it is important to plan the overall mix of these. For example, what are you going to say to your regular supporters? Are they to be taken for granted and not written to or thanked and otherwise left alone? Or treated just like any other supporter? The illustrated mailing plan gives an idea as to how different groups might be treated. It also indicates some of the themes that might be chosen to give a balanced view of the organisation's work.

Another task is to ensure that the mailings are producing the expected results and keeping within budget. Control can be exercised in a number of ways. Costs should be monitored through the normal financial management process. You should get competitive quotes for all items of expenditure and your suppliers should keep within this. Costs will normally be referred to as per thousand mailed for comparison purposes. Income can be best estimated by breaking down the results achieved on the last comparable occasion for each segment of the mailing list. Though costs will rise with inflation, there can be no such certainty that income will keep pace. Every extra penny given has to be worked and planned for carefully. Useful measures of income are:

- the **response rate** (the percentage of people mailed who respond)
- the **average donation** (how much each person gives)
- the **combination** of these factors, which is the yield (the money received per hundred mailed).

A Mailing Strategy

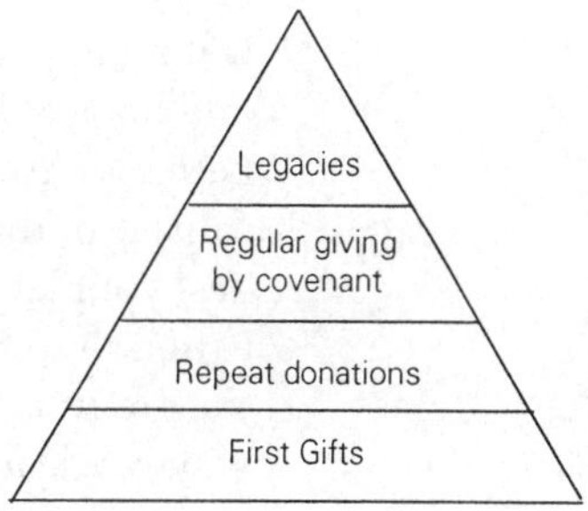
Legacies
Regular giving by covenant
Repeat donations
First Gifts

This is the approach used by many charities. The idea is that the whole thrust of appeals should be to move individual supporters up through the pyramid. Getting the first gift may be done on a continuous basis with cold mailing, advertising or other mass appeals. Regular appeals thereafter should aim to upgrade supporters to the next level of the pyramid.

'The Good Mailing Guide'

1. Use emotion in your writing.
2. Include stories about individuals.
3. Ask for money, directly.
4. Use simple language, avoid jargon.
5. Make all written material visually attractive.
6. Portray your beneficiaries as 'doers' rather than as 'victims', not as helpless, but needing your help.
7. Catch the reader's attention immediately, perhaps with a snappy headline.
8. Use someone specific as the signatory – this could be someone well known, your director or chairman, or a frontline worker.
9. Get the timing right.
10. Make the reader give.
11. Appeal to the reader's conscience.
12. Read what you are sending before sending it – would you give in response to your own appeal letter?

This is a list of success factors developed by Oxfam after studying ten years of appeals to supporters.

It is usually better to focus on both response rate and average donations – as you can do different things to improve each. Improving the response rate is part science and part judgement. The science is in the appropriate testing of your mailings. You can test almost any aspect of what you send and hope to be able to tell with a fair degree of certainty whether it can be bettered. You do this by sending a slightly different message to a small sample of the total that you are mailing, and then comparing the results. Test your letter, your message, how you personalise it, and test one group against another. Whatever you do, test just one thing at a time, and ensure the group is large enough to give a statistically valid result. Testing is the way you learn from experience and improve your performance over time.

Getting started

The real difficulty in direct mail is getting started. Once you have a large donor base and an active mailing programme, it is a question of good management. However, there are considerable sums of money which will need to be spent in advance and this means greater risk. Here are a few tips.

- Find as many ways as possible of **capturing the names** of supporters: people who write to you or visit you; people who have participated in a fundraising event and volunteers who are giving their time. Keep their names and addresses on a database.
- Get these **existing supporters** to suggest friends who might like to be written to.
- Try to get a **sympathetic organisation** to let you mail their list for free. This is a reciprocal mailing without giving something back in return.
- Acquire **other lists**, but test them first. It is a good strategy to send a small test mailing to several lists in order to see the response, then if they do respond well, you can mail the rest of the list later on.
- Use **directories**. This does not always work. For example, if you were to use a telephone directory and target people who lived in a certain area, you will be writing both to responders and to non-responders – some people never respond to direct mail. If you wrote to someone else's mailing list, they would all be known responders. This is why people prefer to rent other people's lists rather than compile them from public information.
- **Hand deliver** where possible to save costs, and start with a simple mailing package – though the message must be powerful for it to work at all.
- **Start slowly**, and build up.

Getting help

Direct mail is a highly technical fundraising method. You will need to be skilled at:

- writing effective copy
- producing a cost-effective mailing package
- knowing how much to ask for
- planning a mailing programme
- selecting the best lists to rent
- testing (and coding) of the response
- knowing what response rates to expect
- evaluating your performance.

You may not have all (or indeed any) of these skills but it is possible to get advice, and the following are possible sources:

- **professional consultants**, who specialise in this medium. Since you are paying for their expertise, it is as well to know precisely what you need, brief them well, and have a contract that sets out precisely what they are expected to do and for how much;
- **direct marketing agencies**. For the hard pressed, a direct marketing agency will carry out all the necessary functions for a fee. This has the advantage of getting the work off your desk, but against that it can be expensive;
- **freelance help**. Designers and copywriters are available freelance, and can be used in conjunction with yourself or with other sources of help and advice;
- **fulfilment agencies or mailing houses**. The mailing can involve a great deal of work sorting out which letters go to which people and putting everything into the right envelope within a reasonable time. Mailing houses will perform these functions at a much greater speed than you are likely to be able to manage, unless your mailing is quite small. Another advantage of using a mailing house is that they can help you claim a postal discount for bulk mailings;
- **other charities** with direct mail programmes, who might be prepared to share their knowledge and experience with you.

As with other areas of fundraising the key to direct mail is start small, experiment and build up. You need constantly to analyse response rates and test new ideas before exposing everyone to them.

4.6 Telephone solicitation and other uses of the phone

If direct mail was the fundraising medium of the 1980s, the telephone is the fundraising medium of the 1990s. In considering the possible uses of the telephone in fundraising, you need to consider both outgoing phone calls and incoming ones. Both are important. Incoming calls include enquiries and telephone pledges in response to an appeal; lines with recorded messages also have a use. Outward telephoning, which requires some skill (and sometimes courage), can be used for a whole range of promotional and fundraising activities. The techniques discussed in this section include donation lines, premium lines, telephone recruitment and solicitation, and phonathons.

Donation lines

When charities first installed special response lines for people to call in and make a donation, it was very much a marginal facility. Over the years and with the increasing use of credit cards, donors appreciate the opportunity to make a telephone donation in response to an appeal or when the mood takes them. Recently, the Charities Aid Foundation have introduced a plastic card which enables people holding donor accounts to transfer money to a charity from their account in exactly the same way as for a credit card payment.

You can use a special number for the response line, which should be answered by someone specially briefed to receive calls. Some lines are connected to a telephone answering machine, which must have a good clear message and long duration answer tapes so as to be able to record a number of calls, and donors need to be told exactly what information to leave. Using an answering machine is not ideal. Some donors want to speak to a real person. Not many people would leave a donation of £1,000 on a telephone recording device, and some might hesitate to leave their credit card details.

Sometimes the calls are routed through to a switchboard or the reception. It is important that there is an effective procedure for taking calls, and that the person receiving the call knows what to do. Especially if you spend a good deal of time out of the office, you will want any information about people phoning in to enquire about giving passed to you quickly.

Premium telephone lines

An 0898 or 0839 telephone line has the revenue shared between the telephone company and the subscriber. The caller pays a premium rate per minute at peak times, and a slightly lesser amount at other times. The line can be used in conjunction with radio, TV or a mailshot promotion, or to receive donations or to give out information. Every call provides a contribution to the campaign.

Other special numbers are available. An 0345 telephone line gives the caller access to you at local rates irrespective of where they call from, and you are charged for this. An 0800 telephone line allows callers to telephone you at your expense. Another facility which may be of interest is the bureau which allocates memorable numbers.

Answering services

For some campaigns, you will want to have a real person answering the phone, but do not have the facilities or staff resources to do this. One option is to use volunteers. There are two problems with this: you may get very little warning of a media appeal which is going to generate a lot of response; and then there is the problem of finding and briefing the volunteers and getting the lines installed in time.

If media coverage is important to you as a method of generating support or recruiting volunteers or involving people in events, then you need to develop a system for responding to these calls. Another option is to use a telephone agency. Some agencies have memorable numbers (such as 200 0200). All have large amounts of equipment and trained operators. Not only will they answer the phone, but for an additional charge they will deal with any follow up mailings and provide a detailed analysis of the response. This can be quite expensive, so be sure to get a quote first. One agency, which is itself a charity and which provides a specialist telephone service for voluntary organisations is Broadcasting Support Services, 252 Western Avenue, London W3 6XJ.

Recruitment and renewals

Outgoing telephoning can be used for a range of purposes. Possibly the most frequent use is for the recruitment of people. Teams of professional telephone callers are now used by some charities to sell raffle tickets, obtain advertising for a brochure, solicit gifts in kind for an auction, recruit house-to-house collectors, recruit and keep in touch with people participating in a fundraising event and so on.

Telephoning existing supporters of the organisation is much easier than ringing people 'out of the blue', and is more acceptable to the person you are contacting. Opportunities to do this include getting a donor to pay a subscription by Deed of Covenant, and renewals of covenants and membership subscriptions. It is also an excellent way to find out why members are not renewing. Problems can be identified quickly, and hopefully rectified. When making such calls, you should be well prepared and have the relevant information and documentation to hand.

You may consider using the telephone simply to find out if your supporters have any questions for you. Too many telephone calls (just as too many fundraising letters) are concerned with what the charity wants

What can be done over the phone

Donors phoned	Response rate	Average pledge
£20+ donors	61%	£51.42
£35+ donors	67%	£65.36
£50+ donors	83%	£102.83

These results were achieved by **Friends of the Earth** in a recent test. They tested 1,250 donors and raised £64,000 in pledges. Two problems confront telephone fundraisers: how do you convert the pledges into reality; and how do you carry the operation out without offending supporters? Complaints are a common occurrence.

to tell its would-be supporter rather than listening to the supporter's ideas, questions and concerns. Why not simply ring people up to find out if they are happy with what they receive from you and whether there is anything else they would like to know? You would be amazed at some of the questions and outcomes. However, if you are going to do this you must be prepared to respond accordingly. If they ask you not to ring them again, don't.

Another good use of the telephone is to raise money in an emergency. If there is a famine and people are dying, then that is a good reason to call. If the medical costs for an operation for a child need to be met immediately, then again the urgency of the appeal by telephone is appropriate. If a spell of bitter weather is causing the elderly to die of hypothermia, again instant action is required, and a phone call seems appropriate.

One technique that is used extensively in the US but has yet to catch on in the UK is the Phonathon, or telephone fundraising campaign. There are two ways that this can be done. One uses a team of volunteers, the other uses professionals who may be selling double glazing in the morning and your cause in the afternoon. Telephone fundraising campaigns work best if the cause is really urgent, or if it can be made to seem so. If the need is obvious then it also becomes simpler to recruit volunteers to do the telephoning.

The telephone is quite an expensive way of contacting people and so it needs to be used with care. It is unlikely to be of value in soliciting £5 donations, but the response rates can be over 50% when calling past donors, which is well in excess of normal mailing response rates. However, the pledge rate may not turn into cash in the bank unless donors are giving a credit card payment option. For those that don't have a credit card or are unwilling to use it to make the donation, you will need to send a letter to clinch the donation. You might expect 60% of pledged donations to be converted into actual support at the end of the day.

Telephone solicitation

Essential requirements for using the telephone successfully are the script and the list. Creating the script is a technical task. Until you have experienced the huge range of responses possible, it is difficult to create a good script but it should contain:

- **information** about who you are and the organisation you represent;
- whether it is a **good time to talk**. Anyone who has received calls at 6pm just as the children are sitting down to a meal, will vouch for the potential hostility that can be generated by a caller presuming that now is the most convenient time to talk; so callers should attempt to ascertain whether this is a good moment to talk. Failure to do this can diminish the results of the call;
- **reference to previous support** or past contact. When calling people, who have supported the organisation before, it is important to refer to their past help and thank them again;
- a short **introduction** about the current needs of the organisation or something else about the development of its work, and this should help set the scene for a further request for help;
- a **call to action**. As with any other form of communication, you should not expect that supporters will necessarily know why you want to talk to them unless you state it explicitly. The call to action must be very direct and clear, and should state precisely what you want them to do. Getting a pledge or a verbal agreement is usually the best you can hope to do over the phone – unless you are seeking a credit card donation (in which case you can complete the transaction there and then);
- a follow up **reminder**. The caller may say any pledge made over the phone will be followed by a letter or form to sign. The follow up should be done immediately to achieve a maximum response.

Creating a list of people to call is not always that easy, since many databases do not include phone numbers. This is something that is changing. If you plan to use the telephone, then perhaps you should include space on the reply coupon or in your promotional literature for the supporter to put a phone number. There is also then the implication that if they give you this, they will not mind being called. With the callers and the script in place, you need a ready supply of phone numbers; you may need someone to look these up in the phone book or other directory, if you do not have a list.

You will need to recruit and train your callers; this is definitely not something just anybody can do. Successful callers have an easy outgoing confidence that is communicated over the phone. Though many people are used to the phone, put them in a situation where they have to ask a supporter to give, and they become reluctant and tongue-tied.

Using an agency

An important decision is whether to do telephone solicitation in-house or subcontract the work to an agency. Clearly, an agency can be very helpful for a major telephone campaign but the use of an agency to solicit funds means that they have to conform with the requirements of the Charities Act (see overleaf). There are other issues of working with an agency.

- You need to be able to produce the scripts and **change and modify** them with experience or changing needs.
- There must be close **supervision** of the process to ensure that the most valuable asset of all – your charity's reputation – is maintained. You may only be aware of what is being said over the phone in your name when you start to receive complaints. If the agency is being paid on the basis of its success, then there is pressure to be a little economical with the truth.

For these reasons, if you are planning a major campaign, it makes a lot of sense to carry out volume trials with an agency. This will incur start-up costs, but will lift much of the burden of the work at this stage from you. If the indications are that it will be a successful venture, you can then look at the logistics of doing it in-house, or recruiting a team of home-based part-time callers, as some have done.

Whichever way you set about it, you need to engage in at least two levels of testing. First you need to test the concept of telephoning for support. It is not guaranteed that your prospective supporters are going

---

The requirements of the 1992 Charities Act

If you employ an agency to make calls on your behalf, then they are a 'professional fundraiser' under the terms of the Charities Act. There are a number of requirements:

- a written agreement between the charity and the professional fundraiser in a prescribed form (the Institute of Charity Fundraising Managers has a model form);
- a statement to be given to potential donors informing them as to what proportion of their donation will be used to pay the costs of the fundraiser;
- a cooling off period. When a professional fundraiser uses the telephone to solicit money or to sell goods to raise money for your charity, and people respond with payments, then the professional fundraiser must, within seven days of receipt of the payment, write to people who have given or paid more than £50 giving them the right to cancel. The donor then has seven days to cancel the gift. This only applies to telephone solicitation by a professional fundraiser or commercial participator, and not to funds solicited by the charity's staff or by volunteers, who are not covered by these provisions;
- when a professional fundraiser is used, donors have to be sent a written statement which details what the money is to be spent on and the basis on which the fundraiser will be remunerated.

(The requirements of the Charities Act are set out in further detail in Appendix 4.)

to be readily available on the phone (or more importantly, cheaply available). So you should test telephoning against other media, such as advertising or direct mail. Having satisfied yourself that using the telephone is a viable option, then a variety of approaches will need to be tested. These should include the use of in-house callers as against an agency, a range of scripts with different messages and calls to action, and any use of pre-recorded messages as part of the call.

4.7 Membership and committed giving

Committed giving

Continued giving by your supporters is what really justifies your direct mail (and other donor acquisition activities). The donor acquisition process is expensive, and unlikely to cover its costs through the immediate income it produces, but it is the first step in building up a supporter base. The follow up mailings are what generate the real revenue – for as we have seen, the people who have given already respond much better to any appeal.

If you can then get your donors to commit themselves to regular donations this will create a continuing stream of assured income. This will help you broaden your fundraising base and move towards sustainability.

Your aim is to:

- get your first time donors to continue to give, by sending them further appeals, only removing them from your donor list when you are convinced that they are no longer interested;
- stimulate their concern for the cause and interest in your work, and this should then lead to an increase in the level of support they are prepared to give;
- help them recognise the importance of giving long-term support to the work that you are doing (your work may take time to yield results, and you need their continuing support to help you do this), and then get them to commit to supporting you on a long-term basis;
- make it easy for them to give on a regular basis. Set up a simple payment mechanism to enable donations to be paid regularly (see below). You might also want to use some form of 'membership' or 'friends' scheme to suggest levels of giving;
- encourage donations to be paid in a tax-effective way (if there are tax incentives for charitable giving available). Explain the tax benefits that are available, and help the donor take advantage of them;
- ask them to think about legacy giving as 'the ultimate gift'.

This was part of a membership flyer that included a free video as well as the three months free membership. New members were expected to compete a direct debit.

This list sets an agenda for you to develop your direct mail and donor acquisition programme, and to turn your first-time giver into a committed and enthusiastic long-term supporter.

Mechanisms for committed giving

Recruiting donors is expensive. Therefore, once you have them you should try and get the most from them. In other words you want them to become committed givers. Also, if you have a good, regular flow of income from friends or members, you can apply it to those parts of your work which are hardest to raise money for. Furthermore, you can demonstrate to other funders that you have a strong degree of support. This will help any fundraising you need to do.

There are three main ways in which committed giving can be developed:

- encouraging donors to give by **Deed of Covenant**, which is a tax-effective mechanism for regular giving;
- a **membership scheme**. This is something that is not necessarily tax-effective but can confer other rights and benefits. Some membership schemes are more concerned with the subscription income that is generated, whilst others seek to recruit large numbers of members to enhance the credibility and campaigning clout of the organisation;
- **payroll giving**, which is also a tax-effective way of giving (this is covered in Section 4.13).

The specific mechanisms available for the actual transmission of money are:

- a **standing order**, sometimes called a banker's order
- a **direct debit** which reverses the control of the transaction. You, the charity, demand from the bank the payments that fall due
- **cash** or **cheque** payments.

Promotion

Not every donor will agree to enter into a long-term commitment, but it is important to give each one the opportunity to do so. Therefore, you need a clear promotion strategy. This should include answers to the following questions:

- what are the interests and motivations of your supporters?
- what are your financial requirements – how much income do you need to raise, and how much do you think your donors will be prepared to give?
- how will you promote a scheme to your existing supporters, to encourage them to make a bigger commitment?
- are there any other prospective committed supporters that you can identify?

- how should you report back to your committed givers, so as to maintain their continued enthusiasm and support?
- what else can you do to get them to feel more involved in the work of the organisation and the cause it is addressing?

A common problem is that once the support is committed, you then begin to take your committed givers for granted. This must be avoided at all costs. You should take every opportunity to keep in touch and tell them what you are doing. You might feel that once a donor has made a commitment it is an indication that they do not want to be asked for further support. A better approach is to view their commitment as an affirmation of the importance of your cause. The trick is always to

---

Promoting committed giving

The following are some of the promotional techniques you can use.

Approaching active givers

If you analyse the response to your appeals, you will see that a number of your donors will have given more than once. They may give each year in response to an annual appeal. They may give more than once during the year. They may respond very promptly to the appeal. These are your priority targets for committed giving. They should be contacted, pointing out the advantages of giving regularly and offered all the appropriate forms. If there are only a few 'prospective targets', then you can do this contacting in person or by telephone.

'Member-get-Member' or 'Supporter-get-Supporter'

This is simply an invitation to an existing member or supporter to nominate or recruit another. Various incentives (such as a free entry prize draw or some form of gift) can be used which are offered either to the original member or to the new one. This relies on the personal enthusiasm of existing members and their ability to persuade their friends and colleagues, but generally works extremely well.

Promoting committed giving more widely to your donor base

One strategy is to undertake one appeal per year which promotes regular giving and encourages payment by standing order or some other system, but this may involve a loss of response from those not in a position to give regularly, and who might otherwise have made a one-off cash donation. Another approach is to mention the value of committed giving in each mailing, and allow people the opportunity to give in this way.

Using child sponsorship and similar techniques

Here the donor is linked to a specific project, community or family over a period of time. In return the donor receives news of the project and the sponsored child, and even letters written by the child. Such an approach works extremely well in fundraising terms, but has to be handled with care. Problems can arise where the donor really wants to help just one individual person (most projects provide support for the whole community), or where the donor builds up an expectation of a relationship with the sponsored child, which may not be what the family wants.

recognise their commitment so that they understand that whenever you approach them, this is because of rather than despite their commitment. On this basis, committed supporters can then be appealed to on a regular basis. This is especially true when there is an obviously good reason for the appeal, such as an emergency; appealing to your list of covenantors or members, you might get at least a 10% response (which is far better than you could achieve by cold mailing).

You will need to report back to your committed givers. You might produce a newsletter or a magazine or send a personalised letter from the chief executive. Committed givers are likely to want to see a minimum of expenditure on unnecessary items, and so should not be approached too frequently or too lavishly. Friends of the Earth has a good way of reporting back to covenantors, which is to invite them to an evening meeting which is addressed by the senior staff of the organisation. These meetings are organised on an annual basis. This not only provides a good

Benefits of membership

1. Membership offers a convenient peg upon which to hang the request for committed and long-term support.
2. Membership can enhance your campaigning ability. Organisations like Amnesty and Friends of the Earth invite people to become members to harness their support for the cause. It is a badge of support for their campaign and it is the members who can be expected to be at the forefront of local action, while donors will be supporting the work of the organisation itself.
3. Membership can open up the organisation to democratic control through annual meetings, giving the members some feeling that they control the direction of the movement.
4. The membership list is an ideal hunting ground for donations. Some membership fees are set deliberately low to attract the maximum number of people, so not much money is raised through subscriptions alone. However, the members have demonstrated their commitment to the cause and so qualify as perfect prospects for obtaining a further financial commitment.
5. Membership can easily be structured to invite different levels of contribution (to reflect people's commitment, ability to pay etc.).

Benefits of Covenants

1. Tax reclaim adds value to the donation and can benefit higher rate taxpayers.
2. The duration of the covenant can be open ended, allowing it to continue beyond the four years until the donor wishes to end it.
3. No link to membership is needed (although membership subscriptions can be paid by covenant, provided that the benefits offered to the member do not exceed 25% of the annual subscription).
4. A minimum commitment of four years creates a stream of assured income for the charity.

opportunity to say thanks, but also enables the most committed to become more involved, get more information and meet other supporters.

When any fixed-term commitment comes to an end, there is both an opportunity and a need to ensure that as many people as possible renew. The usual way to do this is through sending reminder letters – one before the expiry and one coinciding with it. The telephone can be used to ask donors why they have not yet renewed; this both reminds those who have simply not got round to dealing with it, and gathers useful information about those who have decided not to renew.

Membership schemes

Some membership schemes are aimed primarily at people who are interested in doing something – helping the organisation campaign, attending cultural events, volunteering their time. The aim of these is not to generate an income, although members may be happy to give when asked. Membership schemes of this type may have their annual subscription levels set deliberately low to encourage as many people as possible to join. Then there are those schemes that have a fundraising purpose – the primary aim is to generate income for the organisation.

There are three main benefits which you can derive from having a membership scheme.

- *Commitment*: a membership scheme is a convenient way to build committed long-term support for your organisation.
- *Involvement*: membership provides a mechanism for democratic control through the right to vote at annual meetings (if this is included in the constitution of the organisation), thereby giving the members some influence over the direction of the organisation.
- *Money*: the annual membership fee provides an income, which you can apply to whatever purposes you wish within the organisation. It can be a really effective means of covering your core costs.

Another important purpose of having a membership base is the indirect benefit it can bring to your organisation. If you wish to mount a campaign, your members are the first who can be called on to participate in it, and

---

Why people become members

There are a number of reasons why people will sign up as members of your organisation.

- *Personal benefit*: the member joins principally because of the benefits they believe they will gain. Examples of this are the National Trust and the RSPB which give discounted entry into their reserves or properties to members.
- *Supporter*: the member joins to express support for the work of the charity. In this case membership is organised to encourage members to subscribe at preferred rates as a way of making their contributions on a continuing basis.
- *Campaigning*: members are signing up to show their support for particular policies or causes. An example of this is Friends of the Earth where members are showing their concern for the environment by joining. Subscriptions are quite modest in this case and have to be renewed on an annual basis.
- *Influence*: members join many local organisations simply to be able to influence their affairs. This will be done through regular meetings and AGMs. Subscriptions are usually quite low.
- *'Clubs'*: the member joins a club – such as the Friends of the Royal Academy – to signal their support for the work and also receive benefits from membership. Subscriptions may be higher in this case and there may be expectations of involvement in activities and events.

your membership numbers indicate the degree of the public support for your campaign or issue. A high membership level can increase your influence and impact.

Frequent giving

The value of committed giving or membership subscription income depends on:

- the **number of donors** or members – the more you have, the better. Once you have established a scheme, your aim should be to find ways of recruiting new donors or members economically;
- the **annual subscription** level. With a membership scheme, this will depend on your objectives – to make money or to involve as many people as possible. Some organisations give the donor or member different levels of annual subscription to select from;
- the **cost of running the scheme**. This includes the cost of member acquisition, and the annual administration cost including the cost of communicating with the member and sending information such as newsletters and annual reports. This should be calculated and budgeted for, so that an organisation has a clear idea of the surplus income that will be generated by each member after the costs of running the membership scheme;
- the **value of any additional income** that is generated from further appeals to members.

The frequency of giving is also of key importance. If you ask for a smaller sum on a frequent basis, you will find that you can get people to contribute much more over the year. For example, ActionAid in one of its most successful promotions asked, "Does this child need 50 p more than you?". They were inviting supporters to give 50 p a day, which seemed a trivial sum, but in fact they were asking donors to enter into a monthly commitment of £15 If they had been asked to give £180 a year, people would almost certainly have refused to do so.

You can ask people to give once every three months (quarterly) or once a term (three times a year, which might be appropriate for a school project), or monthly (which is the frequency of many people's pay) or even weekly (for the real enthusiast!). You might even suggest a certain level of donation, and ask the donor to select the frequency. The value of encouraging frequent giving is something that can be tested quite easily in one of your mailings. The usual outcome is that requests for monthly or quarterly giving will be no less effective, and will produce dramatically higher average annual donation levels for you.

Categories of membership

One of the key issues is the way in which membership and committed giving is priced and styled. Membership fees have to take into account the possibility of attracting large numbers of people who are prepared to be identified with your organisation. They also need to allow concessions to people on low income and encourage higher levels of support from those wealthy supporters, benefactors and corporate members.

Many organisations have several categories of membership with different levels of annual subscription. Other categories of membership can be created such as a sponsor or a patron, or special categories like those produced by the Royal National Lifeboat Institute's 'Shoreline', for people who can be expected to give more. One organisation has three categories – 'Friends', 'Good Friends' and 'Best of Friends', another has 'Gold', 'Platinum' and 'Silver' membership. One challenge for the fundraiser is to lift members from one category to the next.

Life membership is an opportunity to get a single large payment in one go, as well as enabling a member to be seen as an important benefactor of the organisation. But life means life, unless you state otherwise, and you are committed to servicing the membership for the duration without any expectation of an annual income. The price needs to reflect this.

Administration

The administration of membership demands a high degree of organisation, especially if you wish to maximise the benefits of your fundraising effort. There are several issues to consider:

1. Membership renewal

How should you organise the task of inviting members to renew their subscriptions? The best system is where the member has to do nothing – the membership continues until cancelled, and the subscription is paid by Standing Order or Direct Debit.

If there is a fixed-term commitment and this comes to an end, you will want to ensure that as many people as possible renew. The usual way to do this is through sending reminder letters, either a few months before the expiry, giving them time to renew, or to coincide with the expiry, to remind them that renewal is due. A follow up reminder some months after expiry, telling them that their membership will lapse if they don't renew, or a further follow up some months later – which is the final reminder – could also be appropriate.

The telephone is also a valuable tool. It can be used to ask donors why they have not yet renewed. This reminds those who have just not got round to dealing with their membership renewal, and it also gathers useful information about why members are not renewing.

Membership renewal can be done on a fixed date each year (with annual membership running from the 1st January to the 31st December, for example), which means that all renewals are handled on one date.

However you have the problem of what to do with members who join during the year – especially with those who join in the later part of the year and feel that they have already paid their subscription. An alternative mechanism is that each member's membership expires exactly twelve months after the annual subscription was paid. This requires more efficient organisation, as you will be dealing with membership matters throughout the year.

If there is a large membership, you will need a reliable computer system to make it work well. A key point is the ability of the system to identify renewal points so that you can mail not only on the point of renewal but also before and after to stimulate the highest possible renewal rate.

2. Raising the subscription rate

A change in the annual subscription rate can be a very laborious process, because members have to be informed of the change and all Standing Orders need to be cancelled and replaced with new ones for the appropriate amount. As a result, some organisations review their subscriptions quite infrequently (perhaps once every three or four years) and take a conservative view of the need to increase rates. This means that membership fees can often lag well behind inflationary pressures and costs.

One way around this problem is to ask for the subscription to be paid by Direct Debit. This is becoming much more acceptable to people as a payment mechanism. The usual procedure is to inform the donor in advance, giving them a chance to cancel their subscription if they do not want to pay the higher amount, and to agree to reimburse any sums debited from the member's bank account in the event of a dispute. A small organisation may find it difficult to obtain a Direct Debit facility from their bank; in such cases, the Charities Aid Foundation offers this facility, but only for organisations that have charitable status.

3. Paying membership subscriptions by Deed of Covenant

A covenant increases the value of any donation by nearly 30% at present tax rates (see Appendix 3), but it can only be used for donations, and cannot be used to pay for goods and services. A membership subscription may offer something in return to the donor. The Inland Revenue offers a concession. 'Ordinary small subscriptions' paid to a charity can be paid by covenant provided that the benefits offered to the donor (which is not the same thing as the benefits actually received by the donor) do not exceed 25% of the cost of the subscription. There is a further concession for heritage and wildlife sites, where the value of free or reduced price access to these sites is not included when calculating the amount of benefit.

If a membership subscription can be covenanted, members should be informed of the extra benefit to the charity of their doing so. Simple pre-printed forms should also be provided. The best type of covenant to use is one where the annual amount due is the level of the membership subscription (which enables the subscription to be raised during the term of the covenant), and where the covenant continues for four years and then until the member cancels. Alongside this, the covenant payments are best paid by Direct Debit.

4. VAT liability on membership subscriptions

When more than an annual report and a right to vote at the AGM are offered to a member in return for their subscription, Customs and Excise will treat the subscription payment as being partly a payment for a service, and some or all of it may be taxable (for those organisations who are registered for VAT, or where the taxable subscription income takes them over the VAT registration threshold). Many organisations are keen to offer benefits to encourage people to subscribe. If you are unsure about the tax implications, you should consult Customs and Excise before finalising the membership scheme. (See Appendix 3.)

5. Maintaining donor records

In your committed givers and members, you have a group of people who will be giving money to you regularly and possibly supporting you in a number of other ways. You need to keep track of their support, so that you are able to identify people who might be able to give you special help when you need it, or to invite to special events such as receptions, or simply to personalise the appeals you write to them as much as possible. This means that you need to keep all the information on one record, and that you should avoid at all costs the mistake of sending them duplicate mailings. You need to merge donor information, which is collected when members make additional donations, with their membership record.

It is essential not to keep just one set of information so that you are able to look up one person in one place to find out how and when they have supported you.

4.8 Personal solicitation

Meeting and speaking to potential donors in person has a great deal of potential as a fundraising technique. There are many different ways in which face-to-face or personal solicitation can be carried out:

- one-to-one meetings at the place of work
- personal visits at people's home
- talks at public events
- making a presentation at private meetings
- telephone calls to supporters.

All these give opportunities for persuasion, for questions to be asked and answered, and for reassurances to be given on matters of concern. The degree of personal interaction between the charity and the donor is what sets this apart from other fundraising techniques.

Warm visiting

Warm visiting involves face-to-face meetings with people who have already supported you or with whom you already have some form of contact. There are two reasons for doing this:

■ **to talk about your work**, find out more about their interests, and develop a warmer relationship with them, rather than to ask for money. This is an investment in the relationship which you hope might lead to more committed giving (or even a legacy) later on;

■ **as part of a major appeal**, when you really do need to get support and are making a personal presentation on the work of the organisation to a potential new supporter. This will involve fixing an appropriate time and place for the meeting and the charity's offices are often the best place because they give people a flavour of the organisation. Alternatively, some people will feel more comfortable meeting in their own homes.

How to succeed at warm visiting

- Have precise **information** on the individual's past support so that you can thank them and tell them what you have been able to do with their money. Try to locate a particular interest or concern of theirs and show how you are working in that field. In other words, listen first and suggest second.

- Be **well briefed** about the work of the organisation, so that you can talk about current efforts and future plans in an informed and interesting way.

- Have some idea of the **support** you need, and the ways in which they might be able to help you so that if the opportunity arises, you can introduce the idea of further support.

- Know about **tax-effective giving** – this can be one excuse for being there in the first place – and tell them how their money can be used even more efficiently, by donating it tax-effectively.

Meeting potential new supporters

If someone has indicated an interest in giving to you, you may want to meet them personally. At this meeting, you will be able to answer all their questions, and suggest ideas for the sorts of things that they might like to support. Such a meeting should be held in an appropriate venue; the charity's offices are not always the best place to meet potential supporters – a site visit where the beneficiaries are around, or a meeting at the offices of an important existing supporter may be better. If it is at your office, make sure everything looks well run and busy – this gives a positive image of your organisation. Alternatively, some people feel more comfortable meeting you in their own homes.

For such a meeting you need to:

- **research the donor** and their capacity to give, so that you know their interests and understand the scale of giving that may be possible;
- have a **list of projects** which they might like to support, so that you can discuss what will most interest them;
- have **good, clear information** about the organisation and its work available, including photographs of the organisation at work and endorsements from prominent people.

Don't be in too much of a hurry. The skilled fundraiser knows when to ask. This may not be immediately, but later, after their interest has been stimulated and they have had time to think about it. Also, the experienced fundraiser listens to what the potential supporter is saying and responds accordingly. Fundraising isn't about telling someone what you think they should know; it's about working together to meet certain needs.

Cold visiting

Much more daunting is visiting people 'cold', where there has been no previous support or expressed interest in giving as a reason for the visit. Though this sounds a thoroughly unpromising way of winning supporters, it can work very well in the hands of trained canvassers.

The technique is unlike house-to-house collecting, in that you are asking for a covenant or some other high value gift, and thus the process needs to take place inside the home rather than on the doorstep. However, like a house-to-house collection, it does require a licence.

A few organisations use teams of volunteers who make visits on their behalf – the Karuna Trust, which raises money for children's homes in India, is one good example. The visitor chooses a likely area and calls unannounced in the evenings. They ask if they can talk to the householder about the cause. Typical experience suggests that more than one in a hundred visits result in a covenant or a reasonably substantial donation.

You need to put in a lot of footwork and be prepared for the usual rejections. It is a particularly suitable method for raising money and support for local community projects where donors can see the need and the benefits on their own doorstep. If this technique is of interest, there are trainers who have experience of preparing visitors for this work.

Telephone solicitation

Asking on the telephone has many of the same characteristics as personal solicitation. It is much more efficient in that you can contact many more people in a given space of time, but less personal. It is even possible to organise mass telephoning campaigns (either warm or cold calling) using your own volunteers, or even a specialist telephone selling agency.

The telephone can be used successfully in many situations and is discussed in more detail in Section 4.6.

Presentations at events

You may have the chance to speak at meetings, conferences or other events. This is an opportunity to speak directly to people about the work of your organisation and its needs. With an experienced speaker, this can also be a good opportunity for raising money. If it is someone else's event, you may need their approval if you plan to collect money or distribute fundraising materials.

The presentation has to be carefully thought out. Why should that group of people be particularly interested in your work? The answer may be that they are not, but would be keen to take part in the activity you have organised. If you don't engage their interest you won't get their support.

Next, you need to work out how your audience is going to respond. After you have spoken, the audience may want to get home quickly or to move on to something else. The seating pattern may inhibit them from coming forward for written information or a donation form. If they don't respond immediately your response rate will not be that high; however well intentioned people are when they leave the meeting, the majority are unlikely to follow any commitment through.

One signal of your need to raise money can be made by organising a bucket or plate collection. Place collectors at the door or at the end of each row but don't forget to announce what you are going to do in your speech! You could keep a register of people who have attended – if it's an invitation event make sure someone notes who actually came – and those people can then be personally visited or written to afterwards. Alternatively, it may be possible for you to arrange for appropriate forms – perhaps a covenant form – to be on each person's seat in advance of your speech. You can then refer them to the chance to support you that this offers.

Your own events

Other people's events offer you new audiences, but you can organise your own events for existing and potential supporters. These can be visits, study tours or open days to see your organisation at work, small discussions with an expert speaker so that they can see the problems you are addressing in greater depth, or receptions of some sort, perhaps at the home of a well-respected donor and possibly with a guest speaker or some sort of presentation afterwards.

Such events can be an excellent fundraising investment. You will make your existing donors feel important, and give them a better understanding of the issues. This may lead them to give more substantial support or commit time to your organisation as a volunteer.

Think carefully about your objectives for such an event, and about your audience and the sort of event that will most appeal to them. It is not just organising the event, but having the right event for them that is important. One idea is to mix existing supporters and people who have expressed an interest at such an event. If you do this, all the new people attending should be told to expect a follow up visit from you afterwards.

What you will need to succeed

Here are some of the things that you will need to succeed in personal solicitation.

- **People** who are really good speakers and presenters. You may wish to provide some form of training for them in presentation skills and asking skills. You might even try to develop a panel of people who are interested in your organisation and good at speaking at meetings.

- **Donors** who are prepared to speak at meetings to be attended by potential donors. There is nothing like having people say "the organisation is great, and I've given to it" in motivating others to give.

- **Volunteers** with similar skills for warm visits.

- Good handout **material** that can be used to illustrate the points you are making. It is important that these show people (people helping, and people being helped). For presentations you may want visual aids (for use with an overhead projector or a flipchart) or even a short video (not more than five minutes long).

Any visit should be prepared with care. Above all, rehearse the presentation thoroughly. You should try to predict what questions will come up and you will need to be well armed with written information. Go prepared with photos, brochures, budgets and plans so that you can use these as prompts. Short videos can be useful too. Finally, remember to leave some prepared material behind. Most people will not make up their minds immediately, and will be guided or reminded or helped to respond by what you have left with them.

The Good Public Speaking Guide

- Find out how long you are expected to speak for.
- Keep sentences short and jargon free.
- Plan your talk. But remember that it is more effective to appear to speak 'off the cuff' than to read out a speech.
- Start with a joke or a story to enliven the proceedings.
- Explain your involvement in the organisation, and inject a sense of personal commitment to the cause.
- Use case studies and personal stories to explain the work. This is far better than a stream of statistics.
- Do not use jargon.
- Appeal to your audience's emotions – their hearts not their heads.
- Ask for support if you need it.
- Have business cards, explanatory leaflets and pledge forms to hand out to those who are interested.
- Tell people to phone you if they are interested, and say that you would be delighted for them to visit you to see your work at first hand.
- Always be positive and upbeat, talk about success rather than failure, and opportunities rather than problems.

Throughout the meeting, you should give people the opportunity to ask questions. If you are not getting much feel for how the meeting is going, ask some questions yourself. Do they feel it is an important issue and that the project will achieve what it is setting out to do?

At some point you need to make the request for money. There are different approaches to this. One is to say that you want them to consider helping in one of several ways. The direct approach dispenses with such niceties, explains the urgency of the need, and simply asks for the money – but always try to ask for a specific amount. The final, and probably the most effective, is when someone who has already given support is making the request, and mentions what their donation has been.

4.9 Legacies

Legacies are an enormously important source of charitable funds, generating around £700 million a year, which is as much as grant-making trusts provide. Legacy fundraising can often seem a mysterious activity which generates large sums of money with apparently little effort for the fundraiser. In fact, some of the largest legacy earning charities have carefully planned strategies for developing their legacy income. Like other forms of fundraising, what you get out depends on what you put in.

Types of legacy

There are several types of legacy. Each is of value in different circumstances.

- *Pecuniary legacy.* This is a simple clause in a will where a gift of money is left to another individual or charity. "I leave £100 to my faithful companion, Rose" is one example. This is easy to arrange, but has the main drawback that over time the value of the legacy is eroded by inflation.

- *Specific bequest.* A donor can give an object or specified item of property in their will which can either be kept or sold by the beneficiary. "I give my Bokhara rug to my favourite nephew, Jamie", for example. Such bequests are good in that they are more likely to maintain a real value over time; though they can be problematic if the Bokhara has long since been sold or thrown away after paint was spilled on it, or if the rug turns out not to be Persian – in which case the beneficiary would get nothing.

- *Residuary legacy.* An alternative method is to bequeath either the whole or a proportion of the residue of the estate after all pecuniary legacies and specific bequests have been made. These legacies are on average ten times larger than when a sum is specified. Residuary legacies will keep up with inflation better (their value is particularly linked to property and other share prices), and many people simply do not know the value of their estate. With the decline in the birth-rate, the increase in life expectancy, and the increase in property ownership, there will be an increase in the number of people with significant assets who are without family to bequeath their estate to. This is a real opportunity for charities.

■ *Long stop legacy*. These stipulate that if all the other provisions of the legacy fail, for example if all the named residuary beneficiaries have died, or if there are conditions attached which cannot be met, then the estate reverts to a charity. Thus, instead of the will failing and the money being distributed according to the intestacy rules, which may not be what the deceased would want, the money goes to a charity of their choice.

■ *Reversionary or life interest*. Where an elderly relative needs to be cared for, a life interest clause is often used such as "My house is given to the Charity with a life interest to my uncle Charles". This gives Charles the right to live in the house during his lifetime but on his death, the right to the property reverts to the charity. This can be a useful way of carrying out a responsibility to the supporter's family while at the same time ensuring a valuable legacy to charity.

■ *Codicil*. A codicil is an addition to a will, containing supplementary instructions, and is drawn up and witnessed in exactly the same way as a will. It is a simple way in which people can add instructions to their will without having to rewrite it. They could for example draw up a codicil to add a £1,000 legacy to your charity. (A model form for a codicil is given in Appendix 3.)

Legacies received		
Types of legacy received	*numbers*	*average value by charity*
pecuniary legacies	53%	£3,230
residuary legacies	47%	£20,040
(Smee and Ford, 1995)		

■ *Deed of Variation*. This is a way of changing a will after the testator has died. This can only be done when all the beneficiaries to the will agree. Thus, if the deceased was a very keen supporter of the environment, then the family could instruct the Executors of the will to make a £500 bequest to an environmental charity out of what they would have received. This has to be done through a Deed of Variation drawn up in a legally effective way, and the amount given in this way to charity is exempt from Inheritance tax.

Promotion

How do you invite your supporters to give you a legacy? Because the process of making a legacy is complicated as compared with sending a donation, a more systematic approach to raising legacies is needed. This demands drawing up a plan before proceeding.

The essence of legacy fundraising is that if you make an effort now, you will get a reward some years later. There will usually be a time-lag of between three and five years before you begin to see anything at all so you must be able to justify making a financial investment in the promotion needed and be prepared to stick to your guns when early returns are not evident and your management committee begins to question the wisdom of the policy. There are a number of ways to promote legacies.

- **Meet donors** to discuss the intricacies of legacy giving in detail. Although it is not always easy to arrange to meet donors in their own homes, this will undoubtedly be much more effective. The pioneering approach by Oxfam in the early 1970s involved setting up a team of volunteers primarily to visit solicitors, but also to visit Oxfam's larger donors to discuss will-making. This could also be done by using paid staff which gives greater control over the process, but costs more.
- Some charities organise **meetings or seminars targeted at professionals** to which they invite a number of their own supporters. This gives an opportunity to discuss will-making. The main professionals involved with wills are solicitors but charities also target accountants, bank managers and financial advisers, who may on occasion be asked for advice.
- The less personal approach of **direct mailing** to supporters and the general public requires a very clear set of objectives, a sensitive package and good administrative back up. Again it is desirable to follow up any interest by telephoning donors.
- **Advertising in the press**. This needs to be well targeted, coded and analysed and needs to carry a challenging message. Small ads as well as display advertising can be used.
- **Advertising in specialist journals**, which are targeted at the professionals mentioned above (this is covered in Section 4.14).

Your target audience

It is stating the obvious to say that to receive a legacy, the person making the will (known as the 'testator' or 'legator') has to die. This means that the charities which attract predominantly older supporters will have the best chance of receiving legacy income. Given that women live longer than men and, if they marry, tend to marry older men, it is more likely that a female supporter will have no direct family to leave her money to than a male supporter.

Before developing a legacy campaign it is important to:

- decide whether you are the sort of charity that might expect to receive legacy income;
- find out who your supporters are, and who legacies are currently being received from. It is also important to note whether it is your existing supporters or people completely unknown to your charity who are leaving legacies to you.

A review of any people who have already made a legacy to your organisation will indicate the sex and location of your testators. It may also give an idea of whether they have been past supporters or members of your charity. As a general average, 60% of charitable testators are unmarried females. The age of a legator is not usually known from looking at the will, but will presumably mirror the national mortality statistics.

There are several questions to answer in respect of targeting. Whether to go for existing supporters, which is where you are most likely to find support, or whether to target the general public with a bias towards elderly females living in the South East, which is where you are most likely to find substantial testators, or whether to target legal advisers, such as solicitors, who help in the drawing up of a will and whose advice may be sought by a legator considering a charitable bequest.

One aim of having a supporter base on which to concentrate your fundraising is to build up a good understanding of them and of how they might help you. If some form of regular committed giving is a natural successor to occasional gifts, then a legacy is the natural step up from regular giving. In the process of communicating with donors over time you will build relationships which will enable you to discuss sensitive issues such as legacies.

You might adopt a slow indirect approach, with regular mentions in a newsletter, or take the bull by the horns and write directly on the subject. One major charity embarked on this route some years ago with extreme caution. They invested in a mailing to 100,000 existing supporters inviting donors to send off for a range of new materials and to indicate their interest in making a legacy. The resulting 3,500 enquiries may represent a huge success or little more than polite interest; only time will tell. However the careful addition, as a defensive tactic, of the alternative of sending a donation if readers were unable to leave a legacy, yielded £100,000 in direct donations.

An alternative strategy is to focus on the general public. This can be done by posters, by cold mailing or through advertising. Although this has the benefit of lifting the awareness of your charity in general, it can be an expensive way of getting the message across unless it is carefully targeted.

Who gives legacies	
Women	69%
Men	31%
Past donors	32%
Non donors	68%

Yet another strategy is to concentrate on the intermediaries and advisers: the solicitor, the bank manager and the accountant. When wills are written these professionals are the ones who are asked for advice. They may be asked to provide information about charities, and certainly will have their own preferences or prejudices which could act as a veto or in your favour. In general, they do not like giving information on particular charities.

There are a number of publications sent free to these professionals which contain legacy advertising by charities in an attempt to influence them. At the very least, these publications (which include directories, yearbooks and special charity supplements) may be left lying around for clients to pick up whilst waiting or to be given if they request information about charities. Due care should be exercised in spending money on such advertising as it may not work, and the pay back period is likely to be many years ahead.

Another approach, which is particularly appropriate for a local cause, is to communicate directly with local professionals through personal contact or by talking at meetings.

The message

There are three main types of message.

1. **Make a will (and don't forget us)**. This approach leans on the fact that a high proportion of people die intestate (without having made a will) and the State then distributes their estate according to pre-set rules. Thus it is in the family's interest to see that a will is made if they wish to have any control over how the money is to be distributed and to minimise Inheritance Tax liability. According to a Charities Aid Foundation survey, 64% of the population have not made a will.

2. **'Remember us by adding a legacy or codicil to your existing will.'** This approach must necessarily be directed at those 36% who have made a will. Will making is a complicated process, especially when there are significant assets and family interests to consider. Thus the value of this approach is that it gets to people who know what you are talking about and who could, at least in theory, do something quite quickly – which is to add a codicil to their existing will. Another advantage is that you can include a codicil form for them to use in your mailing.

3. **'Make a pledge to support us when you next write your will.'** This approach has several advantages. It allows you legitimately to keep the supporter on file and to keep in touch about the subject, whilst also allowing you to get a very direct measurement of the effectiveness of your promotion. Most importantly it can imply some sort of

commitment on the donor's part to the process which can be stressed in future communications. Your aim is to get people thinking of leaving you a legacy to send you a signed pledge form.

Other ways of promoting legacies

There are a number of barriers to making wills. Some can be overcome by being creative.

- **Suggest a solicitor.** Some people who do not already have a will are prevented from writing one by not having contact with a solicitor they trust. A number of charities get the local Law Society to offer names of local solicitors for supporters to choose from.

- **Provide an executor service**. Some people do not have access to executors and feel inhibited about inviting a professional to do the job. Again, some charities will provide this as a service if they stand to benefit from the will. In a similar vein many charities, especially those with shops, offer a house clearance service, and will eventually benefit from this by turning the donated goods into cash.

Analysis of wills in UK	
All wills:	194,068
Wills with charitable legacies:	26,263
Total charitable legacies in these wills:	73,604
Distributed as follows:	
Health and social welfare:	17,171
Animal welfare:	10,996
Physically disabled:	7,376
Cancer research:	6,048
Medical research:	5,643
Religious:	5,061
Child welfare:	4,597
Services and marine charities:	4,473
Aged welfare:	2,643
Overseas aid:	2,436
Environment:	2,301
Educational:	1,099
Mentally disabled:	958
Arts:	541
Others:	2,261
(first published in 'Codicil')	

- **Assist people to draw up a will.** Perhaps the ultimate inducement is to provide assistance with the drafting of a will. This should only be done through a solicitor, but is something some donors prefer as they feel it will minimise the loss to the beneficiary charity. Some national charities and the Law Society have banded together as 'Will Aid' to provide a free will making service. The charities benefit by being associated with this promotion, and the solicitors will benefit if they are appointed as executors for which they can levy normal professional fees. It is possible to organise such a promotion on a local basis by working with a prominent local firm of solicitors.

- **Provide pre-printed forms.** One simple step is to print sample wording for a clause in a will or a codicil to a will in leaflets, which can then be used by a solicitor who is drawing up a will for a client. (Sample wording is given in Appendix 3.)

Memorial giving

Another variant is memorial giving, where the gift commemorates a person who has recently died. This can be an important source of income for local amenity societies and conservation charities. Local parks or galleries can have seats or rooms named after individual benefactors or supporters and memorial plaques abound. Educational charities may institute memorial lectures or bursary funds in the name of the deceased. This is particularly appropriate for charities where the deceased is known to have had a strong interest in the cause. If your charity does not readily lend itself to this type of memorial you can keep a memorial book, which is used to inscribe the names of benefactors and those being remembered.

Memorial giving is usually done by the friends and family in memory of the deceased. It can be done in a number of ways:

- **small ads** are regularly placed in the personal columns of the newspapers inviting friends an family to send donations to a favoured charity rather than to send flowers. This can yield a continuing flow of donations;
- **funeral directors** can be useful intermediaries, providing literature to the family of the deceased. This has become a tradition in Watford, where the Watford flower fund encourages donations in lieu of flowers which is then put into a community trust and distributed to local charities;
- a **Deed of Variation**, where all the beneficiaries of the will jointly agree to a variation in the will such that a bequest is given to a charity, can be negotiated in return for some form of memorial. This needs to be done within two years of death, and professional help in drawing up the Deed of Variation is recommended. The negotiation process needs to be handled with tact.

Getting started

The first thing you need to do before you can expect anybody to leave you money, is to produce some literature outlining your needs and showing them how they can leave you a legacy. Important points to make are:

- the tax exemptions for legacies to charity
- the legally correct forms of words
- the importance of the work and the need for support, as it relates to the viewpoint of potential testators
- the importance placed by the charity on legacies as a source of income.

These can either be mailed out or be used as information for enquirers.

You will need an efficient administrator. Getting people to make a legacy is only the first step. You will want to keep in regular touch with those who have pledged to support you or told you that they have mentioned you in their will. A good deal of administration may be needed once the legator has died. The process can at times be extremely protracted especially when you are sharing the residue with others, or when the will is contested. It is important to have someone carrying out an effective accounting and chasing function as well as someone who can deal sympathetically with bereaved families.

Issues

One of the issues often confronted by fundraisers is to decide how much to invest in legacy fundraising. It takes time to see any return – most people will, on average, die three to five years after having made their latest will. However, each legacy you receive will be larger than you could expect from a lifetime donation – the average amount of each legacy may be between £1,000 and £10,000 – but you can never link the promotion with the results with any degree of certainty. If you do nothing, you are not likely to see any development of your legacy income.

> ### The Smee and Ford service
>
> Smee and Ford, a firm of legal agents, provides two services to charities on a commercial basis which are useful to any charity receiving legacy income. The 'Will Notification Service' informs the charity when it has been mentioned in a probate will, so that the charity can notify the executors of its interest and press for an early distribution. The 'Discretionary Will Service' notifies charities of situations where money is left for charitable purposes to be distributed at the discretion of the executors, rather than to a named charity. Here the charity can send an appeal to the executors and hope that it will be considered favourably.
> Smee and Ford can be contacted at 2nd Floor, St George's House, 195-203 Waterloo Road, London SE1 8UX Tel 0171 928 4050

One idea is to use a percentage (say 10%) of your current legacy income for promotion. Another is to set a target for the number of pledges that you will receive each year. As time goes on you will find out both how many turn into legacies and how much it costs to get a pledge. The most common way is to look at what was spent last year and add a bit – not the most scientific approach!

To get an idea of the returns from any of your long-standing promotions, you can code the response so that you can identify a bequest with a particular promotion. You might use a variation of your address such as a room or box number which may then be included in the text of any bequest in your favour. This will help you monitor your marketing methods, but is of debatable value when you are changing your promotions every few years.

4.10 Schools and young people

Fundraising from children and in schools is virtually synonymous. If you want to reach large numbers of young people and harness their enthusiasm, then schools are the best place to start, but there is a word of warning. If you are planning to raise money from young people and in schools, remember that you are dealing with a vulnerable and impressionable group. You need to approach them with care and be sensitive of their needs. You should not put undue pressure on them to support you or to get their parents and family to support. Instead you should try to get them to understand your work, the reasons for it and why it is important.

What children are likely to have is time rather than money, and access to support from their families and friends. The link between the nature of your work and their educational interests is important, as the relationship will work much better if you can encourage their understanding of the cause or need you are addressing, rather than simply ask them to raise money for you.

Fundraising will take different forms depending on the type of school. Parents and teachers will both be concerned about the conduct of any fundraising and the pressure being put on the children. In primary schools, the ideas must naturally be very simple and have a good educational content. When dealing with the 9 to 13 age group, children are beginning to do things on their own initiative. Sponsored fundraising activities are very popular at this stage. At secondary level, fundraising becomes even more independent, for example young people organising discos or sleep-outs for charity.

In targeting young people, you will be:
- **generating money for your cause**, although this will not always be a huge sum;
- **involving young people** in your cause, giving them a better understanding of the issues involved and the work you are doing;
- **laying an important base for future support**. If people get involved in supporting charity when they are young, this can influence what they do and choose to support in later life;
- **reaching adults** through children. Raising money through young people inevitably includes their parents and parents' friends in a way that you otherwise might not be able to.

Ethics

Raising money from children is a delicate matter for a number of interconnected reasons and there are a number of issues to consider.

- **Legal issues**. Young people under the age of 18 are not able to enter into legal agreements, and should not be expected or invited to make contributions of any contractual nature (such as a Deed of Covenant).
- **What you can expect children to do** in school. This is well covered in the Institute of Charity Fundraising Managers (ICFM) code of practice on fundraising in schools (see Appendix 5). Obviously the role of a school is to prepare young people for their future life. Though charity and charity appeals are certainly part of the outside world, exploring this may best be done by classroom work rather than through some fundraising event. The school must be the judge of what is appropriate, and many now have quite tough stipulations on accepting charity appeals.
- The **pressure that children apply** implicitly or explicitly on their parents to give money or participate in an event. Most fundraising by children involves getting parents and close relatives or neighbours to contribute. Parents may react negatively to the number of times and the purposes they are asked to give to through their children, and may even try to prevent their children from taking part.
- **Safety issues**. Children should not be encouraged to solicit support of any sort from people outside quite a narrow circle of family and neighbours for personal safety reasons.

Making the approach

To obtain access, you will usually need the permission and support of the headteacher (or the support of a committed class teacher, who will persuade the headteacher). You can make the approach directly; or there might be a committed supporter or volunteer who is a parent or a teacher, who could do this for you.

Most heads will be receiving a large number of approaches from charities (some of the larger charities even have departments which concentrate on this form of fundraising), and will want to ration the number of activities taking place in the school. Although the local education authority plays little part in determining what happens in any particular school, some charities find it useful to be able to say that they have the approval of the education authority.

It is unlikely that you will be able to involve a school more than once a year, so you will probably need to contact as many schools as possible in order to get a reasonable number involved in raising money for you. A personal visit is the ideal way of making the approach. If this is not practical, a telephone call will be better than a circular letter, which is likely to find its way into the bin.

Some Fundraising Ideas for Schools and Young People

Auctions
Carol singing
Contests
Discos
Litter picking
Picnics
Raffles
Rag days
Recycling
Sponsored events
Summer fete with:
　face painting
　name the teddy
　high jumping
　puppet making
　treasure map
　book stalls
Tea bars
Treasure hunts
Tugs of war

Ideas for fundraising

No school is going to invite you in if the only thing you plan to do is raise money. A useful guide is to make your activities:

■ firstly fun;

■ secondly educational;

■ and only thirdly fundraising.

The usual starting point is to offer to give a talk about your organisation, the work it is doing, and the needs that it is dealing with. This is usually to a school assembly or to a relevant year group. You will need to make your presentation as attractive and interesting to the children as possible because this introduces the next step – the invitation to fundraise. This will either be taken up by the school or by particular classes if it fits into some other aspect of their educational programme.

For infant and junior schools you will need to offer very clear set of fundraising ideas if they are to succeed. Help the Aged, for example, has a series of quizzes for different age groups which are changed every year or so, and are designed to fit in to the curriculum as closely as possible. Sponsored competitions are popular as they give the child the opportunity to learn and to obtain sponsorship for the number of questions answered correctly. For secondary schools, the children themselves are in a better position to decide how funds should be raised and then to organise the process.

Sponsored events, such as walks and swims, are always attractive to the young as there is an element of physical challenge.

Fundraising by schools

Not only is there an increase in competitive pressures, with more and more charities competing to raise money from a fixed number of schools, but there is also a whole new sector of organisations seeking to raise money through young people and their parents – the schools themselves. As local management of schools has become established, schools have realised that the only way to expand or improve the quality of their education or to provide for extras is to raise money themselves.

It is natural for the school to have first call on the generosity of both the children and their parents. Raising funds for the school itself can be carried out in a whole range of ways that are covered elsewhere in this book: fetes, discos, sales, quiz evenings, Christmas cards, entertainments, and 100 clubs have all proved popular and effective. Mostly this fundraising activity is carried out by Parent Teacher Associations, which comprise a group of active and already committed parents. They are also able to raise money tax-effectively by getting parents to give regularly by deed of covenant.

Publications for schools

A number of the larger charities produce publications for children. These fall into two categories:

- school packs of teaching materials specially designed for use in the classroom (where they must be linked somehow to the curriculum). With many schools chronically short of books, producing good educational material (either for sale or for free circulation) can get your cause into the school. You also have the opportunity to get the cost of this paid through sponsorship;
- simple information aimed at young people, which is sent to young people in response to enquiries or as a thank you for a donation. This could include books, pamphlets, newsletters and information sheets. You might even consider setting up a junior supporters 'club' to nurture the interests of young people – for example a junior environmentalists' club. 'Young Gateway', a four-page section of the Children's Society magazine, sets out to motivate children to become further involved by showing what other young people around the country are doing for the charity. The 'Red Nose Club' does the same for Comic Relief. Barnardos have a 16-page full colour leaflet informing children about the work of the charity; laid out in cartoon format it demands the child's attention and includes a well-designed quiz. These undoubtedly build a strong loyalty to the organisations concerned and are an important ingredient of their fundraising programme.

National competitions

National and the larger city-wide charities have another opportunity; to design and develop a national award scheme for young people – an essay competition, an art competition, an ideas competition, for example.

You will need to offer prizes, which can be to the young people, or to the school – or perhaps to both. The prizes might be in cash, books, bursaries, or travel opportunities. You will need to reach schools with information about the award scheme – which may require a media sponsor, such as a newspaper – you will need to have the money to do this. The prizes will usually represent 25% or even as little as 10% of the total cost of running the award scheme, since you have to pay for publicity, printed material, the judging, the awards ceremony, and all the administration involved. However this can be a suitable vehicle for sponsorship, as it will appeal to sponsors who are looking for ways to reach young people and obtain the credit and good publicity form having supported an exciting award scheme.

4.11 Gambling

Since the arrival of the National Lottery (covered in Section 3.5), gambling has taken on a whole new meaning for fundraisers. Whereas previously there were only a few small charity lotteries and the football pools,

---

Some definitions

Lotteries come in many forms, and have different names:

- **Lottery**: formal name for a game of chance by sale of tickets. This could be a private lottery, a small lottery, a society lottery, a local authority lottery or the National Lottery
- **Raffle**: colloquial name for a lottery, usually with non-cash prizes
- **100 Club**: a group of 100 people participating in a lottery on a monthly basis. Tickets are purchased by monthly subscription and the draw is each month
- Tombola: a small scale game of chance at an entertainment event, usually involving the purchase of tickets to win bottles and other donated goods. Each ticket usually wins a prize
- **Sweepstake**: a lottery where the winner is decided (for a sweepstake on a horse race) by whether the participant has drawn the name of the horse that wins a race
- **Skill Game**: where the outcome is decided by some measure of skill (including a tie break to choose the winner from all those submitting correct answers). Sometimes the element of skill required is very small, and the format is used to get around lottery regulations
- **Competition**: the same as a skill game. Skill games and competitions can also be free entry, where they are used extensively in sales promotions. A recent variant requires entrants to ring a premium telephone number, where the cost of doing so generates a return for the promoter. Because a measure of skill is involved, these are not technically lotteries, which are games of chance
- **Free entry draw**: this is a skill game or competition used in sales promotion, where there is no charge for entering.

Gambling activities

Activity	Definition	Authority	Act
Raffle	No skill, with entry fee	Gaming Board	Lotteries Act
Scratch cards	No skill, with entry fee	Gaming Board	Lotteries Act
Slot Machines	n/a	Gaming Board	Gaming Act
Prize Draws	Skill, with entry fee	Advertising Standards Authority (ASA)	Code of Advertising Practice (CAP)
Free Draws	No skill, no entry fee	ASA	CAP

gambling has now become a national obsession. The National Lottery benefits good causes, with 28% of the total being distributed for arts, sports, charities, heritage and millennium projects. But charities can and still do raise money from gambling, mostly from some form of lottery, but also from scratch cards and competitions.

A lottery is covered by the Lotteries and Amusements Acts and is carefully regulated by the Gaming Board and local authorities. It consists of a promotion where there is a sale of tickets with an equal chance of success and there is no skill involved. Scratch cards are instant lotteries and are similarly controlled by the Gaming Board. Competitions – which are games of skill – are regulated by the British Code of Sales Promotion. Free entry draws are unlikely to be of interest to fundraisers. The exact status of any activity is very important as there is a wide range of regulation to be considered.

This envelope contains two books of raffle tickets, a reply envelope and a request for further books

Lotteries and raffles

Lotteries can be used successfully by both large and small organisations. They do not have to be big affairs, and can be a useful fundraising technique at even the smallest charity event.

For the purpose of regulation, lotteries are divided into four categories (apart from the National Lottery which is separately regulated by OFLOT).

- *Small lotteries*. A small lottery is one in which the activity is incidental to an event (such as a dance, meeting, sporting activity etc.) where tickets are only sold at the event. No money prizes are allowed and no more than £250 can be spent on prizes. In this case, there is no regulation involved at all.
- *Private lotteries*. A private lottery must be limited to all those people who belong to one group or who work or live in the same premises. There are a number of regulations concerning promotions and tickets, but these lotteries do not have to be registered either.
- *Society lotteries*. A society lottery is the category most likely to be used by larger charities, as it allows for extensive promotion. This is balanced by the need for registration and reporting. Registration is required with your local authority if ticket sales are to be less than £20,000; if in excess of this, then with the Gaming Board.
- *Local authority lotteries*. A local authority lottery is one that is promoted by a local authority.

Each type of lottery has a different set of regulations which are covered in full in the Gaming Board's publication *Lotteries and the Law*.

Basic lottery rules

■ **Small lottery**

Incidental to entertainment; £1 maximum per ticket; no registration required; sale of tickets on premises only; no money prizes, and £250 max on purchase of prizes.

■ **Private lottery**

Limited to one group of people or one location; £1 maximum per ticket; no registration required; sale of tickets only to members.

■ **Society lottery**

Promoted by one society; £1 maximum per ticket; sales up to £20,000 requires registration with Local Authority; sales over £20,000 requires registration with Gaming Board; returns and audited accounts must be submitted.

■ **Local Authority lottery**

Promoted by a Local Authority; £1 maximum per ticket; sales up to £20,000 registration and reporting requirements as for Society Lottery.

The prizes

Many people buy tickets because it is another way of supporting your charity. Others may be attracted to winning one of the prizes. As a lottery gets bigger, the lure of prizes becomes more important. You can either give cash or non-cash prizes.

Getting goods or services donated as lottery prizes can be quite a good way of getting support from companies, though it takes time. For a small or a private lottery, prizes can be collected from local companies and shops, and need not be more than £5-£20 in value. Bottles of wine, toys, toiletries, luxury food items, vouchers for local restaurants and hairdressers are all attractive in a small raffle. Use volunteers who are local to the event to visit shops and local companies, calling door-to-door to collect possible prizes. Having a wide range of prizes that you can display at the event will help sell the tickets. It is not usually necessary to offer cash prizes.

For larger raffles you will need to focus on a smaller number of better prizes. These are what will encourage people to buy tickets. There is little research as to whether large money prizes are more attractive than non-cash prizes to a similar value. It is quite possible to get substantial prizes in kind donated by friendly companies, which cost the company far less than the retail value. An unusual and imaginative prize will almost always be more attractive than a money prize, and sometimes will not cost a lot to organise. For example, a museum supporters group might arrange a personal tour with the Director followed by a smart dinner. An arts organisation might persuade leading painters to paint a portrait of the winner (free of charge).

You should allow at least six months to find your prizes. They should be of interest to your audience and consistent with your organisation's aims. The prize of a mountain bike for a Friends of the Earth raffle would be eminently sensible, or a free trip to a game park in Africa for a wildlife charity. In approaching potential donors you should prepare an outline of your plans. For major raffles, it may be worthwhile producing a special brochure highlighting the advantages to being associated with the raffle. You should contact potential donors well before the event. Asking for support in kind is always likely to be more successful than seeking cash. One organisation achieved a 1 in 4 success rate with those approached.

Some companies will expect more from donating a prize than just a warm feeling of having supported a charity. They will want good publicity for their support. This can be provided in a number of ways. Newsletters can be used to recognise their generosity. The face and back of the tickets has space to mention the prize and its donor, and this will be reach quite large numbers of people. The prize giving offers an opportunity to give warm thanks. Finally, their generosity can be mentioned in the local press and publicised in the company's own employee newsletter.

Promotion

Everything hinges on selling as many tickets as you planned. If the prizes are right and the price not too high (£1 per ticket is the current maximum that you can charge), tickets are best sold on a personal basis. For small raffles where the tickets are sold at an event, this is not difficult but needs careful planning. Identify a group of key volunteers for the evening and ask them to go round and visit everybody at the venue. You can also contact supporters prior to the event, and ask them to ask their friends at their place of work.

For a society lottery where you aim to sell tickets to a wider public, more will need to be done. The usual method is to use your mailing list to send out raffle tickets. Though many people get irritated by this practice, sometimes as many as 10% will actually accept the tickets and sell them on or buy them themselves. As an example, in one raffle 20,000 members were sent two raffle books each. This resulted in 100 people returning their books and a total sale of 96,000 tickets. The end result was an income of £60,000 with costs of £12,000.

In addition to your own mailing list of members or supporters, local groups or volunteer fundraisers are often excellent at selling raffle tickets. They will have contact with other groups: for example people connected with a company can go round their workplace and sell tickets there; hospital workers can sell tickets to colleagues and so on. The best way of contacting supporters or recruiting new volunteers is by telephone.

Some organisations offer incentives to those who are engaged in selling lottery tickets. In one example, a computer was offered to the person who sold the most tickets – although the organisation didn't in fact know whether this incentive made any difference to the number of tickets sold.

The draw

In a small raffle, the draw for the prizes is the key moment of drama. It is important to build the timing of the draw into your plans for the event. It should be announced at regular intervals leading up to the draw as an aid to selling tickets. Ideally, the draw should be the finale, thus encouraging people to stay to the end of the event.

The choice of some sort of celebrity to present the prizes can add to the excitement and encourage people to buy tickets – although from the presenter's point of view, there can be little as tiresome as presenting dozens of prizes at the end of a long day.

For a larger raffle the situation is different. Few members of the public will want to attend the draw, although the date and place should be clearly publicised on the tickets. This is a time to look forward and build bridges. There is an opportunity to use the draw to invite donors and sponsors to meet senior staff and trustees, and to try to enlist their support for the next year. At the same time there is a good opportunity for photographs of prizes being presented. It is important not to miss this. You should invite a photographer from a local paper to record the event, or use a member of staff with reasonable photographic skills to take shots of prizes, prize winners and celebrities.

To gamble or not to gamble

Organisations with a strong religious tradition (and some others) may find this area of fundraising difficult. Even with the prevalence of the National Lottery, they may not wish to be involved in any form of gambling. It is not important what you personally think about selling lottery tickets, or whether there is any evidence that links buying lottery tickets with addictive gambling. What is important is that you are clear about your organisation's attitude. If there are good reasons to believe that gambling might be a contentious issue, you should get the management committee to agree a policy.

4.12 Television and radio appeals

In the rapidly changing world of radio and television broadcasting, new opportunities for raising money or getting support are opening up almost daily. These include both paid for advertising (which is covered under 'Advertising for support' in Section 4.14) and free coverage of one sort or another. The following media currently exist:

- terrestrial television. There are currently five channels. The BBC has some regional programming; Channel 3 is divided into 14 regions with separate coverage in London for weekdays (Carlton) and weekends (LWT), and a separate company (GMTV) responsible for early morning programming on a national basis. Channel 5 is national, but does not yet reach every part of the UK;
- satellite television. Those with a satellite dish can receive the many channels broadcast or transmitted by BSkyB;

- cable television. In some areas people are able to receive their programmes through cable networks, with the cable station also able to produce its own programming in addition to transmitting broadcast and satellite channels. With the cabling of new communities moving ahead rapidly, the coverage here will progressively increase;
- radio, which is divided into three sectors: commercial stations, BBC national and local radio and community radio. At the time of writing,there are some 44 commercial stations, 30 BBC stations and a growing number of community radio stations.

Strategy for broadcast appeals

Type of Appeal	Large national charity	Small national charity	Local charity
Lifeline TV Appeal	✗	✓	✗
Editorial TV	✓	✓	✓
Public Service Announcement	✓	✓	✗
Community Action programming	✓	✓	✓
Telethons	✓	✓	✓
Editorial Radio	✓	✓	✓
Week's Good Cause	✗	✓	✗
TV Adverts	✓	✗	✗
Radio Adverts	✓	✓	✓

Television appeals

Because of the nature of the medium and its huge audiences, TV is potentially the most powerful way of getting a message across, but it is difficult to use TV to raise money directly. The opportunities for free appeals are limited, and paid for advertising (covered in Section 4.14) is expensive. However, there are many ways of using TV to get your message across in ways other than a direct appeal; these can, if well coordinated, enhance your other fundraising work. The main opportunities for using TV are:

- The Lifeline appeal
- Community Service Announcements
- Editorial appeals.

The Lifeline appeal

Lifeline is the name used for BBC TV appeals, but the mechanisms are similar for ITV appeals. To get an appeal you must apply either to the

Results of Lifeline Appeal on BBC1

Sick Children's Trust	Gary Lineker	£16,416
World Vision	Gavin Campbell	£83,090
Camp Quality UK	Gaby Roslin	£21,684
Music Therapy	Rolf Harris	£6,131
Homeless International	Robert Lindsay	£24,000
Sequal Trust	Nigel Havers	£19,484

(some appeal results during 1996)

BBC or the Independent Television Commission. Both are advised by the Central Appeals Advisory Committee about which appeals should be given air time. Appeals are allocated TV time on the monthly slots, usually on Sundays. There are opportunities for appeals nationally as well as regionally in Scotland, Northern Ireland and Wales.

You are allowed to apply once every two years to the BBC and to the ITC, but you can never guarantee that you will be granted a slot. You have to fill in a simple form, and since this involves little effort and there is nothing to be lost if you feel that your charity has significant public interest and appeal, then why not apply every two years? If you are successful, the publicity and the financial support generated can be considerable – you might expect to raise anything from £5,000 to £130,000. If you aren't successful, then hope for better luck next time.

If you obtain an appeal slot, you next need to think about how to make the most of it. The first step should be to meet the producer allocated to you by the broadcasters. You will want to discuss with them the general approach to the appeal, the presenter, and how the script will be developed. Clearly it is not expected that all charities will have the required broadcasting skills readily available to them, so the broadcasters offer these services. You may feel that it is more appropriate to develop your script in-house, based on your more intimate knowledge of the organisation and its work.

An important decision is who will be the presenter. Actors are very suitable, as they can bring most scripts alive. The person should also be credible to the audience perhaps through some existing connection with your charity or cause, or because they have the right style. The broadcasters will be able to suggest possible names to you and help you make the approach. The actual production of the appeal will be organised by the broadcasters, who will provide you with a producer with the appropriate skills. All that remains for you, the fundraiser, to do is to ensure that you have enough staff, or preferably volunteers, who will be able to handle the donations and enquiries that arise.

Looking at the results of past appeals, it is not clear that the popularity of the charity has much to do with the response. In 1996 Gavin Campbell spearheaded the star appeal which raised £83,000 to aid World Vision's work in Mozambique. The strength of the subject matter was thought to have accounted for this unusual response. Gary Lineker's appeal for the Sick Children's Trust had an about average response of £16,416.

You can contact the BBC and ITC appeals offices at these addresses:

- BBC Appeals Office, Broadcasting House, Portland Place, London W1A 1AA.
- ITC Appeals Office, 70 Brompton Road, London, SW3 1EY.

Community Service Announcements

Viewers of network TV can hardly fail to notice what look like rather unpolished efforts to recruit volunteers for local charities. These are known as Community Service Announcements (CSAs). Volunteers to visit deprived families and helpers in Citizen's Advice Bureaux have been some of the many people who are recruited in this way. They are an extremely good way of recruiting volunteers and they are free. The Media Project of Community Service Volunteers works closely with TV and radio broadcasters to provide this service. Approach your local independent TV station.

Community action programmes

A number of TV and radio stations broadcast community action programmes. These are short programmes which cover the work of voluntary organisations, and are not appeals for money. Each station has its own format. Central TV currently has a five-minute advice programme, also called Lifeline, which is shown on Sunday mornings. Some organise weekly or monthly programmes, each of which covers a specific local issue.

For the most part, these programmes do not focus on the work of any one organisation. Opportunities lie in the chance to get the issues you are dealing with on air, to help in the research for the programme, to get coverage for your work, to produce or be included in the printed material that is made available to responders, and in providing volunteers to deal with enquiries.

Other opportunities exist where there is a series of programmes on a particular theme which relates to your work. These are often backed up with materials and include contact points, and these are sent to responders and distributed in the community – to schools, churches and so on. One charity, for example, was invited to produce a guide to services for people who had suffered sexual abuse.

Editorial appeals

Each year, especially at Christmas, some magazine and news programmes on TV feature some sort of appeal. Usually they do this only once a year and they always plan well ahead. *Blue Peter* is the best known example, supporting charities that appeal to children. In their case money is rarely sought – stamps, clothes and other convertible items being the usual object of the appeal. Local and regional news programmes have similar appeals.

To get your charity featured, you must make yourselves known to the producers of the programmes, and in the first place to their researchers. This should be done at least six months in advance, and preferably well before then. Where there is a link between the audience and the appeal, you are more likely to be successful.

Special fundraising telethons

Telethons were a feature of the 1980s and 1990s and look set to continue to raise relatively large sums. They are to an extent a counterbalance to the pulling power of the large charities, as most of the proceeds are distributed to smaller and local charities.

- The **BBC Children in Need** appeal began appearing annually as a TV and radio appeal in 1980, and consistently raises over £20 million for children's charities.
- This was followed in some style by **Live Aid** in 1984, which was run as a one-off to raise money for famine relief in Africa.
- **Comic Relief** has been run every second year from 1986 by Charity Projects, and raises rather more than Children in Need for development projects in Africa and selected causes in the UK.
- The **ITV Telethon** started in 1988, but ceased when the franchises were renegotiated in 1994, as the new style TV companies just did not have the staff to do the work.
- Channel 5 started the **Give 5** telethon in 1997, supporting five named causes.

There are opportunities for charities to be featured as part of the telethon broadcasting, but the main chance is to apply for and get a donation of money after the event, in exactly the same way as from a charitable trust. The chances of success are reasonably high if you match their criteria.

Disasters Emergency Committee

The Disasters Emergency Committee (DEC) provides an opportunity for the major overseas charities to get air-time when there is a major disaster. Members consist of Oxfam, Save the Children, Christian Aid, CAFOD and the British Red Cross, supplemented by Help the Aged and Action Aid from time to time. This is a self-selecting club which has been notoriously difficult to get into despite, or perhaps because of, the very high sums raised (from £500,000 to £10 million per appeal). New rules now mean that the income can be shared with non-members on occasions.

Radio appeals

Radio must surely rate as the most under-exploited fundraising medium, as it holds many opportunities for the imaginative and energetic fundraiser. Possibilities include:

- **'The Week's Good Cause'**, the BBC radio appeals slot on Radio 4
- Community Service Announcements. The procedure is the same as for television
- **Paid advertising** (see Section 4.14)
- **Editorial Coverage**. Nationally there are opportunities in programmes such as 'Does he take sugar', 'Costing the earth', and 'You and yours'; locally, news and chat show programmes present the best opportunities
- **Phone-ins**. It is always possible to phone in to a chat programme, or to get your supporters to do so, to express a point of view, promote an activity or make a request for support.

The Week's Good Cause

Each week Radio 4 dedicates a five-minute slot on Sunday mornings to an appeal known as 'The Week's Good Cause'. The procedures for getting an appeal are identical to that described for the Lifeline Appeal (see above). You can never guarantee that you will get a slot, but as for Lifeline appeals on TV, there is nothing to be lost, and you should consider applying every two years.

Examples of 'The Week's Good Cause' appeals on BBC

Arthritis Research	Dinah Sheridan	£5,866
Befrienders International	Chad Varah	£5,511
Reach	Lady Howe	£2,990
Phab	Rolf Harris	£3,634
Nairobi Hospice	Desmond Tutu	£58,774
Contact-a-Family	Michael Aspel	£5,133
Muscular Dystrophy	Derek Nimmo	£5,215
Council for the Protection of Rural England	Jonathan Dimbleby	£3,500
Mediathon UK	Rosemary Harthill	£3,500

(some appeal results during 1996)

Getting editorial coverage

The cheapest way of getting publicity for your appeal is to harness the editorial power of the media (see also Section 7.6 on public relations). If you are doing something newsworthy, you might try to get coverage for this as a news item. TV and radio news, locally and nationally, requires a large number of stories each day. If yours can be one, you could gain everything that a commercial gives you for a fraction of the cost. Indeed if you are mentioned on the news, it confers extra kudos and respectability. It is generally reckoned that editorial coverage is worth at least seven times the value of the equivalent paid space.

News items are picked up because they are relevant nationally or locally, because you have announced an important new piece of information (resulting from your research, perhaps), because it fits into a topic of real current concern, or because you are doing something unusual. If all this is accompanied by film or taped interviews, then it makes it easier (and cheaper) for the broadcasters, but it also ensures that you get the sort of coverage you want.

The first contact should be with the news desk, which should start the ball rolling. There can never be any guarantee that you will get coverage, but the producers of the programme will help you identify whether you have something of interest to them. Offering good spokespeople always goes down well, and this can be a very powerful way of getting your organisation's cause across.

Getting an issue covered on a 'soap'

Some of the television 'soaps' reach eight-figure audiences. Many charities and pressure groups are keen to get their issues highlighted in the story line as a means of raising awareness. The schizophrenia of Joe Wicks in EastEnders on BBC1 was developed in consultation with the National Schizophrenia Fellowship, to ensure that the condition was portrayed accurately. EastEnders has also highlighted AIDS; Coronation Street on Channel 3 and The Archers on Radio 4 have both covered domestic violence; and Brookside on Channel 4 has dealt with incest, rape and drugs.

If you want to get your cause covered in feature programmes on TV or radio, you will need to make contact with the programme makers. For small radio stations you might talk to one of the station presenters; for TV stations you will need to be in touch with researchers, and later the producers.

Although the media do not like charities to make a direct appeal to the public in programmes – this is against the broadcasting rules, but these are occasionally broken by a sympathetic presenter – any appearance or interview should always be seen by you as an opportunity to make an appeal. You should always have worked out exactly how you might mention your specific needs, and how to give a phone number for those who are interested to call. This can help ensure that your appearance will not only build general awareness, but will also give the public an opportunity to respond directly.

Radio is a medium which, especially at a local level, has a great deal of potential for charities. News and current affairs programmes can give you coverage and are often happy to accept speakers from your organisation. For a local charity, they may be prepared to consider doing some sort of on-air activity for your benefit. This could range from a direct appeal, to radio auctions, to publicising a fundraising event. You should get in touch with the programme producer to explore all the possibilities here.

National organisations, who are interested in reaching across the country, can produce tape recordings, possibly using a celebrity's voice. These can then be mailed to radio stations who may use them to fill any gaps in programming.

Credit card donations

Credit card payments are increasingly used by charities as a response mechanism because of the immediacy of response and ease of payment. The 1992 Charities Act covers credit card donations or payments for goods in response to a charitable appeal on TV (and also on radio) where the appeal is made by a commercial participator (see Appendix 4) or a professional fundraiser. If the donation or payment is over £50, there is a cooling off period. Donors have the right to cancel the donation or return the goods for a full refund less any administrative expenses. Note that the cooling off period does not apply to donations or sales in response to an appeal made by the charity itself

4.13 Giving at Work

Giving at work has been around for many decades in Britain. Originally it involved large numbers of workers in factories being asked to give just a few pence per week, which many were happy to do since not a lot of money was involved and all that they needed to do was sign an authorisation to have the amount deducted from their wages each pay day. Barnardos was one of the more successful national charities raising money in this way, and on Merseyside a community trust, United Way, had successfully used this technique to raise money for a central fund which was then distributed to local good causes.

In 1987, the Government created a new scheme for tax-deductible payroll giving. This was a part of the Government of the day's policy of encouraging charitable giving, and was seen as an opportunity for charities to mobilise support from the millions of people in employment. This gave what had been a very marginal form of giving a completely new lease of life. Although the new payroll giving scheme has not delivered all that was expected of it and still does not generate huge amounts of money for charity, it is now an established way of giving and does provide the opportunity for smaller as well as large charities to solicit regular committed income.

The Charities Aid Foundation estimates that in 1995 a total of £18.5 million was given from 345,000 donors – an average donation of £63 per annum. There are nearly 5,000 employers who operate payroll giving schemes for their employees, who between them employ around 10 million people.

How payroll giving works

The payroll giving scheme involves a number of different parties.

- *The donor*. The donor has to be an employee on the permanent payroll of a company or some other employer, such as a local authority, central government, a hospital trusts or even a charity. A company pensioner who is also on the company payroll can also give through the scheme. The donor can use the scheme to make a donation to any charity or charities of his or her choice, which is done by signing a form authorising the employer to make deductions each pay day from the employee's salary or wages for donation to selected beneficiaries. The donor can alter the beneficiaries or increase or reduce the monthly amount or even cancel the arrangement at any time. A maximum of £1,200 can be given by any donor through the payroll giving scheme in any tax year.

- *The employer*. The employer has to agree to run a payroll giving scheme through an 'agency charity'. If the employer does not run a payroll giving scheme, the employee cannot give to charity using this method, and there is no way that the employer can be forced to run a scheme – even where there is a substantial interest from their employees for them to do this. The employer makes the monthly deductions from the employee's salary as authorised by the employee, and passes the money to the agency charity together with the employee's instructions for distributing the money.

- *The agency charity*. The job of the agency charity is to receive the money from the employer and distribute it to the charities selected by the donors. Thirteen agency charities have now been licensed by the Inland Revenue to operate payroll giving. The purpose of this procedure is to provide assurance to the Inland Revenue that the money is going to bona fide charities. There are certain operating requirements for an agency charity: the administration charges must be kept within 5%, the money must be passed to the beneficiary charities within 90 days, and a donor must be able to support any charity in the UK using the scheme. The two main agency charities are the Charities Aid Foundation (the 'Give As You Earn' scheme) and the Charities Trust (the 'Work Aid' scheme).

- *The beneficiary charity.* A charity may simply receive money through the scheme on the initiative of any donor who wants to support it, or it may actively promote the idea of payroll giving to its existing supporters, through its fundraising and by approaching employers to undertake promotions at the workplace. It may raise money for itself on its own, or it may join with other charities to form a consortium where the promotional work and the proceeds are shared.
- *The Inland Revenue.* The role of the Inland Revenue is to ensure that the money passing through the payroll giving scheme is received by a charity and spent for charitable purposes. The design of the scheme, using licensed agency charities as intermediaries, is to ensure that this happens. In addition, the Inland Revenue sets the rules within which the scheme has to operate. Initially, these were quite restrictive, but

Payroll giving in British Telecom

BT has been involved with the payroll scheme since 1987, and has actively promoted it to its employees. The initial response was poor, with only 1% of the company's workforce participating. In 1988, the BT board decided that the company should re-promote the scheme. This included a decision to match pound for pound all employees' donations, as well as paying the agency charity's administration costs. This decision was announced at a meeting hosted by the Chancellor of the Exchequer.

The first promotion took place at BT's London HQ. The Charities Aid Foundation, Barnardos, Oxfam, Scope, and the Samaritans were approached to help plan the campaign; later on other charities were involved. 'City Lifeline' was the title given to the consortium of charities, and each member of the consortium undertook to share equally the work and the income that arose. The company required that employees should have the freedom of choice to choose any charity they wished to support, but many were happy to support the consortium.

Employees were approached personally by representatives from the participating charities and encouraged to give their support during a two-day promotional campaign. At the end of the promotion, the HQ staff's participation in the payroll giving scheme had risen from 4% to 25%, with the total contributed exceeding £40,000 per annum.

Other promotions followed in other BT locations, and in some of these, local charities were involved. One of the most successful was in Liverpool, where eight local organisations formed a consortium called 'Active 8', and raised almost £60,000 per annum. The promotions were especially successful when enthusiastic volunteers were used.

Payroll Giving is seen as a part of BT's community programme, and all employees are given information about the facility upon joining. The total amount donated to charities by BT employees via payroll has now reached £1.9 million including the company's matching contribution. The response rate from staff has averaged around 6.5% and a total of 9,400 donors have used the scheme.

were relaxed later on when charities were allowed to print their own deduction forms to circulate to potential supporters (who would then hand them in to the payroll department at work), suggest monthly amounts, and advertise the charity and its work.

The scheme works in the following way. The employee agrees to give, say, £10 per month to one or more named charities. The payroll department then deducts this amount from the employee's monthly wage and passes the money to the agency charity. The sum so given is allowed against the employee's income when calculating his or her tax liability, but it does not affect the amount of National Insurance contribution that has to be paid, which is calculated on the employee's gross income. With a 23% Income Tax rate, the £10 given would cost the employee £7.70 after taking into account the tax saving of £2.30. Assuming an administrative charge of 5% made by the agency charity, the charity selected by the employee would receive £9.50, which amount would be credited to its bank account each month.

How Compton Hospice encourages payroll giving

Terminally ill patients receiving treatment from the Compton Hospice are benefiting from over £140,000 raised each year through payroll giving. The money is raised by a team of fundraisers, who try to identify successful local firms and those active in the community. They always approach the senior person in the company, writing first to try to arrange a meeting to request an opportunity to canvas staff face-to-face. Posters are put up in advance, and a small exhibition is arranged. They ask for a minimum of 25p per week. The result is an average of £30 per donor and a near 30% success rate.

Promoting payroll giving for your charity

There are several different approaches that you can employ:

■ circulate details of the scheme to your supporter list, suggesting this as a way of giving regular support for people who are not doing so already. The problem here is that not all your supporters will be in employment or working for an employer who is running a payroll scheme;

■ ask your existing payroll supporters to canvas support from their colleagues at the workplace;

■ use your own staff to contact companies, and ask them to allow you on to company premises to canvas employees;

■ use a commercial promoter to put your cause alongside others;

■ join a consortium which then employs a commercial promoter to reach employees;

■ use leaflets inserted in company magazines to recruit employees direct, who can then go around the workplace signing up colleagues.

Approaching employers directly

Employers have two main attitudes to charities who ask for access to their employees. Some are happy to select a charity or charities to recommend to their employees for support. This may be where a company adopts a 'charity of the year', or it might be to supplement the support that the company is giving through a major donation or sponsorship. Other employers prefer to leave it to the employees to decide what to support, and are wary of giving one charity the opportunity to canvas support at the workplace. Sometimes an incentive is added by the employer, such as matching the employee's support with a contribution from the company on a pound-for-pound basis. This might be for nominated charities, or it could be to match any donation made by an employee to any charity (as with BT). One selling point though is that you are not asking for money (which can be a relief to them), but you are helping them improve their community relations and giving them the opportunity to associate themselves with an important and worthy cause.

The majority of employers in the UK, and particularly the smaller and medium-sized companies, still do not offer payroll giving facilities to their employees, nor are they likely to know much about the scheme. In such cases, the company has to agree to establish a payroll giving scheme first – and this means putting them in touch with one of the national agency charities (from your point of view it does not matter which) – but all this takes time to sort out.

When approaching a company, you will want to do the following.
- Research the company; what is does, who makes the decisions, whether they undertake any charitable giving. You will also want to find out whether they operate a payroll giving scheme, which you can do by asking the person responsible for charitable donations.
- Approach the person who has the authority to allow you to set up a meeting to discuss your plans. For smaller companies, this would be the Managing Director.
- Discuss with that person how you might promote payroll giving to their staff.
- Arrange your payroll giving promotion in the company.

Canvassing options

The only really effective methods of promoting payroll giving are those where you can communicate with employees face-to-face. Indirect methods such as memos and posters will not work on their own, partly because the system appears so complicated. You need to agree with the employer precisely what access you will be allowed to the staff. The ideal is to be able to go round the offices or shopfloor and ask employees individually. This is rarely allowed, but you may be able to address staff in their lunch breaks, as they arrive for work or when they leave at the end of the day, or mount an exhibition in the entrance foyer. Here are some options for promoting payroll giving:

- one-to-one discussions with employees at the work place
- being escorted around the workplace by the employer
- small group presentations or organised promotional sessions
- the use of a room set aside for employees who are interested to visit you to find out more
- an information desk in the canteen
- at clocking in points
- in the lobby or display area
- circulation of leaflets to employees, putting up posters on notice boards, and so on
- contact made via unions or staff representatives
- contact made via personnel department.

(List courtesy of Bell Promotions)

Commercial promoters

There are now a number of commercial organisations who specialise in promoting payroll giving to employees. The most usual mechanism is as follows:

- you enter into a contract with the commercial promoter;
- they put information about your charity alongside that of up to 20 other charities;
- they approach employees and attempt to interest them in supporting one or more of the charities they are representing;
- they charge you for each donor who signs up to support you.

There is now an organisation of payroll giving promoters and consultants to help ensure that standards are maintained. This is the Payroll Giving Association, 4 West St Helen Street, Abingdon, Oxon OX14 5BL. It is an obvious starting point for engaging a promoter.

Consortia

For smaller charities, the use of commercial promoters is problematic, since the charity will have very little public profile. When a prospective donor is faced with a choice from amongst 20 charities, those which are unknown are the least likely to be supported. This is a situation in which a consortium approach can be helpful.

A consortium is set up by a group of charities specially to promote payroll giving. Donors are encouraged to support the consortium (which is usually constituted as a charity in its own right), and the proceeds are shared between consortium members, either equally or according to some formula agreed at the outset. The consortium might comprise a group of national charities who want to promote payroll giving nationally, sharing the costs, the work, the risk and the proceeds, or it might be formed by a group of local charities with the aim of getting local support. There are also cases of national charities joining together with local charities, which combines national profile with local interest. There are two important advantages of promoting payroll giving as a consortium:

■ **the costs are shared**. This is a form of fundraising where many organisations do not have any previous experience, so operating in this way can be less risky;

■ **the consortium is benefiting a range of charities**. Ideally there should be something to interest everyone, which can also make it easier for a consortium to gain access to the workplace, because the employer may not want to be seen as favouring one charity over another.

A charity wanting to get involved in payroll giving, but not wanting to go it alone, could attempt to join an existing consortium, or it could consider setting up a new consortium with others. The consortium should have a catchy name, and comprise a compatible group of similar charities who are happy to collaborate.

Donor relations

It is all too easy to concentrate on finding new payroll donors. However, when new donors have been acquired, they should not be taken for granted.

■ **Thank the donor** and keep them regularly informed about the work of the charity. Each payroll donor should be added to your mailing list. You will have their work address, and if you don't, you should be able to obtain this from the agency charity. All records should be marked to indicate that they are supporting you in this way.

■ **Ask for further support**. Donors can be continually solicited for further support, as you would do for any other name on your mailing list. You want to ensure that they continue to give and you want to persuade them to increase their level of giving, and possibly also to give in other ways. Payroll giving has one great advantage – it is an inertia form of giving, which continues for so long as the donor does not cancel the arrangement. The disadvantage is that the arrangement will cease automatically when the donor leaves the employment.

- **Suggest to the donor that they ask their colleagues at the workplace to sign up for your charity**. Donors can also be asked for advice on how best to approach the company to request an opportunity to promote your charity to the workforce. In addition, if you are receiving significant support from a company's employees, this is something you could mention in any application to the company for financial support; they are more likely to be sympathetic to a charity which their employees are interested in than any old charity sending in an appeal 'out of the blue'.

How to get started

There are a number of important decisions to make when considering whether to develop payroll giving.

- You need to decide whether payroll giving is important enough as a potential source of money for you to be bothered. There are opportunities, but remember it is not a major source of charitable giving and it takes time and explaining to get going.
- You need to decide whether you should do it yourself using your own staff, or whether to engage a commercial promoter.
- You need to decide whether to promote your charity on its own, or whether to become part of a consortium.
- You will need to prepare promotional materials, including an explanatory leaflet for employees, which can include a deduction form to hand into their payroll department, and a poster to put up at the workplace.
- You will have to consider how to fund the development costs, bearing in mind the long lead time involved before you actually begin to receive a flow of income.

4.14 Advertising for Support

This advertisement appeared in the Financial Times and is reported to have raised £122,000 at a cost of £2000, a remarkable achievement by any standards

Paying for an advertisement in a newspaper or magazine can be a powerful way of promoting your cause or raising money but it can be expensive. You can raise money off the page directly through making an appeal for money, or indirectly by recruiting members, volunteers or those seeking further information (who you will later persuade to give to you).

Nine questions to ask before you advertise

I find it useful to start work on appeal advertising by thinking of myself as a person to person fundraiser; about to set off, ringing the doorbells of potential donors. Like a salesman (for that's what I am), I ask myself these questions:

- Which are the best door bells to ring?
- How have I identified them?
- What kind of people live behind these doors?
- What's the best time to 'call', remembering the clamour for their attention?
- What's their lifestyle; their attitudes, discretionary income; knowledge of, and sympathy for my organisation's work?
- How do I best get a hearing?
- How do I get them to open the door and invite me in?
- What shall I ask them to do and how can I most successfully get them to do it?
- How do I retain their continued interest and practical support?

Not until I have answered these questions am I ready to see how my charity's need can be translated into the 'calls' I'm going to make in printed advertisements.

I'm not writing to a mass audience. I'm writing to individuals; to the reader, my press ad (like my mailing), must come as a personal message, telling her or him of a need, so that it evokes a personal reaction and response. But the initial impact needs to be swift, or it will never retain attention.

From **The Printed Fundraiser** by Harold Sumption.

Advertising can be extremely successful in raising money at the time of a disaster or when an issue has hit the headlines. Your advertisement will reach people at a time when they know that something needs to be done – and you are offering them a way of helping.

You can also use advertising to build awareness of your charity through a promotional campaign on what you are doing. You can sell greetings cards and other products which you are using to raise money for your work. A further use is to invite people to support you with a legacy.

Advertising can take the form:

- **press advertising** – taking space in national or local newspapers, through display advertising or small ads;
- **advertising in magazines and journals** (general interest or specialist);
- **inserts** in a magazine;
- **posters** (both billboard advertising and smaller posters displayed on notice boards or flyposted in the street);

How big a space should you use?

Space size	Responses
1/4 page	48
1/2 page	71
3/4 page	87
full page	100
Double page	141

This table illustrates what research and practical experience has shown about the disproportionate effect of using small spaces in advertising. The responses are those you would expect to receive indexed against a full page. You should bear in mind that you may be able to get a larger space for a greater discount and thus counter the advantage of taking a smaller space.

Taken from **Commonsense Direct Marketing**.

Newspaper advertising

The main problem with the use of the press as a medium for advertising is that the cost is high, even for a limited amount of space. As a result, the messages are much shorter than is possible in a leaflet or brochure, and must be more striking if they are to be noticed and responded to.

Press advertising has the advantage that you can select your audience by reference to the known readership of the paper or magazine; you can also predict whether your issues are likely to be given editorial coverage and, if so, whether or not this will be done sympathetically.

The most you can hope for (except in very exceptional circumstances) is that an advertisement in the press will give a 3:1 revenue to cost ratio. Most organisations will not achieve anything like this, and many find that the returns are substantially lower than the costs. It may be that what you can achieve with advertising, would also be achieved more cheaply with effective and well-targeted public relations.

Opportunistic advertising

Possibly the most exciting aspect of advertising is its flexibility. You can place an advertisement extremely quickly. Thus if a disaster or some other high profile event happens one day, you could be appealing for help the next day at the breakfast table.

What is a disaster? It is not what you think is a serious emergency, it is what your public is being told is serious by the newspaper itself and by other news media. A famine overseas is an obvious example, or the domestic disasters that occur from time to time, such as the Dunblane massacre or a major oil spill. Then there are the regular 'disasters' that are perceived or stage managed, such as Crisis with its Christmas appeal for the street homeless at a time when the weather is getting cold and public sympathy is high, or the NSPCC focus on the levels of child abuse at around the time of its winter appeal.

Timing is everything, and one estimate is that as much as 30% of your response is likely to come from getting the timing right.

Acquisition advertising

This is all about finding new supporters who can then be put on your mailing list and profitably appealed to at a later date. The rationale for the many organisations who do not break even on the initial proceeds of their advertising. They regard it as an investment in their mailing list, which eventually does much more than break even. As an example, the Refugee Council has taken full pages in the papers to invite you to send donations to support destitute asylum seekers in this country. Very little surplus was made over the costs of the advertising yet hundreds of new donors gave support. Many of those responding will go on to give more substantial sums on a regular basis. Beyond this, the space allowed the organisation the opportunity to talk about its work at a time it badly wanted to raise the profile of the issue.

You should decide before you start how much you can afford to spend to recruit a new supporter. Some organisations are happy if they can find new supporters for £50 each. The precise sum for your organisation will depend on how much you can expect to raise on average subsequently from each supporter you have recruited.

Awareness advertising

If no one knows much about you or if you want to launch a new campaign, then your objective may be to build awareness first, rather than attempt to raise money or recruit supporters. Awareness advertising is both expensive and difficult to measure, and it often demands the use of very large spaces with the advertising continuing over a period of time.

Although this approach is often used by large companies, is it the best way of using very limited charitable funds? Many would say that the effective use of public relations will buy a good deal more awareness than any amount of advertising. The advantage of paying for the space is that what appears is exactly the message you want to appear at the time you want it.

Legacy advertising

A good deal of pressure is exerted on charities to advertise for legacies in the specialist media. Before you say yes, read the advice on legacy fundraising carefully in Section 4.9.

Loose inserts

One of the main problems with buying space in newspapers is the size constraint. The purchase of a 20cm space across two columns in a national broadsheet may cost in excess of £4,000. The cost is high, so the space you can afford is very limited. The use of loose inserts addresses this problem. Depending on the publication, anything from a small leaflet to a Christmas gift catalogue can be inserted or bound into the publication.

There are four important differences between an insert and an advertisement.

■ There is much more space available to you and you can even include an envelope with the insert, although there may be restrictions on the weight of the insert imposed by the publisher, and the print cost will vary with the size of the insert. This makes inserts an ideal medium to describe your work and set out the different ways of supporting your organisation. Inserts can work extremely well for membership drives, campaigns for committed giving such as child and community sponsorship schemes, and those appeals that demand space if they are to be promoted effectively.

- The cost per recipient is much higher, but inserts can be extremely cost-effective because of the combination of the space available to you, cost and value for money factors, and the ability to design a powerful response mechanism as part of the printed insert.
- Inserts take time to arrange and produce. Thus they cannot easily be produced to take advantage of topical events in the same way that an advertisement can.
- They can be easily detached from the publication, without damaging it; on the other hand, they can fall out and get lost, or thrown away.

Inserts can also provide excellent opportunities for testing the message or format of the appeal.

Posters

Posters fit least well into the fundraising area, largely because they don't allow for an immediate response, but they are nonetheless a useful promotional medium. They can range from the huge 96 sheet hoardings visible on main roads right down to the smaller posters and handbills used in windows and on notice boards.

1. Commercial posters

Posters are an extremely potent communications medium: a whole industry exists to plaster huge images of products and ideas across the land. Their impact depends on the size of the image and the extent of the coverage, but naturally it requires a great deal of both to get a message across and this is expensive. Charities can use the medium in small bursts to highlight a week or the launch of a campaign, either nationally or in a chosen area or, like political parties at election time, they can rent a site for a day to promote a poster which will generate controversy and media coverage.

It is also important to understand what posters cannot do. By and large posters cannot be used in rural areas – most sites being in towns and cities. Perhaps more significantly, posters do not allow for any direct response, except via a phone number. In any event, the time for which people see a poster, either in a car or walking around a town, is extremely short and in neither case are they well-placed to respond to your appeal. Thus, at best, posters can only act as an awareness medium to support other activities.

2. Free posters

For a long time the poster industry has organised itself to offer free poster sites to charities on the basis that it's better to display something than have empty and torn billboards. These are usually the smaller and less popular sites such as those that go on building ends. The things to consider with free sites include:

- are the sites available when you want them?
- where are the sites, and are they in the right place?
- is the cost of printing posters too high to make it worthwhile?
- would it be useful to produce cheap run-on posters in addition to those required for the sites?
- can you get the posters sponsored?

3. Mini-posters and handbills

In a different league from the commercial poster industry are the small posters or handbills which are used to publicise almost anything locally. These are attractive for fundraising, since they can be printed cheaply and displayed free. One commonly used idea is to print a poster as a part of one of your leaflets – possibly the back or inside.

Depending on what you are promoting, these mini-posters can be targeted at whoever you want. They can be put in windows, in local shops, on library notice boards, in community centres, in schools, or anywhere you feel you can reach your target audience. Volunteers can distribute thousands of posters and leaflets and create a highly visible campaign at little cost.

Evaluating the results

Fundraisers should always try to evaluate the effectiveness of any advertising they pay for. The way of doing this is by using a coded coupon, reply address or phone number on the advertisement. The coding should be done for the campaign as a whole and for each separate promotion in the campaign. This is the only way you can find out which medium works best for you. Results can then be measured in terms of:

- income raised per £ of media cost
- cost per new donor recruited
- cost per legacy notification generated (for legacy advertising).

In the case of awareness advertising, research can be conducted before and after to measure the increased awareness generated by the campaign – however, this can be expensive and can only really be considered for major campaigns by large charities.

How to improve your commercial

- Advertise between 9am and 4pm
- Advertise in films and current affairs programmes
- Be the last ad in any break
- Buy a very short 10 second slot or a long one, over 30 seconds
- Advertise your phone number for as long as possible
- Use 0800 free phone numbers where possible

Advertising on TV

Because television advertising is immensely expensive, so it is important to identify realistic objectives for any advertisement. If you simply wish to promote a message, then you may succeed; but be aware of the Independent Television Commission rules on what you are allowed to say (the ITC is the regulator for commercial TV, and of course you can't advertise on BBC). Alternatively you may want to advertise activities going on in the regions or around the country. The Children's Society and Christian Aid have both used TV advertising to support their national fundraising weeks. This can give your volunteers moral support and make the public aware in advance of a flag day or house-to-house collection. So far, there is little evidence of the cost-effectiveness of doing this.

TV advertising can also be used to support other appeals such as press advertising or a direct mail campaign. Again there is currently little evidence of the outcome of doing this. Over the last few years, direct response advertising on TV is becoming more widely used and this has relevance for fundraising. This differs from the classic commercial in that it invites you to send in a donation now, using the phone and your credit card.

The medium can be bought in a wide range of ways. Individual spots can be purchased, but are extremely expensive at peak times. However the evidence suggests that off-peak times are better for charity advertising, such as afternoons and late at night. In this case, packages of spots might be purchased at a good discount.

The choice of media depends on your objective: if it is to get a message across to a national audience then the independent network, breakfast TV, or a satellite channel can be used. If you are to test in one region, then use just one independent TV station.

Getting the message right can be difficult. If it has little impact, you risk wasting the chance to bring your charity to the attention of millions, but if you attempt to make it too strong and emotive, you risk having the advertisement turned down by the broadcasters or the regulators (as happened with the some of the Party Election Broadcast by the Pro-Life Alliance). They are still feeling their way on what are acceptable limits for 'cause advertising', and it is likely that in the future controls will be relaxed somewhat. Make sure your advertising agency checks carefully with the appropriate authority on what is acceptable, before committing you to too much expense.

TV commercials are expensive to run, costing anything from £15,000 upwards to produce, depending upon whether you can do the shooting in a studio or need to take a film crew to the Amazon. To cut down on costs, you can try asking the professionals to donate their services free, use existing film or slide based material, use a personality (preferably in a studio), find a partner to share the cost, or get the advertisement sponsored.

Advertising on radio

Advertising on radio has the advantage that it is much cheaper than television, and is much more localised. It also reaches a much smaller audience and although it lacks the visual element, it can be especially useful for supporting local or regional events. For example, a concert can be promoted on local radio stations in the catchment area for the audience. Shops, or indeed a charity week, can be usefully promoted on radio too, as the information does not require any visual treatment.

Radio time is bought in exactly the same way as TV time, and national packages are also available. It would be quite normal for your advertising agency to place adverts with a dozen or so radio stations to cover one part of the country.

The creative possibilities with radio are considerable, but require the help of professionals. Ask your radio station whether they can help you prepare your commercial. Radio lends itself well to competitions, to celebrity voices and to repetition. You can expect well-known voices to give their time free, if properly approached. The cost of production may be from hundreds of pounds to a few thousand. If you have to distribute tapes widely, this will be an additional cost.

Issues in advertising

1. Seeing it through other people's eyes. In fundraising, it is necessary to illustrate the cause in some way. Images of the beneficiary and their needs will often provide the most powerful means of generating a response. The question then arises as to the effect this might have on the beneficiaries themselves or on public attitudes towards the cause. The views of British children on the Third World are cited as an example, with public images and attitudes to these countries largely being formed by disaster advertising. It is notable that organisations dealing with the problems of disability use much less harrowing pictures, especially when they are controlled by the people who suffer the disabilities. An alternative approach is to use very positive and optimistic images.

2. Free or fee? There remains the option of declining to pay for advertising. A number of campaigns have been developed using free space

A number of campaigns have been developed using free space whenever it becomes available (for example, the advertisements by the Friends of John McCarthy during his time of imprisonment in Lebanon). The disadvantage is that you have no control over the intensity or timing of your campaign.

Getting started

Once you have decided to use advertising, there are two key decisions to take. How to design and produce your advertising and how to place it. Both can be done by you, but you will never be able to purchase media as cheaply as a media buyer or an advertising agency. Developing the creative approach and producing the design have traditionally been the function of the advertising agency. Many are interested in taking on charity clients on a *pro bono* basis. This can provide a creative challenge to their staff, but they may be less interested in taking on a very small charity. Also, selling fast cars and having an unlimited budget at their disposal may not make them as sympathetic to the nuances of your work as a friendly local designer who is familiar with what you are doing.

4.15 Advertising as a fundraising tool

Getting companies and individuals to advertise in souvenir brochures and programmes for events, or in newsletters, annual reports and other publications is a tried and tested way of raising money. For companies, it allows them to make the payment as a business expense, without the bother of having to organise the gift by Deed of Covenant or Gift Aid. For the charity, it provides an opportunity to ask for a specific amount, and to offer something in return – an association with a prestigious and successful event, and good publicity. It can even be a mechanism for reaching a specialist market – for example a national society of bellringers might be just the right marketing opportunity for a manufacturer of earmuffs, and the Campaign for Oxford, the National Trust or the Friends of Covent Garden all have highly sought after membership lists, which can attract advertisements for the newsletters and magazines which are sent out to them.

Advertising can be broken down into two quite separate categories:
- *Goodwill advertising*, where the primary purpose of the advertiser is to support a charity, and is seen to be supporting a cause, which creates goodwill with the readers as well as with the charity;

- *Commercial advertising*, where the advertiser wishes to reach the audience that the charity's publication can deliver, and the decision is made for purely commercial considerations.

Opportunities for advertising include:
- **newsletters, magazines and journals**. These come out regularly, and you may be able to get advertisers to support each issue;
- **annual reports**. This is a publication you have to produce, so defraying the cost through advertising or by taking sponsorship can enable you to produce a better annual report and demonstrate your cost-consciousness;
- **an annual publication or yearbook**. This can be a definitive guide to a specialist market, and as such be attractive to both goodwill and commercial advertisers;
- **wall charts**, year planners, diaries and other publications specially produced to generate an advertising revenue. These may generate an income, and there are several commercial companies which specialise in publishing these for charities, but remember that mostly they look quite tacky and are usually thrown away rather than used so if you are conscious about wasting resources, then this may be something to avoid;
- **conference folders and pads.** This is a form of goodwill advertising that can help subsidise the cost of the conference;
- **programmes** and souvenir brochures produced for fundraising events. For many events, the income from the event only covers the cost of putting it on. The surplus is made from raffles and auctions, and from the souvenir brochure (as long as it is not too expensive to produce);
- **posters**, including educational wall charts. The benefit of these is that they are displayed, and some form of sponsorship or a limited amount of advertising can be included without affecting the poster design too much;
- **publications** produced specially to generate an advertising revenue. These will typically be free circulation publications for a specialist market – such as restaurant guides for hotel visitors. These are often produced commercially, but there is no reason why a charity might not do something similar.

What are you offering to advertisers

Before getting down to selling the advertising, it is important to recognise what you are offering the advertiser. If it is goodwill advertising, then the prestige of the event, the nature of the audience, location and any celebrities who will be present will all be major incentives. Correctly pricing the advertising is less important than the work of the charity and advertiser will want to know the circulation of the publication and its readership, any special characteristics of that readership and any particular connection between the readers and the product. A reader survey could be useful in gathering such information. Here the price is really important in that the advertiser is paying for a commercial service so would expect the price to reflect this.

Pricing the advertising

The first consideration when pricing the advertising is the format of the publication. An A4 souvenir brochure is very different from an A5 annual report, and this in turn is very different from a tabloid-format newsletter. There are two factors to consider when deciding the cost of the advertising:

- how much do you want to raise? Divide the target sum by the number of pages of advertising to get a page rate;
- how much are advertisers prepared to pay? For commercial advertising this is especially important. You should try to define and point out the worth of your audience to them. For goodwill advertising, you need to think about the type of audience and their

Advice on being successful

My maxim is "It's always yes until it's no". You'll stand the best chance face to face but telephoning anyway to try to get a commitment will improve your chances considerably. Try to follow up your mail out with a phone call as soon as possible. Don't delay until the mood hits you; determine to do a certain number of calls each day and keep a log to record progress. One good method is to keep an alphabetical card index of 'possibles' with space for comments. When people say "yes" or "no" take it out and put it in the appropriate file. Whatever system you use, keep it up to date.

You won't be able to remember everything people tell you on the phone, so write it down and diary it. Along with the commitments and refusals, you will get replies such as:

"Ring back on Friday"

"He's in Tokyo until Tuesday"

"We decide our advertising budget in two weeks time"

"She's on maternity leave, but you can ring her at home"

"He's broken his leg skiing".

These aren't just excuses, they are clues, and they will give you an 'in' next time you ring. Instead of saying "I'd like to speak to Mr Gillings", you could say "Hello, Mr Gillings, I hope you had a good trip to Tokyo" or "I am so sorry to hear of your broken leg". This sort of approach may seem to you to be a little brash, and if it makes you uncomfortable, don't do it. But selling is just like any other form of human contact – the more you know about the other person (however little that is), the more easily you will get through to them.

Audrey Semple in *Sell Space to Make Money* (now out of print) ability to be generous, but the type of event will also influence the decision to give support.

Once you have decided a page rate, you will:

- offer smaller sizes, but at slightly higher than *pro rata* rates. For example, if the page rate is £250, then a half page might be priced at £150, a quarter page at £85, and eighth page at £50;
- ask for higher sums for special positions, such as the back cover, the inside front cover and facing the contents page;
- for a regular publication, you could offer a series discount for taking space in several issues.

Getting the advertising

You will need to produce a rate card which contains all the information that the advertiser needs to know, including:

- deadline for agreeing to take space
- deadline for receipt of artwork and address where it is to be sent
- publication size
- print run
- use of colour on cover and inside pages (four colour, two colour, black and white)
- page rates, including special positions, size of advertising space, and whether VAT is chargeable
- payment details.

The covering letter

On the last Friday of every month, come hail, rain or shine, our team of 150 volunteers pushes a copy of the 'Community News' into each and every one of the 5,000 letterboxes in NewTown. We know our readers eagerly await its arrival, because they write and tell us, telephone us, and stop us in the street to tell us so.

There are many reasons for its continuing popularity – lots of local interest stories, on-the-spot photographs, and our fearless reporting of local issues without political bias of any kind. Our regular features – the crossword, gossip, cookery and gardening columns, the over 60s angle and Young Mum's Forum have all helped us make 'Community News' NewTown's No.1 Good Read, and we aim to keep it that way.

Advertise your company's products and services with us and get your message into 5,000 letterboxes each month. An advertisement rate card is enclosed with full details. If you have any queries, please don't hesitate to call me.

From *Sell Space to Make Money* (now out of print)

You will need to think carefully about paper quality and use of colour, and the general design of the publication. No advertiser will want to be associated with something shabby. You will also produce a simple brochure or covering letter which sets out the reasons why an advertiser might want to advertise. These will be sent out by post to potential advertisers, your existing supporters, a mailing list of local companies and any specific contacts you have who might be interested. However, these will elicit little response. The tried and tested method of selling advertising is on the telephone, where you make a call to follow up a letter you have sent. You may find that they have thrown away the letter, and ask for another letter to be sent; this will then require a further telephone follow up. For larger advertisers, you might try to arrange a personal visit.

You have to find the right person who can make the decision, grab their attention, persuade them, and not get off the line or go away until you have a commitment. Of course, the majority of people you approach will say 'no'; but your job is to persuade a significant proportion to say 'yes', and to get them to take a larger space than they might instinctively go for. To do this requires a good telephone manner, a degree of persistence, and a well worked out argument. Telling people about who else has agreed to take space can also influence the decision; nobody likes to be mean if others are being generous.

Of course you will want a confirmation in writing, and you should try to get this as soon as possible. Then there is the question of ensuring that the artwork arrives on time, allocating the advertising to specific pages in the publication, ensuring that payment is received by the due date and acknowledging this and supplying a copy of the publication to the advertiser. Always show them a copy of the proof, and get them to sign it as 'approved'. In this way, if there is a mistake, you cannot be blamed. For smaller or very local companies, you might offer to design the advertisement for them. You can make an appropriate charge for doing this which will help the advertiser who does not have existing artwork or facilities for designing an advertisement.

Issues to consider

There are a number of important issues to consider before deciding to take advertising.

1. Whether to take advertising at all

A publication with advertising will look different from one without advertising, and there may be a suspicion that the editorial content has been trimmed to make it more acceptable to advertisers.

2. Ethical issues

In taking advertising, you are implicitly endorsing a message to your readers. Is the product that is being advertised one that you are happy to promote? For example, the Pre-School Playgroups Association has been running a magazine for parents called 'Under-5', which is paid for by the advertising revenue it generates. Would you be happy to see sweets manufacturers, for example, take pages of advertising in the magazine? Every organisation will need to develop a policy on the sort of advertising it does not wish to accept.

3. Tax

Advertising is not the same for tax purposes as the receipt of a donation, and there may be a liability for VAT for those organisations who are VAT registered or whose income is sufficient to bring them over the VAT registration threshold. Customs and Excise offer two concessions. They treat advertising revenue as donation income if:

- the advertising is in connection with a one-off fundraising event
- the publication is a brochure published by a charity and has the characteristics of fundraising exercise
- the payment for the advertisement is excessive by normal commercial standards in relation to the space taken and the circulation of the publication
- the motivation of the advertiser is to support the charity
- the brochure contains a significant proportion of advertising paid for by private individuals.

4. Whether to use a professional firm or consultant to solicit the advertising

Getting advertising is very different from other fundraising techniques and requires specialist skills and experience, as well as an ability to get on the phone and be persuasive. Faced with this, many organisations have turned to outside professionals to help them solicit advertising. This has often been done by payment of a percentage of the revenue raised. The 1992 Charities Act sought to control fundraising means by placing certain requirements on the charity (see Appendix 4).

There are two main points to bear in mind: an agreement in a specified form between the fundraiser and the charity is required and when soliciting advertising, the fundraiser must state the basis on which they are being remunerated. This second point makes it difficult to pay the fundraiser on a commission basis, as advertisers are less likely to advertise if they are told that 20% or 25% of what they are paying is going as a sales commission, especially in the case of goodwill advertising. Also, if the fundraiser is being paid a fee, then this involves a greater degree of risk to the charity.

Anoraks or donors?

2.35 million people in the UK have used the Internet in the last 12 months

80% were ABC1s

35% earned more than £25,000 pa

34% were between 25-34 years old

33% were between 35-55 years old

(from Third Sector, 12/12/96)

4.16 Fundraising on the Internet

Since the first edition of this book, the Internet has arrived from nowhere. Though academics and computer buffs had known about it, most people in the voluntary sector had not. Now there are few fundraisers who are not aware of it, but also few who understand its relevance to fundraising. Over the next few years, we can expect a dramatic growth in usage to continue, and the Internet beginning to develop its full potential as a fundraising medium.

Whether the Internet becomes a serious medium for fundraising will depend upon a number of factors:

- the continuing growth in the number of homes equipped with computers with modems;
- the numbers of people signed up to one or another of the Internet service providers;
- the development of cheaper, faster telephone lines.

All these appear to be developing rapidly at the moment. It seems inconceivable that what we are seeing is just a temporary craze, rather that the Internet will develop into a common communications medium and a threat to the traditional post and fax.

Two issues will determine exactly how useful the Internet will be to fundraisers. The first is the development of secure payment systems. The obvious way of transferring money over the Internet is to use a credit card. However, the opportunity for fraud is considerable. To counter this, there are already systems of encryption available, which must be installed at both ends of the line and most members of the public are not equipped for this yet. If charities encourage members of the public to commit their credit card details to the Internet, and then that information gets picked up by unauthorised users, then everyone loses. Until this is a demonstrably secure system of money transfer, it will be difficult to promote fundraising on the Internet.

The second is the idea of the Internet Bank. The first banks are emerging and are already being used by voluntary organisations in the US. It will not take long before these institutions and others that may spring up in this country earn the confidence of British givers and thus offer new ways of giving over the Internet.

Possible uses of the Internet

For fundraisers, the Internet presents a number of opportunities, and more will undoubtedly emerge in the next few years.

- It is an ideal medium to **explain the details of your work** to those who are interested. At the time of writing a number of charities are already on line, and visitors to their sites can see a description of both their regular and latest work. For example, Friends of the Earth publish news about their latest campaigns on their well visited web site, which is well visited. Equally, you can find out about Oxfam's current disaster responses in Africa. The medium lends itself not only to providing this sort of information, but to linking it with all other aspects of the organisation's work, such as the recruitment of new members, or encouraging enquirers to attend events. Naturally, the information can be displayed in such a way as to appeal to donors.

- For those **organising events**, the Internet provides special opportunities. One US charity has organised a silent auction. Bidders send in bids for donated items and within a given period, the bids accumulate. At the end of the period, the highest bidder wins each of the items being offered. For large sponsored events, such as the Friends of the Earth "Bike to the Future", Internet publicity can be used to publicise all aspects of the event. It can show the various starting points and illustrate the route; it can inform individuals how to register, and advise them about safety or other requirements. For the charity Children with Diabetes, the Internet is allowing them to publicise all the events in a particular locality, so that local supporters can get involved. Comic Relief used the Internet to publicise the 1997 Red Nose Day with full graphics and a complete description of what went on.

For organisations looking for more direct financial support there are a number of methods already in use.

- *Simple appeals.* The British Library has used a very simple format to set out its 'Adopt a Book' appeal. The appeal is simple text on the Internet, and the response requires the browser to access the appeal and then respond to it by sending a cheque to the Library.
- *Plugged in appeals.* This variant of the simple appeal risks the wrath of the Internet community. It involves sending a simple appeal by e-mail to as many other Internet users as possible. In order to avoid annoyance to others, the appeal has to be prefaced in suitable terms. It is then posted on as many bulletin boards and conference groups as possible.
- *Printed appeals.* Many Internet users will be able to print the contents of screens that they have downloaded from the Internet. This is used by a number of organisations to solicit support. For example, the screen becomes a donation form, a membership form, or a standing order form. The browser fills this in with relevant information. This is then printed out at the browser's end to become a fully completed pledge form. The drawback of this is that it still requires to be put into the post – and so still has many of the problems of direct mail – requiring an envelope, a stamp and a trip to the post box.
- *Credit card giving.* Undoubtedly the way of the future lies in being able to commit support immediately over the Internet. This is being pioneered by Friends of the Earth, where you send them your credit card details and the amount that is to be given. Most equipment cannot

yet cope with the encryption, and for the moment the system is very unsafe for donors. This will change over time, developing this into a powerful fundraising mechanism.

Getting onto the Internet

The first step is to ensure that your organisation is equipped to get connected. For the smallest of organisations, this may simply involve finding a volunteer who is already connected. The equipment required is not sophisticated and works with most Personal Computers, which are already widespread in fundraising offices. You need a fax/modem which is either built into the computer already, or can be bought separately as a small box. Connection to the Internet is carried out through one of the many service providers. It is likely to cost £10-£15 each month to subscribe plus a connection charge. You may also need an extra phone line if you are likely to be using the Internet to any great extent. With this simple equipment you are in a position to monitor what other organisations are doing and send e-mail messages to others.

Further information and ideas are contained in Howard Lake's book *Fundraising on the Internet* published by Direct Connection (http://www.fundraising.co.uk).

The next step is to create your own web site. Each page is a screenful of data which you publish and which can then be visited by anyone else on the Internet. You can have one page with a small announcement of your existence and work; or you could consider a complex of pages linking your work, your services to clients and your fundraising requests. To create the pages that are necessary for this, you can either find an individual who understands the programming involved, or go to one of the organisations that offer this as a service. One World Online, Voluntary Organisations Internet Server and Greennet are all possible choices, or you could get listed on the extensive Charities Aid Foundation Internet site. As the Internet interest in the voluntary world increases, more organisations will undoubtedly offer to help charities get started on the Internet.

Campaign phases

A campaign to raise any sort of significant sum must be properly planned and is likely to go through a number of clearly defined phases.

- The planning stage
- The case document, which sets out and justifies the purpose of the fundraising
- The business plan or feasibility study, which sets out the plan and time scale for the fundraising
- The research
- The recruitment of an appeal committee
- The private giving phase, in which major gifts are sought
- The launch
- The public giving phase
- The consolidation.

The importance of going through all these stages is not just to ensure that the appeal is properly organised, but also to allow a reasonable time scale for the appeal, and to link this with your expenditure plans and deal with any cash flow shortfalls. It may take at least two years from start to finish, and a very large appeal may well take longer. There is also the question of investment and risk. When plans have been approved and the staff have been taken on, trustees may begin to get nervous about the chances of the original outlay being recouped. This is quite a common occurrence, and demands both an understanding of the appeal process and an act of faith in the people charged with its success.

4.17 Capital appeals and big gift campaigns

Charities have always been able to attract big gifts, but recently attention has turned on big gift fundraising as one of the principal components of a capital appeal. The techniques tend to be used in the context of a single, large one-off appeal. Some charities have tried to apply them to their on-going fundraising needs, but this has not always been so successful. Typical examples range from £200 million raised for Oxford University through the Campaign for Oxford, and the Wishing Well Appeal for the Great Ormond Street Hospital, which raised around £70 million.

With responsibility for care and welfare shifting away from the state, either because it has become too expensive to provide or as a consequence of the contract culture, charities are going to find themselves needing more and more capital funding. Schools, which are now self-managing, and hospitals, will want money to develop their facilities or for equipment; organisations caring for the elderly will need to extend their facilities to meet the needs of a growing elderly population. In addition, the National Lottery has funded a large number of national, regional and local projects where there is a requirement for matched funding, particularly for arts and heritage projects. All this suggests that we will continue to see capital fundraising accelerating. This could result in a decline in responsive rates and a resistance to giving but it also means that those seeking funds in this highly competitive climate should be looking for ways of improving their effectiveness.

Planning an appeal

Planning an appeal will involve a number of activities. These include:

1. **Planning the development**, with drawings and costings. You need to be able to justify the development as being vital to your work and the future of your organisation. If you can't make the appeal sound really important, you are unlikely to be able to persuade people to give. You will also need to do a business plan for the development, to assure yourself that you can raise the money and that there will be enough to keep going once the development has been completed. Too often a new building has to close or a new piece of equipment lies idle because there are not sufficient running costs to pay for its use.

2. **Establishing the feasibility** of running the appeal. Many organisations will decide to take on a consultant to offer advice on how to conduct the

appeal. One of the first steps a consultant will take is to conduct a feasibility study which will, apart from anything else, advise on whether the appeal is likely to be successful. This is an important process, as it will serve to highlight any inconsistencies or ill-conceived ideas.

3. **Planning the structure** of the appeal. This is likely to involve an appeal committee to lead and oversee the appeal. The key appointment is the Chair of this committee. The function of this committee is to raise big gifts, and people should be appointed for their asking capacity rather than for any other quality. You may also want to establish sub-committees to oversee the running of events, the publicity and media campaigns, and in order to harness volunteer help. These committees will be supported by a professionally staffed office to provide the back up that is needed.

4. **Reviewing the likely funding sources**. A vital planning tool is a table setting out the number and size of donations needed. This lists the gifts that you plan to acquire, helps you identify possible donors and gives guidance on the level of support to ask for. You will need to develop a plan for raising the money you need: through soliciting major gifts, via a mailed appeal, or through fundraising events and activities.

5. **Documentation and research** to back up the above. For the major gifts, you should undertake some preliminary work at this stage on your fundraising potential. You should certainly explore possible government and aid grants.

6. **Preparation of the case statement**. This is a vital document, which will be the strategic plan for the appeal. It will include sections covering the following:
- a background to the charity and its history
- a description and justification of the project
- the costs of the project
- the individual components of the project, costed
- the gifts needed to achieve this target
- the plan to meet the needs and raise the money
- the sources of money expected.

This should be well produced as a report, and you may wish to produce some overhead projector slides as visual aids for presentations.

7. **Identifying the people** who will lead the appeal, and approaching them to ask them if they would be prepared to help. This is usually done by drawing up lists of leading businessmen and other influential people

gleaned from a wide range of sources, including personal knowledge and contacts. They will meet infrequently, but are there to help solicit the largest gifts through their contacts and credibility. Once again, the appointment of the Chair is critical as he or she will be the public figure leading the appeal. Some appeals have even failed simply because they get this appointment wrong.

8. **Ensuring the support** of your trustees. One key issue is the degree to which your trustees are committed to the development and to the appeal. It makes it extremely difficult to approach people for their support if many of the trustees are known to be half-hearted about the venture.

Leadership

The leadership of the appeal campaign is enormously important. There are two important principles to bear in mind.

- People respond better when asked by people who are at or above their own level in society – this is called peer group giving.
- People respond better if the person who is asking has already given and given generously. One question they will ask is "Have you given?". If the answer is "no", then it is far easier for them to refuse.

The qualifications to look for in the Chair and in Appeal Committee members are that they have the resources to give major gifts on the scale you need (either personally or through the company or foundation they are associated with); that they have important contacts; and that they are able and willing to ask others to support the appeal both in person and by letter.

The first stage is to identify people to help you plan the appeal. Since you are asking for advice, it is easier for them to say "yes" and later on you can ask them for money! A group of two or three senior people with an interest in your work can be invited to act as a planning group. Their role is either to act as the formal leadership of the appeal or to select that leadership. They should be people who are well-respected in the community and who may have not been associated with a similar appeal in the recent past – if they have, their asking capacity will have been diminished. They should have plenty of contacts. One of their tasks will be to select other people to form the nucleus of the Appeal Committee.

You need to understand why important people might want to work for your cause. Research seems to suggest that almost every motive under the sun will be present. Some people find themselves genuinely supporting the cause; others find the approach from a senior person in the community difficult to resist; others find the link with other business people attractive for their own purposes; some are motivated by the notion of some sort of recognition for what they have done at the end of the day;

and some just like the challenge of achieving something rather unusual and worthwhile. All those involved at this level are likely to appreciate efficient administration and being provided with the back up they need. This will ensure that they spend the minimum amount of time in committee meetings and that their time is effectively used.

Many people don't know how to ask effectively, and you may wish to provide some training in the principles of effective asking as well as an induction into the work of your organisation and its importance.

The private phase

With the building blocks in place, you should be ready to begin the slow yet vital task of solicitation.

The first task is to get the commitment of those on your Appeals Committee. It is important that your early gifts are of a sufficient size to give a lead to those that follow. Through the process of developing and refining the appeal document, most committee members should now be

---

Table of Gifts needed for Appeal

It is always sensible to break down the total appeal target into the numbers of gifts of different sizes that you will need to raise. This table is an example showing how this might be done.

	No. of gifts	Amount p.a. £,000	4 year value £,000	Total over 4 yrs £,000
	2	25	100	200
	8	10	40	320
	20	5	20	400
	40	2	8	320
Total	70			1,240

---

aware of the scale of donations that are needed. They will have been engaged in discussions about what is expected of other prospective donors, and will be familiar with what might be expected of them.

Once they have made their own commitment, they should move on to the task of approaching others. For this purpose you will have drawn up lists of prospective donors. They will be able to help by adding new names and deciding how an approach can best be made. The role of the fundraiser is to provide smooth administration; the actual task of asking for big gifts is best done by the committee member. Once you have identified who is the best person to approach a potential donor, a wide variety of methods can be used from an informal sounding out at a dinner party to a personal letter to a round of golf. The one you choose will be that which the person doing the asking feels most comfortable with.

Big donations usually take time to be decided. This will be particularly true of big donations from public sector sources. A decision should not be expected within the course of a single meeting. However, what might happen is a series of meetings – starting perhaps with a reception, followed by informal chats – that culminate in the prospective donor being asked to help and offered a range of possible ways of doing so. Not only can they be asked to give money, they can be asked to give support in kind and can suggest other people to be approached.

The objective of the private stage of the appeal will be to collect promises of between 25% and 50% of the appeal target. This will give a tremendous boost to the appeal when it is launched. Indeed, you should not actually launch an appeal to the public until you are confident of its success.

The public phase

The public phase starts with the launch. This can be done in any number of ways depending on how the campaign is structured. It should certainly involve a press conference and might also involve an event to which you invite prospective donors.

In the public phase of the appeal, much of the money will be raised from large numbers of people in smaller donations. This phase will have several objectives: to take the appeal to a wider audience; to assist the task of the big gift fundraising, and to give those who were unable to give at a high level the opportunity to give at a more modest one.

A press and public relations campaign is important to give your appeal a continuing profile. Some of the bigger appeals recruit PR committees and involve a range of PR professionals on a voluntary basis. You should certainly have someone working hard on public and media relations, as this will underpin your other fundraising activities.

Events are an important component of an appeal. They can attract good media coverage, and can reach a large audience who will become aware of the appeal in this way. However, they should be organised by a group of volunteers (perhaps an Events Committee). This will ensure that your time is used effectively. It is easy to get swallowed up in event administration, when the real money is coming through personal solicitation.

Mail shots are also useful as they can be targeted to those that your personal approaches have not yet reached. It is important though that these be left towards the end, so that nobody gives a small donation in response to a mail shot who might otherwise have given a bigger one if asked personally.

For the very large national appeals, a regional committee structure may need to be set up to harness the many possible appeal opportunities at a regional level. The regional chairpeople are appointed as part of the appeal structure, and they then recruit people in their area. Their role will mainly be in the public phase of the appeal helping to stimulate and co-ordinate events and to give support and publicity to the campaign in their area.

The consolidation phase

Consolidating what has been achieved in the first stages of your campaign will ensure that you can make the most of the efforts and the contacts you have made for your continuing fundraising. This phase includes a number of key steps:

- **bringing in all the promised money**. During the appeal you will have received pledges and promises of support which may not yet have materialised. This is the time to chase these up;
- **closing the appeal.** When the appeal has hit its target, or a revised higher target if the appeal has been a success, then is the time to announce the fact, to get publicity for the success of the venture, and to celebrate this through some sort of reception or entertainment event. Key volunteers, prominent supporters and sponsors, staff and others who were centrally involved in the appeal can be invited;
- **thanking everyone involved**. This includes committee members, volunteer helpers, donors, staff. Everyone should be thanked for their contribution to the success of the venture;
- **setting up a development committee**. You may have generated your income on a somewhat *ad hoc* basis up to this point; the creation of the right structure for the charity and its future fundraising can help ensure that the momentum is not lost. This may involve setting up a permanent development committee or a connected foundation whose job it is to carry on the fundraising or a high level advisory committee. During the course of the appeal, you will have gained the confidence and enthusiasm of a number of business and other leaders. Those who have been particularly effective should now be encouraged to take more permanent places within the structures that you have created so that they can continue to help you;
- **further fundraising**. With these people and structures in place, you are in the position of approaching the many people who did not give to the appeal, and to begin to tap those who did give for further support.

The issues

One issue is the degree to which a major appeal will interfere with your ongoing fundraising and affect future fundraising prospects. This will vary with each organisation, and depends on the appeal strategy and the relative sizes of your capital and revenue fundraising budgets. For a £50 million a year charity raising £5 million of capital, there is likely to be some overlap. Also, it is a point of major commitment for your existing supporters. Having made a substantial donation on this occasion they may want to be left alone for a while.

However, for a small charity raising a relatively big sum, the momentum, excitement and interest that is generated by the appeal will probably add to the regular income received rather than detract from it.

A further issue to consider is the difficult cash flow decisions that may need to be taken. There will be considerable costs involved in the early months especially if a professional consultant is retained. It is important to recognise that no appeal is cost-free, and to budget for the necessary administrative and back up resources you will need to make the appeal a success. A properly planned and resourced appeal will stand a much better chance of success. This all needs to be budgeted for. If the appeal is on track for success, then all that is required is faith in the plans and budgets, and a strong nerve. There may come a point at which you may question whether the appeal will succeed. This should be well before the public phase. If you take the view that it will not, then you should pull out. This is not an easy decision and one which the organisation has to make up its own mind about. However, it is better to withdraw at this early stage than to be seen to fail very publicly.

5. Fundraising Stategy

5.1 Developing your strategy

Your strategy is the backbone of your fundraising. Getting it right demands a good deal of attention at an early stage or you risk wasting your time and efforts and ultimately failing as a fundraiser. Developing your strategy is best done with the widest possible involvement of people inside and outside your organisation, especially if you have major fundraising ambitions. If you simply need £250 for equipment, all you need is a couple of successful coffee mornings or a few people taking part in a sponsored event. Such a strategy is perfectly simple and quick to plan. However, if you have a wider hopes or major existing commitments to fund, you will need to spend more time and be more creative in developing your fundraising strategy.

Strategy is about organising your ideas to produce a viable plan which will take you forward for a period longer than one year. Your strategy will indicate where you wish to get to in a period of (say) five years and it will indicate the route you think best to achieve your aims. Not everything will go according to plan, and you will have you to make changes from time to time. In any case, you should aim to produce a new strategy every few years and expect to revisit the strategy every year to make minor adjustments and incorporate new ideas.

Your strategy should be seen as an inherent part of the long term plan for your organisation and your business plan, if you have one.

> **Headings for a fundraising strategy paper**
>
> Review of the current position
>   Current strengths and weaknesses
>   Past fundraising experience
>   Existing fundraising strengths and resources
>
> Projection of fundraising needs
>
> Overall funding strategy
>
> Proposed new sources of income
>
> Suggested methods to meet fundraising targets
>
> Resources needed to do this

Outlining the needs

The starting point for any fundraising strategy is to define the needs of the organisation. This can be done at three levels.

1. Just to keep going
What are the financial requirements if the organisation is to continue its

work programme at the present scale of operation? How much money is already assured, and how much will need to be raised to meet spending requirements?

These calculations will usually take the form of annual and rolling budgets for the short and medium term (up to three or even five years ahead).

2. To expand to meet growing need

Most organisations believe that they are only scratching at the surface of the problem, that if they had more resources, they could do much more to meet the need. Alongside this, the need may be growing or the problem getting worse. Starting with the human or societal needs being addressed by the organisation, you might ask the following questions:

- what exactly is the current level of unmet need?
- what are the consequences or implications of this if nothing is done?
- how are the needs growing and what changes do you foresee happening over the next few years?
- who else is doing something to meet the need?
- what should you be doing to respond to the challenges of the future?
- how does your plan fit in with what others are doing?
- is what you propose to do an effective way of addressing the need given the limited resources that are likely to be available?

Future plans should be discussed and developed. Is it just a question of expanding what you are doing, or will you need to develop new mechanisms for addressing the problem? If the need is not important and your role not clear, then developing a good fundraising 'case' can become very difficult.

3. The future development of the organisation's work

Most organisations do not stay still. There is often a momentum to expand and develop. Success with one project not only gives the organisation a feeling of confidence; it will also throw up ideas for other things that the organisation might do, and bring greater credibility with funders and public bodies who might wish to create closer working partnerships with you.

What developments will you want to consider for the future? What new services or projects will you want to run? Will you want to export your work into other regions? Will you want to enter into major collaborations with your funding partners to extend your work? Will you want to enter into partnerships with governmental authorities, working with them on a much wider scale to address the problem?

If you are a community development organisation, there is also the relationship with the people you are helping to be considered. Are you empowering people to help themselves? If so you are, how will you be planning to operate once local people have the structures and skills to organise their own development? Will you extend and develop your work and maintain your development role? Or will you develop a withdrawal or exit strategy?

The future of your organisation starts with what you want to do. It is up to your Chief Executive to plan this, with input from other senior staff and from yourself. Then it is up to you, the fundraiser, to get the resources that will be needed to put the plans into action.

However, it is vital that you do not do things simply because you can get money for them. You must be led by the work that you want to do, the needs you want to meet, rather than the money you think you can raise. If you are not, you will soon find that you have lost your commitment and sense of direction and will be in grave danger of simply fizzling out.

Different approaches to fundraising strategy

Besides funding the work, you will also need to fund the organisation and its future. There are several factors to consider.

1. Capital developments

Capital developments can have an impact on future fundraising needs in three ways. On the plus side:

- they can create a stream of income from fees and charges arising from their use or from letting out space;
- they can generate a greater capacity to fundraise. By organising a major appeal, you will be developing important contacts which you can mobilise later on for further support, building a mailing list, and developing fundraising expertise and systems.

On the minus side:

- they almost always increase your revenue costs as they require the money to run them. You will need to bear this in mind when planning your fundraising.

2. Endowment

Many organisations plan to develop a corpus fund or an endowment – that is, a capital reserve which can be invested to produce a regular income for the organisation. Some approach major donors for contributions to this fund, others set aside some of their income each year. They feel that this will give them greater financial security, remove some of the fundraising pressure or act as a nest egg for the unexpected. Most trusts and companies prefer to fund your work directly rather than have money tied up as an investment. However it is possible to raise endowments as these examples show:

The Campaign for Oxford has succeeded in getting several professorial chairs endowed. The money raised for each is sufficient to generate the annual income needed to support a professor.

Community Links, a community-based project in London, organised a major appeal to take over a town hall in Canning Town and turn it into a community centre. The building was seen as an asset which could continue to be exploited for community benefit.

Although having an endowment seems an attractive option, it takes a lot of hard work to raise the money. Might it not be better to spend that money on undertaking exciting and successful work? This would make the organisation more attractive to funders and make future fundraising easier.

3. Reducing dependency and developing independent sources of funding

There is a fundamental difference between an organisation that receives all its money from one source, and an organisation which has developed a wide range of sources each contributing towards the total requirement. Too much dependency on one source can give the donor too much power to dictate how the organisation should be working and where it should be going. It can put great pressure on the organisation to meet the agenda and the objectives of the donor, rather than stand up for what it wants to do (where this is different). It creates a risk of failure – that the organisation will not be able to survive if the grant is cutback or withdrawn.

It is for this reason that many organisations seek to extend their fundraising base, bringing in other major donors and developing new sources of funding. You need to decide whether your organisation's funding base is too narrow, and if it is, then how you are going to broaden it. You will need to think about all the possible sources of funding, and decide which are the most sensible for your organisation to develop.

4. Developing a membership and a supporter base

This is another aspect of financial independence, where the organisation attracts large numbers of individual supporters. This not only brings in money, but it also strengthens the organisation by:

- **creating a constituency of support** (the numbers of people who support you matter);
- **building a local base** for your organisation (the relationships with the local community will be different if the funding is drawn from it rather than obtained externally);
- **creating opportunities** for further fundraising. Each donor can be asked to give regularly and to give more generously. They can also be asked to recruit other donors, to volunteer their time and skills to help the

organisation, to donate items of equipment, or even to leave a legacy. The more people who support you, the greater the opportunities.

Some key concepts

Before deciding exactly which sources and techniques you could be using there are a number of general issues to be considered. Some of these will help you see which approach to funding you should take or which sorts of funders might be most relevant for you.

- *Be cost conscious*. Everything should be done to save money both in the organisation and in its fundraising for two good reasons. First there is a moral imperative upon the fundraiser to ask supporters for only what is strictly necessary, and to use as much of the sums given as possible on the work of the organisation. Many donors really do give the equivalent of the widow's mite, and good stewardship is owed to them. There is a pressing practical reason too. If fundraisers are striving for a return ratio of say 5:1 of income to expenditure, then to maintain this ratio requires either extra income from the fundraising effort or lower costs.

  All fundraising activities should adhere to some cost effectiveness ratios. For mature fundraising schemes these may be as high as 10:1; other types of fundraising will never be able to do much better than 2 or 3:1. It is not sensible to expect new ventures or recently recruited fundraisers to produce these returns. Thus sliding scales of cost effectiveness are often used such that in year one a ratio of 2:1 is required; in year two 3:1, and so on. Only with very clear planning are fundraising targets going to be met. Donors and trustees would undoubtedly prefer not to spend anything to raise the money. The reality is that an expenditure of 20% represents a norm (a 5:1 ratio) that is often acceptable to most donors.

- *Someone has to pay*. An important decision is whether to charge for any services being provided. Many charities exist to provide a service to beneficiaries, and it is a part of the purpose of the organisation to do that on a free or highly subsidised basis. This then means that the amount raised determines the volume of work that can be undertaken. You will have to decide for yourselves how appropriate it is to charge and the levels of subsidy that can be offered. This must be reviewed frequently as the services provided are often the principal drain on the charity's resources. It is important however, to cost what you do carefully and accurately. Someone has to pay for it. Your funders, your sponsors, your donors or the users.

- *Avoid risks*. The cash used for fundraising purposes is intended ultimately for the beneficiaries of the charity. Naturally they would be pleased to hear that this money had been invested wisely to generate funds for the charity, but they would not be at all pleased to hear that their money had been lost on a high risk venture. It is important that fundraisers do everything to reduce risk. This might involve piloting or testing new fundraising ideas where this can be done; it demands that you identify the worst possible thing that can happen in an event and insure against it, and that you scrap the activity when it looks set to fail. For example, an event like a concert in the Albert Hall will depend on the sale of tickets for its success. If very few tickets are sold, the losses will be very large. In this case, the best insurance would be to get a sponsor to underwrite all the costs. You can then give the tickets away if you can't sell them to ensure a full house.

■ *Don't be dependent*. It is a problem to be over-dependent on only one source of funding. If this fails, then the organisation can go into a financial crisis from which it may prove difficult to recover. One approach to this problem is to diversify your fundraising activities and sources. This is one reason why so many charities were so interested in the prospects of payroll giving by employees when it was introduced and, more recently, the National Lottery. Both seemed to promise new sources of continuing income.

■ *The long-term approach*. Most organisations are not just interested in the results this year alone but in the income which can be secured for the future. Fundraisers have a choice: they can concentrate on getting cash now or they can devote some of their resources to ensuring a continuing flow of funds for the future. Among the areas of fundraising where this is necessary is the development of charity shops, appeals for legacies and the use of covenants. There are inevitable costs in the short-term but the experience of most fundraisers is that the value of long-term giving soon outweighs that of casual giving.

■ *The multiplier approach*. A good way to multiply fundraising results is to cascade. For example, many charities over the last 20 years have operated regular collection schemes. In these, householders are visited monthly by a local collector and give their 50p or so. These are collected by an area representative and in turn sent in to the charity HQ. In this way one person at the centre is able to mobilise literally thousands of people and raise what in some cases has been millions of pounds. The cascade effect can multiply the number of people supporting you and the amount you can raise.

■ *Sustainability*. Sustainable organisations are structured in such a way as to minimise the need for permanent fundraising. For most, this is a mere pipe dream, but if you can put any of these ideas into practice you will reduce your fundraising needs later. The ultimate problem is when you are dependent on a small number of income sources and

they withdraw their support. Thus there are a number of ways of making yourself more sustainable:
- arrange for your core costs to be funded separately
- develop a range of income generating activities
- develop partnerships with larger bodies – government for example
- raise an endowment fund
- raise volunteers and get support donated in kind
- develop repeatable income sources such as memberships or regular events.

- *Time*. A key element within the strategy is to be realistic about how long things take. To go from £0 to £100,000 a year from grant-making trusts may require years of patient fundraising effort. To land your first major company sponsorship requires professionalism and good relationships that you may well not yet have. Be realistic on how long things take.

5.2 Analysing your position

Analysing the present position of your organisation and its work is an important starting point for any strategy. Not only will it help you answer some of the difficult questions you are often asked by funders, it will also help you see your work in new ways and to better understand its strengths and weaknesses. In analysing your position you should first try to answer as honestly as possible some questions about the nature of the work which you are seeking to fund.

- What is the need that your work is addressing?
- Who are the ultimate beneficiaries of your work?
- What difference to the beneficiaries does your intervention make?
- Are there competing agencies, and how does what they are doing fit with what you are doing?
- What is distinctive about your approach to the work ?
- Is the need expected to increase or change over the next few years and how will you respond to these changes?
- What are your medium-term plans?
- Is the need you are addressing an on-going social need or is it occasional, seasonal or one off?

Projection of financial need

The next step is to make a financial projection of the resources you will need to undertake your planned programme of work over the medium term. This must take in all the expenditure you plan to incur and all the

Example of a funding projection for a small organisation

Source of income	Current year	Next year	2 years' time	3 years' time
Current local authority grant	10,000	10,000	5,000	5,000
Grant from charitable trust	2,500	2,500	nil	nil
Membership subscriptions	250	250	250	250
Total committed income	12,750	12,750	5,250	5,250
Reserve at start of year	500	2,050	2,050	1,550
Current operational costs	10,000	12,500	15,000	15,000
New project costs	1,200	3,500	5,000	5,000
Projected Fundraising Target	nil	3,250	14,750	14,250

The example shows that your funding position for the current year is good, and that you have a small target to meet next year which is a realistic goal for your fundraising. However in two years time, as your major grants run out, you will need to find alternative funding, or develop new ideas for the organisation.

sources of funding that are probable. It should aim to show you two things. The first is the funding gap that needs to be met, and the second is to indicate the possible fall-back options if funding is not received. This can best be illustrated by way of the example set out in the box.

Analysis of your environment

There are a number of tools that are useful for analysing the environment in which you will be doing your fundraising. It is better to have a small group of people involved in each of these exercises as the analysis will benefit from a brainstorming approach.

1. SWOT analysis
The first, and most commonly used tool available is SWOT analysis. This involves trying to identify the:

Strengths
Weaknesses
Opportunities and
Threats

to your organisation. Strengths and weaknesses are internal to your organisation – those things that you know to be true which either give

An example of a SWOT analysis for a small organisation

	Strengths	Weaknesses
Internal factors	Established team Experienced management Good relations with local authority Good reputation	Limited contact with funders Existing grants running out No evaluation undertaken
	Opportunities	**Threats**
External factors	Public attention on your issue National Lottery round coming up	Change in benefit regulations Local agency expanding aggressively

you an advantage or hold you back. Opportunities and threats relate to the external world and how, both now and in future, they will impact on your work and funding opportunities.

2. PEST analysis

To explore the external factors in more detail, a PEST (sometimes also known as STEP) analysis can be useful. This works in a very similar way to SWOT analysis (see above). In this case though, you will be looking at the trends in society which are going to affect your fundraising and your work generally. This is done under the headings:

Political
Economic
Social
Technological.

Its orientation is both future and external and focuses on changes in the world which may at some stage affect you. For example:

- *Political*: what impact will the change of government in 1997 have on the voluntary sector? Will the privatisation of social services make fundraising easier or more difficult?
- *Economic*: what effect will the next budget have on fundraising? If public spending continues to be under pressure how will this impact on voluntary organisations?
- *Social*: what will be the impact of the growth in the elderly population? What will be the results of the continuing fragmentation of the family?

PEST Analysis of a small employment charity for people with disabilities

Political: change of government may bring advantages

Economic: improvements in economy will bring more work opportunities

Social: car based society will continue to disadvantage those on low incomes and with mobility problems

Technological: it will be possible to do more work at home

If these are the main factors that were identified, you then have to consider what impact they will have.

- *Technological*: what opportunities arise as the move towards home banking continues? Does the Internet offer new opportunities? Will the advent of Channel 5 and new satellite and cable channels bring new opportunities?

All these factors and others of a similar type may affect the organisation and its fundraising. There may be little you can do about some, but all are important to bear in mind as you develop your fundraising strategy.

3. Stakeholder analysis

Stakeholder analysis simply involves consideration of all those groups who have a particular interest in your organisation and in its funding. For example, a refugee service concluded that it had a number of key stakeholders. They included:

- the local authority who might otherwise have to provide support to refugee families;
- members of the organisation, who are members because they feel strongly about the issues being tackled;
- refugee community organisations, who already provide direct support to new refugees;
- second generation refugees, who have stayed on and made good in Britain and who wish to put something back to help other refugees.

The usefulness of this exercise is to help you identify who has a particular interest in supporting your work and what is their reason for this? This sort of analysis can be a useful starting point for your fundraising and for the development of a new strategy. It seeks to answer the two questions:

- who do you think should be funding you?
- what is their particular interest in doing so?

4. Audit of your existing fundraising

In order to make a proper evaluation of what fundraising sources and techniques are worth exploring, you first need to have a good understanding of the present position. Even the smallest and newest organisation will have some sort of fundraising experience and there will also be the known history of similar groups which have had similar starting points and whose experience may be useful. Having done this there are two frameworks which you can use, both relying on common sense: the Ansoff matrix and the Boston matrix. Both will help throw light on your existing fundraising experience and future plans.

Listing your fundraising sources

Source of funds	funds received		% of	
	Previous year	Last year	This year	Total
Central government				
Europe				
Local government				
Trusts				
Companies				
Membership				
Individual donations				
Fundraising events				
Legacies				
Charges and fees				

You can also include volunteer inputs and support in kind, if you wish. This gives a better picture of the total resources you are deploying.

5. Analysing the existing sources

A simple analysis of your existing funding sources should be made to give some indication of where you are currently getting funds from, where you might be able to get more from and whether you are especially vulnerable to any particular source disappearing or being cut back.

To this list you should add as a note any particular problems that may have experienced with each of the sources. The trends highlighted by this analysis may also be revealing.

6. Competitive analysis

A good deal of information can be gleaned by an intelligent look at your collaborators and competitors. Those that are successful may have tried already to develop some of the fundraising sources you are considering and failed; or they may be succeeding with a fundraising source or technique that you have not yet considered. Although most organisations reveal much about their fundraising sources in their annual reports, they do not say much about their methods. This can best be discovered by reading the trade press, talking with your colleagues in other organisations and being prepared to ask them how they are doing. One idea is to phone them and enquire about making a donation and see what happens.

Ansoff Matrix

New source	Known source	
New technique	High risk	Medium risk
Known technique	Medium risk	Low risk

Boston Matrix

Effort in	Market growth		Fundraising Efficiency
	HIGH	**LOW**	
HIGH	STAR QUADRANT e.g. the growing payroll scheme	PROBLEM CHILD e.g. recently launched sponsored event	HIGH
LOW	CASH COW e.g. postal appeals to existing donors	DOG e.g. your original penny a week scheme in workplaces	LOW

Balancing the new with the old: the Ansoff Matrix

The Ansoff Matrix shows the risk associated with combinations of new sources of funds and new fundraising techniques. The more changes you introduce, the more risk there will be. The safest way of proceeding will be to use known methods of fundraising from known audiences. An example is to appeal to your past donors to ask for a repeat donation. Slightly more risky is to use new methods with existing supporters – for example by launching a covenant scheme for your existing donors, or to extend existing methods to new supporters, for example launching a fundraising drive to sign up new supporters. Most risky is to use new methods targeted at new audiences, for example soliciting legacies from people who have not previously supported the organisation.

Assessing existing fundraising: the Boston Matrix

The Boston matrix is a way of comparing a portfolio of fundraising activities, and it implies ways in which they can be supported. The original idea, which was conceived by the Boston Consulting Group for the analysis of product portfolios, envisaged an analysis by market share (x) and market growth rate (y). In this version, we suggest that these are changed to an analysis of market growth rate against cost effectiveness ratio. Elements of your fundraising – if you have several – are then located on the grid. Each quadrant is named according to how you should view that aspect of your fundraising. For example:

- a **dog** is a fundraising scheme that is operating in a low growth or declining market and which is expensive to operate. The implication of this is that you should endeavour to withdraw from this scheme unless you can move it into a different quadrant;
- a **problem child** is a scheme that has yet to prove itself and which may need further time. However you should expect to concentrate on it in order to move it to another square on the grid before too long;
- the **star quadrant** is for schemes that are not only doing well, but which are also operating in an expanding market. A scheme of this kind should have maximum attention and investment made to ensure that the greatest returns are made;
- finally a **cash cow** is a successful scheme operating in a stagnant or declining market. With a fundraising scheme of this sort you would wish to put a minimum of new investment in, but to expect high yields in the short term.

Assessing the opportunities

In constructing a fundraising strategy a useful starting point is to identify your likely funding sources in relation to what you have been obtaining, and what is on offer. These include:

- a grant from a central government department
- a grant from a non-governmental agency (such as the Arts Council)
- a grant from a local authority (county or district) or local health authority
- a contract with one of the above to deliver a specified service
- a contract with another body (perhaps a commercial organisation or another voluntary agency) to deliver a service
- fees and charges from users
- support from individuals through membership or donations, and legacy income
- support from individuals raised through collections, fundraising and entertainment events and other fundraising activities
- grants from trusts and other independent grant-making bodies
- support from companies (cash, kind, sponsorship, facilities, skills, secondments)
- support from individuals who donate their time as volunteers
- investment income and interest.

These are the main types of funding available to you, although what is most appropriate to your organisation will depend on many different factors. You will have to think through which ones you should aim to develop. Below are some of the factors to take into account.

- **Past experience**. The results of your fundraising so far provide a good indication of both what to do and what not to do. Things that have gone well can be developed to do even better. Donors that have supported you can be encouraged to continue their support, perhaps at a higher level. New donors can be brought in to match the support you have got from existing donors. Effort and resources can be invested in the development of those areas of fundraising that appear to work.

- **Scale of need**. Large needs may require large funds. These can be raised in large grants from a few sources, or in multiples of smaller gifts from a large number of donors. You will need to develop fundraising sources that have the capacity to make a realistic contribution to your overall need.

- **The attractiveness of the cause**. Some causes seem able to sell themselves. People working with cuddly animals or starving babies have causes that are extremely compelling. If you are associated with such a cause, then all types of fundraising become much easier. If not, then you have to work hard to make your cause seem important, to present it effectively to donors and make it seem compelling as something to support.

- **The style of your work**. Are you radical or conservative? Young or old? Innovative or steady? Every organisation will be able to identify institutions and individuals that share its vision and outlook. Equally there will be those that don't, and these will be much less likely to give their support.

- **The resources and skills available to you**. Do you have the people to mount a collection, the contacts to develop a big gift campaign, or the organisational ability to run a major event? It will always be best to do what you are good at doing.

Assessing possible funding sources					
Source	*Past Experience*	*Competitors' Experience*	*Relevance to cause*	*Resources Needed*	*Rating*
Central Govt					
Local Govt					
Trusts					
Companies					
Individuals					

- **Your natural constituency of support.** Is this government? Trusts? Individuals? Who has a stake in the problem or need you are addressing? Can you get them to share in its solution by becoming an investor in your work?
- **The type of organisation you want to be.** A membership organisation is very different from an organisation that is funded by government, and a fundraising organisation very different from one that relies onearnings from the sale of its services. Your fundraising enables you to do what you want to do. Your fundraising strategy will help you become the sort of organisation you want to be.
- **Short term and long term**. Some sources are essentially short term, whilst some can develop into long-term relationships and partnerships. If you are there for the long term, you will need long term sources of income. You will want to get as much as you can committed on a long-term basis. You will want to turn supporters into regular supporters. You will want to organise a successful fundraising event even more successfully next year.

Clarifying the constraints

In fundraising, action will be limited by a range of constraints, some which stem from the nature of the organisation, some which are internally generated, and others which are externally imposed. Many touch on areas which are also some of your key opportunities.

- *Geography*. An important constraint is the geographical remit of the organisation. Some sources only give to organisations with a national remit, others only give locally. Some companies may give nationally through head office, but make smaller local grants through local plants or branches; local people are concerned about their own local communities, but are also concerned about wider issues in society. This precludes some sources, but opens up opportunities for others. If what you are doing locally is particularly innovative or interesting, it may catch the interest of national funders, both because they like being associated with excellence and because the project may provide the answers to similar problems in other areas.
- *Appropriateness*. Some sources are completely inappropriate because what the donor stands for is the complete opposite of what the charity stands for. The British Heart Foundation will take sponsorship from margarine producers but not butter producers; cancer charities will not accept support from tobacco companies. If they did so, they would create bad PR for themselves and problems with their donors. They could not be seen to be endorsing a product which causes the problem. There may be other reasons for refusing a grant. For example, a

campaigning organisation might not wish to be seen in the pocket of a vested interest or the government; and it might gain strength in its campaigning by being seen to be supported by a large membership. It is often quite difficult to draw up an all-embracing set of rules on where you can and where you can't fundraise. It is important to discuss and try to agree the constraints before you set about asking, rather than creating problems for yourself afterwards.

- *Resources*. The resources available to you determine what you can and can't do. If you are planning to organise a public collection, do you have sufficient people to rattle the collecting tins? If you don't, and you can't find them, you will find it difficult to make a success of the venture. Money is another important resource. Much fundraising involves investing resources now to achieve a result later. Some fundraising, such as a direct mail or an advertising campaign or even a large building appeal, can require a substantial immediate expenditure. Anyone soliciting legacies is unlikely to see their efforts rewarded for several years. You need to know how much it is going to cost and when the results will come in to see if you can afford to do it. Although lack of resources can be a constraint, to some fundraisers it is a challenge. They will find the people or the money they need to mount a campaign somehow.

- *Contacts*. The contacts that you have can lead you to sources of money. If you have good contacts in the business world, this can lead to you generating useful sums of money from businesses. If you have celebrities waiting to get involved, you might use them as an anchor in a fundraising event. If you don't have the contacts you might want to consider how you can develop them as a major resource for your fundraising.

- *What other organisations are doing*. What others are doing affects what you do. Not many organisations can expect to get away with being imitators of others. In some way they must distinguish themselves. Two ways of doing this are by differentiation and by focus. Take, forexample, charities in the overseas development sector – Oxfam, Action Aid and WaterAid. Action Aid has a strategy of differentiation and WaterAid a strategy of focus. All three support remarkably similar work. Action Aid target support directly towards children and make much of it in promotional material; WaterAid focuses on both fundraising and assistance in the water sectors; on the other hand, Oxfam succeeds as the market leader by doing neither.

5.3 Putting the strategy into operation

Possible fundraising methods

Depending upon the choice of sources of funds, you will already have reduced the many options open to you for fundraising methods. The next stage of the process involves setting down the most plausible methods that will be available for each of the sources. A simple pro forma for this activity is set out below.

Fundraising start up

Most fundraising techniques require some investment to make them work. If you wish to make appeals to charitable trusts, for example, you will need to invest a good deal of somebody's time in researching the proposal, writing it up, getting others views on it and finally getting the presentation right. Other methods of fundraising may well require that you print leaflets, buy collecting boxes or lay out money before you can get it back. The box gives some rough and ready start-up costs for different methods. All are very dependent upon the scale at which you choose to do them and whether you are lavish or frugal in your purchasing.

Just as there needs to be money invested in getting the fundraising going, so it will take time before you see the income. Thus, for a collection, you may need to organise collecting boxes and leaflets in the month before you are able to carry out the collection. On the other hand if you want to carry out appeals to charitable trusts, it may take you several months to get the proposals and applications properly organised. If that is not slow enough, you will find that many of the smaller charitable trusts do not meet more than quarterly. This could add up to six months to the time before you hear whether you have succeeded.

Equipping a fundraising office

In order to succeed as a fundraiser there are some essential items of equipment which are needed. Some other items may also be useful. All of them can be acquired from a range of sources and need not be found before you start. In some cases you will be able to borrow from friendly organisations or supporters. In others you may be able to get equipment cheap or second hand. The main items of equipment are:

Start up costs for successful fundraising methods

1-5%	5-15%	15-40%
Donor mailings	House to house	Temporary shops
Appeals to trusts	Lotteries	Events
Payroll giving	Collection boxes	Radio/TV appeals

40-70%	70-100%	100%+
Permanent shops	Advertising	Cold mailing

1. A **telephone**. Without a telephone you are at a serious disadvantage. It should, if at all possible, be a line of your own and not be a telephone shared with others, because of the volume and length of both your outgoing and your incoming calls. It is an advantage if the fundraiser's telephone is in a quiet place, where calls can be made in privacy. Busy and effective fundraisers are constantly on the move and likely to be out of their offices for a significant proportion of the time. To catch all of those incoming calls that might otherwise go unanswered requires some form of answering service. The best idea is undoubtedly to arrange for someone to answer your calls. Failing that, an answering machine will cost upwards of £50, and incoming calls can be checked remotely. There are also now answering services available that can easily be arranged.

Planning times for fundraising

1 Month	Advertising for support, postal appeals, house to house
2-6 months	Lotteries, events, appeals to trusts, radio/TV appeals
6-12 months	Government grants, payroll, covenants
1 year +	Legacies, Christmas cards

2. A **PC** or **word processor**. This is a vital piece of equipment which will help you produce high quality letters and proposals as well as storing your database of supporters. You will also need a printer that will produce high quality output. The price of these machines is falling daily. Perfectly satisfactory equipment can be bought in the high street for around £1,000.

3. **Desk Top Publishing** (DTP) is the software and hardware required to be able to produce simple leaflets and other printed materials rather than sending it to a studio. If you already have a computer of moderate power, the software can be readily added at extra cost. However, beware of spending hours playing around with designs as an alternative to getting on with the hard fundraising graft!

4. **Photocopier**. If you are writing proposals and letters to people, then a copier will be very valuable. It will not only enable you to keep good

records of your appeals and correspondence, it will help you prepare large volumes of printed material for circulation to supporters.

5. **Fax**. In a modern office an increasing proportion of communications are sent by fax. It is fast and cheap and is well worth considering as a means of instant written communication.

6. **Annual reports and brochures**. Most institutional donors such as companies and trusts will want to see a copy of your annual report at some point as well as your annual accounts. It does not need to be expensively produced, but it should be well prepared and presented. You may also wish to have a small range of information leaflets for the public which include reply coupons to encourage a direct response.

7. **Books** and **directories** on fundraising (including handbooks, technical information on tax and grants guides) are very valuable. These should include directories of trusts and companies.

8. **Cash collection facilities**. At its simplest you must have a bank account so that donors may send donations and you can safely deposit gifts. If you expect to have large sums on deposit for any length of time you should have a high interest account. If you plan to do house to house or street collections you will need to have the appropriate envelopes or collecting boxes.

9. **Letterheads**. Most organisations will need to have a set of stationery which includes letterheads, compliments slips and return envelopes. Letterheads now need to include certain information for example name, logo, legal status and registration number. You should spend some time designing your letterhead as it is the first point of contact for many people. It also offers an opportunity to spread your message through a strap-line explaining your mission or through an outright appeal.

10. **Display equipment**. This is useful to take advantage of the many opportunities that may arise to have a small exhibition of your work. Fairs, exhibitions and shop windows can be a good way of gaining more interest in your work.

Setting up an office can be expensive. Asking suppliers or supporters may be an effective way of getting what you need. Borrowing is another option. Try the following:

- ask your management committee and volunteers if they are able to give you what you need;

- ask local companies, who may have good, surplus equipment or furniture. Banks are especially worth approaching;
- approach local suppliers and ask for a heavy discount.

The most expensive items are the copiers and computers which are difficult to get donated. You may need to allocate a budget for their purchase, but remember to drive a hard bargain.

If you have a major donor funding your work, you should prepare a shopping list of your needs and then present it to them as an investment package. It is in their interests to get you set up as a fundraiser and reduce your dependency upon them.

Who should do the fundraising

There are several options to consider.

1. The management committee

These are the people who are legally responsible for ensuring that the organisation has sufficient funds to carry out its work and that it doesn't become insolvent. They have to ensure that the fundraising is done effectively and on time, but that does not mean that they have to do the fundraising work, although in many smaller organisations, it is the committee members who will be doing most of the fundraising.

2. The chairperson

The chairperson of the organisation occupies a special position of leadership. Part of the responsibility of heading up the organisation may be to deal with major donors, along with the director, and to attend various meetings with foundations and businesses where this will be helpful.

3. A fundraising committee

Where the fundraising is being done by committee members, it is important to remember that some people don't like doing fundraising or are no good at it. This leads some organisations to appoint committee members for their fundraising skills and personal contacts. This is not always a good strategy. Any committee needs to include people with a range of skills, expertise, and standpoints, as it has responsibility for the proper management and strategic direction of the organisation as well as to ensure that the organisation has sufficient funds.

It might be better to form a fundraising committee or development committee with people who are interested in the organisation and are also keen to help raise money for it. This group can then be charged with overseeing the fundraising, and even undertaking much of the fundraising work.

4. The director

The director of the organisation is the senior staff member. As such they are in a good position to do the fundraising – with an expert knowledge of the work being done and sufficient seniority to be an effective persuader. Fundraising can also be a creative process. If you are dealing with donors, you will be testing out new ideas and getting feedback, negotiating different forms of support and having to think creatively about how to turn people's goodwill into support. All this is extremely useful for a successful director.

One problem is the lack of time, which means that the fundraising will not be given sufficient priority. One solution is to give the director sufficient administrative assistance so that the fundraising part of the job can be done well.

5. A member of staff

Organisations of sufficient size or where fundraising is to be given a high priority, may decide to create a specific post of fundraiser within the organisation. This will ensure that a person with the required skills and with sufficient time to do the job properly is responsible for fundraising.

However it is easy to delegate a job that nobody really likes doing and then forget about it. There are many instances of organisations appointing a fundraiser and telling them to get on with the job, then a couple of years later finding that nothing has been achieved. If you decide to delegate the job of fundraising to a professional, both the director and the management committee need to keep management control of the process setting goals and monitoring progress, providing active support where needed and giving encouragement.

6. A volunteer

Another option is to find a part time or even a full time volunteer who is prepared to do the fundraising. Some organisations have been able to do this successfully. A recently retired business person might find this a challenge.

Volunteers are more often given responsibility for a particular aspect of the fundraising, such as organising a fundraising reception or a charity gala film evening. This has the advantage that a slice of the fundraising work can be handed over to someone else who takes full responsibility for it, but the volunteer should be set targets and held accountable for performance if the arrangement is to be a success.

7. A fundraising consultant

Fundraising consultants or consultancy organisations are in business to help voluntary organisations with their fundraising – for a fee. Some specialise in major appeals, some in event organising, some in direct mail campaigns, some in corporate sponsorship and joint promotions, and some in working with smaller organisations to help them clarify their approach to fundraising and get started. Using a consultant can be quite expensive, as you are having to pay for their expertise as well as their overheads. But particularly where you are developing a major initiative, they can provide an extremely useful input of experience and knowledge which can add value to your fundraising efforts. It is rarely the case that you will hand over all of the fundraising work to an external consultant.

When you need a fundraiser

It is not essential for every voluntary organisation to appoint a member of staff as a fundraiser. Many grant-aided bodies will neither need nor want the expense of fundraising staff. They can leave the task to the senior worker or to trustees and board members. For others, volunteers will be able to raise all the funds they need. For many their growth and the pattern of their funding will lead to a time when a decision is needed on whether to recruit a professional fundraiser.

For voluntary supporters to take at least some responsibility for the fundraising remains a desirable option whether or not there is any staff time devoted to this function. For organisations with more than a handful of staff, the overall responsibility for seeing that the money is raised will need to be concentrated in the hands of a senior executive.

A combination of executive responsibilities and volunteers doing most of the work allows the organisation to develop without undue emphasis on fundraising, and staff can concentrate on the development of the organisation's programme. While the funding still comes from a small number of large donors, this structure remains possible. However, as soon as it is decided that support from a wider section of the public is needed, then staff will almost certainly be needed to undertake or organise some or most of the fundraising work.

The main consideration when deciding the right time to employ a fundraiser is a financial one. Can you afford to, and what effect will it have on the administrative costs of the organisation? Not many organisations are lucky enough to obtain sponsorship for their fundraiser, so you will have to consider the costs involved. On the other hand, can you afford not to? As a rough rule of thumb, to employ a junior fundraiser on a full-time basis will cost at least £15,000 plus overheads. To justify such an expenditure, you will need to generate in the region of £50,000 a year in extra revenue as a result of this appointment – although it can take some time to achieve results on this scale.

In the early days it may appear that much of what a fundraiser is doing is to raise the costs of their own salary. This is a difficult psychological barrier at the best of times, and it is far better if the fundraiser's salary can be paid out of general funds. In any case, those appointing a fundraiser for the first time should take a long-term view. It will take several years to develop the full potential of the fundraising effort put in. Any appointment of a fundraiser should be seen as part of the organisation's longer term strategy, and the fundraiser should be set targets for the money to be raised in each of the first few years of the appointment

Recruitment of a fundraiser

Once you have decided to recruit a fundraiser, you should consider the following:

1. Objectives

What are the objectives for the fundraising post? Is it to develop alternative sources of funds to replace grants which are known to be coming to an end? To launch an expansion programme? To run a major capital appeal? To develop a corpus fund or endowment? To develop independent and local sources of funding? To create a large and active membership? To develop corporate support? Or to organise high profile events which will raise awareness as well as money? You need to decide quite clearly what your objectives are. This will help you write a job description and a person specification, so that you recruit someone with the experience and capability to do a good job for you.

It is also important to recognise that realistic objectives should be set – objectives that recognise the fundraising needs of the organisation and the opportunities that exist, but which do not present an insurmountable obstacle to success. There will also be an inevitable learning process at the start when nothing much happens, whilst the fundraiser familiarises himself or herself to the work of the organisation and begins to build experience and contacts. It is also important that results should begin to flow, even if the successes are quite small initially, as this will demonstrate that things are beginning to work.

2. Budget

As has already been mentioned, the budget for fundraising will be more than the salary costs of the fundraiser. A sensible budget needs to be set aside to resource the post and pay for all the promotional work that is needed.

3. Recruitment

So you've decided your objectives and produced a written job description.

Where do you find this paragon you are looking for? You will need to identify someone with the right:

- experience and expertise
- personal skills and qualities to do a good job
- ethical values and commitment to the cause.

Of these it is the last two which are really important – especially in countries where there is not yet that much experience of fundraising except raising money from international donor bodies. Expertise can be acquired and experience gained, but the personal skills and ethical stance come with the candidate. (The personal skills required in a fundraiser are discussed in some detail in Section 2.2.)

When you decide to recruit someone, there is always a chance that the arrangement will not work out – that they will be the wrong person for the job despite having got through the job interview and selection process. You may want to have a six month probation period for the newly recruited fundraiser.

Where to recruit a fundraiser

- Circulate information about the job opportunity to your staff. This job might be something that a current member of your staff team might like to do.
- Circulate information about the job opportunity to your existing supporters and volunteers. They already have some commitment to the organisation. Someone might be just the right person for the job.
- Advertise in the local newspaper, the business press and in marketing journals. These will reach the sorts of people you are looking for.

---

4. Induction

The fundraiser is selling the organisation to donors. It is important that there is a satisfactory induction process, which might include:

- meeting the Management Committee
- meeting senior staff
- site visits to projects to see the organisation at work
- discussing and agreeing what the organisation stands for and how it should be projected to the public
- discussing where the organisation is not prepared to solicit support
- agreeing the fundraising strategy and the targets for the first year, and sketching out what might be achieved over the first three years
- reviewing existing donor support, identifying problem areas and opportunities, and being introduced to any key contacts.

Management and motivation of fundraisers

Fundraising is a tough and demanding job and often a lonely one. With all the difficulties in raising money, and with a steady flow of rejections, it is easy to get downhearted. Proper management of the fundraiser's job means:

1. Keeping in touch with the work of the organisation

The fundraiser should keep in regular touch with those doing the front-line work of the organisation, visiting projects to see the work, talking to project workers and beneficiaries to get a feel of the need and the quality of the work being done, and to understand the issues and the particular approach and ethos of the organisation. This interchange of ideas also has the effect that those spending the organisation's money learn more about the fundraising process and begin to recognise the concerns and interests of the donor.

2. Setting targets and monitoring progress

Targets should be agreed with the fundraiser rather than imposed, and progress should be regularly monitored. If targets are not being met, then this will need to be discussed and the causes identified. Perhaps they were over-optimistic in the first place. Perhaps a particular fundraising approach or technique is not working well enough. Perhaps things could be done better or there was a mistake to learn from. One idea is to create a small fundraising advisory group who will take a particular interest in the fundraising with whom the fundraiser can discuss issues or refer problems.

It is also important to keep track of the time and effort put into each fundraising initiative. There is a tendency to spend a lot of time chasing after sources which are marginal or unlikely, and too little time developing those which are really important to the organisation and its future. There is also the problem of organising fundraising events which take up a lot of time but yield little in terms of money raised. So it is important to find out whether you are using your time effectively – since your time is usually the biggest fundraising cost you will be incurring.

3. Giving fundraising due importance

It is important that fundraising be recognised in the organisation as an important function, and that the fundraiser be given the support that is needed to do a good job. Fundraising which is just delegated and forgotten about will rarely work well. Fundraising which is starved of resources – it will always take money to raise money – is also likely to fail. So the Executive Director and the Management Committee need to have confidence in the fundraising process and the abilities of the fundraiser, and then provide support for them in whatever way is appropriate.

4. Access to information

The fundraiser will have to represent the organisation and answer on its behalf in a whole range of different situations. They will need to be able to speak authoritatively to any interested parties. Therefore, any fundraiser must be kept informed of what is going on, how the organisation is doing financially and what new initiatives are in the pipeline.

5. Recognising success

When a fundraiser achieves success, this should be recognised by the organisation. How this is done is up to you. Some organisations offer incentives to fundraisers in the form of some form of commission or performance bonus based on the amount of money raised. This is not always wise, nor might it be the best way of motivating a fundraiser, and it can sometimes lead to a conflict of interest. It can also alienate other staff who cannot guarantee bonuses in the same way.

6. Training and meeting other fundraisers

There are now courses on aspects of fundraising being run in most countries, and the International Fund Raising Group runs active training programmes worldwide as well as annual conventions. These are good places to brush up on basic skills, to share ideas and experiences, and to meet and network with others doing a similar job.

7. Finding out what others are doing

A fundraiser should be encouraged to find out how other organisations are seeking to raise money, and should try to get hold of copies of annual reports and promotional brochures from rival organisations.

8. Free time to think

Some of the most creative fundraising comes from thinking about what you are doing, chatting to people about your ideas, meeting people and talking about your work (with no immediate intention of asking for money, but to develop a contact and a relationship). With the pressure to raise money, it is often this creative time which is lost. The successful fundraiser will make sure that he or she has sufficient time to do all of these things by building this into the work schedule.

Getting outside help with your fundraising

At various points your organisation will need help with its fundraising. It may help to tackle a particular campaign; or you may need advice on new fundraising schemes that you have in mind; or it may be that you need help devising a new fundraising plan.

There are a number of possible sources each with their own advantages and disadvantages. Apart from employing your own fundraiser, you can employ an individual consultant, a company, or you can use peers to get free advice. The wrong choice will involve considerable expense and, most of all, large amounts of management time wasted.

If it is more than just a few words of advice that are needed, you need to be clear about what sort of help you want. You could have someone to produce a piece of theoretical work such as a fundraising strategy. The outcome, in this case, would be a report. You may want someone to help set up fundraising systems or support a new fundraiser; this would require some intensive work in your offices. Equally you may wish to take on some help with soliciting money in person or by writing letters. Each of these types of task will demand different skills and have different costs associated with them. In each case, your briefing to any potential consultants should make this clear.

Networking

When dealing with smaller problems or ones that only you can resolve, using informal networks can help. The main body that can help facilitate this is the Institute of Charity Fundraising Managers (ICFM) with its 3,000 members. There is a strong culture of one fundraiser helping another despite the highly competitive nature of much fundraising today.

The best way of accessing the network is to join ICFM. With membership, you can get access to its list of members. An additional suggestion for newer fundraisers is to deliberately attend fundraising courses or conferences run by ICFM or by the Directory of Social Change, where you will meet people in similar situations to yourself.

If you are the senior staff member of a small organisation charged with fundraising, you could use another network, the Association of Chief Executives of National Voluntary Organisations (ACENVO) which encourages the same sort of networking. For international contacts, there is the International Fund Raising Group, which organises an annual workshop in Amsterdam and other events. Contact details are given in the Useful Addresses section at the end of this book.

Independent fundraising consultants

Many people are working independently as self-employed fundraisers. There are at least 500 members of the Institute of Charity Fundraising Managers (ICFM) who are independent consultants, as well as more who are outside this group. Some of them will be moonlighting from current employment while others will be dependent upon commissions for their work.

Consultants themselves will say that their costs are likely to be small compared with the returns. However they would also admit that their costs are the only certain element while their returns are never guaranteed. Costs are likely to range from a low of £250 a day to highs in excess of £600 plus VAT. The only way to be sure is to ask (see below).

Since there are plenty of possible consultants around, it is not difficult to find names. There are three main areas to look initially:

- The **ICFM** members handbook entitled *Who's Who in Fundraising*. This lists all current members and those that are independent consultants. In addition to this it has a number of advertisements offering relevant services. Contact the Institute of Charity Fundraising Managers, Market Towers, 1 Nine Elms Lane, London SW8 5NQ.
- The **Association of Fundraising Consultants** (AFC) This is a grouping of consultants which combines both independent consultants and consultancy companies. It has developed its own code of practice. Contact the Association of Fundraising Consultants, The Grove, Harpenden, Herts AL5 1AH.
- The **National Council for Voluntary Organisations** (NCVO) maintains a list of consultants. If approached, NCVO will produce a short list for any member wanting to employ a consultant. Contact the National Council of Voluntary Organisations, Regent's Wharf, 8 All Saint's street, London N1 9RL.
- The **specialist press**. You can use this to see who is contributing in print. Many consultants of all sorts write pieces with a view to raising their profile or generating contacts. Others advertise and clearly set out their areas of expertise. Recommended magazines are *Third Sector* and *Charity*.

Consultancy Firms

Over the last decade a number of international and home grown companies have emerged. Their interest is to provide a range of fundraising services to charities. This usually means that they expect to carry out more work for their clients and are likely to be more expensive. They will all have some sort of track record to demonstrate and a reputation to maintain.

The logic of using a firm is that they have a greater capacity to work for you and they may have access to a wider range of skills. It thus makes little sense to employ a company to provide a small amount of help in one particular area. Areas in which fundraising or other companies are used include advertising, capital giving, direct mail, payroll giving, design and video or print production.

In order to find a consultancy firm, use the same sources as those for individuals listed above.

Working with consultants

In order to be sure that you get exactly what you want, it is essential to set out a brief prior to choosing any consultant. This can then be the template against which to compare quotes from different people. It is common practice in this field to be expected to quote for the business and no consultant worth their salt will object to this process.

Once you have identified whom you wish to appoint, ensure that you agree precise terms of business with them in the form of a contract. Surprises are easier to deal with at this stage than later when you are completely committed. The ICFM has a useful set of guidelines for charities wishing to appoint a consultant. The usual basis is to employ on a time and materials basis, which is put into the form of an agreed quote for the work.

Payment by results

One common problem in using a fundraising consultant is the temptation to pay on a commission basis. Although this removes any financial commitment on your part – you pay if and when the fundraising is successful – there are certain problems that you need to consider.

- Under the Charities Act **the arrangement has to be declared**, and this can affect the chances of getting support. A donor, who might fully understand that fundraising has a cost attached to it, might be unwilling to hand over 20% of the donation (or even 10%) as a fee for the fundraiser. However, note that this part of the Charities Act only applies if the consultant actually asks for money. If they simply advise on strategy or write out the letter for you to sign, then no declaration needs to be made.
- The **Charity Commission is not keen on commission fundraising**. They feel that the charity should make a decision to employ someone based on their competence to do the job and the expectation that they will succeed, and that the consultant be paid on this basis, possibly including a success fee if certain targets are achieved (this is a much less direct link between payment and results).
- If you have not made a financial commitment, there may be less incentive for you to manage the consultant effectively.
- The fundraising consultant might cherry pick – get those donations you were expecting anyway, and do little or no more.

If you just don't have the resources to make a commitment to a professional fundraiser, which is a situation that many small organisations find themselves in, then you could:

- look for **sponsorship** to cover the costs of the consultancy. You can show it as an extremely cost-effective input;
- seek a grant for a **feasibility study**, as a first step. The Charities Aid Foundation provides money for this purpose;
- **find someone prepared to do the work for nothing**. This is a long shot;

Selecting an adviser

Whoever you decide to choose, there are a number of steps to go through:

1. Be absolutely sure of what your problem is and what sort of service you actually need. Do you need someone to help you devise the strategy only? Do you need both the strategy and help with its implementation? Do you have a specific task you need done, and require someone to do it for you? Or do you just need advice?

2. Write a good brief and clear job description. This should cover what needs to be done, the timetable, and the specific objectives.

3. Wherever possible, make sure you have a good selection of people or companies to choose from – so as to ensure that you choose the best.

4. Agree the basis of remuneration. Is the budget acceptable? What control over success and failure will you retain? How will expenses be charged? How much notice is required to terminate the arrangement if you are dissatisfied?

5. Get references and follow these up to find out the quality of their work for other similar organisations. If you do not get good – or indeed any – references, proceed only with the greatest caution.

■ **do the work yourselves**, but gather around you a number of people with the required expertise to act as mentors to you.

Regulation of Consultants

Using paid consultants to solicit money for you will require some care as the law now sets down that this be declared. This means that if you are paying someone directly to send appeal letters on your behalf, to visit donors or to make phone calls to donors, their status and their reward must be declared. The regulations in the new Charities Acts state that there should be a written agreement in a prescribed form between the charity and the professional fundraiser. In addition to this, potential donors must be given a statement to inform them of what proportion of their donation will be used to pay the fundraiser.

5.4 Measurement and Control of fundraising

Strategy is not forever even though you may feel that after all the effort in creating it, you never want to see the document again. But things do change and it does need updating from time to time.

The first step with a new or revised strategy must be to ensure that everyone understands it and agrees with it. Not everyone in your organisation will feel able to contribute to the process of producing the fundraising strategy. Therefore it is important before you start work on it or before you present it to your committee, that it be widely discussed. The process of consultation will ensure that those who are involved in various aspects are more likely to feel committed to the outcome.

Once you have started work on implementing the strategy it will be necessary to review it, possibly on an annual basis. This does not mean that you will have to go through the whole analysis each year. However, you will learn more about what works and what does not, who will be in a position to help you. Additionally, other things may change in the environment which will change your basic assumptions. All these should be reviewed on an annual basis and the whole plan completely rewritten possibly every three years.

Monitoring strategy

Without a strategy or a detailed plan, it is hard to provide any detailed monitoring of how you are getting on. Monitoring is important:

- to check your overall returns
- to compare the effectiveness of different aspects of your fundraising
- to justify the level of investment that the charity is making
- to help indicate the fundraiser's performance.

Monitoring can be carried out in a large number of ways but mostly it will be with monitoring the financial data. There are several pieces of information you should monitor:

- cash received
- costs incurred by each fundraising method
- pledges of future support received
- offers of help from target groups
- individual fundraising methods or appeals.

Monitoring is easier in a small organisation but can be surprisingly difficult in many established charities. This is because the systems are not usually designed for the convenience of fundraisers. They usually describe reasonably the total costs and the total income. For monitoring purposes what is needed is to isolate the data for each separate method so that you can easily compare the effectiveness. Mostly it will not be possible or necessary to do this on a weekly basis; monthly should be sufficient. A sample monitoring form is shown below.

Detailed measurement of fundraising

There are a number of ways in which you can measure the effectiveness of your fundraising, although no method provides the definitive answer. Usually a combination of measures is helpful in getting the sense of how you are doing. Not all measures are appropriate to all fundraising situations.

The two main ways in which people measure their fundraising effectiveness is by using the cost ratio and by calculating the profit.

The cost ratio is the measure which most readily identifies the efficiency of any fundraising method. It is calculated by taking the direct income generated and dividing it by the direct costs. This can then be expressed as a ratio (viz 5:1) or a percentage such as 20%. These are confusing labels as in one case you are looking for an increasing ratio while in the other you are happy to decrease the %.

Monthly monitoring sheet

Appeal Type	Income this year	Income budget	Income this month	Direct costs	Profit Ratio
Collections					
Postal appeal					
Sponsored event					
General income					
Office costs					
Total					

The main drawback of this measure is that it does not give you a clear idea of how much you have raised. For example, you may discover that your efforts in public speaking to a wide range of local groups and appealing for their support raised £2,380 and cost only £340 (a ratio of 7:1 or 14%). On the other hand, the very long time you committed to raising money from trusts yielded £17,200 but cost you an estimated £6,500 (a ration of 2.6:1 or 38%). This is quite misleading from two points of view.

1. You may have exhausted all the local speaking possibilities and so you cannot repeat the success even if this is your most effective method of fundraising.
2. Your most efficient fundraiser has actually only generated £2,010 for your work where your trusts work has generated £10,700.

For fundraising which involves appealing to larger numbers of people and where you have the opportunity to try out different approaches, there are some further measures that are useful.

If you are using the phone to recruit collectors for your flag day or for house to house collections, you will be interested in how efficient your phoning is. This is measured initially by the response rate to your request. It is simply measured by the number of successes divided by the total number approached. This could be used in postal appeals, payroll giving and collections for example. If you can change your technique in such a way as to increase the response rate without affecting other things, it will be beneficial.

Knowing how many people will respond is, in itself, not enough. You also need to know how they respond and how much have they given. It may be good to get 10 people in 100 saying yes; but if they only then give £1 each, you will still be disappointed. The average donation is the measure of how much they give. Trying to increase the average donation is something you can do easily with very little cost. For example, when you ask a member or covenanter to renew, why not suggest the amount and mention that you were hoping they might increase their gift; when doing sponsored events you can suggest the sorts of sponsorship people may give. Ask them to sponsor by minute rather than by the hour, and they will give more. Ask a standing order supporter to pay by the month and you will receive more than you would if you did it by the year.

The other useful measure when hundreds of donors or supporters are involved is the response rate. For example, if you send an appeal to 1,000 supporters and you get only 25 responses back, your response rate is 2.5%. In this event you will wish to try out new approaches to see if you can increase the response. A further version of this is the yield. This is the income received divided by the numbers approached in the first place. Thus, if the same 1,000 donors had sent in responses worth £350, the yield would be 35p per donor mailed.

Finally you will need to have some way of measuring the impact of appealing to supporters and getting four-year covenants back. How do you evaluate the later years; and what will happen if they renew their pledge after four years? This is a complicated area and it can take a statistician to calculate the lifetime value of a supporter. Probably the simplest way to do this is to look at the commitment that is made and add the value of this in to the income. To this you should make some allowance for inflation which over four years can be very considerable even with low rates.

The lifetime value is very helpful because it can help you justify expenditures on promotion and fundraising which you would otherwise not be able to afford. For example, the cost of writing to all your supporters now (let us say that this costs you 50p x 1,000 supporters) may not appear to justify the response. Five reply with covenants worth £60 per year gross, giving you a fundraising ratio of £300/£500 =0.6. However if we assume that each covenanter will pay for four years, ignoring inflation, and the costs of covenant administration, then the ratio becomes £1,200/£500= 2.4. At this ratio you may decide that is worth investing the money. This doesn't even take into account those who will want to continue giving when their covenant expires.

6. Working with people

6.1 Working with volunteers

Volunteers are extremely important to many charities. The National Centre for Volunteering estimates the value of formal volunteering (which is defined as any voluntary activity undertaken through or for an organisation or a group) as being worth £25 billion a year. Clearly the input of volunteers is a major resource for any voluntary organisation.

Some organisations are run entirely by volunteers, and do not employ staff. Some use volunteers to carry out the service delivery, but use paid staff for administration and coordination (the Samaritans, which runs a national telephone help-line for people who are despairing or suicidal, and the British Trust for Conservation Volunteers, which undertakes practical conservation work, are good examples). The Citizen's Advice Bureaux, on the other hand, use both volunteers and paid staff for advice giving. Many others use volunteers on an *ad hoc* basis, or to bring in extra expertise.

Volunteers can also be used to raise money for the organisation, and research shows that this remains the main way in which volunteers are used – to run charity shops, to organise local fundraising activities, and to act as a support group. There are a range of fundraising tasks which could not be carried out without the use of volunteers – either because the organisation would not have sufficient time or the capacity to do the fundraising in the first place, or because if volunteers were not being used, the money could not be raised cost effectively. Volunteers can also assist the fundraiser by providing all sorts of administrative support and back up.

Volunteers are important in fundraising in all sorts of ways. Volunteer management means more than just finding the people to do the work for you. In order to get the best out of your volunteers, they need to be chosen well, placed with imagination, given satisfying work to do which matches their skills and interests, and managed with skill. They are not simply there to be deployed as cheap labour in all the worst jobs. Rather, they can add hugely to the resources available to you, enabling you to do more with less and to do it better.

If you use volunteers, you can also take advantage of this fact in your fundraising.

- You can **show the numbers of volunteers** and the amount of volunteer time you are mobilising. This shows an enthusiasm for what you are doing, as well as good sense in mobilising people's time for your cause.
- You can **illustrate the worth of the volunteering** to your organisation by estimating the value of the time put in, or the value of the work done by the volunteers, or both. Many agencies that require some form of matched support for their grant are increasingly willing to have their financial contribution partly matched by the value of the volunteer contribution calculated on some basis that seems to make sense – perhaps the cost of having to pay the going rate for the job.
- In your annual report you can **show the value of the volunteering** and the proportion of the total resources that the organisation is consuming represented by volunteering in the report, and try to illustrate how this enhances the service you are providing and makes it more cost-effective.

The economic value of volunteering

Volunteering has an economic value, which the National Centre for Volunteering has tried to estimate.

- The economic value of volunteering measured in terms of its wage value is £25 billion per annum. This is calculated by using an hourly rate of £7.83 (based on average earnings in 1993) to multiply the total hours worked, as indicated by the 1991 national survey of voluntary activity.
- Men and women make a similar economic contribution through their formal voluntary work. Whilst men are slightly less likely than women to volunteer, they contribute slightly more hours.
- All age groups make a significant contribution. People in the youngest age group (18 to 24) and in the older age group (65 to 74) are less likely to volunteer than those in the middle age ranges, but contribute more hours to volunteering. The 2 million volunteers aged 65 to 74 make a larger economic contribution that the 5 million volunteers aged 25 to 34.

Alongside the value of volunteering, there is a cost of using this pool of 'free labour'. This includes the cost of recruitment, induction, support and training, and the payment of out-of-pocket expenses and project costs.

Work that volunteers can do

1. Committees

Most voluntary organisations are controlled by a Management Committee or Trustees, whose roles include:

- deciding the vision, mission, strategy and priorities for the organisation and overseeing its work;
- ensuring that it meets its charitable objectives and being accountable for the proper expenditure of any funds donated to it.

This committee normally consists of volunteers, many of whom will also get involved in other aspects of the organisation's work.

Committees or sub-committees may also be set up to supervise and develop particular areas of the organisation's work such as a Development Committee to plan a major appeal, a Business Committee to develop links and partnerships with local businesses or an Event Committee to plan and run an important fundraising event.

The committees of new organisations usually consist of the founders and perhaps a few friends to assist them. As the organisation develops, there is the opportunity to set out precisely what skills and experience you are looking for in your committee members, and then to go out and find the people that meet your requirements.

2. Administrative tasks

The administrative office of most organisations is usually an extremely busy place, where there is more work to be done than people can cope with. There are all sorts of ways in which volunteers can help:

- addressing and stuffing the envelopes for the 1,000 addresses you are sending your appeal to;
- dealing with the response – banking the proceeds, sending thank you letters, and putting the names of those who responded on to the database;
- reminding members whose subscriptions are about to lapse that they should renew their membership, either in writing or on the telephone;
- answering the telephone or acting as receptionist or being in charge of the library;
- editing the newsletter;
- all sorts of research;
- organising a public meeting.

Volunteer jobs should match the skills of the volunteers you are using, and the volunteers will need supervision and support if you are to get the most out of them. You will find, if you ask, that there are a great many people who are prepared to help.

3. Volunteers who raise money

One of the most important ways in which volunteers can help in fundraising is by helping raise money for the organisation. Again, there are all sorts of ways in which they can do this:

- house-to-house and street collections, where success depends on the numbers of collectors that you can produce;
- organising a fundraising event, such as a sponsored walk, a fair or a dinner dance, where a team of volunteers can be entirely responsible for running the event;
- contacting local companies and shops to get prizes donated for a raffle;
- selling raffle tickets or Christmas cards.

Much of this fundraising work can be done largely unsupervised by fundraising groups. Many people really enjoy this sort of local fundraising work, doing something useful in their spare time and working with a group of like-minded people. Inevitably, they will be representing the charity and people will ask them about what the organisation is doing. It is important that they understand what the organisation is doing and share its values, as in a sense they are acting as your ambassadors. Some induction training is quite helpful, so that they can be briefed about the organisation's work and meet some of the staff and beneficiaries.

4. Peripatetic volunteers

Another sort of volunteer is someone with time to give, but who wants to help at times more suitable to themselves. It is possible to design volunteer jobs for such people:

- visiting donors to offer thanks and explain the organisation's work in more detail;
- speaking at Rotary Lunches and other similar events, or in schools.

You will need people for these jobs who are highly motivated and articulate, and who are happy to be given a large degree of responsibility.

Who volunteers?

All sorts of people volunteer for all sorts of reasons.

- You may find that the people who are prepared to volunteer are the **people with least time** on their hands. Busy people like to keep busy.
- People who have a particular connection with the cause may be willing to volunteer out of a **sense of commitment**. For example, someone whose child has recently died of leukaemia might be willing to volunteer for a cancer charity.
- Recently **retired people** may have time on their hands, and be willing to do something useful and challenging. There are a number of schemes which promote senior volunteering and which act as a link between the volunteer and the organisations looking for volunteers. The best known of these schemes are REACH (the Retired Executives Action Clearing House, which is an independent charity) and RSVP (the Retired and Senior Volunteer Programme, run by Community Service Volunteers).
- **Employees**. There is an organisation called Action – Employees in the Community, which was formerly known as the Action Resource Centre and is now part of Business in the Community. It promotes and supports employee volunteering. Many companies encourage their staff to volunteer. A very few, including IBM, offer time off during the working week, but most expect the volunteering to be done in the evenings or at weekends. Some have a grants scheme, which entitles employees to a grant for the organisation they are volunteering with. One or two of the very largest companies, such as Shell with its Better Britain and Livewire projects, encourage employees and retirees to contribute to programmes they are sponsoring.
- **Professional skills volunteering**. Lawyers, accountants, surveyors and others are encouraged to volunteer by their professional associations,

using their special skills for the benefit of a community or charitable organisation. Many lawyers work with law centres and citizen's advice bureaux, for example, and Lawyers in the Community, which is a scheme run by Action – Employees in the Community, encourages lawyers to become trustees and committee members.

- **Unemployed young people** such as recent school-leavers and graduates yet to get their first job might be persuaded to volunteer just to keep active. You can tell them that they will develop new skills and this can improve their job prospects. Some of the leading charities receive a steady flow of requests to volunteer from recent graduates seeking a career in the voluntary sector. They hope that volunteering will be a gateway into a paid job, and this is often the case. There is a proposal for a National Citizen Service scheme which would encourage and provide opportunities for young people to volunteer as their contribution to society. This scheme is being piloted by Community Service Volunteers. The Prince's Trust also runs The Prince's Volunteers which is a scheme that aims to involve 25,000 young people working on groups on volunteer assignments.

- **People between jobs**. The expectation of lifetime employment no longer exists for most people, and temporary unemployment or part-time work are features of modern life. People between jobs need to maintain their confidence and keep their skills; people with part-time work may have time to spare; women with children growing up may find they have time available and want to start thinking about a second career. All these groups are potential volunteers, who see volunteering as providing something useful for themselves.

- **Young people** at school and college or in youth organisations. There is a thriving Student Community Action movement and a new Federation of Youth Action Agencies, and schemes such as Changemakers encourage young people to become involved and develop social enterprise skills as an important part of their informal education. The Rank Foundation runs a 'Gappers' scheme which provides bursaries for young people to work with a charity during a gap year after school and before work or further education.

- If you need something done and **it sounds interesting**, then just ask. If you ask enthusiastically, then you may find that people are prepared to help out. It is just as with fundraising, where the main reason people give for not volunteering is that they were never asked!

- **People arriving on your doorstep or ringing up** asking to volunteer. They probably share an enthusiasm for what you are doing and want to help. Some may be from overseas, and these provide a special opportunity later on for your organisation to begin to develop overseas linkages.

Volunteer recruitment and selection

The recruitment and selection of your volunteers is an important task. Exactly as for the recruitment of a new member of staff, there should be a proper job description for the volunteer job, and the volunteers should be selected according to their ability to do that job. You need to decide your policy on remuneration – whether you are going to offer to reimburse out-of-pocket expenses or even give some sort of honorarium or allowance. There are two important points to consider.

- **Equal opportunities**. If you don't offer expenses, or if you put pressure on volunteers not to claim expenses, then this could have equal opportunities implications. You may also want to actively encourage the participation of certain groups of people as volunteers, such as young people, the unemployed, ethnic minority people, disabled people, elderly people, and to develop ideas for actively recruiting from such groups.

- **Unemployment benefit**. If you recruit unemployed people for voluntary work, you will need to adhere to DSS requirements; otherwise the volunteer may lose benefit. These requirements relate to availability of work, the level of any remuneration received and whether there is any liability to pay National Insurance. With the introduction of the Jobseekers Allowance, the requirements have been relaxed in an attempt to encourage volunteering by unemployed people. Details are available from the local Job Centre or contact the National Centre for Volunteering.

1. Recruiting people locally

Where you need a number of volunteers in one place – perhaps to help in the office or help out on a fundraising event – a range of recruitment opportunities exist. People occasionally turn up at your office or telephone you for information. If they seem interested, then you could ask them directly if they would like to help as a volunteer.

Your publicity leaflets – or an article in your own newsletter which ask for support – may offer the option of giving support in time as well as in cash.

Public meetings and other speaking engagements, including your organisation's annual general meeting, are opportunities to make your need for volunteers known. Those attending might offer, or know someone who might be interested.

You might try to get a feature article on your organisation, its work and its need for volunteers in the local newspaper, or you could consider taking paid advertising space just as you would for a paid job. A letter to the editor stating the importance of your work and your particular need is another option.

Many local radio and television stations run social action programmes with the help of Community Service Volunteers, which assist organisations recruit volunteers. As with a newspaper, you can also try to get feature coverage, or ring a phone-in programme and make your request on air.

The *Guardian* runs a volunteer recruitment page once a month on Wednesdays, which offers a low-cost advertising opportunity for those seeking to recruit a volunteer.

2. Recruiting people with specific skills

This needs a rather more directed approach, as you need not just a person but a person with particular skills. Each will have its own particular opportunities.

- To find an accountant you might well seek the help of the local bank manager or accountancy firm; or for a lawyer, contact a local law firm.
- Professional bodies and associations are a good hunting ground for recently retired people with time on their hands. You could offer to give a talk, or suggest an article or a free advertisement in their newsletter.
- If you know exactly what you want, then by asking specialist people if they know anyone who could do the job, you may eventually find someone prepared to do it.

Unsuitable as well as suitable people will volunteer. So the next step is selecting from the people you have identified – which you may want to do through an interview and taking up references, just as for a paid job. Don't lower your standards simply because someone offers to help you. You need to take particular care where people are expected to represent your organisation in public or where they will be involved in handling money.

You will need to agree terms and conditions, and set these out in some form of 'contract':

- the nature of the job to be done
- the hours expected
- the supervision and support offered, and any training that will be given
- grievance procedures
- what expenses are to be paid
- any notice to be given on termination of the arrangement (by either side).

All these need to be discussed and agreed.

Before you volunteer...

Being a volunteer can be demanding and frustrating. The deeper you get involved, the more the organisation will depend on your contribution. A strong sense of commitment and patience will help ensure that you do not tire too soon and drop out, or grow cynical.

Most issues pertaining to children are complex and must be understood thoroughly by those wishing to help. Plan to spend time talking and reading to understand the issues involved. Also be ready to get involved in whatever needs to be done, rather than going with preconceptions of what you will do. Here are some suggestions that will make you a better volunteer:

- make a list of your skills and resources before approaching a voluntary organisation
- be clear about how much time you can spare
- don't expect to be paid. Voluntary organisations usually do not pay volunteers. Check if they will pay for work-related phone calls, travel and so on
- be prepared to work as part of a team. Voluntarism usually means teamwork.

Adapted from advice by CRY – Child Relief and You, Bombay

People volunteer when asked

- 55% of people said that they had volunteered in the last three months
- 55% of people said they would be prepared to be involved in further volunteering activity
- 1% of people said they would not like to volunteer.

These figures were taken from the Charity Household Survey in Britain. Every type of good cause activity uses volunteers. The survey asked people whether they had volunteered and what voluntary activity they had undertaken during the previous month. Of those who said that they had volunteered, 28% had been involved in religious activities, 25% in sports and exercise activities, 25% with children's education and schooling, 25% with young people outside school, 21% in a social welfare activity, 21% in the arts and recreation, plus lesser percentages in other categories.

Management of volunteers

Volunteers work for charities for a wide range of reasons. Some do it because they believe in the cause and want to do something, while others do it because they want to get something out of it. Some will be there because they have nothing better to do or because they desperately crave human company after the death of a husband or wife or on retirement from a job. All can be useful members of your team. But just like paid members of staff, they will need managing.

- A volunteer should have a **clear job description**.
- You should set them **objectives**.
- There should be an **induction** process, so that they see and understand the work of the organisation, meet members of staff (who will also need to appreciate the role and contribution of the volunteer).
- You should **train** them in what they have to do, so that they can do the job effectively, and continue to provide on-the-job training as necessary.
- You should ensure that they have enough **information** to do their job, and that they are **briefed** about recent changes and developments in the work you are doing.
- You should **supervise** their work, give them feedback on how well they are doing, and congratulate them when they have made a positive contribution. They are just like any other human striving to do a good job. They need to know what the job is, how to do it and whether they are doing it right. Because they are not being paid, they need other forms of reward – recognising and appreciating their contribution is extremely important.

6.2 Working with patrons and celebrities

Associating your organisation with a well-known personality, could lift you from obscurity into the limelight.

Celebrities can help in many ways. Their presence at any function will draw others. For example, the fundraising dinner, which supporters are paying premium prices to attend, will become very much more attractive if there is a smattering of TV stars, media people and other personalities in attendance. They can inspire members and donors, and can turn your fundraising event into a roaring success.

Probably most important though, is the advantages they confer in attracting media coverage. If, for example, a well-known broadcaster is prepared to lead a press conference announcing a new campaign, the press is going to be much more interested than when an unknown charity executive says the same thing. Similarly photo editors of national newspapers are more likely to publish a photo of a well-known and attractive actress opening some new facility, than when a local councillor is doing the same thing.

Many organisations ask well-known people to help them for these reasons, and celebrities are prepared to give their time to the organisation for precisely the same reasons that anyone else wants to support it – they think it is worthwhile and that their contribution can make a difference. However, it is not just having celebrities associated with your organisation, but the way you use your celebrities that will have an impact.

> **Celebrities who can attract people to your cause include:**
>
> - Sports personalities
> - TV and radio stars
> - Film stars
> - Pop stars and musicians
> - Business leaders and prominent philanthropists
> - Politicians and retired politicians
> - Journalists
> - Writers
> - Academics and experts.
>
> The list can include anyone who has a high public profile and is well-liked by those sections of the public you hope to draw support from.

Using celebrities effectively

You should try wherever possible to find a relevant celebrity. People who have had some direct experience of the problem (if you are working with disabled children, for example, someone who has had a disabled child) will be a much more powerful advocate for the organisation and the cause. Celebrities should also be matched to your target donor audience.

Well-known people can be used in a wide variety of ways – from becoming a patron or joining your board of trustees to appearing in photo calls, launching publications, giving out prizes or participating in fundraising events.

Be opportunistic

People flit in and out of the limelight; you need to capitalise on their 15 minutes of fame. For example, in the spring of 1997, Chesterfield Town Football Club – from the second division – found themselves in the semi-finals of the FA Cup. For about the two weeks leading up to the game, every member of the Chesterfield team was a potential celebrity. Once they lost the game they faded back into the relative obscurity of life in division two. But during those two weeks, if a member of the Chesterfield team had spoken out on a charity issue, it would have received national coverage partly because footballers so rarely make such pronouncements but particularly because Chesterfield happened to be in the news. You cannot plan this kind of opportunity; you simply have to be alert and seize the moment.

When asking a celebrity to help, you need to think carefully and discuss with them how best they might be used. They want their association with you to be a success, but the time they can offer might be quite limited.

You also have responsibilities to them. Celebrities have their own reputations to consider, so they do not want to become associated with bad publicity or with controversy. They may be used to a level of personal support and attention that is difficult for small organisations to sustain – everything from being given detailed instructions for what they are expected to do, to having speeches written for them, being collected by taxi or car and driven back after the event, and being accompanied and looked after whilst they are there.

Managing Celebrities

It is often said that celebrities are the most difficult of people to work with and that their presence can result in major cultural clashes. This is undoubtedly true for some organisations, but couldn't be less true for others. Some well-known people demand to be treated as celebrities in all aspects of their lives; others can be deeply appreciative of the opportunity to be involved at all. It is important to build your relationship with such people carefully, as indeed you should do with anyone who contributes to your organisation in any significant way.

Because celebrities can bring you great benefits, you should treat them professionally and politely and try to make sure that their contribution is meaningful for you and satisfying for them. In an organisation of any size, it is important to control access to your celebrities tightly. This is to help prevent them being asked to do too many things too frequently, or indeed being asked to do things that they have specifically declined to do.

For performers, the question of whether to pay them for appearing at an event may arise. If you want to avoid having to pay large fees in future, then it is wise not to start doing so now. Most performers do not expect or want to take fees from charity events, and certainly should not be encouraged to do so. As a general rule, you should be prepared to pay reasonable expenses (but not for a convoy of air conditioned limos for them and their friends, which can gobble up your funds but also create bad publicity for you) and only consider paying the most nominal amounts as a fee, and then only in exceptional circumstances and possibly as a donation to a charity of their choice. The possible exception to this rule is in the use of musicians at entertainment events.

If you are recruiting someone for an event, they will need to have a very clear idea of what is going to happen and precisely what is expected of them. Is a speech going to be necessary? Who is going to write it for them? Will a car be provided? At what time must they arrive? When can they discreetly slip away? Who will greet them and look after them whilst they are with you? Will there be a presentation of flowers or a public thank you? Do they have to shake hands, speak to and be photographed with your main sponsor? Who will brief them on what to say? Who will be responsible for formally thanking them afterwards on behalf of the organisation? And so on. They will also want to be told how much their presence has helped: how many extra people have come this year; how much extra money was raised, and how many reporters covered the story. Any professional will want to know that they have really been able to help and that you have got the most out of their presence.

Sometimes it is not possible to deal directly with the celebrity. You have to get to them via an agent or personal assistant. Working with an agent can be both a help and a hindrance. They will be more concerned with fees and payments, and may not want their client to do something for nothing. On the other hand, being associated with you can bring the celebrity a lot of good publicity and help create an image of a caring person. So there is some benefit to their client. Attempt to get a direct line to your celebrity supporter as soon as you can, but the agent can be helpful in identifying long-range opportunities and availability; they can also help you get an idea of what the person concerned is looking for, as well as their likes and dislikes.

6.3 Working with Trustees and Committee Members

Most organisations need outsiders to provide fresh energy and new thinking, and to contribute their particular skills to the running of the organisation. The obvious place for such people is on the Management Board of the charity, or on one of its Advisory Committees.

For many organisations, Management Boards are often a self-selecting group of people which has more to do with the history of the organisation than with its current needs. They can become stale and out of touch with what's happening, and can soon forget that they have a crucial role to play in the organisation's success. A properly structured, well-briefed

Support and training for trustees

The National Council of Voluntary Organisations (NCVO) undertook research and produced a report on trusteeship in the voluntary sector. They found that most Committee Members and Trustees did not understand their role and that there was a need for better information and training, both for trustees and for the senior staff who they would be working with. This was published in 1992 in a report entitled 'On Trust'. As a result of this, the NCVO set up a Trustee Services Unit to promote better trusteeship, to act as an information point for trustee training, to produce and publish information (including a newsletter listing training for trustees), and to deal with important aspects of policy and practice, such as trustee liability and insurance. Contact NCVO, Regents Wharf, 8 All Saints Street, London N1 9RL

At the same time, the Directory of Social Change published a three-part handbook for trustees under the title *The Effective Trustee*, together with an accompanying training programme, again in three parts, and a 'Trustee Organiser', with basic information for trustees and for filing papers. These are available from the Directory of Social Change, 24 Stephenson Way, London NW1 2DP.

The Association of Chief Executives of National Voluntary Organisations (ACENVO) provides training on managing the sometimes difficult relationship between Chair and Chief Executive. Contact ACENVO, 31-33 College Road, Harrow, Middlesex HA1 1EJ.

and motivated team of people can play a hugely important role in the life of the organisation.

You may also find that your Management Board is overwhelmingly white, middle-class, middle-aged or elderly, and male. If you have an equal opportunities policy, this should extend to recruitment of Board Members just as much as to staff, and there may be particular categories of people, such as users, that you are interested in having on board. This is not just a matter of recruitment; when you hold the meetings and whether you offer travel and other out-of-pocket expenses can also be an important consideration. If you are approaching the National Lottery Charities Board, this has particular importance. The application form for a grant includes a question on the composition of your Management Board, and you get extra points in your assessment for ethnic diversity and for involvement of disabled people and users.

One of the roles of the Management Board is to ensure that the organisation has sufficient resources to carry out its work and that it is doing all it can to meet the need it is seeking to address. This means having a strategic view of the organisation's fundraising potential, and ensuring that there is sufficient expertise and administration within the organisation to raise the money that is needed. So for the fundraiser, it is imperative to get people on to the Management Board or Fundraising Sub-Committee who will ask the right questions, think long-term, advise on crucial issues, suggest useful contacts, and bring clear thinking to the fundraising.

If your Management Board seldom meets, what do you do if it does not understand its role and has lost interest? There are several steps you can take.

- The staff team, including the Executive Director and of course the Fundraiser, should recognise the potential contribution that an effective Management Board can make to the running of the organisation and to the fundraising.
- The matter might then be discussed with individual Board Members who share the concern that the Board is not operating effectively, and who are committed enough to want to do something.

- You could then undertake an 'audit' of the skills and expertise that you would like to have amongst your Board Members.
- Fresh people might be identified and approached who are willing to become involved as Board Members bringing these skills and expertise.
- A plan can then be drawn up for reforming the Board, replacing those who have lost interested with new people, setting an agenda for the Board, and allocating roles and responsibilities to individual Board members.

The role of the Management Board

1. **Giving direction** to the organisation: setting and reviewing the mission of the organisation, developing priorities and agreeing plans, monitoring progress, steering the organisation through good and bad times.
2. **Managing people**: being responsible for the performance of the Chief Executive, and ensuring that the organisation is getting the best out of all its people – paid staff as well as volunteers.
3. **Making the organisation accountable**: ensuring that the organisation accounts to all those who have a stake in it, including the community it is serving and those providing funds for its work.
4. **Keeping within the law**: ensuring that the organisation abides by its governing instrument and fulfils its objects and purposes as stated in its constitution, and that it operates within the law at all times.
5. **Managing resources**: ensuring that money and property are used properly and to best effect, and that there are sufficient resources to cover all liabilities and for the organisation to keep going and develop its work.
6. **Managing itself**: ensuring that the Board operates successfully as a team, that its meetings are effective, and that all individual members are contributing and involved.

Who to put on the Management Board

1. Professionals: accountants, lawyers, teachers, welfare workers, architects, and so on.
2. Experts in the service you provide.
3. Clients who have benefited from your work.
4. People drawn from your local community.

Qualifications required

1. A genuine interest in your organisation and what it is doing.
2. Specialist skills which your organisation can benefit from.
3. Contacts and access to people that will be able to help you.
4. Time to devote to your work.

Remember, not every committee member is expected to be able to do everything. However, when put together the committee as a whole should give you a wide range of skills, resources and expertise.

Fundraising Committees

Besides appointing people to serve on the Management Board, there are other ways in which you can bring outsiders into your organisation. One is through the Fundraising Committee. There are a number of different models for such committees.

- **The Fundraising Strategy Committee**, which reports to the Executive Committee. Its role is to monitor regularly and improve the fundraising across the whole of the organisation. Its role is purely supervisory. This group will not raise money for you.
- **The Fundraising Advisory Committee**, which is a looser grouping which may meet less frequently. It consists of 'ideas people' drawn from different walks of life, chosen because of their occupations or talents. It can be a useful source of ideas for the fundraiser and can sometimes be a means of getting new ideas taken up by the organisation.
- **The Event Committee**, which can play a crucial role where any sort of fundraising event is being organised. It is likely to be an *ad hoc* group specifically created for the purpose of running a ball or film premiere or other activity.
- **The Appeal Committee**, which can be most effective where individuals are recruited specifically to help raise large amounts of money for a major appeal. Members of this group are chosen because of their ability to give substantial donations themselves and for their willingness to ask others to give (the rich, the important philanthropists, the leaders of industry and commerce, and those in charge of government programmes). Meetings are likely to be rare, and the role of the Chair in leading the group and ensuring that the money is raised is crucial.
- **The Local Committee**, which is a group that acts as the local representatives of your organisation. They will consist of the activists in a given area and will usually be prepared to get involved in any activity that is needed, including fundraising, public speaking and media work.

The role of the committee must be clearly thought through. Getting the right brief for the committee is as vital as recruiting the right people. It is much better to start with the right concept of what the committee is going to do, than to try to change the approach or brief once members of the committee are in place.

How to get the most out of your Committee Members

Collecting a group of skilled and experienced people to help you is only the first stage. Getting the most out of this group of people and ensuring their continuing interest and involvement is equally important. Too often voluntary organisations simply assume that committee members instinctively know what is expected of them or hope they will find a fulfilling role. It is much better to spell things out from the start so that everybody is clear. Here are a few things to consider doing.

- Give each new person a proper induction, showing them the work of the organisation, introducing them to some of the clients and beneficiaries, so that they understand the impact the organisation is having on people's lives, introducing them to members of staff so that they understand who is responsible for doing what, and giving them printed literature about the work of the organisation.
- Discuss with each person how best they might contribute to the success of the organisation and what personal objectives might be set for them. It is better to ask for specific contributions and commitments than just ask people to help as required and to get people to do something significant for a limited period of time than to continue doing little until they grow old. If you set performance targets, then they will be able to recognise their achievements.
- Agree matters like regular attendance at meetings, remuneration of expenses, training or attendance at conferences, and so on.
- Review their contribution (as a group if everything is going well, or individually if it isn't) on an annual basis.
- Find ways of keeping them motivated by continuing to impress them on the importance of the organisation's work, showing them its successes and achievements, involving them in discussing matters of current interest or concern, and continuing to expose them to the organisation's front line work.

6.4 Getting the most from your donors and supporters

Your existing donors and supporters are a really important part of your fundraising future. They have demonstrated their commitment to you through giving, and you should try to retain this commitment and develop their involvement in your organisation. In this section, we look at two important aspects of developing your relationship with your donors and supporters – saying thank you, and involving them further.

Saying thank you

Saying thank you to your supporters is both an essential courtesy and a piece of enlightened self-interest that fundraisers forget at their peril. This applies as much to grants from donor bodies (such as government departments or international donor agencies) as it does to donations from individual supporters and participants at fundraising events.

Saying thank you makes donors feel good about their giving; it tells them that their donation has actually been received, and that it is being put to good use; it gives you the opportunity to find out about the depth of their interest, and perhaps some of the reasons why they have decided to support you; it enables you to tell them more about your work and your future plans; and all this will help you to get further support from them in the future. Your best prospects for a donation are those people who have given you a donation. So the thank you process becomes crucial. There are many ways of saying thank you:

1. By letter

Some charities reply to all donations, while others reply only to certain classes or levels of donation. The cost of replying can make it expensive to reply to smaller donations but there are important advantages in thanking all donors in some way if you can – a small donation now may turn into a large donation later, or for the donor, what is a small amount of money to you may be a major commitment of money and concern for them. If you are worried about cost, you might ask donors to tell you if they do not want a reply (to save administrative costs).

When you do say thank you, make your reply swift – say within three days of receipt of the donation. Make the letter personal to the donor, and recognise their giving history (the length of time they have been supporting you and their level of giving). A word processor can help here, using standard forms of thank you letters as the basis, and adapting these as necessary.

Some organisations wait to get the Chairperson to sign the letter. This is not necessary – your smaller and regular donors are probably much more interested in building up a personal link with your donations administrator, who they will be able to contact if they have a query or want further information.

2. By telephone

To give a really fast and personal response, little can beat the telephone. This is not recommended for small donations, but is an important medium for thanking larger donors. As soon as you receive an exceptional gift, ring the donor and thank them personally. Reassure them that their cheque has arrived safely – donors often feel concerned about committing their generosity to the vagaries of the post, find out what prompted the gift and find out what they think of your organisation.

Fundraisers will need to use the evenings to do this, as donors will often be out during the day. When making a phone call, try to create a sense of excitement, enthusiasm and urgency – the money will really help, it is being put to good use immediately, and it will bring real and important benefits

3. By visit

Personally visiting donors who are likely to be of importance to the organisation is likely to be a very time consuming business. However research shows that it can be an extremely worthwhile way of saying thank you. You need to be able to identify those whom it will be worth your while to visit and those whom it is possible to visit geographically. The visit can be made by the fundraiser, by a Management Committee or Fundraising Committee member, or by a trained volunteer. A preliminary phone call can be made to announce when they are going to be in the area, and an appointment can be set up.

Donors may be wary about the object of such visits until they have actually received one. A simple chat to tell the donor more about your work and to thank them for their gift will often naturally lead on to discussion about committed giving or how they might help as a volunteer – and even about the possibility of leaving a legacy – without your having to introduce the subject yourself or ask directly.

4. By meeting

Where personal visits are not possible, some charities set up meetings, receptions or open days for much the same purpose. Supporters in a particular area are invited and refreshments laid on. A senior person from the organisation will give a short talk. It is important then to have staff, committee members or other volunteers present to chat to those invited to the event.

One possibility is to hold the event at your office, where all your staff and committees are available. People are always interested in seeing your offices and your facilities. Such events are usually very well received, even when all they are able to see are desks and filing cabinets. Another is to organise a site visit to see a project at work and enable the donors to meet some of the beneficiaries or the local community. It is the people that donors and volunteers most enjoy meeting at such events.

5. By gift

Some fundraisers offer some inducement or token in return for gifts of a certain size. There are two distinct circumstances: one is heavily promoted by the charity to encourage a particular type or size of response, whilst the other is a token of thanks used to build commitment and help spread the message to others.

Paper items of low cost and high perceived value are more frequently used for this purpose. A special Christmas card from the president; a certificate for a pledged legacy; or a wildlife print in return for a donation of more than a certain amount. Though giving is often a private matter, some supporters welcome opportunities to discuss their favourite cause with their friends. A thank you token or certificate of support which they can display in their home can help them do this.

6. By public acknowledgement

A further way in which thanks can be given is through a public announcement – such as an advertisement in a newspaper, or a mention in your newsletter, magazine or annual report.

The use of the annual report is sensible. Not only are you able to thank your donors, this sends signals to others too that you are interested in receiving donations and publicly acknowledging the support you receive. If you indicate the level of their gifts, this will create a certain peer group pressure for others to give at similar levels. Perhaps more important is the credibility factor – "If they have given, then it must be a good organisation". As an organisation grows, this is no longer feasible, as the number of donors gets too large to be able to list everyone. Even then the major donors can be listed or mentioned.

Taking paid advertising to thank donors can be expensive but can be worthwhile if there are other messages to communicate (for example that the cause has widespread or prestigious support). Remember always to get the donor's permission before you do this, as most do not expect to see their names publicly in print (and may become frightened that they would then receive an avalanche of appeals from other good causes).

We are grateful to...

Arab British Charitable Trust
Association of University Teachers
Austcare
BandAid
Britten Pears Foundation
Comic Relief
Christian Aid
DES...

A well used way of recognising the role of major donors to your organisation is to publish a list in your annual report. This is the beginning of a longer list published in the World University Service Annual Report.

Getting donors involved

Donors and supporters are likely to give more generously the more they understand your cause. If supporters are aware of the issues and policies behind your work, of your difficulties and failures as well as of your success, then they are much more likely to become firmly committed to your work. Fundraising effectiveness can be enhanced by using a number

---

Involving Your Supporters in the Campaign

The Anti Apartheid Movement needed both to raise money from its members and to make a political point about sanctions against South Africa. They invited both their supporters, and also the supporters of the Campaign for Nuclear Disarmament, to send a donation and to send in a card printed in the shape of an orange with their name on. A thousand oranges, each one addressed to the Prime Minister, were then hung on a huge model tree and taken to the Prime Minister's official residence. Using this method they both persuaded more members to give a donation and got more of them active than they would otherwise have done.

	Cash response	Responders sending oranges
AAM members	7.5%	20.0%
CND members	3.0%	7.8%

---

of devices which give the donor a feeling of much greater involvement in the work and the concerns of the charity.

There are a number of ways of giving them a fuller picture of what you are doing that will build their commitment and their support.

Regular mailings to supporters

Sending mailings to supporters is a necessary and vital form of communication. it keeps them in touch with what's happening. It reports back on your progress, and by implication how you have been able to use their money. It highlights successes and achievements, including major grants that have been received. It sets out future plans and further opportunities for giving support.

In communicating with your supporters, you want them to read what you have sent, and you may also want them to respond in some way. Both these are difficult in a world where people are constantly receiving unsolicited information from all manner of sources. So you may want to find ways of improving the communication process. Here are some possible ways.

- *Questionnaires*. Where you have a large number of supporters, you have an opportunity to use the strength of their numbers, both to inform yourselves better on what they think (and who they are), and to use their views to make important campaigning points. Sending a questionnaire to supporters in a regular appeal mailing can increase response rates. Some people will be motivated by the appeal and some will be motivated by the request to provide information. You can also use questionnaires to ask donors how they want to be involved and/ or how they want to be mailed – including not at all.

- *Campaigns*. Asking supporters to return cards to a government minister or to a planning authority, either directly or through the organisation's offices, can achieve much the same.
- *Contests and competitions*. A quite different way of encouraging involvement is through some form of contest or competition. Competitions where the skill is knowledge of what your organisation stands for can often develop greater understanding of what you are trying to do, but use this technique with care. Attractive as it may be to get supporters looking at every line of your copy for the answer to a clue, some tests have indicated that large and regular donors do not respond well with this sort of device, which they might find too childish. There are other sorts of competitions that you might consider – for the best idea or suggestion on some matter that concerns the organisation and its work, for example.

Other involvement techniques

There are also other ways in which you can try to involve your supporters much more in the work of the organisation. These seek to provide a greater understanding of the organisation and its work and to expose the donors to the people behind the organisation (staff, volunteers, clients, beneficiaries and the local community where the projects are based).

- *Visits*. Most supporters never get to see the work you are doing. You can build their commitment by inviting them to visit you. This can be done in a number of ways. Open days at your office will yield a surprisingly high level of interest, even if your office is remote from the projects you are organising. If possible, site or project visits are even better. Overseas development charities have for years organised project visits for their staff, donors and volunteers, not because the projects want it, nor because they enjoy the administration involved, but simply because the excitement and understanding that is generated by such a visit can never be replicated through less direct means.
- *Events*. Inviting supporters to events such as annual meetings or celebratory receptions can be another way of getting them involved in your work. Try to ensure that you have enough explanatory literature around, and that members of staff make a point of meeting people and discussing the work of the organisation with them.
- *Lectures and talks*. This is another form of getting their involvement, where you lay on events for your supporters where they can hear experts discuss the problem or issue. This gives them the chance to understand more fully the cause you are addressing, and makes them feel that their contribution is important and useful. You can tactfully introduce the notion that you are looking for support to develop some new initiative whose importance has been highlighted in the talk.

However the essential purpose of such a meeting is not to raise money, but to build interest and involvement.

- *Involving donors in your fundraising.* On the principle that the best person to ask is someone who has already given, you might try to find ways of inviting donors to accompany you to fundraising meetings, particularly where you know that their support is enthusiastic. If they can convey something of what motivated them to get involved, it can encourage others; equally importantly, it will cement their relationship with you.
- *Friends groups.* By 'enrolling' donors as members of a friends group or a supporters club (either free or for a subscription) and sending them a regular newsletter which focuses as much on the donors and what they are doing for the organisation as on the work of the organisation, you can create a sense of belonging. You can then organise special events for these key supporters and also develop special appeals where you ask your existing supporters to raise a sum of money for a specified purpose. By giving them the responsibility for doing this and a target to achieve, this will encourage them to give generously.
- *Campaigning.* Many voluntary organisations have as part of their brief a message to communicate to both public and government alike. The campaigning is usually spearheaded by the paid staff, but can often be reinforced by volunteers. Involving donors in this can also build commitment. Those who become involved in advocating a cause, will develop a much deeper commitment to it. It is exactly these people that are likely to become your best supporters in the long term.

Challenges for the fundraiser
1. To get the donor to give again.
2. To get the donor to give regularly and frequently, on some form of committed basis.
3. To get the donor to increase the level of giving.
4. To get the donor to give in several different ways at the same time.
5. To encourage the donor to think of giving a legacy.

Fundraisers should never allow fundraising to become divorced from the advocacy of the cause. It is important to ensure that there are a number of different ways for people to support an organisation: giving money, volunteering, fundraising, and campaigning. Some people will only be able to do one of these things. However many want to do more, and by becoming more involved they will strengthen their concern and commitment to you.

Recruiting volunteers from your donors

It is sometimes assumed that volunteers and donors are two separate categories of supporters which should not be mixed. Many charities feel that they should not ask their donors to volunteer, nor their volunteers to give money. This assumes that people compartmentalise their concern and their response, which is plainly not true.

From the fundraiser's point of view, two things need to be borne in mind. The first is that all those who are giving their time should also be given the opportunity to support the organisation by giving money. If you feel that they should be protected from other requests and encouraged in their existing support for the organisation, then you might consider doing some simple market research to find out whether they would like to be asked to give. The second is that donors can be invited to become involved as volunteers in some way. Most will not have the time available or wish to, but some will, and they will continue as donors too. Even if they don't, their support may be reinforced by their being told that other local people are working as volunteers for the organisation.

7. Communication skills

7.1 Producing effective printed materials

The creation and production of effective fundraising and publicity literature is one of the fundraiser's most important tasks. Good fundraising ideas can be destroyed by poorly prepared or presented material. Good writing skills and an understanding of the design and production processes are vital.

The process of creating any printed material usually follows a similar path. The stages include:

- conception or visualisation (which may include producing a dummy or sample copy), and you need to ensure that you are working to an economic format
- setting aside a budget, and later on in the process getting estimates of costs
- copywriting and gathering together of photographs and other visual material
- design
- print and production
- distribution.

Many of these stages will be carried out by outsiders and each stage might be produced by someone different. This creates considerable opportunities for getting things wrong – deadlines can be missed as a result – and also for losing or watering down the original concept during the process.

You need to decide who does what. There may be many people, even within a small organisation, who feel they can write effectively. However, you need specific writing skills to present a good, clear, logical case and to express your ideas forcefully. This may require an outside professional in advertising or marketing. You may also be dealing with promotional consultants and designers. They may have the skills you need, but you have to brief them properly and be happy that they can produce what you need within your budget.

Principles of effective communication

You must have a clear idea of what you are trying to achieve. It is worth writing down the objectives of any particular piece of communication and including this in the brief to the writer and designer (if you are not doing it all yourself).

Who is it intended for?

- Volunteers and supporters?
- Funders?
- Professionals and others interested in the cause?
- Other stakeholders (name them)?
- The public at large?

And is it:

- To generate awareness?
- To convey information? If so, what information?
- To get a response of some sort?
- To raise money?

You may answer "all of the above". If so, you will run into problems. The message will fall between lots of stools. Decide what you are keenest to achieve (e.g. raise money) and do that. Other things will follow (e.g. raising awareness), but the primary purpose is clear and the main message will come across.

This is especially important when it comes to annual reports which may have to serve a number of purposes for several audiences. If the objective is to raise money, then there must be a clear understanding as to how this is to be done. Is the brochure to be sent through the post and a postal response sought from the addressee? If so, will that response be a cash donation, a membership subscription, or a legacy pledge?

The next stage of the process must be to identify who you expect to read the material. If they are readers of a magazine or a particular mailing list, then you will know something about them and their interests. Have they had any previous contact with you or knowledge about your work? Your past donors might be expected to be fairly knowledgeable, and what you say to them will differ from what you say to those who know little or nothing about the organisation. For your existing donors, you could try to get some picture of who they actually are. Some simple research will tell you something about their age, sex, interests and preferences, and also something about their degree of commitment to the organisation.

Ten suggestions for writers

1. Get to know your audience.
2. Use simple, direct and everyday language.
3. State your proposition boldly and clearly.
4. Feature real, identifiable cases and people.
5. Communicate the need.
6. State clearly what the reader's support will enable you to achieve.
7. Remember that cleverness rarely pays.
8. Avoid seeming too professional.
9. Remove any unnecessary detail.
10. Give a clear course of action.

Ken Burnett, a communications consultant, gives this advice to his staff and clients.

You will also need to bear in mind budget factors. You may have limited space (in an advertisement, for example) to get your message across, or if you are sending out a mailing, the cost of printing all the material and postage weight limits will be a factor. Printing in full colour will be more expensive than in one or two colours. If you want to include photographs, will these need to be taken?

The next stage is to set a clear deadline for when you need the materials. This is especially important if the material is going to be mailed or presented at an AGM. Things usually take longer than you think so give yourself room for slippage, but make sure that everyone involved tries to stick to their deadlines.

Conception

The concept stage of producing any fundraising material is important. This will generate a creative approach, a visual theme, a style and a headline or slogan.

Themes, headlines and ideas can be generated through a brain-storming approach. This involves putting a number of interested people together in a room, identifying the object of the exercise and the rules of the brain-storming process, then asking those present to contribute as many ideas as possible. Some may be zany, others can be done at speed, but all must be written up so that new ideas build on old. Then there is a process of refinement to select one of the suggestions or develop the approach out of several of the ideas. Out of this will come the general strategy which will in turn generate the actual copy.

An ActionAid leaflet asking people to sponsor a child or make a donation

At this stage, you will need a designer to produce roughs. This is an important stage, as it is the last major point at which you can turn back. If you don't like the rough design, you should ask for a new approach before too much time has been spent. If you pass this stage and then decide a new approach is needed later on, this will cost money and you may miss your deadlines. The visualisation need be no more than the front cover for a leaflet with a sample page – enough to give you an idea of how it will feel and look.

Writing

Not everybody has the skills to write copy, though almost everybody needs to communicate in writing at some time. A good copywriter can really make your words come alive. However, small organisations do not always have the means to hire copywriters, so fundraisers will usually have to write their own materials.

A good copywriter requires a clear understanding of your cause and a proper briefing of what you are trying to say to whom, and the objectives of the communication. When hiring an outside consultant, always look at their portfolio to see what they have done for similar organisations. Some will have an instinctive understanding of your work, alongside their flair with words, while others will be better at selling condensed milk. Though good copywriters are expensive, you may be able to find one as a volunteer.

If you are writing the copy yourself, there are a number of things you will have to remember. The first is about structure. An acronym is useful here – A.I.D.A. This describes the process of persuasion and communication.

- **Attention**: the reader's attention has to be attracted.
- **Interest**: if you don't identify a reason for the reader to be personally interested, you will lose them.
- **Desire**: to support your cause.
- **Action**: the practical steps they will take to deliver this support
  Headlines, pictures or strong ideas can all create the visual attraction that you will need to claim the reader's attention in the first place. Their interest can be gained by showing them why you exist and the needs you are serving. Don't imagine that your supporters will continue to support you without a continuing reminder of the importance of what you are doing, or the human cost of ignoring the problem. Desire to support your cause is likely to be generated by an understanding that things can be changed if they give their support. Action demands that you tell them what you want them to do and what sort of gift they are expected to make.

Keep everything simple and understandable. One problem is that organisations tend to develop shorthand ways of describing their work. These are useful when talking to colleagues, but can involve language that is quite meaningless to outsiders. Jargon should be avoided at all costs.

Find someone to read your first draft who does not have anything to do with your organisation. Ask them to feed back what they have understood – and what they have not understood! A problem may arise when you have to agree the copy with others. Most people's reaction to checking someone else's text is to check for typographic errors and false statements, and then add their own thoughts. The result can often be an accurate but heavily qualified text that loses all its punch and impact. Accept their comments, but remember that effective text cannot be written by a committee. They may have skills in providing the service or in running the organisation; yours are in fundraising and communication.

Design

The design gives the printed piece its character. Good designers can lift the central idea from a piece of text and make it something infinitely more compelling. The elements of this include the copy, the headlines and sub-heads, the photographs and illustrations used, as well as the design style. There is also the number of colours to be used (and whether it is to be printed on tinted paper), and the use of colour with text reversed out and blocks of the page overlaid with a tint of the colour.

> **The KISS principle**
>
> An important principle is that of simplicity. KISS is the acronym often used to remind us of this:
> **K**eep
> **I**t
> **S**imple
> **S**tupid!
>
> And remember:
> - Pythagoras's Theorem was written in 24 words.
> - Archimedes Principle was written in 67 words.
> - The Ten Commandments were written in 179 words.
> - The US Declaration of Independence was written in 300 words.
> - A recent European Commission Directive on a minor food matter was written in 3,427 words!

You may already have a house design style, including the use of logos. If you do – and consistency is always important – then ensure that designers are clearly briefed about this. Maintaining a consistent house style will help build up a feeling of continuity and reassurance, and will convey the message of dynamism, safety or whatever is implicit in your house style.

The important elements of the design include the format, colour, layout, type faces, the heading and signposting of the various parts of the text, the use of space and how the various sorts of illustration are used.

Illustrations can take many forms and help bring a design to life. Photographs are the easiest to use but don't use them if they do not make a point or are not of good quality. Photos should always be captioned, as captions are among the most read parts of any publication. The best are those that involve people doing things – and not pieces of equipment, buildings or groups of committee members posing for the camera. Illustrations, diagrams and plans are a good alternative, and can also be useful for illustrating things that cannot yet be photographed (such as the building you are planning to put up).

A good designer will integrate all these elements for you and, having taken your brief, should be able to satisfy your needs. If you are using an outside designer, do ensure you get a clear quote for the design cost before agreeing to proceed. These days all but the most complicated designs can be produced on a Desk Top Publishing system.

A good illustration can make a point far more forcefully than the written word

Newsletters, handbills and leaflets that are produced regularly in a similar format can often be produced in-house to a pre-designed format created for you by a professional designer.

Getting it into print

The final stage in the process is to get the written material into print. You will normally want to seek quotes from any outside printers (and from designers if you are using them). With printers, try to obtain three quotes in order to get the best price possible. It is surprising how much the prices vary, even on the most tightly defined jobs. This is a lot to do with how much the printer wants the job and whether what you are producing fits their capacity and their machine size. Do not be embarrassed about asking printers you are dealing with regularly to quote on new jobs. It does not demonstrate mistrust, rather it shows good business practice and a keenness to get the best price. When asking someone to quote, you should have a clear understanding of the following.

For dealing with designers:
- date of text and instructions to the designer and date of receipt of completed job
- visuals needed
- format, size and price guidelines for the job
- copywriting and who does what and by when
- photographs needed: what is required and by when
- illustrations needed: what is required and by when.

For dealing with printers:
- **date** that the completed artwork will be sent to the printer and date required for receipt of completed job;
- **paper size** (printers will use standard size sheets of paper; the less the wastage, the more economic the format);
- **print quantity** (the more you print the cheaper each one becomes and short runs are particularly expensive; but it is more expensive producing extra copies you have no need for);
- **paper quality** (it usually pays to print on stock paper used by the printer which is bought in bulk). Think about the colour of the paper (tinted paper is more expensive than white paper). Glossy art papers, card and heavy papers, and special finishes (such as Conqueror Laid) are usually much more expensive, and should only be used in appropriate situations;
- **number of print colours** (one, two or four). One colour can look dull (although there are some shining exceptions to this), and one colour printed on tinted paper can look old fashioned. Four colour is

expensive, and the use of special inks (such as silver or gold) can also involve substantial additional cost. Two-colour offers lots of opportunities for creative design, and is reasonably cheap;
- **illustrative photographs and halftones** (this can add to the cost, but increase the effectiveness of the communication). You need good illustrations which reinforce the points you want to make;
- **Folding** (complicated folds will usually be more expensive than simple folding; scoring or perforation can also add to the cost);
- **Packing and delivery** (the price usually includes delivery to one address).

Every decision you make about the design and print quality of a book, leaflet or letter says something about your organisation and its ethos. A most obvious current issue is whether to print on recycled materials. It is hard for an organisation that claims to be concerned with the environment not to be doing this, whatever the economics (and it is usually more expensive). There will be a perception of inconsistency if you don't.

A similar problem surrounds the use of seemingly expensive or glossy paper. Donors expect that when charities communicate with them, they should not waste money. Though they say this, donors will always respond better if what you send them looks nice and appears professional, or something that stands out. So if your printed material looks expensive, then one way of showing financial prudence is to get it sponsored. Remember too, to communicate effectively with new groups of people, you will need to have something much more substantial and well laid out than you would for your existing donors.

7.2 Writing an appeal letter

Letter-writing is fundamental to any successful fundraising activity. It is not simply a question of raising money because all letters create some sort of impression whether or not the recipient responds. This awareness building is an important factor, particularly when 98% or more will not respond.

Remember that direct mail appeals should aim to raise money at a cost ratio of 10:1 from a warm list, and if the communication is got right, then this fundraising technique can be one of the best sources of continuing income available to any organisation.

However, there are various other elements to the appeal: the envelope, the salutation, the entry, the appeal, the call to action, the postscript and the supporting literature. Though only a few of these are actually contained in the letter itself, they all play their part in making the appeal effective.

1. The envelope

70% of people never get beyond opening the envelope. Some charities include a slogan or a teaser line on the envelope to try to create a sense of intrigue and curiosity, thereby enticing the recipient to open the letter to find out what is inside. Alternatively, you may feel that since no personal mail ever has advertising copy on the outside, a plain envelope with a stamp may be more compelling to open, rather than immediately thrown away as a piece of 'junk mail'. Only a knowledge of your audience and careful testing will determine the best approach. However, the more personal the letter seems, the more likely it is to get immediate attention.

2. The salutation

The salutation (Dear...) should be as personal as possible. When writing a small number of personal letters, you can top and tail letters personally with the salutation at the start and signature at the end. You may get volunteers with good writing to do the topping and tailing for you – this can be very effective.

If none of these is possible, then fall back on "Dear friend" or "Dear supporter". Both of these are an admission a circular letter is being sent, and that you can't do more than treat the recipient as a statistic. Still try to make it as personal as you can. Most word processor systems have mail merge software that enables you to link a list of names and addresses with a given letter.

3. The entry

You need to grab the reader's attention immediately. If you don't, the reader may not get beyond the first paragraph. A letter from a respected celebrity or an amazing statement may make people read on, or an intensely emotional opening to the letter can do the trick.

Grabbing attention

"More men are guilty of committing intestacy than adultery."
WWF (UK) advertising for legacies. The message startles, perhaps because the reader confuses 'intestacy' with 'incest'. But the point is clear; most people die without making a will, and a charitable bequest can do a great deal of good.

"1 in 4 marriages will end in heartache"
The British Heart Foundation telling people that there is a 1 in 4 chance of a marriage ending due to the death of one of the partners through heart disease. This is considerably lower than the probability of the heartache of divorce, though!

*"Do you really need 50p more than he does?...
... 50p a day won't get you very far. But use it to sponsor a child in need, and it could go a lot further than you ever thought possible. Just £15 a month helps us provide clean water, health care, basic education, seeds and tools for growing food... all things that could make life better, not just for one child, but for everyone in the community."*
ActionAid showing how much can be done for so little.

*"You hold in your hand an instrument of torture...
... it can also be an instrument of change."*
An Amnesty International advertisement featuring a pen, which can be used by a torturer to gouge out eyes, but also by a donor to commit financial support.

4. The appeal message

Once the reader's attention has been gained, it must be held. The appeal must be simply written. It must be well laid out with short words, short sentences and a variety of paragraph sizes. Key ideas should be underlined, indented or highlighted. In terms of content, you need to:

- state the problem
- show how you can help resolve it
- demonstrate your credibility by showing what you have achieved in the past and others who have helped you
- indicate how much you expect the donor to give and what this will achieve
- make the call to action clearly.

(See section 2.3 Writing a fundraising proposal for further ideas on what to put in the letter.)

5. The call to action

The call to action is crucial, and where many otherwise well written appeal letters fail. Perhaps it is to do with the reluctance to be direct in asking for precisely what you want. Yet that is exactly what is required. Start flagging up the call to action early on in the letter. Repeat it throughout the letter and make it absolutely plain near the end. It should consist of:

- what you want
- how much you want them to give
- how you want the amount paid
- when – how soon must it arrive (usually immediately, to create a sense of urgency)
- who to send it to (a personal name to reply to will always be better than an anonymous department)
- where – the return address.

6. The postscript

Save an important idea for the postscript (or PS). This is one of the most read parts of the letter and a good PS doubles the response. So use it for your final argument to clinch their support or reinforce the message. This can be produced in a printed typeface or a reproduction of the same handwriting used for the signature.

7. Supporting literature

Supporting literature should be used to reinforce the message of the appeal. Don't be drawn into the temptation to squeeze in thousands of words of text that you couldn't find space for in the letter. Use all the same fundraising considerations. It is often a good idea to have

The call to action

■ If you love art it'll be the best £25 you spend all year...
... when you join the National Art Collections Fund
All these benefits for just £25.... free admission to more than 170 permanent collections which charge for admission, free publications, exclusive offers and events...and you'll be a valued patron of the arts. Since 1903 our members' subscriptions have helped buy more than 100,000 works of art for hundreds of museums and galleries all over the country. Your membership will secure even more.

■ If you're on our side, say so!
...Instruct your Bank to strike a blow for justice
Whether it is war or bombings, attacks on the street or beatings that go on behind closed doors, the effects can be devastating. Yet despite their difficult circumstances, many women are organising to stamp out the violence that threatens them and blights the lives of their children. All of War on Want's projects are run by local people with the support of the community. They need our help – please don't forget them this Christmas. Please will you send a donation today? Or better still take out a standing order with your bank, so that we can give these women and children the lasting solidarity and support they need to rebuild their lives.

■ Help them build a future free from hunger and disease...
... for just £2 a month.
People in the Third World don't want to live on handouts. All they want is the opportunity to work themselves out of poverty – and the chance to live dignified and independent lives. Your £2 a month will help these people in their daily struggle to help themselves. Please fill in the coupon below. (Oxfam)

■ Your next decision could affect a child for the rest of their life
When you sponsor a child through ActionAid, 90% of your money is spent directly on our development work. We work closely with people, providing long-term solutions to poverty – and so creating a situation in which people can begin to support themselves. In return for your help, you'll gain a valuable insight into the lives and needs of poor communities in the developing world. And, of course, you'll know you've played your part in improving the life of a child and the lives of everyone in the community.

Each of these examples illustrates a direct call to action. What the charity wants the donor to do is clearly spelt out. The text is simple and direct. The examples show how you can write good copy to appeal to your donors – showing the benefits that will be obtained by responding, confronting prejudices, and illustrating the cause in an attractive way.

photographic material with little text. Don't forget to repeat the call to action.

8. Response mechanism

There will need to be some way of donors getting their reply and hopefully their donations back to you. This could be a simple reply envelope, or a credit card hot-line, or an instruction to pay money into your bank account. Make the options clear and remember the resource implications – if people ask for a receipt, send it promptly; if you offer a credit card hot-line, make sure it is properly staffed.

7.3 Writing an annual report

Every organisation has to produce some sort of annual report. This can be an extremely useful publication for your fundraising. The annual report is an opportunity for your organisation to promote your strengths, highlight the importance of the need, demonstrate your effectiveness, celebrate your achievements and also raise money both directly and indirectly.

An annual report and accounts are a legal and fundraising necessity. All your major funders will want to see them, as will the Charity Commission, Companies House or whoever you report to. However, try to see it as a useful promotional opportunity rather than a chore. Here are a few important points:

- **don't use the annual report to complain.** Use it to promote and celebrate;
- **use illustrations and photographs** liberally. They can convey more than the printed word;
- **don't start with long lists** of supporters and committee members. You are writing the annual report to create interest in your organisation;
- on the other hand, **do list major donors.** This recognition (and you will be sending them a copy) will encourage them to think about giving a repeat donation, and encourage others (to whom you could send a copy of the report with your appeal letter) to give;
- think about who you might send a copy to, as good PR for your organisation or to **create interest** as a prelude to making an appeal;

Thirteen criteria for the ideal annual report

1. A well planned structure.
2. A clear statement of objectives.
3. A clear understandable financial picture.
4. Visible economy, demonstrating sensible use of resources.
5. Instant appeal.
6. Legibility.
7. Good design.
8. Well written copy.
9. Good use of photos and illustrations.
10. Overall appropriateness of style and feel to the organisation.
11. Empathy with principal audience.
12. Completeness: all components working well together.
13. A sense of excitement.

Source: 'Charity Annual Reports' by Ken Burnett

- annual reports are good vehicles for **sponsorship**. It is a reasonably small amount to cover the costs of design, production and dissemination. The sponsorship is visible, and will be seen by key supporters. And with sponsorship you could mount a more effective PR campaign using your annual report;
- if you want to **use the report to raise money** directly, either print an appeal at the end of the report or enclose an appeal leaflet inside the report.

Many of the standard fundraising techniques also apply to your annual report. For example, try to be positive and communicate a sense of enthusiasm and achievement. You have more space than an appeal letter so you can use a range of techniques to get your message across. For example, why not try to include the following.

- *Drama*. Voluntary organisations revolve around dramatic issues – the fight against disease, giving children a chance in life, protecting the environment from destruction or whatever, but so many annual reports are dry! Tell some good stories about what you have done.
- *Human interest*. Charities are about people, people in really fascinating situations. What about the odd case study, interview, profile, testimonial, quote or whatever?
- *Support*. Show how many people love you, either through the messages they send or the endorsements they give. Ideally have a picture of them alongside the quote to make it real.
- *Boxes alongside the text*. Many annual reports are A4 and look a really daunting read. Try to break up the text with boxes which have facts, quotes, snippets of information, key points or other simple points.

You will have your own ideas as well. However, annual reports should be attractive and easy to read, even if some of the content may sometimes be challenging or even shocking. Don't forget to use lots of sub headings, bullet points and short sentences.

7.4 Market research

Too often charities assume that they know what all their supporters and potential supports think, what they are interested in and what they want to know from the charity. This simply is not true. You need to find out what your supporters really think about your charity, the things you do and the services you provide. In other words, you may need to undertake some research.

Market research is vital if a charity is to maximise the funding and support it receives from its donors and from the public. The more you can find out about your donors and potential donors, the more you will be able to communicate effectively with them and to motivate them to give.

There are many different types of market research that you can carry out, and for a wide variety of purposes. In this section we look at researching your own donor base, finding out what the public thinks of you, and using research to seek out new supporters.

All research involves collecting data gleaned from small groups of people and making extrapolations from that to derive views about the attitudes of the public at large. There are three basic types of information that are used:

- **demography** refers to the vital statistics of age, sex and location of individuals in the general population;
- **psychographics** denotes people's attitudes and preferences, as shown by newspaper readership, church going, voting patterns and so on;
- **opinion** research usually refers to the attitudes of the public to given questions. This might be put in a question such as "Do you think stray dogs should be shot" – agree, disagree, don't know.

Donor research

There will often be a group of supporters upon whom the organisation's well-being depends. These may be volunteers, donors, sponsors or others. When an organisation is very small, it is quite often just a small group of enthusiasts and well-wishers who are involved. At this stage, it is possible for the organisers to keep in touch with all their supporters personally, but as numbers grow, this becomes more difficult.

It is at this point that the organisation will need to find out more about its supporters. You will want to know who they are and what they think of you. You are dependent on their time or money to carry out the organisation's work. If they are becoming disenchanted with what you are doing or can no longer meet your expectations, you have a problem which you will need to address. Knowing who your supporters are will also help you identify other sorts of people you might try to recruit as new members – and it could indicate people that have not yet been influenced by your message.

You can always chat informally to your supporters at events and open days, or indeed whenever you come into contact with them. You should be doing this as a matter of course, to show that you are interested as well as to find out more about what your supporters are thinking, but you may want to do a more formal research survey. A postal survey is the most usual form of supporter survey. If you have a mailing list or can enclose the questionnaire with a newsletter, then this is relatively easy and cheap to do.

There is an important issue behind interpreting results: to what degree are the results of those people who responded representative of the whole (including those that didn't respond)? The responders are likely to be people who are more keenly interested than an average sample. If only a minority has responded, they have one thing in common – that they have responded. Do they also have other things in common? For example, if it was a long questionnaire, then only those people who had the time might have responded, and thus your results could be biased in favour of older people or those not going out to work. Poor survey techniques can produce misleading results.

Examples of questions you might want to ask in addition to those that seek to find out their attitude to your organisation and its work, might include:

- age
- sex
- marital status
- number of children
- income band
- working status
- job
- newspaper readership
- voting habits
- religious membership
- trade union and other membership
- giving methods to the organisation
- frequency of giving
- preferred areas of support
- other good cause organisations supported
- voluntary support (whether and how much time they give)
- legacy support.

With this information, you can also begin to build up a profile of a typical supporter, which will help you do two things:

- communicate more effectively with them. If you have a picture in your mind as to who they are, then this becomes easier to do;
- think about where else you might look to recruit people with a similar profile as your supporters.

Surveying your own supporters is a great deal cheaper than doing the same job for the public at large. It can be relatively easy to carry out yourselves, especially if you pay attention to the question composition and to the methods of getting the responses back to you with a minimum of effort (by making the survey seem important and easy to respond to, by enclosing a reply paid envelope, or by offering some incentive to those responding, such as a free entry into a prize draw).

Public opinion research

Finding out what the public at large feels is more difficult and expensive but for some organisations it can be essential – for example, if you are trying to change the government's environmental policy, it will add weight to your argument if you can show that the public feels extremely concerned about the present state of affairs. There are a number of ways this can be achieved. Postal surveys are not usually effective here, and so are not often used. Omnibus research is one useful technique: this is where a research company puts together the questions from several organisations and sends interviewers out to ask all the questions in one survey. If you want to know just a few things, then this can be cost-effective and can be done quickly. If you want to know how the public are likely to react to a given appeal or style, then focus groups will be better (see below). This is what is called qualitative research which ends up with different sorts of answers, and is particularly useful for situations where yes/no answers will not do.

Interviews

Interviews take time, require professionals and are expensive. However, the findings can be invaluable. Using this type of research, an organisation can learn how it is perceived, how it is compared to others in the same field, who are its prospective supporters, and what their attitudes are to the cause and the work being done. The interviews are invariably conducted by professionals, as is the construction of the questionnaire to which they work. You should get responses which are well-balanced and results that are reliable. One important result that can be derived from this sort of survey are the differences between supporters and non-supporters. If you depend upon high levels of current public awareness of your cause for your success, then this type of research will tell you how well you are doing. Prompted and spontaneous awareness are two useful measures of how well your publicity is working.

Focus groups

Focus groups are useful when you have a new strategy that you want to explore prior to launching it. It works by gathering a number of people in one place for a period of discussion. There should always be an experienced facilitator to help steer the conversation and record the results. A new name of the charity, new advertising strategies, and attitudes to important issues can also be explored in depth this way. The groups themselves are formed in different locations to give balance and compare different types of supporter and public. Reports and transcripts are made available to the client. The results can prove extremely interesting, and you can use this technique to test out the response to proposed fundraising materials.

Sources of data

Regular information is available to the keen observer from a number of places. The National Archive or the public library system is always a good starting point. Reports from censuses will contain a wide range of research at a national level. For other information about people's behaviour and buying habits market research companies may produce interesting reports which may be available in business libraries. Your local reference library or university social studies department should be able to tell you about any local research that has been carried out and help you find out about relevant academic research that has been published. This information can be particularly important in highlighting the importance of issues and social problems.

Statistics

Not all research data is reliable. Proper samples are needed to give meaningful results. Samples can suffer from several forms of bias. One is associated with the nature of the sampling process. For example, does it cover all the areas of the country? Does it cover all age and income groups? And is the sample self-selecting, or have you only selected those who answered?

Equally important is sample size. For example, if you were to ask two people about their views and hope that they were representative of a group of four people, then you might be in for a shock. The question may be a simple yes/no attitude question, such as, "Do you agree with hanging as a punishment for murder?" Suppose that two people said yes, and two no. Researchers using a sample of two might get two yeses, or two nos, or one of each. In all cases they would have got the answer completely wrong if the actual split in the population as a whole was 70:30. There are statistical formulae to determine the sample size required to get it right 95% of the time. You might be able to find a university lecturer or graduate to help you as a volunteer to design your sampling procedures.

7.5 Marketing

Marketing is not the exclusive concern of aggressive companies, nor is it just about selling. Fundraising demands marketing skills and a full understanding of the principles of marketing will help the fundraiser a great deal.

Marketing is often described in terms of the five P's. These are:
- planning
- product
- price
- place
- promotion.

Though the term may not be familiar, the whole of this book is in fact about marketing – about marketing a cause to someone who can contribute money and time to supporting it. This section simply sets out the link between marketing theory and fundraising. Most of the points covered here are dealt with in more detail elsewhere in the book.

Planning and market analysis

A key part of the marketing process is the planning that precedes it. This should start with a clear understanding of the organisation and its work, the market in which it is operating, the competitor organisations (in the non-profit, the public and the private sectors), and the attitudes of potential supporters. Useful tools for this include:
- **SWOT analysis** which gives a picture of the strengths, weaknesses, opportunities and threats to your organisation;
- a **positioning map**, which plots where you are in relation to other organisations, and significant variables such as reliability, urgency, and so on – derived from how you perceive yourselves and from market research based on the public's perception of you;
- **market share analysis**, which measures what proportion of a given sector of donated income you are currently receiving – for example, how much support is given by local companies, and how much of this your organisation is receiving;
- **market research**, which identifies the attitudes of your potential or actual supporters to giving to the cause in general, and to your particular charity.

The outcome of all this analysis should be a picture of those groups in the population which are the best for you to target.

Product

The service provided by your organisation is, in marketing terms, the product. It consists of the following ingredients:
- the actual 'tangible' product or need which your charity exists to meet;
- what the donor gets from association with you;

- the frills: the invitation to meet the child you have helped; the attendance at a special function each year, and so on.

All these can be added together, so that the concept as a whole appeals to your target audience. The point is, you are competing for a share of the disposable income of your supporters. You have to tempt them to buy your product, rather than someone else's. You need to make your product as attractive as you can to your supporters.

Each product you create will have a life cycle. According to marketing theory, you will need to re-promote your product from time to time to keep it attractive and in people's minds. Equally, theory teaches that every product will eventually run out of steam and have to be replaced by another – although, in practice this is not always the case.

Just as each company will produce a range of products, so any charity is likely to have a range of its own fundraising products. These might include a big gift scheme with recognition for major donors, membership subscriptions for the mass support, a friends group for committed supporters, and a schools fundraising scheme for the young. These can all happily co-exist, so long as they are not in competition with one another.

Price

Donors do not automatically know how they are expected to respond, nor how much they are expected to give. Your role as fundraiser is to steer them towards what is likely to be achievable and affordable to them, and at the same time ensure you meet your own needs. This is a vital part of the process.

The most obvious way of doing this is to ask for a precise amount. "We are asking each person to give £10", for example. However this is not always satisfactory as it begs the question of "why £10?" The response to that is to offer a specific example of what the money will do – "£10 can buy a new walking frame for a disabled child". The donation may not actually be spent on that, so the wording has to be carefully constructed if you are not to create a binding obligation to spend the money in precisely the way you have indicated or commit a breach of trust. There are three useful approaches.

- A **shopping list** which illustrates a range of things at different prices that their money might be spent on.
- A **range of levels** of support from which the donor can choose. Each will be set in such a way as to confer a greater status to those who give more (for example, friend, good friend, best friend).
- A **range of possible frequencies** (annual, quarterly, monthly, or even weekly). You will find that smaller amounts given more frequently yield larger amounts to you. This is because people respond to the headlined figure more than to the actual cost.

Not only does the price you ask determine the type of supporter you get, it also determines the amount of benefit you generate for your organisation. This will be the amount you ask for less any costs of raising the money and administering the donation. A £5 subscription will cost as much to service as a £25 subscription and a £5 donation might be immediately swallowed up by administration costs. There is often a tendency to ask for too little. Generally people are far more generous than you think. Then there is the opportunity cost. For major potential donors, you will do yourself a disservice asking for only £50. Not because it is expensive to administer, but because they might have given £5,000!

Place – the type of gift

The place of giving refers to the channel through which the support is given. It will usually be closely linked to promotion. For example, a personal request to help provides an opportunity to write a cheque and hand it over. A request made in a speech or over the radio should also include a way of giving support (a return address).

The place – the way the donor makes a commitment and gets their help to you – is always important. Whether it is providing pledge forms on each table, a bucket at the door, a credit card hot-line or a well-placed advertisement, this needs to be thought about when the promotion is being devised.

The place will determine not just what you can ask for, but how they see the charity. For example, a charity that decides to raise money from running a series of balls or dinner dances will only interact with a certain range of people in a particular atmosphere. Equally the same charity could appeal to a wider audience by running a series of village fetes. The two approaches might ultimately achieve the same result in terms of money raised. However, they would have done this by using completely different techniques, from quite different sources, using different resources and helpers, and in the process creating a completely different organisation.

Promotion

Promotion of your cause is about how you project yourself to the public. It is not only the medium, but the message too. The message is conveyed by a whole range of things within your control. Your name – or at least the title of your appeal – sends an important message, particularly if you have made this name well-known. People recognise World Wide Fund for Nature (WWF) or Save the Children, and these names evoke images of what the charity is doing.

How you present yourself creates an impression of credibility, urgency, dynamism, and so on. Most important is how you express your needs in your written and visual material. Is it a rational or emotional appeal? Is it supported by human content that makes it personal? Good designers and copywriters can create the image you require for your organisation, if they are well briefed.

The medium of your promotion is another important ingredient. Are you going to rely on personal recommendation to get your message across? Or are you going to use other means of communication? Possible media include TV, radio, newspaper advertising. public relations, direct mail posters, house to house calling, exhibitions, company promotions, booklets, events, speaking at meetings and many others. The five P's of marketing are in fact all interdependent; if one factor is changed then it will affect all the others.

7.6 Public relations

Good public relations can create a positive climate of opinion and counter negative feelings or images that people may have about your organisation, its work and the cause it is addressing.

Effective PR is an essential ingredient of successful fundraising. For a fundraiser the value of PR lies in two things. First, it can draw the public's attention to a cause or a need, whether this is national or local. Without this attention and understanding, the task of the fundraiser becomes much more difficult. If when you get to see the head of the local company there have recently been articles about the good work that your organisation is doing in the press, you will already be starting from the point where that person accepts your cause as being serious.

PR can also help position the organisation in relation to other organisations in the same field. "Why do we need so many charities, all apparently researching the same diseases? Shouldn't they all combine?" will be a natural response of the public. Good PR can help identify the special importance of your work and its particular ethos and contribution as against all the competing organisations, and get this recognised by the public. This can help eliminate an important barrier to public generosity.

Damage limitation

The media relishes a good story which blackens the name of a charitable organisation. You need to ensure that you are capable of countering the bad press and media coverage you may occasionally receive. There are a number of possible situations all of which need proper handling.

A newspaper might publish an article claiming that you are badly administering your money or that someone has run off with it. The readership and reputation of the newspaper will be enough to do you a great deal of damage. In such cases, action needs to be taken quickly.

The first people to contact are your donors. They need to be reassured that what they have read is not true; and they need to be given the facts. Next you should reply to the offending article as quickly as possible. Though the damage at this point has already been done, it can be mitigated by an article or letter in reply. Then you should issue a statement to other papers and to your own staff and trustees setting out the facts of the matter.

On some occasions you will get advance warning of media interest. On these occasions you should establish the facts; identify a spokesperson to put your case to the media, making sure you keep the message consistent; or consider inviting the senior management of the paper or the television station to withdraw the offending article.

If the bad coverage has some element of truth in it, you are in a less defensible position. In such circumstances, a different approach is required. You should accept responsibility for the situation, identify the immediate action that has been taken to remedy it and invite the paper to do a follow up in a more positive vein to help rehabilitate the organisation.

In all these situations there are a number of useful guidelines:

- **ensure that the staff of your organisation do not speak to the media** unless they are specifically authorised to. There is nothing so damaging as the leaked report or the inept interview from a well-meaning staff member;
- make sure that the **facts are established** at an early stage and are accurate. Then make them well-known;
- make sure that your **internal communication** systems are working well, that you can get any new twists of the story across the colleagues speedily, and that trustees and supporters are kept informed;
- if you haven't already got one, draft an **emergency plan** in which you anticipate the possible disasters that could happen and allocate responsibilities accordingly.

Campaigning and PR

For organisations that do campaign, PR is clearly a major tool to help them achieve their aims. This also has important implications for fundraising. Sometimes campaigning and fundraising are seen as two separate activities that require different people and skills. The truth is that if the campaign is seen to be an intrinsic part of the organisation's reason for existing, then when the campaign gets good coverage, good fundraising results will follow.

Most not-for-profit organisations do not see campaigning as the primary part of their work, but many need to campaign on particular issues from time to time or have successfully set themselves up as experts in a particular area. This creates an interesting opportunity, since the media will naturally turn to the organisation when there is a story and they need informed comment.

You can also try to get the name of your organisation mentioned in the media, as many times as possible, hopefully in a good context but almost irrespective of whether there is any informed comment on the cause. This can be done by:

- issuing press releases;
- setting up stunts and events which will naturally attract publicity. Better still may be to use these same skills to set up interesting fundraising events that the media will want to cover;
- holding press conferences;
- writing letters to the letters page of newspapers and magazines (see below).

Timing is all important in media work. Not only because of the deadlines of the different media, but also because of the need to use the coverage to enhance your own fundraising. Thus the media exposure should ideally be timed to happen just before you launch a major fundraising initiative, targeted towards the people you are approaching for support and in whatever form you can obtain it.

Letters

One of the most helpful ways of creating a positive climate of opinion about your cause is to write letters to the newspapers. This can be done by staff, or better still by volunteer supporters.

The best papers for a local organisation or a local branch of a national organisation to target are the local newspapers in the area. In this way you can spread the word about your charity quite widely for little cost. The theme of any letter should ideally by topical. If it is linked to a local event or signed by a well-known local personality, your letter is more likely to be published. However letters just alerting readers to new needs or services you provide may also be published.

Answering letters that others have written to the press is another opportunity. A letter of thanks for local help after a flag day or other event can give you the opportunity to show how successful the event was, how efficiently the money was raised, and how well it is going to be spent.

Similarly, you can use local radio phone-in programmes where you or a volunteer can ring in to make a point, announce a development or even appeal for support.

News releases and press conferences

When you have something new to report, sending a press release to a selected list of newspapers, radio stations and TV channels is one of the most effective ways of publicising it. This can be in response to a recent development in your work, a major donation received, a new publication produced or research completed, a celebrity supporter joining your ranks, or some form of stunt designed specifically to highlight your work or generate publicity.

An effective press release answers the questions who, what, when, where, and why. To be effective at a local level, it should have a clear local angle. Ideally, you should write it in the form of a short article, so that editors can use it verbatim, if they wish. Some might be really interested in the story and want more background information, which you can include separately. Picture editors will appreciate good photos.

If the event is of real interest, then you might consider holding a press conference. You invite the press to come in person to hear your story, and you can expect to be closely questioned on the project and your organisation.

The timing of the press conference is critical. Its proximity to other important news stories can make or break yours, though you may have relatively little control over this. For example if there is a major political development or financial scandal, there will be little room in the newspaper for other news breaking at the same time. The timing is also important, in that you need to know the schedules and deadlines that the journalists are working to. If you are not sure, then talk informally to a journalist or newspaper editor first before planning your PR initiative.

Location is extremely important. An interesting venue can add to the feel of the story – launching a campaign on climate from the roof of the Meteorological Office would be ideal. The venue should also be easily accessible to journalists. You might want to hold a press conference at an event which is guaranteed to get good coverage itself – such as a national conference.

One way of making the press conference go with a swing is to announce that it will be given by some well-known people, renowned either for their entertainment value or for their serious interest. An actress or celebrity will often use pithy words for journalists or be well rehearsed in the photo call for photographers. Similarly, reporters will know that senior figures at press conferences can usually be drawn on the issues.

If you are using a celebrity, having a conference chaired by a senior person from your organisation will help control the questions and steer them away from the celebrity who might not know the answer. To get your message across with no deviation or hesitation, there is nothing quite like a dry run first. If you can't manage this, you will have to give the spokesperson a full briefing.

For those who don't get to the conference, you should compile a briefing pack. It often transpires that some of the fullest coverage from a press conference comes from journalists who have not even attended. But you might never have got this coverage without having organised the conference in the first place!

Photocalls and events

The media are always attracted to the unusual, the famous and the picturesque. Sometimes it is necessary to express your needs in this way, rather than expect that your campaign or fundraising message alone are in any way newsworthy.

If your main way of raising funds locally is to run coffee mornings, how might you use the media to help boost those events? Apart from a one-line mention in the local paper, nobody in the media is going to take much interest. One answer is to use a celebrity. Celebrities do not have to be major national names to be of interest to the local media, though it does help if they are. You could find out which celebrities live in your area and who will be visiting the area at the time you plan to hold the press conference. Just by getting them to pose for an appropriate picture you can raise the chances of getting coverage for your coffee morning. Another possibility is to get photographers to come to a coffee tasting to select the best brand. Another is to hold a coffee morning with supporters drinking from a huge coffee cup. It is the extra dimension that makes the event newsworthy, and the visual aspect will attract the photographers.

A development of this is to organise a stunt of some sort. This need not depend on a well-known person, but can use the stunt's uniqueness to attract attention, and its visual excitement to attract TV or radio coverage. A stunt built around your coffee morning campaign might have a group of air cadets having a coffee morning in the back of a airforce transport plane in flight, or someone leaping off a bridge (with the usual strong elastic attached!) sipping their coffee as they go as if nothing were happening.

The challenge with these sort of activities is not just having to set them up, but also selecting an activity that is relevant to your work so that any publicity can be linked to it to good effect. Needless to say, dangerous stunts should not be encouraged. There is the additional risk that if anything goes wrong your organisation will receive the blame, whether it was your fault or not.

Managing public relations

Ideally, the control of your public relations should be integrated with the fundraising work. Some organisations see the two roles as being quite separate – with the result that the PR person does not maximise the fundraising potential of the organisation, nor does the fundraiser maximise the PR potential. If there is someone who has a specific PR role, they should be asked to produce plans to show how they can best support the fundraising needs, as well as meet the PR objectives of the organisation.

In small organisations, PR will not be a separate function, and will probably be carried out by a senior member of staff or even a committee member. This is as it should be, but everyone should be encouraged to give PR the importance it deserves, recognising the effectiveness of good PR in generating extra funds for the organisation.

One option is to appoint a PR agency to handle your public relations. You may find some which work mainly with the non-profit sector, or you may find a commercial agency interested in your cause and willing to take you on as a client at a reduced fee or even for free. Any agency you use needs to be briefed well, if they are to present your work as you would wish them to. You can monitor the results of your PR through the use of a press cutting agency. This will show you whether you are getting your money's worth.

However you handle PR, there should be proper co-ordination. Links with the press should be handled only by designated people, and preferably be channelled through one individual. The risks of any well-wisher discussing confidential issues, getting information wrong or just appearing ill-informed are just too great to allow.

Appendices

Appendix 1 – Using computers

The uses of computers can be as diverse as their types. The most important uses for fundraising purposes are:

- databases for appeals and big gift fundraising
- word processing
- spread sheets for figure work and for general use
- desktop publishing (DTP).

Databases

The main purpose of having a database is to conduct appeals more effectively. In its most simple form, the database holds a list of donors or supporters, with information on their past giving, trading purchases, standing orders and covenants, personal information, their address and telephone number, and so on. This information will be used at different times for differing reasons. Your database should be able to do the following things:

- add names
- amend donor information
- add new types of information
- delete donors when they have lost interest
- provide fast access to any donor.

All of this is necessary just to keep a list of names up to date. To be truly useful the database needs to do a number of other things as well:

- select particular combinations of donors
- output information in various formats, for example as address labels
- produce letters of thanks and receipts
- print out donation statistics
- print an analysis of response rates
- print out analyses of donor characteristics
- print out a tracking analysis or donor history.

Only in the last five years has it been realistic to consider a sophisticated database on a PC. This is now possible and there are a number of specialist software packages for fundraising work now available.

For big gift fundraising programmes, a database is essential. While the basic usage is the same, you are able to make links between the many people who have given you support, who have expressed interest, and those who you want to attract. Your supporters may be members or trustees of an organisation like Rotary or a charitable trust. If you can discover any such links, this can help you make contact at the right level. The ability to record background detail on your supporters can be helpful when you make approaches to them. Your computer system should be able to help you by regurgitating background information, personal contacts or anecdotes about the people you are approaching at the touch of a button.

If you need some sort of database, there are several different options you might want to consider. These are:

- buying a package off the shelf
- employing a computer whiz to write a system for you
- designing a simple system linking, for example, Word and Excel.

Word processing

Word processing packages are a great boon to an efficient fundraising office. They can be used to produce a formal letter, and also vary and personalise a standard form of wording for different recipients.

To make a word processor work well for you, you need to develop good keyboard skills and have a good printer. The software package can come in many forms. The top word processing packages are WordPerfect, and Microsoft Word. However, there are a wide range of other programmes, some at a considerably lower cost all of which are perfectly satisfactory.

As time goes on and word-processors get more sophisticated, each is able to read data from the others. This means that there is less pressure to have the same sort as every one else has.

You should do three things before purchasing a software package. Try it out for yourself, check that it has got all the facilities you need and see that there is someone to give you support when you need it. Facilities you might need are:

- mail merging for form letters
- the ability to take and send files to other machines
- on-screen help when needed
- spell checks
- the ability to move large blocks of text around
- windows to see several bits of text simultaneously
- replacing and searching text.

Types of printers available include inkjet and laser. Cheap printers cost around £200 and cheap laser printers around £600. The inkjet (also known as bubblejet) printers are slow, but produce crisp characters.

Laser printers can be very quick and quiet and the quality is excellent but they are more expensive to buy. Most come equipped with a standard set of typefaces. If you need special fonts, then the cost will be more.

Spreadsheets

Spreadsheets are an electronic means of manipulating figures. They will be useful for a variety of jobs including:

- budgets
- appeal results
- 'what if' calculations
- inflation adjustments
- graphs
- charts.

The main functions that you may want to specify when buying spreadsheet software are:

- graphical functions for drawing charts and graphs
- database functions to help make large lists
- whether it can talk to other computers.

Excel is the name of the ubiquitous Microsoft spreadsheet which is very powerful. Its main opposition comes from Lotus 1-2-3.

Communications

Computers can be useful as communication tools in several ways. These are:

- networking
- using the computer as a fax machine
- using your computer for e-mail
- using your computer to access the Internet.

Networking is the way in which computers in the same office talk to each other. Networking your computers can be very costly and so care needs to be taken to ensure that you are getting networked for good reasons. If it is important that you are able to send each other messages within the office, then it could be for you. If you need to share data or files but cannot keep several copies, then it can be useful. You are likely to need a specialist to help you get set up as well as new hardware and software.

You may well decide that you want to have a fax machine as a part of your office. One way of doing this is to install fax software. This will either connect with an internal modem (a small device that turns analogue signals into digital and vice versa) or an external modem box. This, when connected to the telephone line, can act just like a normal fax machine. It will not be cheaper to do unless the modem is already in your computer.

While you can send what is effectively digital paper down the fax line, e-mail allows you to send the data so that it can be much more easily manipulated. For example, if you are working with someone at the other end of the country on a fundraising strategy paper and you want to let them do the next draft, then e-mail could be the thing to have. By sending them a copy of the paper, it stays in their post box until they are ready to access it. When they are, they can use a file that can be worked on by your word processor.

To sign up to e-mail, you will need to be linked to one of the major providers who operate this system. Academics get it through JANET. Most other people get it through Internet services such as CompuServe.

The Internet itself is covered more fully elsewhere in this book (see section 4.16).

Desktop publishing (DTP)

Another benefit of the computer is its ability to design and print to a very high quality. To be effective, you will need a mouse attached to your computer, a proprietary DTP programme, and a laser printer. The programme will enable you to use headlines, text and simple designs in an attractive form suitable for publishing. If printed out on a laser printer the quality of the finished artwork is surprisingly good.

DTP is useful for producing newsletters, leaflets, posters and other display material. Using a laser printer you can provide good quality artwork to send to the printer or run off on the photocopier. You can add photographs or small line drawings to the artwork subsequently. There are a range of proprietary DTP programmes. Before buying, test them out on a computer similar to your own.

Quite sophisticated designs can be produced from the main word processing packages. Before investing the time and money in your own DTP package you should ensure that you cannot do the work much more simply through your existing software.

Implications

However enthusiastic you may be, you will have to share that enthusiasm with everybody else in the office too. Your staff and volunteers will need to be properly trained to use your equipment. Security is the other major issue to take note of. You will need to undertake a series of procedures to ensure that your information remains safe and secure. These will include everything from resisting balancing coffee mugs on the machine, to regularly backing up all your files. Finally you must make sure that the machinery is physically secure. Small modern computers are very attractive to thieves.

Buying computers

There are several ways of buying computers. PCs are now commodity products which can be bought off the shelf. So if you know what you want, it will certainly be cheaper to order a PC in this way.

If you do not have that confidence, you can go to a small local supplier and specify your requirements. This way, you will have a name and a phone number to ring if it breaks down. The value of this is in the training and back-up support they should be able to supply.

If you are looking for something altogether more sophisticated or custom-built, you will need to go a different route. This will involve getting a full systems specification, and then putting it out to tender. You will then have the surprisingly difficult task of choosing who to get to do the work and of paying the very substantial bill for it.

Appendix 2 – Targeting and profiling

For those large charities undertaking fundraising campaigns through the mail, the question of how to find new supporters and where to focus your efforts can be assisted by targeting. For smaller organisations, the principle of targeting can be useful in many fundraising methods.

The development of large databases has brought a whole range of new tools to the aid of fundraising. These started with the advent of geographic analyses such as ACORN, which set out as a classification of residential neighbourhoods. This was later supplemented by financial systems that focused on the wealth of people and most recently have developed into what is called lifestyle information.

Targeting enables you to:
- identify where to carry out house to house campaigns
- decide where to hold street collections
- decide which existing donors to mail
- identify where to find new supporters

The general approach is to use the information that you already have about who supports you to extrapolate this to other fundraising that you wish to do. The idea can be used across quite disparate types of fundraising with more or less accuracy. To be sure that the way you are using your data will accurately pinpoint new possibilities you should:
- ensure that the basic information you are depending on is reliable
- ensure that the fundraising activity is not too far removed from the fundraising which generated your data
- check that responses to the new campaign reflect the original data

Three steps to targeting.

- Carry out a survey of your list of existing supporters
- Draw up a profile of who they are, where they live, what they read, and so on
- Match this profile to the targeting of any new fundraising.

Geographic systems

The first system of interest to mailers was the ACORN system which works from the electoral register. The system maps information about the type of housing in which people are living onto the information already contained on the register. Comparing housing type with incidence of your existing donors will suggest where you should be prospecting in future. This is a useful system for house to house collections and mailing work. However it works only at the postcode level and assumes that everyone in the same postcode behaves the same. Also, the classification is based on census data and thus relates heavily to the number of rooms in a house and similar information and can also become quickly out of date. Pinpoint is a development of this system using more up-to-date methods which brings in demographic data.

These systems are useful for targeting volunteer based fundraising such as house to house. The principle is that if you know who has given to you in the past, you can make some informed judgements on where they might live. This then may dictate where you knock on doors and where you don't. Obviously there are other considerations such as whether parts of the town or country are safe for collectors, whether drives are too long and so on. One useful indicator that you can find out from existing supporters is what newspapers they read. This can then be checked with local newsagents. Once you have got a body of practical experience you can target your collections more accurately on where collectors are getting a good reception.

Financial and Lifestyle systems

The other targeting system is that built around shareholders of British companies and large scale surveys of consumers. Since the onset of privatisation, the shareholder lists of the large privatised companies are of a size and contain the type of person of particular interest to the direct mail fundraiser. A number of products map the wealth and social preference of the names on these share owner lists in the same ways as for the electoral register. The current names include MOSAIC and Super Profiles. Lifestyle systems have been built up from large consumer surveys which offer all sorts of coupons as incentives to people to complete the forms. They gather data on buying and reading and lifestyle habits all of which helps build a picture of a person. These lists are most useful if you have a mirror image of the donor list; this requires that you have answers to the same questions that they have data on. This can again be done by surveying your list or, if it held on computer, an analysis can be run to do the work for you. This works in a different way: although you will not have details of peoples shareholdings, their newspaper readership and so on, many of the larger systems hold national databases with the names of all adults. They can then check your donors against their list and thus supply the additional data needed to provide a profile.

Donor Targeting

These techniques can also be useful in determining who you should be appealing to from your own list of supporters. Even quite small organisations have lists of supporters that have been built up over a period of years. These lists are very valuable if you contact these people periodically to ask them to give again. However, even the most successful appeals may not get a response of more than 10% of those you write to. That may be very profitable for you, but it still involves the wastage of the 90% who fail to respond. Many of these may not even bother to open the letter: if only you knew which they were, then you could save the cost.

The RFV approach provides a tool to do this. It is not easy to apply without the help of a computer and some expert advice, but the concept is simple and can be applied at various levels of sophistication. The idea is that the three main determinants of responsiveness are:

- recency of the last gift
- frequency of response over a period
- value of the last gift.

The simple method of using this is to review responses to your last appeal against each dimension. For example, you could look at the response to an appeal at different levels of last donation or date of last gift. With a table of response rates you should quickly be able to identify the groups of supporters it is not worth writing to.

More sophisticated approaches which require computer analysis involve looking at previous results and determining a score which indicates the probability of getting a certain response from a given supporter.

Targeting for Legacies

If you are fundraising for a small organisation which does not have many years of operation then you can target for legacies using the known data nationally. For example, it is known that most legators are female; many of the largest legacies are received from spinsters; and that people are more receptive to the notion of giving legacies as they get older. Thus if you have decided to have a push on legacies, you should be targeting these people within your support group.

For organisations with some history of receiving legacies, you should build up your own profile of who has made legacies, where they live, and what they are like then target more like them. Frustratingly, legators appear to be predominantly non-donors within their recent lifetime, which means that you may have little further information about them. It is still worth talking to donors and supporters about legacies.

Appendix 3 – Tax-effective giving

You can increase the value of a donation by over 30% if it is given tax-effectively, provided that:

- the donor pays UK income tax
- the recipient is a charity, and recognised as such by the Charity Commission or the Inland Revenue.

The rules for tax-effective giving are extremely complicated – and you must always remember that tax is not normally the primary reason why people give to charity; they give because they want to support the cause. Nonetheless, getting a donation paid tax effectively can provide an additional incentive for people to give.

There are three main ways in which an individual in the UK can give to charity tax-effectively during their lifetime:

- by making a regular payment for at least four years under a Deed of Covenant;
- by donating a larger gift – of at least £250 – given under the Gift Aid scheme;
- as a deduction from wages or salary under an approved Payroll Giving Scheme.

Legacies and bequests to charities made on death also attract Inheritance Tax relief.

As a fundraiser, you will need to understand the tax rules, so that you can present the information to donors and answer any questions. If you are working for a smaller organisation, you may also need to prepare all the pre-printed Deeds and forms you will need, and even handle the administration of tax relief.

Deeds of Covenant

A Deed of Covenant is a binding legal agreement by a donor to make regular payments to charity out of taxed income. Tax relief is obtainable provided that:

- the Deed is drawn up and executed as a valid legal document;
- the Deed is entered into on or before the date of the first payment;
- the donor contracts to continue to make payments for at least four years;
- the donor cannot unilaterally revoke the arrangement (during the first four years);
- the donor should not receive any 'appreciable benefit' in return for the donation;
- the donor signs a 'Certificate of Deduction of Tax', confirming that tax has been paid on the amount given to the charity.

Let us consider each of these in turn.

1. A valid legal document
A Deed of Covenant must be drawn up and executed in the following way to be legally binding:
- the donor must be aged 18 years or over
- the signature of the donor must be witnessed (the rules for Scotland are slightly different, where no witness is required, but a special form of wording is used whereby the donor states that the Deed has been drawn up as if it were in his or her own handwriting)
- the Deed must state that it is a 'Deed'. This is usually done by heading the document Deed of Covenant
- the Deed must be 'delivered'. This means that it must be signed under the words "signed and delivered by". The term 'delivered' is an old English term which confirms that the donor intends to be bound by the undertaking.

Most charities will have pre-printed covenant forms, but you should check that the wording is in the required form. If it isn't, then you can find that your tax claims will be disallowed. The Inland Revenue treat this seriously, as they are only empowered to grant tax relief if relief is due under the law. No tax relief can be granted under an invalid Deed, however trivial the discrepancy.

2. The Deed is entered into on or before the date of the first payment
This is a legal requirement. The Deed of Covenant cannot take effect retrospectively. You cannot receive a payment, bank the money, send the donor a Deed for signature and claim tax relief. If you receive a donation and would like the donor to consider making it a first payment under a Deed of Covenant, then you should hold the money whilst sending the donor a Deed to sign; and only when you have received back the Deed, properly signed and witnessed, should you pay the money into your bank account. Alternatively, you can pay the money

into your account immediately, and then write to the donor proposing that they continue to give for a further four years, and the next payment will be the first under a Deed of Covenant which you will encourage the donor to enter into.

You should ensure that there is a procedure for dealing with any donation, of say between £25 and £249, that comes into the office. The money should be held in a safe place, the donor written to, and a period of say three weeks allowed for the donor to reply. If there is no response, you could try telephoning. Donations of £250 or more qualify for Gift Aid relief, and can be banked immediately, with tax reclaimed via the Gift Aid procedure; you can then write to the donor suggesting continuing support by Deed of Covenant. For very small donations tax recovery will not be worthwhile. The lower limit will depend on circumstances, for example whether you use a volunteer or paid staff to handle the administration, and might be between £10 and £25.

3. The Deed of Covenant runs for at least four years

The wording of the Deed should require that payments be made annually for at least four years. Each annual payment may be made in several instalments (quarterly, monthly or even weekly). It is good practice today to use a form of wording that enables the donor to continue to make payments beyond an initial four years until they decide to terminate the arrangement. This means that if payments continue, no new Deed has to be signed and tax relief can continue to be reclaimed. The sample wording for the Deed given here allows for this.

The payments are best made by some sort of Standing Order where the donor instructs the bank to make the promised payments on their due dates. The main mechanisms for this are Banker's Order and Direct Debit. Small charities may find it difficult to get a Direct Debit facility, but the Charities Aid Foundation offers this as part of their service.

4. The donor cannot revoke the Deed unilaterally

A Deed of Covenant which can be unilaterally revoked by the donor during its first four years is not eligible for tax relief. There should be the intention by both parties at the outset when the Deed is signed that payments be made according to the terms set out in the Deed. If the donor gets into financial difficulties and is unable to continue making payments, then the charity should try to negotiate that the payments be rescheduled over a longer period. If this is not feasible, then in theory the charity could sue for any amounts due, but in most circumstances probably would not want to do so in practice (both because of the cost and of the bad publicity that this might bring).

5. The donor should not receive any appreciable benefit

A Deed of Covenant payment cannot be made to a purchase of a service. The rules are that there should be no appreciable benefit to the donor. This usually means that:

- a reasonable acknowledgement can be made;
- the donor can receive an annual report, a supporters newsletter and a right to vote at an Annual General Meeting of the charity.

For ordinary small membership subscriptions, there are more specific benefit rules agreed by the Inland Revenue.

6. The donor signs a Certificate of Deduction of Tax

Before tax relief can be claimed, the donor has to sign a certificate (known as a Form R185) stating that the amount of the payment has been made net of income tax, and that the donor will account for the tax so deducted. Most donors pay income tax at the basic rate or above on their income or on bank (or building society) interest or share dividends they receive, and this document simply confirms that the covenant payment has been made out of taxed income.

If a donor signing this Certificate does not pay income tax at least at the basic rate (currently 23%), then he or she will be liable to pay the amount of tax due in respect of the covenant payment. This is the same tax that the charity will then reclaim. The form requires that the donor supplies their Inland Revenue reference number.

Donors who are not UK taxpayers should not be encouraged to give support to a charity through a Deed of Covenant. If they have signed a Deed of Covenant, then it should be pointed out to them that they should not sign the R185; in such circumstances, tax will not be reclaimed and the support will be equivalent to a regular donation paid by a Standing Order.

Donors who pay tax at the lower rate (currently 20%) will probably not encounter any difficulty if they sign a form R185, as the difference between the tax they have paid (at the lower rate) and the tax that the charity then reclaims (at the basic rate) is too small for the Inland Revenue to bother with.

Reclaiming tax

If all these conditions are met, then the charity is able to reclaim the Income Tax at the basic rate on the amount received by the donor. The sum received is a net sum which is received out of the donor's taxable income. The charity is able to reclaim Income Tax calculated at the basic rate from the Inland Revenue (23% in 1997-98).

Where a donor is a higher rate taxpayer (the top rate of tax is currently 40%), he or she will be entitled to reclaim the difference between the basic rate and the higher rate, thereby reducing their tax bill. The benefit of basic rate tax is received by the charity; the benefit of the difference between basic and higher rates is obtained by the donor. The thinking behind this is that tax affairs are confidential, and any system for reclaiming tax which indicated the tax status of the donor would be a breach of confidence.

Tax benefits of covenant giving

The tax benefit on covenant giving depends on the prevailing rates of tax. These have been falling progressively since 1980, and the two main political parties are both committed to further reductions when the time is right. The Labour Party are proposing a 10% level for the lower rate, and the Conservative Party would like to see a 20% basic rate. It is the basic rate not the lower rate that counts for tax purposes, and the amount of tax reclaimable is calculated as follows.

At a 23% basic rate of tax, for every £77 of donation received, the charity can reclaim £23 in income tax. For a £10 donation, the amount of tax reclaimable calculated on this basis is £2.99. The value of the donation is increased by 29.9% as a result of being made by Deed of Covenant. The impact of changing tax rates is shown in the table below.

Basic rate	Tax benefit
25%	+33.3%
24%	+31.6%
23%	+29.9%
22%	+28.2%
21%	+26.6%
20%	+25.0%

The benefit of higher rate relief is as follows. A donation of £76 would be made out of a gross sum of £100 – as the basic rate tax deducted would be £24. With a top rate of tax, the total tax paid by a donor on £100 of gross income is £40, leaving £16 of tax relief for the donor. This amounts to 21% of the amount actually paid by the donor. So for a £10 covenant payment, the amount of higher rate relief benefiting the donor is £2.10. The impact of changing tax rates is shown in the table below.

Basic rate	Higher rate tax benefit at 40%	Higher rate tax benefit at 50%	Higher rate tax benefit at 60%
25%	+20.0%	+33.3%	+46.7%
24%	+21.0%	+34.2%	+47.4%
23%	+22.1%	+35.1%	+48.1%
22%	+23.1%	+35.9%	+48.7%
21%	+24.0%	+36.7%	+49.4%
20%	+25.0%	+37.5%	+50.0%

Membership subscriptions paid under Deed of Covenant

The annual amount payable under a covenant must be a predetermined sum. This usually means that the same amount is paid each year for the duration of the covenant. However, it is possible to fix the amount as being 'the annual membership subscription at the time the payment is due'. With this form of wording, the donor will be committed to pay the amount of the membership subscription (and this payment could be made by Direct Debit, where the amount due is simply debited from the donor's bank account on the donor's authority).

As with any donation, the value of a membership subscription paid by covenant is increased by over 30%. Many charities try to provide some inducement to people to join. The same benefit rules apply regarding any benefit offered by the charity in return for membership. The Inland Revenue require that for most ordinary membership subscriptions, the benefits offered in return for the membership should not exceed 25% of the annual membership subscription. In calculating the value of the benefit, any right to visit a historic property or a wildlife reserve is not counted as a benefit. This was introduced as a concession to major charities (including the National Trust) when the Inland Revenue tightened up its rules on covenant benefits.

Customs and Excise will want to charge VAT on the amount of the membership subscription if any appreciable benefit is offered. The VAT rules operate independently of the Inland Revenue rules, although in recent years there has been a greater degree of coordination between these two taxation authorities.

A life membership subscription cannot be paid under a Deed of Covenant, as covenant payments have to be made out of income, and this would be deemed a 'capital' sum.

Frequency of payments

Payments under a Deed of Covenant must be made annually, and the annual payment can be made in several instalments. The advantage of having a more frequent payment is that the donor is likely to give more. A major factor influencing a donor is the 'headline amount' of the gift. A donor is more likely to agree to give £5 each month for four years than £60 per annum for the same period.

ActionAid in their sponsorship scheme advertise it by asking whether a child needs 50p more than the donor. The donor is then invited to give 50p per day. This adds up to £180 per year, which is requested in monthly instalments of £15. With tax relief, the annual amount asked for is nearly £240.

Probably the most effective way of increasing the amount of income a charity obtains from its base of regular supporters is to invite people to take up monthly covenants. The administration is slightly more complicated, but the increased yield makes this more than worth while.

Administration of Deeds of Covenant

To obtain tax relief, the charity must administer the process in the required way and be prepared to have the administration audited by an Inland Revenue inspector from time to time. Proper administration means that:

- a covenant register must be kept, logging all payments and creating an audit trail from the donor to the charity's bank account;
- all correspondence should be kept, including the signed Deeds;
- claims should be made in the appropriate way. This means using forms required by the Inland Revenue, copies of which can be obtained from Claims Branch or generated through one of the software packages for covenant administration that are available. The Inland Revenue produce a guidance pack on covenant administration, which is beyond the scope of this book.

There is always going to be a cost of administering Deeds of Covenant and reclaiming tax. This means that you should set a lower limit for the size of covenant you ask for and are prepared to administer. This lower limit will vary according to your costs. If you have an efficient volunteer to do the administration, you might accept covenants of as little as £10.

The Charities Aid Foundation operates a covenant administration service for donors, where they arrange for payments to be made by direct debit, the collection of the money, obtaining tax relief, and all reporting and documentation. There is a charge for this service, and it is not particularly suitable for charities with just a few covenants. Details from the Charities Aid Foundation, Kings Hill, West Malling, Kent ME19 4TA.

Gift Aid and single donations

1. Single payments of £250 or more

The Gift Aid scheme was introduced in 1990 to enable single gifts to be made tax-effectively. There is specific legislation which defines what payments can qualify. The rules are that:

- any qualifying payment must be £250 or more, and be made to a UK charity. This lower limit for Gift Aid may be varied from time to time. It was originally set at £600 when the legislation was introduced, and has been lowered twice since then to its present level. A payment of £250 made in two instalments of £125 each would not qualify;
- the payment must be made by a single taxpayer from their own money. For example, you cannot pay all the proceeds from a sponsored event into an individual's bank account and get that person to pay the same

amount in under Gift Aid – the money hasn't really come from them. Neither can two people (say husband and wife) pay £125 each;

- the donor can receive only minimal benefit in return. This is set at 2.5% of the payment or £250 in total on all Gift Aid payments made by the donor to the charity in any tax year, whichever is the lower amount;
- the payment must not be linked to the transfer of an asset. This is to prevent tax abuse on gifts made in kind.

The administration of the tax reliefs is similar to that for covenant giving, except that:

- a special form must be used, which is obtainable from the Inland Revenue Claims Branch. Different versions are used for individuals and companies;
- nothing need be done until after the gift is made. A donor makes a payment. The charity sends a Gift Aid form for signature. Tax relief is then reclaimed – you have up to six years to do this. With covenant giving, a valid Deed of Covenant covering the donation must exist at the time the money is paid;
- a separate form must be provided for each qualifying payment.

2. Single payments of less than £250

Single payments of less than £250 (the current minimum for Gift Aid) do not qualify for Gift Aid tax relief. However, there is a mechanism for obtaining tax relief on such payments, which is known as the 'deposit covenant' or 'loan covenant'. This works in exactly the same way as a four-year covenant, except that all four instalments due under the Deed of Covenant are paid over immediately. The following is then required:

- the donor must sign separately a Deed of Covenant and a Letter of Loan. Both documents need to be witnessed. These forms can be pre-printed, for the amount to be filled in and for dating and signature by the donor;
- in the first year, the amount of the first annual instalment is treated as income, and the remainder of the sum paid is held in a special 'loan account'. Tax relief in the first year is obtainable only on the amount of the first annual instalment;
- each year the annual payment due is transferred from the loan account to general funds. This requires a book entry. The amount transferred qualifies for tax relief, which is reclaimed in the normal way.

Because of administrative costs it will seldom be worth encouraging such arrangements for payments of below £50 or £100; as the minimum qualifying payment for Gift Aid continues to be reduced, so the deposit covenant will begin to become obsolete (until Gift Aid, it was the only way of obtaining tax relief on a single payment).

Payroll giving

The third mechanism for obtaining tax relief on money donated to charity is by using the Payroll Giving Scheme. This requires:

- an employer (public as well as private sector) to operate a payroll giving scheme. If your employer does not do so, then there is no access to this form of giving;
- the donor to agree to have regular deductions made each payday from their pay. These are passed in the first instance to the payroll giving agency, and then distributed to any charity or charities selected by the donor. A small deduction is made to cover administrative costs.

The charity receives a sum regularly in its bank account. The total paid by the donor is deducted from the donor's taxable income when calculating tax liability. It is the donor who receives the tax relief under this scheme, and not the charity. The cost of £100 given this way each year to a donor at various possible tax rates is as follows:

Tax rate	Cost of £100 donation
20%	£80
21%	£79
22%	£78
23%	£77
24%	£76
25%	£75
40%	£60
50%	£50
60%	£40

Assuming a 5% deduction for administration, which is the maximum permitted, the benefiting charities will get £95.

The Payroll Giving Agency which receives the donation from the employer and passes it on to charity has to be approved by the Inland Revenue. There are two main agencies that operate payroll giving schemes on a national basis:

- Give As You Earn: operated by the Charities Aid Foundation, Kings Hill, West Malling, Kent ME19 4TA.
- Work Aid: operated by the Charities Trust, which is associated with the Littlewood's Group, PO Box 15, Kershaw Avenue, Crosby, Liverpool L23 0UU.

Cross-border giving

There are increasing opportunities for obtaining support from overseas or international donors, but in general tax relief in any country is only available on donations made to charities in that country. There are some exceptions – for example there is a tax treaty between the UK and Eire allowing gifts made from one country to another to be deductible. These exceptions are few and far between, and have been surveyed in the information service *The Tax Treatment of Cross Border Donations* published by the International Bureau for Fiscal Documentation, PO Box 20237, 1000 HE Amsterdam, the Netherlands.

However, in most countries it is possible to give to a charitable trust in your own country and then remit the donation overseas to an organisation which falls within the definition of a charity in your own country. There are two possibilities here.

- To establish a charity in the overseas country where you are fundraising to receive the money and remit it to your organisation. For example, the Royal Academy and the Royal Opera House have both established US charities for their US fundraising. Individuals and foundations can give tax-effectively to these charities, which then process the donations and remit them to the UK. Equally, Mother Theresa's Sisters of Charity has established support groups across the world. Many of these are independent charities, which again can receive money tax-effectively and remit it to Calcutta.

- To use the services of the Charities Aid Foundation (CAF). CAF is in the process of establishing foundations in other countries, so that money can be paid to a CAF foundation in one country and distributed by a CAF foundation in another country. There are CAF foundations in the USA and Russia, and CAF hopes to set up arrangements in South Africa and India in the near future, and in Germany, France and Belgium CAF has made arrangements with equivalent organisations in those countries.

VAT and giving

Charitable donations fall outside the scope of VAT, but where the money is a payment for a service, then this falls within the VAT net. The charity would have to include VAT in the amount of the donation and pay this over to Customs and Excise (this only applies if the charity is registered for VAT or is obliged to register because this income brings it over the threshold for VAT registration).

The key question is when is a donation a donation, and when is it a payment for a service. Reasonable acknowledgement of the donation, membership which confers the right to vote at an AGM and to receive an annual report are not considered benefits. Any benefit given by the charity of its own free will and which has not been promised to the donor when the donation was made is also acceptable. Customs and Excise, which administers VAT, has become more flexible on the use of company logos, where they can now be included in an appropriate size as part of a reasonable acknowledgement.

The VAT situation affects four types of giving.

1. Sponsorship and commercial promotions, where the charity is offering benefits over and beyond what is permitted. This will only affect charities whose taxable income is sufficient to bring them within the VAT net. Most sponsors are themselves registered for VAT, and it is beneficial to both parties that sponsorship payment be invoiced to the sponsor for the agreed sponsorship sum plus VAT.

2. Dinners, balls and other entertainment events organised for fundraising purposes. There is a special concession for one-off fundraising events, where the ticket price will not be subject to VAT but for fundraising events which fall outside this concession, there will be a liability for VAT on ticket sales (if the charity has sufficient taxable income to bring it over the VAT registration threshold). Any VAT liability can be reduced by dividing the ticket price into two elements: an admission price to the event, which is subject to VAT, and an optional donation, which is not. Customs and Excise have guidance for this: the admission cost must be a reasonable sum in relation to the nature of the event, and the donation element must be truly optional (even if everybody in fact ends up paying it) and a suggested form of wording is given in their guidance.

3. Advertising, where Customs and Excise offer two concessions in treating advertising revenue as donation income: either if the advertising is in connection with a one-off fundraising event, which is specially relieved from any tax liability (see above), or, for other types of advertising, where the following four conditions are met:
- the publication is a brochure published by a charity and has the characteristics of fundraising exercise;
- the payment for the advertisement is excessive by normal commercial standards in relation to the space taken and the circulation of the publication;
- the motivation of the advertiser is to support the charity;
- the brochure contains a significant proportion of advertising paid for by private individuals.

4. Membership subscriptions. Many charities try to provide a range of benefits to tempt people to take out membership, and thereby become regular committed supporters. Customs and Excise regard any benefit above and beyond an acknowledgement and membership which confers a right to vote at an Annual General Meeting as a benefit to the donor, and will ask for an apportionment of the subscription into a chargeable element (representing that proportion of the subscription which is in return for a benefit), a zero-rated element (if publications are supplied), and a donation element. Any charity designing a membership scheme should seek advice from Customs and Excise as to whether the subscription income will be taxable and what proportion of the subscription will be chargeable to VAT before launching the scheme; but remember, this only applies to charities that are VAT registered or if the subscription income would bring it over the registration threshold.

Note that the Inland Revenue takes a different position on whether a subscription is a donation or a payment for a service when it comes to allowing membership subscriptions to be paid by Deed of Covenant. For Inland Revenue purposes, the benefit on "ordinary small subscriptions to a charity" should not exceed 25% of the amount of the subscription, if the subscription income is to be considered a donation for tax purposes. Note that this is calculated on the benefit offered, and not the benefit actually received by an individual member which might be much less.

The best advice is to understand the tax position of donated income and to take professional advice or seek the advice of the taxation authorities when in doubt. This is far better than ignoring the tax position and having to deal with the consequences later (which could include a penalty as well as having to pay the arrears of tax).

Sample Deeds
1. A four-year plus covenant
2. A subscription covenant
3. A gross company covenant
(see overleaf)

Suggested Net Deed of Covenant for use by individuals

DEED OF COVENANT

To.. *Name of charity*

I promise to pay you each year during my lifetime the sum of

£....................after deduction of tax at the basic rate

Insert amount you wish to give

for a minimum period of four years from the date hereunder or until such later time as I give notice in writing

Signed and delivered ....

Date ....

Sign and date the document in front of a witness

Your Name/Address ....

....

Insert your full name and address

Signed in the presence of

Witness's Signature ....

The witness to sign

Witness's Name/Address ....

....

---

1. This version of a Deed of Covenant is valid in England and Wales from 31 July 1990.

2. Northern Ireland charities should use the words 'Signed, sealed and delivered'.

3. Scottish charities should delete witnessing clause and the line starting 'Signed and delivered' which should be replaced with the following:

   t...

   Signature ....

   t Please write here in your own handwriting before signing the words 'Adopted as Holograph'.

4. The date on which the deed of Covenant is signed should be on or before the date on which the first payment is made (see Banker's Order).

5. The donor pays the sum stated on the covenant form. If you pay Income Tax at the basic rate, tax will already have been deducted. If you do not pay Income Tax you should make your donation by Banker's Order, and not make out a Deed of Covenant.

BANKER'S ORDER

To .... *Insert name of donor's bank*

of .... *Insert address of donor's bank*

re my account no....................................... *Insert donor's bank details*

sort code..

Please pay to... *Insert name of charity's bank*

of.. *Insert address of charity's bank*

for the account of..................................... *Insert name and bank details of charity*

(a/c no...................... sort code.....................)

the sum of £.................... (...................pounds) *Insert sum to be paid in figures and words*

and the same sum on the same day each year for a period of four years starting today

Signed... *Donor signs here*

Date... *Insert day/month/year*

NOTES

1. The sum to be paid should be the same as that stated in the Deed of Covenant.
2. The date that the first payment is to be made should be on or after the date of signature of the Deed of Covenant.
3. The Banker's Order should be returned to the charity with the Deed of Covenant, and NOT sent to the charity's bank.

Suggested form of wording for covenanted subscriptions

DEED OF COVENANT

I promise to pay .... *Name of charity*

hereby known as 'the Charity', for four years or during my lifetime, whichever period shall be the shorter, such a sum as after deduction of Income Tax at the basic rate is equivalent to the annual membership subscription of the charity as at the date on which the payment falls due. The first such payment to be made today, and subsequent payments to be made on the same day in each year thereafter.

Signed and delivered.. *Signed and dated in front of witness*

Your Name/Address.. *Insert your full name and address*

....

....

Signed in the presence of

Witness's Signature.. *The witness to sign here*

Witness's Name/Address..

....

....

NOTES

1. This form of wording is valid in England and Wales from 31 July 1990. Scottish and Northern Ireland charities should adapt the signing and witnessing clauses as for the model individual covenant.
2. Any scheme has to be acceptable to the Inland Revenue. This includes the terms and benefits of membership and how the scheme is promoted. There are many 'grey areas' and there is not necessarily any guarantee that a particular scheme as used by one charity will be given the green light when used by another charity. Our best advice is that a charity wishing to prepare a covenanted membership scheme should discuss its proposed scheme with the Inland Revenue as to its acceptability before the scheme is launched.
3. Payment is best made by Direct Debit Mandate, as this allows the annual subscription rate to be raised without demanding the payment instrument.

BANKER'S ORDER

DIRECT DEBIT MANDATE

I/we authorise you, until further notice in writing, to charge to my/our account with you unspecified amounts which the

(insert name of charity) ....

may debit thereto by Direct Debit in respect of my/our annual subscription to them.

Signed.. Date....................................

Name and Number of
account to be debited..

The Charity will normally undertake with the member to repay any payments debited to the member's account in error or where there is a dispute. Members should also be given advance notice in good time of any subscription rate change.

This Mandate will continue indefinitely, and the covenant with the wording as suggested will continue until the member resigns. The charity will need to get an agreement from the bank before it is able to collect subscriptions income by Direct Debit.

Suggested Gross Deed of Covenant for use by companies

DEED OF COVENANT

We.. *Insert company name*

of.. *Insert registered address*

hereinafter called 'the Company' hereby promise
that for four years from the date shown below the
Company will pay

*Name of charity you
wish to support*

....

the sum of £................................less Income Tax at
the basic rate

*Insert the amount you
wish to give each year*

Executed by the Company as a deed by the
signature of

....

being a Director of the   being a Director*/the   *The Deed to be signed by
Company   Secretary* of the Company   two authorised
                               (*delete as appropriate)   signatories who should
                                                            write their names and
                                                            addresses where
                                                            indicated*

of................................... of...................................

....

Signed

....

Date.. *Insert date of execution
of the covenant*

NOTES

1. The date that the first payment is made should be on or after the date of
   execution of this Deed of Covenant.
2. The Company must deduct Income Tax at the basic rate for the time being in
   force from the amount of the annual payment under this Deed of Covenant.
   The net amount after deduction of tax is sent to the Charity, and the Income
   Tax is remitted to the Inland Revenue. Where payment is being made by
   Banker's Order, the Order should instruct the bank to deduct Income Tax at
   the basic rate for the time being in force from the gross amount covenanted
   when making the payment.

BANKER'S ORDER

To...
Insert name of company's bank

of...
Insert address of company's bank

re our a/c no...........................sort code.....................
Insert company bank account details

Please pay to...
Insert name and account number of charity's bank

for the account of..

(a/c no...........................sort code...........................)

the sum of £........................ (...........................pounds)
less income tax at the basic rate
Insert amount of covenant in figures and words

On...199...............
and subsequently on the same day in each of the following three years, making a total of four payments in all.
Insert date of first payment

Signed... Date........................
Signed and dated by authorising officer of the company

On behalf of...
Insert name of company

Important Note: The sum the Bank should pay is the sum stated less Income Tax deducted at the Basic Rate in force at the date the payment is made.

NOTES

1. The sum stated in the Banker's Order should be the same as the sum stated on the Deed of Covenant.
2. The date of the first payment should be on or after the date of signature of the Deed of Covenant.
3. This Banker's Order should be returned with the Deed of Covenant to the charity, and NOT sent to the charity's bank.
4. In the event of the bank refusing to handle an instruction to pay a sum less income tax, you should delete the 'less income tax at the basic rate' and put the net amount due under the covenant. If tax rates change, a replacement Banker's Order with the appropriately revised net sum should be sent to the bank for signature.

   A different form of wording for the covenant and the bankers order should be used for a net company covenant.

Suggested wording for charitable legacies and codicils

A clause for a pecuniary legacy contained within a Will

I give the following charitable legacies absolutely:
(1)   to...................... (name of charity and registration number)
          of...................... (address of charity)
          the sum of £..............................
(2) etc.

In each case for the general purposes of the charity and with the full power to expend capital as income for such purposes and I direct that a receipt of the Honorary Treasurer or other authorised officer for the time being of the charity shall be a good and sufficient discharge to my Executors for the payment to each of the above named legatees.

(Note: Where a gift is made for a specific purpose, then the condition under which the legacy is made should be described in the Will.)

A clause for a bequest in kind contained within a Will

I give the following charitable gifts absolutely:
(1) to...................... (name of charity and registration number)
      of...................... (address of charity)
      .... (a clear description of the item to be bequeathed)
(2) etc.

In each case with the full power to realise such assets and to apply the proceeds for the general purposes of the charity and I direct that a receipt of the Honorary Treasurer or other authorised officer for the time being of the charity shall be a good and sufficient discharge to my Executors for the payment to each of the above named legatees.

(Note: The items to be bequeathed should be described in clear unambiguous terms so that there is absolutely no doubt as to which items are intended as the bequest. If no item can be found to match the description, then the bequest will fail.)

A clause for a residuary bequest contained within a Will

I devise and bequeath all (or a share of) the residue of my estate absolutely to.. (name of charity and registration number) hereinafter called 'The Charity', such sum to be applied for the general purposes of the charity and with the full power to expend capital as income for such purposes and I direct that a receipt of the Honorary Treasurer or other authorised officer for the time being of the charity shall be a good and sufficient discharge to my Executors for the payment to each of the above named legatees.

(Note: There will be no Inheritance Tax payable on the charity's share of the residue and the charity beneficiary should make sure that this benefit is not apportioned equally amongst all the residuary beneficiaries when calculating the amount due to each.)

A Codicil to a Will adding further charitable bequests

I........................ (name of testator)
of...................... (address)
declare this to be a first (or second, etc.) Codicil to my Will dated and made (date of Will). In addition to the legacies given by my said Will I give the following charitable legacies absolutely:
(1) to............................ (name of charity and registration number)
     of............................ (address of charity)
     the sum of £..
(2) etc.

In each case for the general purposes of the charity and with the full power to expend capital as income for such purposes and I direct that a receipt of the Honorary Treasurer or other authorised officer for the time being of the charity shall be a good and sufficient discharge to my Executors for the payment to each of the above named legatees.

In all other respects I confirm my said Will.

In witness whereof I have hereunto set my hand this (date).

Signed by the above-named as a first (or second, etc.) Codicil

to his (or her) Will dated (date):
.... (Testator's signature)

In the presence of us both present together
at the same time who at his (or her) request
and in his (or her) presence and in the presence
of each other have hereunto subscribed
our names as witnesses:

First witness's signature...
Name..
Occupation...
Address...

Second witness's signature...
Name..
Occupation...
Address...

Appendix 4 – The Charities Act and fundraising

The 1992 and 1993 Charities Acts introduced new controls on fundraising. The main points are summarised below.

1. Registered status of the charity

Where a charity has a gross annual income of £10,000 or more there is a requirement to state that the charity is a registered charity on certain official documents, including notices, advertisements and other documents issued by or on behalf of the charity which are intended to persuade the reader to support the charity. In practice it is best to put your registered charity number on all pieces of paper you send out.

2. Returning appeal monies when insufficient funds are raised

Where the charity raises money for a specific project and is not able to raise sufficient to enable the project to proceed, and if the appeal does not specify how the money will be used in this eventuality, then it has to be returned where the donors are identifiable. Money raised through collecting boxes, lotteries, competitions and other similar mechanisms is presumed to come from unidentifiable donors. The Charities Act 1993 – The Charities (Cy-pres Advertisements, Inquiries, and Disclaimer Regulations) Regulations 1993 explains what needs to be done to identify donors and how the money should be returned. A proper wording of the appeal will avoid this problem, and it may be worth taking professional advice on this. There are similar problems with dealing with surplus funds, where a 'Charity Commission scheme' may be required to allow the funds to be used by the charity for alternative purposes. Again, this problem can be avoided by careful wording of the appeal.

3. Use of professional fundraisers
Part 2 of the 1992 Charities Act and The Charitable Institutions (Fundraising) Regulations 1994 cover the use of professional fundraisers. The Act defines a professional fundraiser as being any person who carries out a fundraising business for gain which is wholly or primarily engaged in soliciting or otherwise procuring money or other property for charitable purposes, or any other person who solicits for reward money or other property for charity apart from:

- any charity or connected company
- any officer or employee of the charity or connected company
- any Trustee of the charity
- any public charitable collector (which falls under the regulations for public collections)
- people who solicit funds on TV or radio
- any commercial participator (where there are separate requirements)
- any fundraiser who receives £500 or less by way of remuneration in connection with a particular campaign, or £5 per day or £500 or less per annum where there is no specific fundraising campaign. This excludes volunteers who are receiving some remuneration. It also means that any salaried member of your staff cannot be a professional fundraiser when raising money for your charity.

The requirements are for a written agreement with the professional fundraiser in a prescribed form (the Institute of Charity Fundraising Managers has a model form), a statement to be given to potential donors informing them as to what proportion of their donation will be used to pay the costs of the fundraiser, and requirements for the transfer of funds raised by the professional fundraiser to the charity.

4. Working with commercial participators
A commercial participator is any person who carries on for gain a business which is not a fundraising business, but who in the course of that business engages in any promotional venture in the course of which it is represented that contributions are to be given to or applied for the benefit of a charity.

This covers joint promotions and some sponsorships (in fact any arrangement in which people pay for a commercial product on the understanding that part of the proceeds go to a charity). The requirements are similar to those for professional fundraising: a written agreement in a prescribed form is required, the public must be informed as to how precisely the charity will benefit, and there are requirements for the transfer of funds to the charity.

5. Telephone appeals

Where money is solicited over the telephone, the charity must ensure that the public are clear about which charity the funds are intended for, and what percentage of the funds will be spent on the objects of the charity (this will be less than 100% when the fundraiser is receiving a percentage of the proceeds). The 1992 Act also contains special requirements for providing written statements, and the donor has the right to a refund if this is requested within seven days of receiving the written statement for donations of £50 or more (a cooling off period).

6. Broadcast appeals

Where a donor makes a donation by credit card or debit card of £50 or more, the donor has a right to a refund if this is requested within seven days of the broadcast appeal.

7. Public collections

The 1993 Charities Act (Part 3) makes provision for new Regulations to be made for governing public collections that will replace the existing legislation on Street and House-to-House Collections. These will cover collections and sale of goods by charities and other benevolent institutions. The Regulations have not yet (as of summer 1997) been introduced.

8. Unauthorised collections

Part 2 of the 1992 Charities Act and The Charitable Institutions (Fundraising) Regulations 1994 also enable charities to obtain an injunction to prevent unauthorised fundraising by a commercial participator or professional fundraiser who is not operating under a prescribed written agreement; in such circumstances an injunction can be applied for without giving notice. The charity can also restrain any other person raising funds in the name of the charity where the fundraiser is using methods to which the charity objects, or where the fundraiser is not a fit or proper person to raise money for the charity, or where the charity does not wish to be associated with the particular fundraising venture; in such circumstances notice must be given in writing at least 28 days before seeking an injunction stating that the charity objects to the fundraising being undertaken on its behalf, giving details of their objection, requesting the person to cease forthwith, and advising that in the event of non-compliance an injunction will be sought.

Further information

- The primary source of information are the Acts and the Regulations made under them. The Government has produced a guide entitled 'Charitable Fundraising: Professional and Commercial Involvement', explaining the rules on commercial participation and professional fundraising in detail. These are available from The Stationary Office (TSO, formerly HMSO).

- The Charity Commission offers guidance and has produced a background booklet on 'Charities and Fundraising'. To obtain copies of Charity Commission publications, telephone 01823-345427. The Commission also operates two telephone helplines – telephone 0171-210 4630 for information and advice on control of fundraising and 0171-210 4458 for information and advice on public charitable collections.

- The Institute of Charity Fundraising Managers has produced guidance on the use of professional fundraisers and model forms of agreement for use with commercial participators and professional fundraisers. Contact ICFM, Central Offices, Market Towers, 1 Nine Elms Lane, Vauxhall, London SW8 5NQ.

- The Broadcast Appeals Consortium has issued a Charter and Recommendations for the conduct of broadcast appeals. This is available from Broadcast Support Services, 252 Western Avenue, London W3 6XJ.

Appendix 5 – ICFM Codes of Practice and guidelines

We are reprinting below the guidance given in the Codes of Practice and Guidance Notes for fundraisers that have been drawn up by the Institute of Charity Fundraising Managers that cover some key areas of fundraising where problems or difficulties may be encountered. These cover:
- fundraising in schools

- house-to-house collections
- static collecting boxes
- reciprocal mailings
- outbound telephone support
- telephone recruitment of collectors
- the use of chain letters as a fundraising technique
- standard contract between charities and fundraising consultants.

For the full Codes of Practice and guidance notes contact ICFM, 5th Floor, Market Towers, 1 Nine Elms Lane, London SW8 5NQ.

ICFM Code of Practice for fundraising in schools

1. The ICFM's policy on fundraising in schools is:

a. To offer the child a positive opportunity for involvement in helping others by raising funds.

b. To put trust at the heart of all fundraising with school children. Clear instructions should be given regarding payment of sponsor money. There should be no harassment of children but the child should be on their honour to pay in all money raised.

c. To ensure that the content of talks given is both educational and non-political and at an appropriate level for each age group.

d. To take into account and to accept the Head Teacher's view of the School's charity commitments and to fit in with it.

e. To make contact with children in or near school premises only with the prior knowledge and approval of the Head Teacher or a member of the School's staff designated by the Head Teacher.

2. Safeguards for children

a. Children should be told both verbally and on printed material not to approach strangers for money and that to go knocking from door to door is against the law. Every effort should be made by the Charity to ensure that parents are made aware of the need for children to approach only friends and relations for sponsorship (see footnotes). Children should be encouraged to discuss fully with their parents a list of whom they may approach, and examples of 'safe' sponsors should be identified and given in the course of the fundraising talk.

b. Participation in any fundraising activity should only be via an authorised adult. For children up to the age of 16, it should be for the parents to decide whether or not a child may take part in a fundraising event.

3. Organisation of an event

a. The use of incentives to encourage or reward individual efforts to raise money is seen as a very sensitive issue, and the greatest care needs to be exercised in offering them to children.

Token gifts, such as badges, may be given provided that they are made available to all participating children, and are given for the purpose of prompting the children and potential donors to think about the work of the charity concerned.

As a general principle, only incentives of purely token value should be given to children. Where gifts of some monetary value have been donated, their distribution should be under the tight control of the charity's representative and only after consultation and agreement with the Head Teacher (see 4a).

b. Particular care should taken with under sevens, who should not be encouraged to compete for badges or any other incentives.

c. Potential supporters should be given the option of sponsoring a child or giving a donation – at a level of their choice.

d. Sponsored events should have maximum limited time/units clearly defined on their printed material in order that the sponsor can determine the maximum level of money promised at the time of sponsoring.

e. Fundraising material should be written in clear, simple language. From time to time special material may need to be prepared for those who do not have English as their mother tongue, subject to the Head Teacher's advice.

4. The fundraiser and the school

Field staff should be instructed:

a. To discuss with the Head Teacher the educational content of the talk to be given and the pattern of the event to be undertaken as well as all other additional arrangements. To go step by step through what is involved for the charity's representative, for the staff, for the children, for the parents. All agreed details, including the financial arrangements, should then be confirmed in writing by the charity's representative.

b. To organise fundraising events to a controlled time limit.

c. To make the organisation of the event and collection of money as trouble free as possible for School staff.

i. If cash is collected, the charity's representative should return on the date promised and call again (or make adequate arrangements) for any late monies.

ii. If the School prefers, monies may be paid in by the use of a bank giro system. The charity's representative should then ensure that guidelines are given and extra giro forms left at the school.

iii. All monies received should be acknowledged promptly by the charity and the onus should be on the charity to ensure that the amount acknowledged is correct.

d. An appropriate message of thanks should be given to the Head Teacher or any staff involved, to the children and their families.

5. General

a. Any letters of criticism received should be dealt with as quickly as possible, and monitored at senior management level in the charity.

b. Head Teacher's comments on events undertaken should be monitored on a regular basis.

c. Field staff should be trained, supervised and monitored on a continuing basis in every aspect of their work.

Footnote: For both street collections and house-to-house collections, permits or a certificate of authority are required. In both cases, collectors must be a minimum of 16 years of age.

ICFM Code of Practice for house-to-house collections

The ICFM Policy on House to House Collections is that:
- they offer a positive opportunity for the general public to actively participate in supporting charity within their own community;
- they enable supporters to raise funds for all forms of charity in an ethical and secure manner;
- they provide an important mechanism for information exchange between charities and their donors.

Planning of Collections

Holders of Exemption Orders are in a relatively privileged position with regard to house-to-house collections. It is recognised that this privilege brings responsibilities that should be fulfilled.

All Exemption Order Holders should:
- establish a clear annual programme of collections
- fix dates a year in advance for all collections
- make every attempt to avoid a conflict in collection dates
- inform relevant authorities of collection dates and, as far as possible, the specific areas to be covered by the collection

- confirm all agreed dates in writing to the relevant authorities
- negotiate any proposed changes in dates with relevant authorities at the earliest opportunity and confirm all changes in writing
- notify relevant authorities immediately, and of any decisions to cancel collection
- where practicable, advise relevant Police Authorities and all other Exemption Order Holders by letter of agreed collection dates at the earliest opportunity
- abide by established collection dates
- ensure that sufficient collectors are available to support an effective collection, in order not to deprive other charities of the opportunity to collect
- charities should be able to provide information on the precise dates and locations of all collections.

Training of Organisers of House-to-House Collections

Effective training of all those engaged in house-to-house collections is critical in assuring a collection that is efficient, effective and accountable to donors. Paid staff of charities, including recruiters of volunteers, responsible for organising house-to-house collections require a clear understanding of their roles and responsibilities and clear guidance to ensure that they work at all times within current legislation.

Training should be undertaken by an informed member of staff on a group or individual basis and be supported by a comprehensive reference manual.

All organisers should be advised of any changes to legislation or procedures at the earliest opportunity.

The information given should include:
- information about the charity in general, its aims and objectives; specific work undertaken in the area in which they work
- details of collection legislation relevant to their work
- clear definition of their role and the extent of their responsibility and authority
- how to plan a collection, on a geographical basis and as an annual or rolling programme
- the importance and necessity of appropriate contact with other relevant bodies e.g. other charities, Police, Local Authorities, Banks, Local Press
- where appropriate, the recruitment, training, monitoring and payment of others engaged in house-to-house collections, e.g. recruiters
- who to approach as potential volunteers and how to approach them, in particular the information and instructions to be given to volunteers

- the recording of collector details
- the issue of personalised authorisation certificates and badges to collectors and the arrangements for their return
- the recording of the collection materials issued to each collector
- the arrangements for the receipt of income
- the recording of the receipt of income which should ultimately provide information for statutory returns
- how to deal with queries from the general public.

Where recruitment of collectors is by telephone, it should be carried out in an appropriate manner; recruiters should be trained in a structured way and monitoring systems established to ensure the quality of their work.

It should be undertaken in accordance with the ICFM Guidelines relating to telephone recruitment of collectors and the ICFM Code of Practice in the use of the telephone in fundraising.

Collection Materials

Every collector should be provided with:
- a collectors badge which should be signed on receipt
- a certificate of authority which should specify the name of the collector, the period of the collection and the specific location in which that collection will take place
- a sealed collecting box or collection envelopes
- clear instructions as to the proper conduct of the collection.

Materials should be dispatched to collectors in good time. All materials should carry the charity's registration number.

Badges and certificates of authority must be standard, supplied by TSO or, for Exemption Order Holders only, of a design approved by the Home Office.

Collection envelopes may only be used by Exemption Order Holders, other organisations need permission from the relevant Police Authority to use envelopes.

To ensure that efficient and effective monitoring of all collections takes place, the issue and return of all materials connected with the collection should be recorded.

Charities should ensure that donors are not placed under undue pressure to give and that all supporting information in leaflets and on posters is clear, concise and conforms, where applicable, to Section III Part I of the Charities Act 1992.

Information and Instructions

All collectors should be aware of their responsibilities and it is preferable to arrange face to face meetings with potential collectors. However, all collectors should receive written instructions as to how to undertake their collection and the procedures to be followed when the collection is complete.

The following points should be included in written instructions.
- How to conduct the collection.
- The exact area in which the collection should take place and that they should only collect in that area.
- The specific dates and times when the collection should take place and that they should only collect in that period and no later than 9.00pm.
- How to use the materials supplied and that they should carry a signed and dated Certificate of Authority; wear their signed collectors badge and only accept sealed envelopes.
- What to do with the monies collected.
- Arrangements for the return of all unused materials and badges of authority after the collection.
- Collectors should be 16 years or over.
- They should be courteous at all times.
- A contact name and address and a telephone number in case of queries or emergency.
- That the collection is being undertaken in accordance with the ICFM Code of Practice on House-to-House Collections.

Collectors should be given sufficient information on the work of the charity and the collection to enable them to answer reasonable questions from householders.

Charities should be able to provide full details of all collectors within a given area including name, address, telephone number and the precise area to be covered and the exact period during which the collector is authorised to collect.

Charities should have an agreed policy regarding insurance for collectors and their collections.

Proceeds of Collections

Charities should ensure that all collectors follow an agreed procedure for the banking of all receipts from the collections and the return of all collection materials.

Charities should establish and execute an agreed procedure for monitoring payments of the receipts from all collectors.

Arrangements should be made for the receipt of the collection proceeds and all used and unused materials connected with it at a specified point authorised by the organiser of the collection.

Collection materials should be opened and the contents counted in the presence of the promoter of the collection or another responsible person and duly witnessed.

A record should be kept of the proceeds collected by each collector and details of the collecting materials returned e.g. in the case of envelope collections, the number of envelopes containing cash returned by each collector.

Where collectors are asked to count the proceeds of their collection, they should have written instructions to open the returned envelopes and count the proceeds only in the presence of the promoter or another responsible person who must confirm the proceeds of the collection in writing. This should include, if relevant, the number of envelopes containing cash returned by that collector.

All proceeds from all collectors should be remitted to the organiser of the collection together with the collectors badge, certificate of authority and any unused collection materials as soon as possible. If the proceeds of the collection are not remitted within one month of the collection, the charity should identify whether or not the collection took place and take appropriate action.

Charities should ensure that all statutory returns are completed in accordance with the requirements of current legislation.

It is the Promoters' responsibility to ensure that all Organisers and Collectors acting for the charity conduct the collection according to the law. It is the Organisers' and Collectors' responsibility to ensure that they comply with all arrangements regulating the collections. Anyone deliberately acting in default of these obligations should not be allowed to participate in future collections.

Accounting

The Institute notes probable changes in accounting practice outlined in Part 1 of the Charities Act 1992.

At this drafting stage, no recommendations are offered for the Code of Practice as these must await specific identification of accounting practices required under the proposed legislation. This Code of Practice applies to current legislation. Amendments will be made in the light of new regulations.

NOTES OF GUIDANCE FOR THE GENERAL PUBLIC
House-to-House Collections are a vital source of funds for many charities and should be carried out efficiently and in conformity with the law.

Charities must ensure that:
- all collectors are 16 years of age or over
- all collectors carry and display a badge and certificate of authority.

PLEASE ASK TO SEE THEM.

To comply with the law the badge must:
- have the name of the charity printed on it
- bear the registered charity number
- be signed by the Collector.

To comply with the law the certificate of authority must show:
- the name and address of the charity
- the name and address of the collector
- the place of the collection
- the date of the collection
- the signature of the collector and the promoter of the collection.

If any of these were missing or if you feel pressurised in any way to make a donation, DO NOT GIVE and contact:
- the charity concerned, OR
- the licensing department of your Local Authority, OR
- the Police, OR
- ICFM.

Never hand over loose money. Your donation should be placed in either a sealed envelope or a sealed collecting tin.

ICFM Guidance Notes on the management of static collecting boxes

Introduction

Public collections undertaken for, or on behalf of, charities and voluntary organisations in places to which the public have general access are regulated by law. Collections undertaken on private premises to which the public are not afforded general access are generally not regulated by law.

Many collections held on private premises to which the public do not have general access are the concern of only a small number of individuals, each of whom are known to one another – members of a family, an association, club, group or small community. If you intend to engage in a collecting activity for or on behalf of a charity or voluntary organisation, always ensure that the collecting activity is undertaken within the requirements of the law.

Where any appeal for money or property on behalf of charities or voluntary organisations is made to a wider public, it is in the interest of everyone involved in fundraising to ensure that the trust and the integrity of voluntary giving is maintained.

The most common form of collection appeals undertaken outside the requirements of existing legislation governing public collecting activity are appeals involving the use of static collecting boxes – either floor standing or on counters in shops, pubs, hotels, hospitals, reception areas etc. Static collecting boxes are among the most effective and efficient forms of fundraising, especially when voluntary workers are employed in their siting and servicing. They also provide visible evidence of a charity or voluntary organisation's presence, and acceptance by, the community.

It is important that the authorities and the general public alike retain confidence in such a valuable source of charitable funds. These Guidance Notes are designed to ensure the proper management and use of static collection boxes and to safeguard the public interest in their use.

General Provisions

- The conduct and control of static box collections shall be the responsibility solely of the charity or fund that is to benefit from the collection.
- The charity or fund will appoint a chief promoter (and designees where appropriate) to be responsible for the collection. The chief promoter must be an official of the charity or fund that is to benefit from the collection.

The charity or fund shall:
- obtain the signed written permission of site holders to collect on the premises;
- issue certificates of authority and identity badges to collectors who are to site and service the boxes;
- ensure boxes are of a suitable material, and are properly labelled, numbered and sealed[1];
- maintain records of where boxes are sited and how much money is collected from each box;
- keep separate accounting records showing money raised through static collecting boxes and any direct expenses incurred in administering them.

Siting the Boxes

- Agreement must be made in writing between the site holder (owner, manager or occupier of the premises) and the promoter.
- The agreement may follow an initial visit to the site by a collector or agent of the charity or fund that will benefit from the collection, at which a box may have been shown or left with the siteholder.
- The promoter must write to the siteholder giving details of arrangements for servicing the boxes. Where possible, the name of the collector should be given in this communication. The promoter must provide an example (overprinted specimen) of the badge of authority carried by the collector.
- Siteholders must be asked to notify the charity or fund, preferably in writing, immediately a box is lost or stolen, or if they wish to end the collection and return the box.
- It is the responsibility of the promoter to be satisfied that siteholders will conduct collections honestly.
- It is the responsibility of the promoter to monitor performance of all collecting boxes.

The Collectors

- Collectors must be 16 years of age or over.
- Collectors must possess a certificate of authority signed by the promoter and bearing the name of the charity or fund that will benefit from the collection together with their own name, address and signature. The certificate of authority must be shown to the siteholder.
- Collectors must at all times undertake their work in a manner which will maintain the high standing of the charity or fund for whom they are collecting and which in no way places undue pressure on potential site holders or donors to participate in collections.
- Collectors must notify the promoter immediately they have reason to believe that the contents of boxes are being pilfered or interfered with in any way.
- Collectors must return the certificate of authority to the promoter on ceasing to act as a collector or at any time on demand by the promoter.
- It is the responsibility of the promoter to ensure that these conditions are adhered to, that collectors perform their duties honestly and that they conduct collections in a courteous and ethical manner.

Servicing the Boxes

- Before opening the box the collector should check for evidence of tampering and, after emptying, ensure the box is securely sealed again before re-siting it.

- Boxes should be opened and the contents counted by an authorised collector and in the presence of the siteholder or their representative.[2]
- The collector must give an official receipt signed by them and by the siteholder to the siteholder with a copy of same to the promoter. The collector should retain a further copy for their own records.
- The official receipt must show the address of the site, the box number, the date and the amount taken from the box.
- Collectors should ensure that boxes are in a good state of repair, that they are clean, properly labelled (see footnote 1) and function correctly.
- Collecting boxes may be repaired or cleaned on site by the collector or may be exchanged for a new collecting box with the knowledge and the agreement of the promoter.
- Boxes should be emptied and the proceeds counted in accordance with a regular, pre-determined schedule provided by the promoter to the collector and the siteholder.[3]

Collecting Boxes

- All collecting boxes must be properly labelled (see footnote 1), numbered and sealed and must bear the name and the address of the charity or fund that is to benefit.
- Collecting boxes used for static collections must be made of a durable material such as metal, wood or plastics. Cardboard or other paper products are not normally adequate for this purpose.
- The seal on the collecting box may be a lock, self-adhesive paper, or some other device provided that any attempt to tamper with or break the seal can be easily detected.[4]

Remitting the Proceeds of the Collection to the Charity or Fund that is to Benefit

- The collector must remit to the promoter the full sum of all monies taken from all boxes without deduction of expenses or fees.
- The remittance should be paid within a given time period specified by the charity or fund that is to benefit from the collection. This period shall not be more than one month from the date of the collection.
- The form of remittance may be decided by the charity or fund that is to benefit from the collection but must be accompanied by relevant official receipts.[5]
- Any expenses incurred in servicing the boxes must be submitted by the collectors separately and refunded by the charity or fund that benefits from the collection according to the terms of agreement between the charity and the collector.

- The promoter must maintain a full list of numbered boxes, and details of the corresponding sites with a record against each box of the amounts remitted.
- The promoter must also ensure that boxes are emptied regularly and that collectors expenses are checked and paid accordingly.

Maintenance of Proper Accounts

- All proceeds from static box collections should be properly recorded in conformity with best accounting practice. Proceeds from static box collections should be separately available and should detail gross income for the year, direct expenses incurred and all fees paid in connection with the collections.
- It is the responsibility of the chief promoter to maintain accurate, up to date records so that income from individual boxes can be traced and direct expenses and fees identified. These records should be certified annually.[6]

Charities Act 1992

Where the management of static collection boxes is undertaken on behalf of charities or voluntary organisations by third parties who receive reward for this activity and who solicit in connection with it, it is important that all parties concerned with the static collection box activity are aware of their responsibilities and obligations under Part 2 of the Charities Act 1992.[7]

Footnotes

1. Section (5) of the Charities Act 1993 requires that all notices, advertisements and other documents issued by, or on behalf of, a registered charity with an annual income in excess of £5,000 and which in any way seeks support for the registered charity, must include a statement (in a prescribed form) to that effect.

Failure to comply with this requirement is a criminal offence. Labels placed on static collecting boxes together with literature that might be associated with the collection and all notices informing people of the collection are likely to be caught by this provision.

For further information regarding the nature of the documents caught by this provision and the form and content of appropriate statements, see *The Practitioners Guide to the Charities Act*, ICFM/White Lion Press 1995.

2. Where it is not practical for the collecting box to be opened and the contents counted by an authorised collector the following procedures should be adhered to:

- the promoter should provide the siteholder with the necessary materials to open, record and bank the proceeds of the box at pre-determined, regular intervals;
- individually coded Giros should be sent to the siteholder with written instructions to open the box and count the proceeds only in the presence of an independent witness;
- the siteholder should take the counted proceeds and completed Giro credit to the nearest branch of a (designated) bank and pay them in;
- a counterfoil must be returned to the promoter as proof of counting and banking of proceeds;
- a further counterfoil should be retained by the siteholder as a receipt;
- all proceeds from all boxes should be banked within a specified period of time not exceeding one month after the previously agreed dates for the collection. If no money is banked within this period of time, the promoter will make the necessary enquiries and take appropriate action;
- on receipt of the counterfoil the promoter will send an official receipt, dated and stating the amount banked to the siteholder for display;
- the siteholder should be provided with the necessary materials to re-seal and secure the box.

3. For further information regarding best practice in the processing of proceeds from collections please refer to the ICFM Guidance Notes on the Handling of Cash Donations.

4. A lock on its own can usually be opened and closed without detection and it is consequently advisable to use some other form of device which can guarantee evidence of tampering.

5. Please refer to footnote 2 for further details of the procedures that should be followed.

6. There is no legal time limit to a static box collection undertaken on private premises, many of these collections are of an ongoing nature and may be undertaken over a number of years. However, there is a legal requirement to include income from static collection box activity for the year in question in the annual return required by the Charity Commission in respect of registered charities.

7. For further information on the Charities Act: see *The Practitioner's Guide to the Charities Act*, ICFM/White Lion Press 1994.

ICFM Code of Practice for reciprocal charity mailings

1. Basis of exchange

The content and character of the lists to be exchanged should be clearly understood. Precise definition of the lists should include:

a. Quantities – numbers to be mailed.

b. Statistical information on giving: how recent; the frequency; the average value of donations; and the frequency of which the list, or parts of it, may be used.

c. Details of past list exchanges with other charities or other organisations (see footnotes).

d. Type (i.e. cash, banker's order, covenant, etc.) and numbers of supporters on the list.

e. Notes so as to avoid duplication in any follow up mailing.

f. An outline agreement reached at the outset about the availability and timing of roll out numbers.

Each party must be sure at the very least that they are exchanging 'like with like' – lists of equal value.

2. Methodology of exchange

It is mailing materials, rather than the actual names and addresses, which should always be exchanged. Therefore each charity mails the other's material to the agreed part of the list, without losing control over their own list. All label or type formats, sizes and positions should be agreed between the two charities.

3. Material

Each charity should indicate their approval of the other's material by signing each item in a sample prior to the actual mailing. Each charity has the right to insist on changes, if they consider the other's mailing to be unsuitable for them to take on.

4. List standards

Each charity should declare the original standard and quality of their list (whether a computer file or a manual index).

5. Unique sleepers

Each charity should put a minimum of ten unique sleepers onto their file – at least one for each different section of the list. This provides security against any possible misuse and because the sleepers are unique ensures that any future misuse is not wrongly attributed.

6. Mailing date

Dates for the mailing should be agreed beforehand and should be evidenced in some way. Any problems in keeping to the agreed dates should be communicated to the other charity immediately.

7. Informing donors

The two charities should make it clear at the outset whether their donors are to be informed that they are engaging in reciprocal mailing. Each has the right to refuse or insist that this happens and it can become a condition of the exchange. Methods and times of informing the donors are the list owner's decision, although the other list owner has the right to see, in order to approve, any such communication.

8. Data Protection Act

Charities carrying out these mailings must register under the Data Protection Act. Each charity should provide the other with a copy of its registration, prior to the mailing.

9. Mailing Preference Service

The ICFM recommend that all participants in reciprocal mailings belong to the Mailing Preference Service to protect their supporters' privacy.

10. Written terms of agreement

Charities should exchange written agreements of the mailing's terms and conditions, setting out step by step the agreements reached under each item listed in the Code of Practice. Whether using letters or contracts to do this, ICFM suggest charities might seek legal advice in this area (see footnotes).

11. Results

Prior to the mailing, the exchange of results and what requirement there is for detailed analysis after the mailing, should be agreed by both charities and adequate resources should be ensured so they are able to carry this out.

12. Supporter response fulfilment/complaints

Both charities should agree procedures and materials for acknowledging response to the mailing. This should also include an agreed standard complaints policy, with discussion taking place between the two charities before non-standard complaints are responded to.

13. File maintenance

All non-delivered items and changes to the supporter file should be returned to the list owner as soon as possible for file maintenance.

Footnotes

1. Charities should be aware of the dangers of entering into reciprocal arrangements with organisations which are not registered charities.

2. In order to avoid any possible illegality under the Data Protection Act 1984, charities should obtain from the Data Protection Register the following notes:

Guideline 4: the Principles

Guideline 19: concerns fairly obtaining personal data

In terms of the fiscal treatment of reciprocal mailings, it is doubtful that the Inland Revenue will be concerned, since for their purposes there is unlikely to be any profit directly bearing from the transaction. However, it may be seen as a trading activity, thus potentially making the charity liable for VAT. However, if both charities are VAT registered then there will be no net gain or loss, as both will pay output tax and reclaim an equal amount of input tax.

3. Please see the Draft Terms of Reference for Reciprocal Mailing. However, it is just a guide and any charity entering into a reciprocal mailing is strongly advised to consult their own professional adviser to draw up a written agreement.

ICFM Code of Practice relating to outbound telephone support

The following code of practice presents a series of criteria by which voluntary organisations should engage in outbound telephone fundraising. The purpose of the code is to enable outbound telephone fundraising to be undertaken in a professional and sensitive manner.

This code of practice applies with equal force to both internal and external telephone fundraising operations undertaken for, or on behalf of charities and voluntary organisations, or in support of charitable benevolent or philanthropic purposes.

Definition of outbound telephone support

For the purposes of this code of practice outbound telephone fundraising is defined as: 'the use of the telephone by a voluntary organisation to actively request support from individuals and organisations using an external agency or an in-house telephone fundraising team.'

For the purposes of this code of practice 'request for support' is limited to telephone calls which are undertaken with the express intention of asking the telephone contact to do something – to donate money or property; to purchase goods or services; to donate time in support of fundraising activities associated with the voluntary organisation.[1]

The code of practice is designed to address warm and cold outbound telephone contacts and the use of the telephone in all outbound requests for support as defined above.[2]

The basis of the relationship between the voluntary organisation and the external telephone fundraising agency or in-house team

Where the telephone is to be used to make contact with existing or new supporters in order to solicit donations or any other form of support: There should exist a written agreement (or contract) between the voluntary organisation and the external telephone fundraising agency or in-house team.[3]

Contractual arrangements with an external telephone fundraising agency or in-house team should be on the basis of an agreed fee for a particular service and not an agreement which involves commission.

External telephone fundraising agencies should provide a written confirmation to the client that they agree to abide by the ICFM code of practice for outbound telephone support.

All parties to these agreements will recognise and respect confidentiality between relevant parties at all times and will seek to abide by all relevant legislation and regulations covering the use of the telephone associated with fundraising practice.[4]

The telephone briefing process

The voluntary organisation and the external telephone fundraising agency (where asked) should agree a detailed brief relating to each campaign prior to any calls being made. It should provide agreement on the following points:

i) The objective(s) of the telephone call.

ii) Details of the target audience.

iii) The process of how the telephone call will actually be made.

iv) The specified process for fulfilment of the telephone call: how the money or other means of support will be collected.

v) The means by which any proceeds resulting from the telephone call will be processed.

vi) The process and manner in which donor details are managed, held and passed back to the client organisation.[5]

1. Telephone Message

i) Telephone Fundraisers should always recognise the right of the other party to terminate the telephone conversation at any stage, and should accept such termination promptly and courteously.

ii) The voluntary organisation and (where used) the external telephone fundraising agency should agree in written detail the content and tone of the telephone message to be conveyed to the target audience.[6]

iii) Once agreed, the external telephone fundraising agency and/or the voluntary organisation and its telephone fundraisers, should not deviate significantly from the agreed script(s) during the telephone process unless with the written agreement of the client and/or the person responsible for the campaign within the voluntary organisation.[7]

iv) The agreed script should not contain any statements or facts known to be dishonest or untrue.

v) The tone, content and style of delivery of all telephone calls should comply with regulations administered by the Advertising Standards Authority.[8]

2. Information Provision.

The following information should always be clearly communicated within the script:

i) The name of the person making the telephone call.

ii) The name of the voluntary organisation for which the telephone call is being made, and if a registered charity, clearly stating that it is such.[9]

iii) That the purpose of the telephone call is to request support.

3. Prompted information

In addition to information automatically provided, if requested by the recipient of the telephone call, the following must be disclosed:

i) The name and address of the external telephone fundraising agency making the telephone call.

ii) The cost to the voluntary organisation of the telephone call.[10]

iii) A contact name and address for the voluntary organisation on whose behalf the telephone call is being made should the recipient of the telephone call require more information or want to lodge an objection or complaint.

iv) Any information relating to the voluntary organisation or the telephone message on which the telephone callers have been previously briefed. If a particular question cannot be answered satisfactorily or is answered unsuitably, a contact name and address for the voluntary organisation concerned to provide a more detailed or appropriate answer should be automatically provided.

4. Target Audience Exclusion

The following categories of potential telephone recipients should be excluded:

i) All those who have registered with the telephone preference service.[11]
ii) In addition, any individual who on a previous occasion has registered an objection to the use of the telephone for soliciting gifts or support for that particular voluntary organisation.
iii) Any person known to be under the age of 16.
iv) Telephone fundraising calls should not be generated by random digit dialling, manually or by computer.

Telephone fulfilment

i) All support solicited by the telephone message should be channelled directly to the voluntary organisation on whose behalf the telephone calls are being made and not to any external telephone fundraising agency making the telephone calls.
ii) The voluntary organisation should acknowledge receipt of the support in line with their own internal policies.
iii) All written material and any other communication sent to the recipient of the telephone call by an external telephone fundraising agency should be agreed in writing, beforehand with the client.[12]

Objections and complaints

Response to objections and complaints should be made in the following manner:

i) **Before the Telephone Call**
a. Where the voluntary organisation and/or the external telephone fundraising agency sends a pre-call letter to prospective telephone call recipients offering the opportunity not to receive the call, all responses to that letter which indicate that the potential recipient of the call does not wish to receive the call, should be recorded and noted to ensure that a telephone call is not made to them.

ii) **During the Telephone Call**
a. The caller should record and note all objections and complaints in connection with telephone fundraising. (If the call is undertaken by an external telephone fundraising agency, this information will be passed on to the voluntary organisation concerned.)
b. The caller should voluntarily disclose a contact name and address of a properly authorised person within the voluntary organisation to whom objections and complaints may be directed.
c. The voluntary organisation should record and note all objections and complaints in connection with telephone fundraising undertaken by it or on its behalf, and comply with the wishes of the recipient not to be contacted again by telephone.

d. The voluntary organisation should respond to all objections and complaints relating to any telephone fundraising appeal undertaken by it or on its behalf.

iii) After the Telephone Call

a. Any complaints received after the telephone call should be passed on to the voluntary organisation concerned.

b. The voluntary organisation should respond to all objections and complaints in line with their internal policies.

Timing

Telephone calls to recipients should not be made later than 9.00pm unless expressly invited by the recipient.

Footnotes

1. Telephone calls undertaken for or on behalf of voluntary organisations which are not made with the express intention of asking the telephone contact to engage in a fundraising, trading or volunteering action in connection with fundraising are not covered by this code of practice.

Consequently, the following telephone calls do not come within the remit of this code of practice: calls undertaken in the course of the administration of support that has already been achieved; calls made to telephone contacts to provide information, thank yous etc.

2. Where outbound telephone fundraising campaigns are undertaken to cold contacts, you are strongly advised to issue a pre-call letter to all prospective recipients of the proposed telephone fundraising campaign. This letter should include within it a clear opportunity for the proposed recipient of the telephone call to cancel the call taking place.

In accordance with this Code of Practice, all requests from proposed recipients of a telephone call who do not wish to receive the call should be recorded, noted and duly observed.

3. Where a voluntary organisation engages the services of an external telephone fundraising agency to undertake telephone fundraising calls on its behalf, if that agency (or any person connected with the agency making the telephone calls) receives 'reward' for this activity, they are likely to be regarded as either Fundraising Businesses, Professional Fundraisers or Commercial participators under provisions contained in Section 58, Charities Act 1992.

Where this is the case, Section 59 of the same Act requires the Professional Fundraisers or Commercial participators concerned to establish a 'written agreement in a prescribed form' with the voluntary organisation(s) on whose behalf they will be undertaking the telephone fundraising activity. The 'prescribed form' of written agreements are set out in Sections (2) and (3) of the Regulations which accompany the Act. These requirements came into force on 1 March 1995.

4. The use of the telephone to attract support is subject to the general regulations pertaining to the use of the telephone as well as specific regulations governing the use of the telephone in support of charities and voluntary organisations.

Any person wishing to engage in a telephone fundraising campaign on behalf of a charity or voluntary organisation should satisfy themselves, in advance, of full compliance with all regulations.

The key regulatory authorities are: Oftel, Data Protection Registrar, Charity Commission and the Department of National Heritage Voluntary and Community Services Division.

The key self regulatory authorities are: Advertising Standards Authority, Telephone Preference Service, Direct Marketing Association UK and the Institute of Charity Fundraising Managers.

5. The Data Protection Act 1984. In all instances, care must be taken to ensure compliance with the requirements of the Data Protection Act 1984.

Compliance with the Data Protection Act is not merely a matter of registration but also requires observance of the Data Protection Principles. Of these Principles the First Principle, which states that personal data should be obtained and processed fairly and lawfully, is of particular importance and imposes certain standards of notification when personal data is collected.

For further information, contact:
The Office of the Data Protection Registrar, Springfield House, Water Lane, Wilmslow, Cheshire SK9 5AX, Tel: 01625-535777.

6. Section (60) of the Charities Act 1992 requires Professional Fundraisers and Commercial Participators to make a statement (in a prescribed form) at each point of solicitation on behalf of a voluntary organisation. Where solicitation on behalf of a voluntary organisation by Professional Fundraisers and Commercial Participators occurs within a telephone call, the appropriate statement must be included in the call at this point.

Failure to observe this requirement in each and every case will lead to a criminal offence being committed by the Professional Fundraiser or Commercial Participator (together with the agency itself) engaged in the telephone call. This requirement applies equally to solicitations of direct support and to solicitations of pledges of support that will be realised subsequent to the telephone conversation itself.

Further requirements contained in Sections (60) and (61) of the Charities Act 1992 govern the rights of recipients of telephone fundraising calls who make payment of £50 or more as a result of those calls, to be entitled to a 'cooling-off' period. During the course of the 'cooling-off' period the recipient of the call shall have the right to a refund (in whole or in part) of their payment, less the cost incurred in administering any such repayment. This only applies where the proceeds (or payment) from the recipient of the telephone call is made direct to the Professional Fundraiser or Commercial Participator.

Additional Regulations accompanying the Charities Act 1992 (Regulation 6), govern the holding and transition of any payments made direct to Professional Fundraisers or Commercial Participators resulting from solicitation undertaken by them on behalf of voluntary organisations. Where this occurs as a result of a telephone fundraising call, these Regulations will apply.

7. Clearly, there might be occasions when time dictates that immediate written agreement cannot be obtained before a script is altered. In such cases, the verbal agreement of a properly authorised person within the voluntary organisation concerned must be achieved, together with an agreed process for subsequent written confirmation of the agreement.

8. For further information regarding compliance with the British Codes of Advertising and Sales Promotion, contact:

The Advertising Standards Authority, Brook House, 2-16 Torrington Place, London WC1 7HN, Tel: 0171 580 5555.

For specific guidance on advertising and promotional campaigns in the press, contact the Copy Advice Department on 0171 580 4100.

9. Particular care should be taken when soliciting support for organisations which are not registered charities. Section (63) of the Charities Act 1992 makes it a criminal offence to solicit support on behalf of a registered charity when, in fact, the organisation concerned is not a registered charity.

10. When a voluntary organisation engages the services of an external telephone fundraising agency, the cost provided in response to a request from the recipient of a telephone call, should be the specific fee paid by the voluntary organisation for each telephone contact. If the fee is on other than a per-contact basis, the voluntary organisation should agree with the external telephone fundraising agency the figure that will be quoted in the case of this query arising.

In those cases where an in-house team is undertaking the telephone fundraising, a figure per-contact should be agreed, including all relevant costs which, will be quoted to recipients of the telephone call raising this query.

In all instances, fundraisers should be able to quote a specific figure. Any accompanying explanation or rationale for the expenditure should be in addition to, not in place of, a clear statement of the costs.

11. Telephone Preference Service. Where charities, voluntary organisations or their commercial agents engage in the use of the telephone for the purposes of soliciting support from individuals who have no existing or ongoing relationship with the charity or voluntary organisation, the charity, voluntary organisation or their commercial agents should subscribe to the Telephone Preference Service and exclude all known subscribers to this service from the telephone fundraising activity.

Where commercial trading companies connected to and controlled by charities or voluntary organisations engage in sales and marketing telephone calls with individuals with whom they have no ongoing or contractual relationship they are required to subscribe to the Telephone Preference Service.

Where charities, voluntary organisations and any commercial companies controlled by them engage with third party commercial companies in joint promotion activities involving telephone contact with individuals with whom none of the aforementioned parties has an ongoing relationship (supporter or commercially based) they should ensure appropriate subscription is made to the Telephone Preference Service.

12. Section (5) of the Charities Act 1993 requires that all notices, advertisements and other documents issued by or on behalf of a registered charity with an annual income in excess of £5,000 and which in any way seek support for the registered charity, must include a statement (in a prescribed form) to that effect. Failure to comply in any instance is a criminal offence. (It should be noted however, that Section 5 of the Charities Act 1993 does not affect the nature of the telephone call itself, merely any information given in the form of a document in support of the telephone call.)

ICFM Guidelines for telephone recruitment of collectors

Introduction

This policy recognises: the value of the telephone to encourage the general public who may not otherwise give; and that it can be both positive and effective in recruiting volunteer fundraisers. Charities will need monitoring and training procedures to ensure it is not abused and funds raised are secured.

1. Training telephone recruiters

Training should be by an informed member of staff either with a group or with individuals. An accompanying manual should include the following: general information on your charity; general information on the structure of the collection; content and style of telephone contact; a standard script; precise details of expectations of collectors; precise details for monitoring contacts – you should include a printed example; how to deal with complaints and queries; and if applicable, clear indication of the payment terms.

2. Monitoring telephone recruitment

Monitoring procedures should be understood by everybody, at all times. Charities should: control who is approached by pre-selecting numbers; know who phones whom; maintain standard record forms indicating number of contacts, identification of each call and the results; and develop a clearly understood method of spot checking.

3. Content and style of telephone calls

All calls should be managed within an agreed structure which conforms to any relevant codes of practice (see footnote). It should include: the caller's name and the charity; the purpose of the call; an unequivocal statement of the non-obligation to participate; no misleading or untruthful statements; an opportunity for the contact to say NO; what is asked of the contact, i.e. dates of collection, areas to be covered and methods of payment; an explanation of what they will receive; an assurance that the contact is over 16, and the name and telephone number of the charity collection organiser.

4. After the telephone call

The results of all calls should be recorded; and the volunteer should have confirmed in writing their responsibilities and duties in regard to the collection.

5. After the collection

All proceeds must be reconciled by the charity with the individual collectors; and charities must identify and investigate collectors who have not banked proceeds within 3 weeks of the collection and be responsible for their security. There must be a procedure for random checks of the witnesses who verify proceeds of collections; and complete collection records must be maintained for at least 3 and preferably 5 years after the collection.

Footnote: The British Direct Marketing Association publish 'Guidelines for Telephone Marketing Practices'. Copies are available directly from them.

Guidance note on the use of chain letters as a fundraising technique

- The ICFM strongly advises charities against using chain letters.
- The ICFM believes that the promotion of chain letters should be discouraged in order to protect the legal responsibilities of Trustees, Fundraising Staff and Volunteer Fundraisers.

Introduction

The Institute has been made aware by ICFM members in the ICFM Northern Ireland Group, that a number of chain letters continue to be used to directly solicit funds in support of a number of charitable appeals.

The Law

Chain letters may be affected by several laws; the Malicious Communications Act 1988 is the most relevant together with the Charities Act 1992.

Malicious Communications Act 1988

A criminal offence will be committed if the letter conveys:

1. A message which is indecent or grossly offensive
2. A threat
3. Information which is false and known or believed to be false by the sender
4. Any other article which is in whole or part of an indecent or grossly offensive nature.

It is unlikely that most chain letters used for fundraising purposes would be regarded as being in breach of any of these conditions. Clearly the most likely manner in which a chain letter could be in breach of the Act would be under point 3. The offence can be committed either by an individual or a corporate entity e.g. a limited company, the charity, a voluntary organisation.

Charities Act 1992

1. Section 3 of Part 1 of the Charities Act places new responsibilities on charity Trustees, fundraisers and volunteers. Anyone issuing a chain letter on behalf of a registered charity will need to comply with the

requirements of Section 3 of the Charities Act each time the letter passes down the chain.

2. Failure to comply, in full, with Section 3 of the Act creates an immediate criminal offence. This offence can be committed both by the Trustees, staff and anyone responsible for the distribution of the chain letter.

3. Under Section 3 of the Act, a statement must appear on all published fundraising material clearly stating that the charity is a registered charity.

The very nature of a chain letter (moving further away from the control of the original sender at each successive contact point), makes it extremely difficult for Trustees, fundraisers and any originator of a chain letter, to guarantee that the statement of Registered Charitable Status appears on each and every copy of the chain letter.

If only for this reason the Institute believes that the promotion of chain letters should be discouraged in order to protect the legal responsibilities of Trustees, fundraising staff and volunteer fundraisers.

The ICFM View

As a result of its investigations the Institute has produced the following guidance on the use of chain letters for fundraising purposes. This note supersedes the interim guidance note issued to members with the March 1992 issue of Update.

The Institute is particularly concerned that chain letters will frequently compromise good fundraising practice on the following counts:

1. They can damage a charity's reputation.

2. Since charities cannot control to whom chain letters are sent, potential major supporters may in fact donate small sums instead of the larger ones of which they may be capable.

3. They often annoy current supporters who feel they have already given or who feel blackmailed into giving additional support.

4. Many people, particularly those who are elderly, living on their own, or of a nervous disposition, do read into such letters an implied threat of 'bad luck' if the chain is broken.

Even where chain letters are successful in raising money there are other considerations that must be taken into account:

a. Under Section 15, Part 1 of the Charities Act, if the appeal is for a specific project and this becomes oversubscribed, the charity might be in breach of trust if it failed to use the money for the purpose a donor intended.

It would be possible to avoid this problem by wording the appeal in such a way that any money raised over the target will be used for similar projects or general works of the charity also covered by its Charitable Objects.

b. It may be that chain letter donors will receive the same letter two or three times from different people. This may annoy donors creating unavoidable difficulties for the charity.

c. It is extremely difficult, if not impossible, to halt a chain letter. Even where this is possible, to do so may imply that the charity no longer needs any form of support, with obvious damaging consequences.

d. Chain letters frequently get drawn to the attention of the press which may result in bad publicity for the charity and for any fundraiser involved with them.

e. The inclusion within the chain letter of an 'urgent appeal to action' limited by time so as to prompt immediate giving, contradicts the mechanism by which chain letters move continuously from one prospective donor to another.

Chain letters are 'open ended' – individuals are asked to donate and also asked to pass on to other potential donors the same letter. Whilst the appeal will have an urgent time limit in order to secure funds, the appeal is ongoing and therefore is contradictory and misleading to donors.

f. It is clearly the case that chain letters provide special opportunities for the unsatisfactory practice of soliciting donations without giving donors clear and precise information about what the money is for and where they may obtain further information.

In addition, the Institute is concerned about a number of more general points:

- it is extremely hard to supervise chain letter fundraising and to know who is fundraising on behalf of a charity using this method. Charities with a clear policy never to agree to this method of fundraising will know that any who do so will be unauthorised;

- chain letters can provide exceptional opportunities for malpractice and fraud by giving incorrect payment addresses with little opportunity for recourse either by charities or by donors;

- negative publicity surrounding the production of chain letters has appeared consistently over many decades. Individual appeals and/or charities that make use of this technique run a considerable risk of being associated with a publicly discredited activity.

New powers to halt the unauthorised use of Chain Letters

- Part 2 of the Charities Act 1992 created new powers enabling charity Trustees and authorised staff to obtain an injunction to halt fundraising activities which are unauthorised and/or unwelcomed by the charity.

ICFM guidance notes for standard contract between charities and fundraising consultants

These notes both safeguard the interests of and provide a framework for agreement between the two parties – the charity and the fundraising consultant.

Preliminaries

1. Have you considered employing one of your own staff, either full-time or part-time?
2. Are you clear which type of practitioner you wish to employ: a Consultant; a Fundraiser; or a Co-venturer?
3. Get advice from other charities who have recently engaged in a similar practice, and ask them who they engaged; if they were satisfied; what if anything went wrong; and whether they would do the same again.
4. If you are not able to do (3) consult the National Council for Voluntary Organisations and get a list of consultants from the Institute of Charity Fundraising Managers.
5. Get a copy of the ICFM Standard Form Agreement.

Considering the short list

1. Draw up a short list of 'possibles' and ask them to indicate: their experience and qualifications; whether they are willing to work for you; how soon they will be available; when they are available; what their charges will be, how they will charge you and when they wish to be paid; what expenses they will ask for, their estimate of these and how they will be controlled; what their views are of your targets and what they would expect to be able to raise; other charities for whom they have worked and referees at these charities; whether they have a copy for you of a standard form of contract; and what provision will be made for premature termination of the contract by either party and the discharge of any outstanding obligations.
2. Consider their responses remembering that they should also have read these guidelines. Do not simply look for the most enthusiastic, but instead for the one that fully appreciates the difficulties to be overcome. What questions do they ask? How searching are they? Do they appreciate your strengths and weaknesses?
3. Look carefully at their estimates of the sums they expect to raise, their time and their expenses. Are they realistic?
4. Ask them what methods they would employ, what they would actually do and how. Do you approve of these methods?

5. If they propose to operate a lottery, make sure the arrangements are legal.
6. Discuss how they will allocate their time to you, amid their other work. Will they be able to do you justice?
7. What other staff will be employed? You must meet them before you commit yourself.
8. Be very careful of anyone who asks to be remunerated by commission on the funds raised. The Charity Commission and others advise against it and it is susceptible to malpractice. A time basis for charging is much more preferable. However, if you do agree to payment by commission, ensure that the consultant is aware that by law, donors must be informed what percentage of their gift is retained by the practitioner. See it is only charged on relevant gifts – i.e. not a legacy or a government grant.

Negotiation with your chosen candidate

1. Ensure you have control over fundraising methods to be used and that they will not bring your charity into disrepute. Make sure that no-one in the practitioner's organisation can claim to be your employee.
2. Ensure all donors are asked to make cheques payable to the charity and not the fundraiser's own organisation and that all cash will be credited to your charity's bank account as soon as possible. Do not agree to any deduction of expenses or remuneration from receipts.
3. Take up a banker's reference.
4. Ask if they have ever been bankrupt, or a director of a company gone into liquidation. Is the contract in the practitioner's or the company's name? If the latter, is the practitioner willing to personally guarantee the company's adherence to its obligations? If necessary, consider making a status enquiry through Dun and Bradstreet Limited or a similar organisation.
5. Ensure the practitioner cannot incur obligations on your behalf without your prior written agreement. Also be sure the money reaches you quickly, so that it cannot be diverted to meet the practitioner's and not your own obligations. If necessary, ask for a bond or fidelity insurance policy.
6. Make sure that information obtained from you or obtained on behalf of you by the practitioner is your property and is not available for their other clients except with your consent.
7. Insist when you are ready, on a written contract. To prevent any unwitting commitment beforehand, make any earlier letters, 'Subject to Contract'.
8. Make sure that the contract is a correct reflection of preliminary agreements, as this is ultimately a binding agreement, over and above previous correspondence or informal agreements.

Further Reading

Below is a list of publications giving information on a wide range of fundraising issues. The abbreviations given refer to the following organisations/publishers:

CAF: Charities Aid Foundation, Kings Hill, West Malling, Kent ME19 4TA.

CAT: Charities Advisory Trust, Radius Works, Back lane, London NW3 1HL.

DSC: Directory of Social Change, 24 Stephenson Way, London NW1 2DP.

EFC: European Foundation Centre, 51 Rue de la Concorde, B-1050, Brussels.

ICFM: Institute of Charity Fundraising Managers, Room 539-544, Market Towers, 1 Nine Elms Lane, London SW8 5NQ.

ICSA: Institute of Chartered Secretaries and Administrators, Campus 400, Marylands Avenue, Hemel Hempstead HP2 7EZ

NCVO: National Council for Voluntary Organisations, Regents Wharf, 8 All Saints Street, London N1 9RL.

WLP: White Lion Press, White Lion Court, 7 Garrett Street, London EC1Y 0TY.

Grant guides and information services

Arts Funding Guide (1996/7), DSC

Central Government Grants Guide (1995/6), DSC

'Community Affairs Briefing', a bimonthly newsletter service for community affairs managers, published by Burson Marsteller and Prima Europe, 14 Soho Square, London W1V 5FB

Corporate Citizen, a journal on company giving published three times a year by the DSC

Directory of Grant Making Trusts (1997/8), CAF

Directory of International Funding Organisations (1996), CAF

Directory of Patrons (1996), CAF

Education Funding Guide (1995), DSC

Educational Grants Directory (1996/7), DSC

Grants from Europe (1993), NCVO

Guide to European Union Funding for NGOs (1996), CAF/ECAS

Guide to Grants for Individuals in Need (1996/97), DSC

Guide to the Major Trusts Vol I (1997/98), DSC

Guide to the Major Trusts Vol 2 (1995/96), DSC

Local Trusts Guides (series) (1996/97), DSC

The Major Companies Guide, with detailed information on 400 leading companies, and *A Guide to Company Giving*, with information on 1,400 companies. From 1997-98, these will be replaced by one volume,*The Guide to UK Company Giving*. All published by the DSC

Scottish Trusts Guide (1996), DSC

The Sponsorship Year Book, from Hollis Publishing, Harlequin House, 7 High Street, Teddington TW11 8EL

Sports Funding Guide (1995), DSC

Third World Directory (1997/8), DSC

Trust Monitor (termly periodical), DSC

Publications relating to Europe

Finance from Europe, available free from the Office of the European Commission in London.

'The Official Journal of the European Union' has a special supplement which covers all the contracts awarded by the Commission. This is available on subscription from the Commission. The journal also publishes a comprehensive overview of the budget at the beginning of each year.

'The Courier' is published by the European Development Fund and can be obtained by contacting DG VIII.

Cultural Funding in Europe (1995), EFC

European Foundation Centre Profiles (1995), EFC

Europe's Solidarity (1996), AICE

Finance from Europe (1995), NCVO

A guide to EU Funding for NGOs, published by Euro-Citizen-Action-Service (ECAS). Available from CAF in the UK

Grants from Europe, NCVO

Networking in Europe, NCVO

More Bread and Circuses, published by Arts Council of England

Information from European networks.

There are now a number of European networks or special interest groups set up to monitor developments in Europe (such as the European Blind Union for organisations of or for the blind). Lists of those operating are covered in 'Networking in Europe' or contact the European desk at the NCVO to see whether there is a functioning network in your line of activity.

The European Monitoring Service is a bimonthly information service provided by the Legislation Monitoring Service for Charities. Subscribers are kept in touch on issues and information of relevance to the voluntary sector. The service costs £64 per annum for charities. Details from LMSC, 12 Little College Street, London SW1P 3SH.

Specialist Taxation Information

'Charitable Giving and Taxation' is a loose-leaf information service from Craigmyle, a firm of fundraising consultants. This is available from Craigmyle and Co, The Grove, Harpenden, Hertfordshire AL5 1BR, and costs £37.50 and an annual cost of £15 to receive updates.

'Tolley's Charities Manual' is a comprehensive guide to the taxation, accounts and audit of charities, from Tolley Publishing Company, 2 Addiscombe Road, Croydon CR9 5AF. This is published in loose-leaf format with regular updates that cover changes in law and practice. The service costs £99.50 for the initial information, plus the additional cost of receiving updates, which will amount to a further £100 to £150 per annum.

Other useful publications

Applying to a Grant Making Trust (1997), CAF

Asking Properly (1996), WLP

Charities Acts Handbook (1996), Jordans

Charities and Trading (1996), CAT

Charities Trading and the Law (1995), CAT

Charity Appeals (1993), Dent (available from DSC)

Charity Shops Handbook (1995),CAT

Dimensions of the Voluntary Sector (1996), CAF

DIY Guide to Marketing (1996), DSC

DIY Guide to Charity Newsletters (1995), DSC

DIY Guide to Public Relations (1995), DSC

Foundations for Fundraising (1995), ICSA

Friends for Life (1996), WLP

Good Ideas for Raising Serious Money (1995), DSC

Image Building and Money Raising (1994), DSC

Irish Funding Guide (1994), DSC

It's Competition, But Not as we Know it (1996), Third Sector

Licensing Deals for Charity Cards (1996), CAT

Meeting Need (1994), ICSA

Millionaire Givers (1994), DSC

National Lottery Yearbook (1997), DSC

Organising Local Events (1995), DSC

Relationship Fundraising (1993), WLP

Running a Local Fundraising Campaign, (1997)

Tried and Tested Ideas for Raising Money Locally (1994), DSC

US Foundation Support in Europe (1994), DSC

Voluntary Sector Legal Handbook, (1996), DSC

Who's Who in Fundraising (1996/97), ICFM

Worldwide Fundraiser's Handbook (1996), DSC

Writing Better Fundraising Applications (1997), DSC

Useful Addresses

1. Arts Organisations

Arts Council of England, 14 Great Peter Street, London SW1P 3NQ.

Scottish Arts Council, 12 Manor Place, Edinburgh EH3 7DD.

Arts Council of Wales, Holst House, Museum Place, Cardiff CF1 3NX.

Arts Council of Northern Ireland, 185 Stranmillis Road, Belfast BT9 5DU.

(Please note that the Lottery Departments for all these organisations are also at the above addresses.)

Association for Business Sponsorship of the Arts, Nutmeg House, 60 Gainsford Street, London SE1 2NY.

2. Community Trusts

The following community trusts are members of the Association of Community Trusts and Foundations:

Berkshire Community Trust, Arlington Business Park, Theale, Reading, Berkshire RG7 4SA.

Calderdale Community Foundation, Dean Clough Industrial park, Halifax HX3 5AX.

Cleveland Community Foundation, Cleveland Business Centre, 1 Watson Street, Middlesbrough TS1 2RQ.

Community Trust for Greater Manchester, PO Box 63, Beswick House, Beswick Row, Manchester M4 4JY.

County Durham Foundation, Park House, Station Road, Lanchester, Co Durham DH7 0EX.

Dacorum Community Trust, 57 Wootton Drive, Hemel Hempstead, Hertfordshire HP2 6LA.

Greater Bristol Foundation, PO Box 383, Bank of England Chambers, Wine Street, Bristol BS99 5JG.

Hertfordshire Community Trust, 2 Townsend Avenue, St Albans, Hertfordshire AL1 3SG (includes Barnet).

Isle of Dogs Community Foundation, PO Box 10449, London E1 9TJ.

Milton Keynes Community Trust, Acorn House, 381 Midsummer Boulevard, Central Milton Keynes MK9 3HP.

Northern Ireland Voluntary Trust, 22 Mount Charles, Belfast BT7 1NZ.

St Katharine and Shadwell Trust, PO Box 1779, London E1 8NL.

South East Wales Community Foundation, 14-16 Merthyr Road, Whitchurch, Cardiff CF4 1DG.

South Yorkshire Community Foundation, Heritage House, Heritage Park, 55 Albert Terrace Road, Sheffield S6 3BR.

Stevenage Community Trust, c/o MMS (Space Systems) Ltd, Gunnels Wood Road, Stevenage, Hertfordshire SG1 2AS.

Tyne and Wear Foundation, Mea House, Ellison Place, Newcastle upon Tyne NE1 8XS.

Wiltshire Community Foundation, 48 New Park Street, Devizes, Wiltshire SN10 1DS.

In addition, the following community trusts are being planned or are in an early stage of development:

The Birmingham Foundation

Caledonian Foundation, Glasgow

Colchester and Tendring Community Trust, Essex

County of Gloucester Community Foundation

The Craven Trust, North Yorkshire

Derbyshire Community Foundation

Devon Community Foundation

Ealing Community Foundation

Essex Community Foundation

Harrow Community Trust

Heart of England Community Foundation, Coventry

Highland Community Foundation, Inverness

Leeds Community Foundation

North East London Community Foundation

Oxfordshire Community Foundation

The Sherwood Forest Coalfield Community Trust

South East London Community Foundation

South West London Community Foundation

Telford and Wrekin Community Trust

Wales (Wales Council for Voluntary Action).

3. Environment and Heritage

Countryside Commission, John Dower House, Crescent Place, Cheltenham GL50 3RA.

Countryside Council for Wales, Plas Penrhos, Fford Penrhos, Bangor LL57 2LQ.

Scottish Natural Heritage, 12 Hope Terrace, Edinburgh EH9 2AS.

Historic Buildings and Monuments Commission for England (English Heritage), Fortress House, 23 Savile Row, London W1X 2HE.

4. Finance and Taxation

Inland Revenue, Trusts and Charities Division, Claims Branch, St Johns House, Merton Road, Bootle L69 9BB. There are 'hotlines' for covenant (0151-933 2778) and Gift Aid (0151-933 2819) enquiries. Enquiries in Scotland should be addressed to Inland Revenue, Claims Branch, Trinity Park House, South Trinity Road, Edinburgh EH5 3SD.

Customs and Excise, VAT Administration Directorate, New Kings Beam House, 22 Upper Ground, London SE1 9PJ. A booklet, 'Charities', is published. Contact should be made with your local VAT office (see Customs and Excise in the telephone directory). The VAT Administration Directorate deals with policy matters.

Charities Tax Reform Group, 12 Little College Street, London SW1 3SH.

5. Housing

Housing Corporation, 149 Tottenham Court Road, London W1XP 0BN.

Scottish Homes, Thistle House, 91 Haymarket Terrace, Edinburgh EH12 5HE.

Housing for Wales, 25-30 Lambourne Crescent, Llanishen, Cardiff CF4 5ZJ.

Northern Ireland Housing Executive, 2 Adelaide Street, Belfast BT2 8PB.

6. Regional Government Offices

East Midlands: Cranbrook House, Nottingham NG1 1EY.

Eastern: Heron House, 49-53 Godlington Road, Bedford MK40 3LL.

London: 3 Marsham Street, London SW1P 3EB.

Merseyside: Graeme House, Derby Square, Liverpool L2 7UP.

North East: Stanegate House, 2 Groat Market, Newcastle upon Tyne NE1 1YN.

North West: Sunley Tower, Piccadilly Plaza, Manchester M1 4BA.

South East: Charles House, 375 Kensington High Street, London W14 8QH.

South West: The Pithay, Bristol BS1 2BW.

Yorkshire and Humberside: 7th Floor, City House, New Station Street, Leeds LS1 4JD.

Wales: Welsh Office, Industry Department, New Crown Building, Cathays Park, Cardiff CF1 3NQ.

Scotland: Scottish Trade International, Farnborough House, 120 Bothwell Street, Glasgow G2 7JP.

Northern Ireland: Industrial Development Board, IDB House, 64 Chichester Street, Belfast BT1 4JX.

7. Special Funds

There are a number of special funds set up to distribute government grants which are operated independently, some in conjunction with large national charities.

The Architectural Heritage Fund, for the preservation of historic buildings, 27 John Adam Street, London WC1N 6HX.

The Charity Know How Fund, to support development work in Eastern Europe, 114/118 Southampton Row, London WC1B 5AA.

The National Aids Trust, to prevent the spread of HIV/Aids, 6th Floor, Eileen House, 80 Newington Causeway, London SE1 6EF.

The National Heritage Memorial Fund, to support nationally important heritage projects(also distributes lottery funds), 10 St James' Street, London SW1A 1EF.

The Opportunities for Volunteering Scheme (England), helping local community schemes, Carriage Row, 183 Eversholt Street, London NW1 1BU.

The Volunteering in Wales Fund, similarly in Wales, Wales Council for Voluntary Action, Llys Ifor, Crescent Road, Caerphilly, Mid Glamorgan CF8 1XL.

The Unemployed Voluntary Action Fund, similarly in Scotland, Comely Park House, 80 New Row, Dunfermline, Fife, KY12 7EJ.

Action on Community Employment (ACE), similarly in Northern Ireland, Training and Employment Agency, Clarendon House, 9-21 Adelaide Street, Belfast BT2 8DJ.

8. Sports Organisations

Sports Council, 16 Upper Woburn Place, London WC1H 0QP.

Sports Council Lottery Unit, PO Box 649, London WC1H 0QP.

Scottish Sports Council, Caledonia House, South Gyle, Edinburgh EH12 2DQ.

Scottish Sports Council: Lottery Sports Fund Unit, as above.

Sports Council for Wales, Sophia Gardens, Cardiff CF1 9SW.

Sportlot Fund for Wales, as above.

Sports Council for Northern Ireland, House of Sport, Upper Malone Road, Belfast BT9 5LA.

Sports Council for Northern Ireland: Lottery Sports Fund, as above.

9. United Nations Agencies

The following United Nations agencies make grants to voluntary organisations:

Food and Agriculture Organisation (FAO), promotes farming, forestry, fisheries, water and land management and rural development. FAO, Via della Teme di Caracalla, 1-00100 Rome, Italy.

International Labour Organisation (ILO), supports projects that promote income generation for the rural poor, vocational training and manpower development. ILO, Route des Marillons 4, CH-1211 Geneva 22, Switzerland.

United Nations Children's Fund (UNICEF), supports formal and non-formal education programmes, and maternal and child health pro-grammes. UNICEF, 866 United Nations Plaza, New York NY 10017, USA.

United Nations Development Fund for Women (UNIFEM), supports women's projects and encourages the participation of women in decision-making in development programmes. UNIFEM, 304 East 45th Street, New York NY 10017, USA.

United Nations Development Programme (UNDP), supports rural development and infrastructure projects. UNDP, 1 United Nations Plaza, New York NY 10017, USA.

United Nations Educational, Scientific and Cultural Organisation (UNESCO), promotes education, science and culture, and supports literacy, libraries, educational and cultural development. UNESCO, 7 Place de Fontenoy, F-75700 Paris, France.

United Nations Fund for Population Activities (UNFPA), supports family planning, maternal and child health, and population policy.

United Nations High Commissioner for Refugees (UNHCR), is responsible for welfare and aid to refugees. UNHCR, Palais des Nations, CH-1211 Geneva 10, Switzerland.

World Bank; the major institution channelling loans for development. The small grants programme supports policy analysis, dissemination, publications and conferences. World Bank, 1818, H Street NW, Washington DC 20433, USA.

World Food Programme runs food for work projects and provides food to vulnerable groups.

World Health Organisation (WHO), promotes health development and prevention work. WHO, Avenue Appia, CH-1211 Geneva, Switzerland.

These are some of the main agencies of the United Nations making support available for development work. They work largely through national governments, but some operate specific grants funds which support NGO work. Information can be obtained either from a regional or country office or direct from the agency itself, but you can also consult the UN Non-Governmental Liaison Service at the United Nations, New York NY 10017, USA.

10. Useful Organisations

ACENVO, 31-33 College Road, Harrow, Middlesex, HA1 1EJ.

Action – Employees in the Community, 44 Baker Street, London W1M 1DH.

Association of Chief Executives of National Voluntary Organisations, 31-33 College Road, Harrow, Middlesex, HA1 1EJ.

Association of Fundraising Consultants, The Grove, Harpenden, Herts AL5 1AH.

Association for British Sponsorship of the Arts, 60 Gainsford Street, London, SE1 2NY.

BBC Appeals Office, Broadcasting House, Portland Place, London W1A 1AA.

Business in the Community, 44 Baker Street, London W1M 1DH.

Charities Aid Foundation, King's Hill, West Malling, Kent ME19 4TA.

Charity Appointments, 3 Spital Yard, Bishopsgate, London E1 6AQ.

Charity Commission, St Alban's House, 57-60 Haymarket, London SW1Y 4QH.

Charity Forum, 60 Laurel Avenue, Potters Bar, Herts EN6 2AB.

Charity Magazine, The Old Court House, New Road Avenue, Chatham, Kent ME4 6BA.

Charity People, 1st Floor, Station House, 150 Waterloo Road, London SE1 8SB.

Charity Recruitment, 40 Rosebery Avenue, London EC1R 4RN.

Commission for Racial Equality, 10-12 Allington Street, London SW1E 5EH.

The Commonwealth Foundation, Marlborough House, Pall Mall, London SW1Y 5HY.

The Commonwealth Relations Trust, 28 Bedford Square, London WC1B 3EG.

The Commonwealth Youth Exchange Council, 7 Lion Yard, Tremadoc Road, London SW4 7NQ.

Community Service Volunteers, 237 Pentonville Road, London N1 9NJ.

Corporate Responsibility Group, 31 Great Peter Street, London SW1P 3LR.

Directory of Social Change, 24 Stephenson Way, London NW1 2DP.

English Partnerships, 3 The Parks, Lodge Lane, Newton-le-Willows, Merseyside WA12 0JQ.

European Foundation Centre, 51 Rue de la Concorde, 1050 Brussels.

European Commission, London Information Office, 8 Storey's Gate, London SW1P 3AT.

Gaming Board for Great Britain, Berkshire House, 168-173 High Holborn, London WC1V 7AA.

Give As You Earn: Charities Aid Foundation, King's Hill, West Malling, Kent, ME19 4TA.

Independent Television Appeals Office, 70 Brompton Road, London SW3 1EY.

Inland Revenue, St John's House, Merton Road, Bootle, Merseyside, L69 9BB.

Institute of Charity Fundraising Managers, 5th Floor, Market Towers, 1 Nine Elms Lane, London SW8 5NQ.

International Fund Raising Group, 295 Kennington Road, London SE11 4QE.

The Lottery and Gaming Board, Berkshire House, 168-173 High Holborn, London WC1V 7AA.

Millennium Commission, Portland House, Stag Place, London SW1E 5EZ.

National Association of Volunteer Bureaux (for the address of your local volunteer bureau), New Oxford House, 16 Waterloo Street, Birmingham B2 5UG.

National Centre for Volunteering, Carriage Row, 183 Eversholt Street, London NW1 1BU. (In Scotland, contact Volunteer Development Scotland, 80 Murray Place, Stirling FX8 2BX. In Wales, contact Wales Council for Voluntary Action, Llys Ifor, Crescent Road, Caerphilly, Mid Glamorgan CF8 1XL. In Northern Ireland, contact Northern Ireland Volunteer Development Agency, Annsgate House, 70-74 Ann's Street, Belfast BT1 4EH.)

National Council of Voluntary Organisations, Regent's Wharf, 8 All Saint's street, London N1 9RL.

National Lottery Charities Board, St Vincent House, 30 Orange Street, London WC2H 7HH.

Northern Ireland Council of Voluntary Service, 127 Ormeau Road, Belfast BT7 1SH.

Payroll Giving Association, 4 West St Helen Street, Abingdon OX14 5BL.

The Per Cent Club (address as for Business in the Community).

The Prince of Wales Business Leaders Forum, 15-16 Cornwall Terrace, London NW1 4QP.

The Prince's Trust, 18 Park Square East, London NW1 4LH.

REACH, Bear Wharf, 28 Bankside, London SE1 9DP.

Rural Development Commission, 19 Dacre Street, London SW1 0DH.Scottish Business in the Community, 42 Station Road, Corstorphine, Edinburgh EH12 7AF.

Scottish Council for Voluntary Organisations, 19 Claremont Crescent, Edinburgh EH7 4QD.

Wales Council for Voluntary Action, Llys Ifor, Crecent Road, Caerphilly CF8 1XL.

Work Aid: Charities Trust, PO Box 15, Kershaw Avenue, Crosby, Liverpool L23 0UU.

Index